HISTORY OF MODERN INDIA

Publisher

PRABHAT EXAMS

4/19 Asaf Ali Road, New Delhi–110 002

Ph. 23289555 • 23289666 • 23289777 • Helpline/ 7827007777

e-mail: prabhatbooks@gmail.com • Website: www.prabhatexam.com

Price

Six Hundred Seventy Five Rupees

ISBN 978-93-5266-745-1

Printed at

Sita Fine Arts Pvt. Ltd., New Delhi

HISTORY OF MODERN INDIA

by Dr. Kamal Bhardwaj

ISBN 978-93-5266-745-1

₹ 675.00

CONTENTS

Section A: Text Matter

Section B: Practice Papers

CHAPTER 1

The Maratha Empire

Introduction

- **Malik Ahmad of Ahmednagar** made friendship with the Marathas and used their best talent and cooperation, both for war and administration. He improved the financial condition of the kingdom and successfully opposed the Mughal advance for a quarter of century. In this grand political struggle, Shivaji's father, **Shahji,** and grandfather, **Maloji,** were associated with Malik Amber in such a manner that they gradually realized their strength and asserted their power in course of time.
- Politically, it formed the ground for establishment of independent Maratha of Mughal armies in the South. The fall of Khandesh, the gradual disappearance of Ahmednagar and the creation of the Mughal viceroyalty in the Deccan affected every aspect of Maratha life, which induced an awakening among the Marathas as a nation under the leadership of Shivaji and others.

Shivaji (AD 1627–1680)

- Shivaji was born in the fort of **Shivner** in AD 1627. He belonged to the Bhonsle family of Poona district. The family acquired military and political prominence in the Ahmednagar kingdom at the close of the 16th century. **Shahji Bhonsle,** the father of Shivaji, was a military officer at first in the state of Ahmednagar and then, from 1636, in the state of Bijapur, where he owned the territory of Poona as a Jagir. His mother was **Jija Bai**, a very religious lady.

Shivaji

Sangameshwar by the Mughal General, Muqarrab Khan, and put to death.

Rajaram (AD 1689–1700)

- At the time of Sambhaji's death, his son **Sahu** was only seven years old. Rajaram, the younger son of Shivaji and stepbrother of Sambhaji, who had been kept in prison by the latter, was proclaimed king by the Maratha Council of Ministers and crowned at Raigarh in February, AD 1689. But, soon thereafter, apprehending a Mughal attack, Rajaram left Raigarh and moving from place to place ultimately reached **Jinji or Gingee** in Karnataka.
- The Maratha Council of Ministers and other officials also joined him at Gingee which, till AD 1698, remained the centre of Maratha activity against the Mughals.
- With his two able generals, **Santaji Ghorpade** and **Dharaji Jadav**, Rajaram launched an attack upon the Mughal territories in Deccan.
- Rajaram's administrative changes included the creation of the new post of **Pratinidhi,** thus taking the total number of ministers, in Ashtapradhan, to nine.
- In October AD 1689, Mughal army, under Zulfikar Khan, launched an attack upon Raigarh. All members of Sambhaji's family, including his son Sahu, were made captive.
- Although Sahu was given the title of Raja and granted a Mansab, he virtually remained a prisoner in t he hands of Mughals till the death of Aurangzeb (1707).
- Jinji fell to the Mughals in (AD 1698) and Rajaram escaped to Vishalgarh (Maharashtra). He died in March AD 1700 at Satara, which had become the capital after the fall of Jinji.

Shivaji II and Tarabai (AD 1700–1707)

- After the death of Rajaram, **Tarabai**, the widow of Rajaram put her other son, Shivaji II on the throne and herself became the regent. Tarabai's energy and ability made her the de-facto ruler. She saved the Maratha state during a period of a grave crisis. Tarabai directed the conduct of both civil and military affairs with equal success.
- During this period Marathas attacked Berara (AD 1703), Baroda (AD 1706) and Aurangabad. In the midst of this confusion and disorder, Aurangzeb died on March 3, 1707, while Tarabai was still in power.
- The Mughals, however, succeeded in dividing the Marathas into two rival camps—one under Tarabai and the other under Sambhaji's son, Sahu, who succeeded in deposing Tarabai with the help of a chitpavan Brahman named Balaji Vishwanath.

Shahu (AD 1707–1749)

- Shahu was released by the Mughal emperor **Bahadur Shah** and this was the beginning of a civil war (AD 1707–14) between him and Tarabai. Tarabai's army was defeated by Shahu at the **Battle of Khed** (October 12, 1707) and Shahu occupied Satara.
- Now, the Maratha Kingdom was split up into two antagonistic sub states. Sahu was the head of the state at Satara while Shivaji II or really Tarabai, was the head of the other at Kolhapur. When Shivaji II died, another son of Rajaram,

Sambhaji II, ascended the gaddi of Kolhapur.

Shahu

- The feud between these two rivals was finally settled by the **'Treaty of Warna'** in 1731, which provided that Sambhaji II should rule over the Southern division of the Maratha kingdom with Kolhapur as its capital and the Northern part with the capital at Satara would be the preserve of Sahu.

Maratha Administration

- Shivaji appointed Hindus on high posts. Marathi was made the state language instead of Persian. He ordered Pandit Hanumant to prepare a dictionary of state craft for official use, titled as 'Raja Vyakaran Kosh'.

Central Administration

- Shivaji laid the foundation of a sound system of administration. Shivaji's system of administration was largely borrowed from the administrative practices of the Deccan states. Most of the administrative reforms of Shivaji were based on Malik Amber's reforms in Ahmednagar.
- The **king** was the supreme head of the state. He was assisted by a group of eight ministers known as the **Ashtapradhan.** It cannot be termed as the council of ministers, as there was no collective responsibility and each minister was directly responsible to Shivaji. The council of ministers could not initiate policy; its functions were purely advisory.
- All the ministers, except of Nyayadhis (Chief Justice) and Pundit Rao usually held military commands besides their civil duties. Shivaji did not allow the high offices to become hereditary.
- There were eight officers in each department to assist the Astapradhan—Diwan, Majumdar, Fadnavis, Sabnavis, Karkhani, Chitnish, Zamdar, and Patnish.
- Shivaji divided the territory directly under his rule (Swaraj) into three provinces, each under a viceroy. He further divided the provinces into Prants each of which was subdivided into Parganas and Tarafs. The lowest unit was the village, and each village had its headmen or Patel.

The Ashtapradhan

Peshwa or the Chief Minister

He looked after general administration and later assumed great importance.

Amatya or Majumdar

Accountant general, he later became Revenue and Finance Minister.

Sachiv or Surnavis

Also called Chitnis, he looked after the Royal correspondence.

Sumant or Dabir

Foreign affairs, and the master of Royal ceremonies.

Balaji Vishwanath (AD 1713–20)

- He began his career as a small revenue official by Shahu in AD 1708 and was appointed as a Peshwa of Maratha empire in AD 1713. He made the post the most important and powerful as well as hereditary. He played a crucial role in the civil war and was responsible for the final victory of Shahu by winning over almost all the Maratha sardars to the side of Shahu.

Balaji Vishwanath

- He concluded an agreement with Sayyid brothers (1719) by which the Mughal emperor (Farrukhsiyar) recognized Shahu as the king of the Swarjaya, and allowed him to collect Chauth and Sardeshmukhi from the six Mughal provinces of the Deccan.

Baji Rao I (AD 1720–40)

- Baji Rao, the eldest son of Balaji Vishwanath, succeeded him as Peshwa at the young age of 20. He was considered the greatest exponent of guerrilla tactics after Shivaji and Maratha power reached its zenith under him.
- His period saw the beginning of the **System of confederacy** and the rise of Maratha Chiefs. Under the system, each prominent Maratha chief was assigned a territory as his sphere of influence, which he was supposed to conquer on his own and which he could administer autonomously.
- Consequently several Maratha families became prominent and got themselves entrenched in different parts of India—(a) the **Gaekwad** at Baroda (b) the **Bhonsle** at Nagpur (c) the **Holkar** at Indore (d) the **Scindias** at Gwalior and (e) **Peshwas** at Poona.
- After defeating and expelling the Siddhis of Janjira from the mainland (AD 1722), he conquered Bassein and Salsettee from the Portuguese (AD 1733). He also defeated the Nizam-ul-Mulk near Bhopal and concluded the **Treaty of Durai Sarai** by which he got Malwa and Bundelkhand from the latter (AD 1737).
- He led innumerable successful expeditions into North India to weaken the Mughal Empire and to make the Marathas the supreme Power in India. He said: "Let us strike at the trunk of the withering tree and the branches will fall of themselves".

Balaji Baji Rao (AD 1740–61)

- Popularly known as **Nana Saheb,** he succeeded his father at the age of 20. After the death of Shahu (1749), the management of all state affairs was left in his hands. Shahu died childless, and though he had nominated **Ramaraja** (A grandson of Rajaram) as his successor, the later was imprisoned at Satara by the Peshwa on the suspicion that he was an imposter.
- An agreement was reached between the Mughal emperor (Ahmad Shah) and

the Peshwa (AD 1752) that the latter would protect the Mughal Empire from internal and external (Ahmad Shah Abdali) enemies in return for the Chauth of the North-West provinces and the total revenues. This agreement brought the Marathas in direct conflict with Ahmad Shah Abdali of Afghanistan.

Balaji Baji Rao

- The 3rd **Battle of Panipat (January 14, 1761)** Resulted in the defeat of the Maratha by Ahmad Shah Abdali and the death of **Viswas Rao** (Son of Nana Saheb) and **Sadasiv Rao Bhau** (Cousin of Nana Saheb) and several other Maratha leaders and 28,000 soldiers. Nana Saheb died on hearing the news on June 23, 1761.

Peshwa Madhav Rao I (AD 1761–72)

- Balaji Baji Rao was succeeded by his younger son Madhav Rao I. Raghunath Rao, the eldest surviving member of Peshwa family become regent to the young Peshwa and de-facto ruler of the state.
- After the death of Madhav Rao, Peshwa-ship had lost its all power.

Later Peshwas

- Narayan Rao (1772–73)
- Sawai Madhav Rao (1773–95)
- Baji Rao (1795–1818)

Administration under the Peshwas

- The secretariat of the Peshwas i.e., Huzur Daftar, was located at Poona. Now the feudal ruled over their jagirs indecently.
- Village was the smallest unit of administration headed by the Patils. Kulkarnis assisted the Patils in keeping the documents of village administration. Potars were appointed to inspect the currency. Balute system of exchange was prevalent in the villages.

Balute System

- Under this system, exchange of services provided, farmers had to make payment in kind, mostly in the form of fixed value of agricultural produce every year after the harvest.
- Taraf, Pargana, Sarkar and Suba were the bigger units of administration. Kamvisdar subordinated him.
- Deshmukh, Deshpande and Darak-hadars were appointed to check corruption.
- The land revenue policy of the Peshwas was based on the interest of the peasants.
- Agricultural land was categorized according to its productivity.
- Mirasdars had full right over the land while Upari undertook agricultural work with the Permission of the Peshwa.
- The Maratha army was also feudalized under the Peshwas.

Maratha Confederacy

- The origin of the Maratha confederacy may be traced to the revival of the **Jagir or Saranjam system** by Rajaram.
- But, it was only in the time of Baji Rao I that the system made a base for itself.
- In this process, Sahu issued letters of authority to his various Maratha Sardars for collecting Chauth and Sardeshmukhi from various parts of India.
- These letters of authority were called Saranjam. The holders of these Saranjam were called Saranjamdars.
- They merely recognized the Peshwas as their nominal head after the death of Sahu.
- But, unfortunately, the Maratha confederacy, owning to internal desertions fell prey to the British imperialism and their confederacy decayed.

Chapter at a Glance

- Shivaji began his first clash with Mughals in 1656 when he invaded Ahmed Nagar and Junnar.
- In 1663, he silently entered the fort of Poona and wounded Shayasta Khan.
- In 1689, Aurangzeb killed Shambhaji.
- In 1750, the Sangola pact was signed and under it the real chief of Maratha Union was Peshwa.
- In Shivaji's first coronation, Pandit Gaga Bhatt came to perform the holy rites. In the second coronation a tantrik named Nishchalpur Goswami performed the holy rites.
- The use of shining tiles on the surface of the store is found in the tomb of Shershah.

Previous Year Question Paper (1998–2017)

1. Who among the following streamlined the Maratha administration after Sambhaji?
   (a) Raja Ram
   (b) Balaji Vishwanath
   (c) Gangu Bai
   (d) Nanaji Deshmukh **(2015)**
2. *A:* Marathas emerged as the strongest native power in India after the decline of Mughal empire.
   R: Marathas were the first to have a clear concept of a united Indian nation. **(2003)**
   (a) Both A and R are true and R is the correct explanation of A
   (b) Both A and R are true but R is not a correct explanation of A
   (c) A is true but R is false
   (d) A is false but R is true
3. The member of Shivaji's Asthapradhana who looked after foreign affairs was
   (a) Peshwa
   (b) Sachiva
   (c) Pandit Rao
   (d) Sumanta **(1998)**

Answers with Explanation

1. (b) Peshwa Balaji Vishwanath, who had an efficient knowledge of both military and finance, streamlined the Maratha administration after Sambhaji.
2. (c) Marathas rose on the spoils of Mughal decline. Aurangzeb's religious policy coupled with growth of Maharashtradharma grew as a power enough to dominate the political scene. But their feudal division was not a true approach to United India concept.

3. (d) Peshwa–Finance and Prime Minister, Sachiva–Master of correspondence, Sumanta–Master of Ceremonies and Foreign Affairs, Pandit Rao–Religious Affairs.
Ref.: 12th Medieval NCERT, K. Reddy.

Practice Paper

1. In Shivaji's Council of Ministers, the Prime Minister was called:
(a) Peshwa (b) Sachiv
(c) Mantri (d) Sumanta
(SSC Grad. 2004)

2. Match List-I with List-II and select the correct answer by using the codes given below the Lists-

List-I (Kingdom)	List-II (Territory)
A. Peshwas	1. Nagpur
B. Gaekwads	2. Pune
C. Bhonsles	3. Indore
D. Holkars	4. Baroda

Codes:	A	B	C	D
(a)	2	4	1	3
(b)	1	3	2	4
(c)	2	4	3	1
(d	4	3	2	1

(SSC Tax Assit. 2009)

3. Shivaji was crowned in the year:
(a) 1664 (b) 1666
(c) 1670 (d) 1674
(RRB Mumbai Supervisor/IESM 2006)

4. Shivaji died in the year:
(a) 1676 (b) 1677
(c) 1678 (d) 1680
(RRB Mumbai Supervisor/IESM 2006)

5. Aurangzeb failed to defeat Shivaji because the
(a) Mughal army grew unmanageable
(b) Marathas were expert in Guerilla - warfare
(c) Mughals had no navy
(d) Mughal generals were treacherous
[Indraprastha Univ. (Delhi) Mass Comm. 2007]

6. Who among the following Peshwas was popularly known as Nana Saheb?
(a) Balaji Vishwanath
(b) Baji Rao
(c) Balaji Baji Rao
(d) Madhav Rao I
(CPF Assit. Commt. 2008)

7. Ashtapradhana was the official council of:
(a) Harihar I
(b) Krishnadeva Raya
(c) Shivaji
(d) Balaji Baji Rao **(NDA 2000)**

8. **Assertion (A):** Shivaji aimed at establishing Maratha rule in Delhi.
Reason (R): Shivaji took the leadership of the Maratha resistance against the Mughals.
Code:
(a) Both A and R are true and R is the correct explanation of A
(b) Both A and R are true but R is not a correct explanation of A
(c) A is true but R is false
(d) A is false but R is true **(CDS 2002)**

9. In medieval India, during the reign of Shivaji, the role of the official called Chitnis was to:
(a) Be the in-charge of King's personal security guard
(b) Be the in-charge of intelligence/ espionage activity
(c) Be the matter of ceremonies in the royal court
(d) Be assisting the king with his correspondence **(CDS 2002)**

10. **Assertion (A):** The British defeated the Marathas in 1818.
Reason (R): The confederate nature of the Maratha State made the Maratha Sardars almost autonomous.
Code:
(a) Both A and R are true and R is the correct explanation of A
(b) Both A and R are true but R is not a correct explanation of A
(c) A is true but R is false
(d) A is false but R is true **(CDS 2004)**

11. The Treaty of Bassein (1802) was signed with the British by Peshwa:
(a) Madhav Rao (b) Balaji Baji Rao
(c) Baji Rao I (d) Baji Rao II
(CDS 2004, 2006)

12. Between whom was the Treaty of Purandhar in 1776 made?
(a) English and Nizam of Hyderabad
(b) Marathas and Portuguese
(c) Marathas and English
(d) English and Sultan of Mysore
(CDS 2005)

13. Who among the following finally removed the Maratha Peshwa from the position, captured his territories and sent him off to a distant place?
(a) Wellesley (b) Cornwallis
(c) Dalhousie (d) Hastings
(CDS 2006)

14. The third battle of Panipat was fought between:
(a) Hemu and Akbar
(b) Humayun and Shershah
(c) Maratha and Ahmed Shah Abdali
(d) Nadir Shah and Mughals
(UP Combined State/Lower Subordinate Special (P) 2004)

15. Arrange the following in the correct chronological order:
1. Chhatrapati Sahuji
2. Rajaram
3. Shambhaji
4. Shivaji II
Select the correct answer from the codes given below:
Codes:
(a) 3 – 2 – 1 – 4 (b) 3 – 2 – 4 – 1
(c) 2 – 3 – 1 – 4 (d) 1 – 3 – 2 – 4
(UP PCS (M) 2005)

16. Shivaji defeated the Mughals in the battle of:
(a) Purandhar (b) Raigarh
(c) Salhar (d) Shivner
(UP PCS (M) 2005)

17. Who among the following Maratha women led struggles against the Mughal Empire from 1700 AD onwards?
(a) Ahilyabai
(b) Muktabai
(c) Tarabai
(d) Rukmini Bai
(UP PCS Special (P) 2008)

18. Who was called 'Chanakya of Maratha Politics'?
(a) Baji Rao II
(b) Balaji Vishwanath
(c) Nana Pharnabis
(d) Mahadji Scindia
(WB PCS (P) 2007)

19. Who among the Maratha Peshwa followed the ideal of Hindu Pada - Padshahi?
(a) Baji Rao I
(b) Balaji Vishwanath
(c) Narayana Rao
(d) Madhav Rao **(WB PCS (P) 2007)**

20. Who among the following streamlined the Maratha administration after Shambhaji?
(a) Raja Ram
(b) Balaji Vishwanath
(c) Ganga Bai
(d) Nanaji Deshmukh **(UP PCS 2000)**

Answers

1. (c) 2. (a) 3. (c) 13. (d) 14. (c) 15. (5)

4. (c) 5. (a) 6. (d) 16. (c) 17. (c) 18. (c)

7. (d) 8. (d) 9. (d) 19. (a) 20. (a)

10. (d) 11. (d) 12. (c)

CHAPTER 2

Later Mughals

Bahadur Shah (AD 1707–12)

- Ascended the throne with the title of Bahadur Shah, at the age of 63 years.

Bahadur Shah

- Released Shahu, son of Sambhaji (captured by Aurangzeb) after which a civil war began between Shahu and Tara Bai.
- *Watan Jagirs* of Raja Jai Singh and Ajit Singh were recognized, but their demand for high *mansab* was refused.
- Granted *Sardeshmukhi* of Deccan to Marathas but failed to grant them *chauth.*
- Made peace with Sikhs by granting Guru Gobind Singh high *mansab.*
- Mughal historians like Khafi Khan gave him the title of Shah-i-Bekhabar.
- A Dutch Representative Committee under the leadership of Joshua Ketelar visited his court in AD 1711. His death in AD 1712 was followed by a fresh war of succession among his four sons—Jahandar Shah, Azim-us-Shah, Rafi-us-Shah and Jahan Shah.

Jahandar Shah (AD 1712–13)

- Ascended to throne by killing Azim-us-Shah, Rafi-us-Shah and Jahan Shah.
- Was helped by Zulfiqar Khan, son of Asad Khan, who became wazir and all supreme in the state.
- Jahandar Shah was a weak degenerate king dominated by his mistress Lal Kunwar.

Jahandar Shah

Farrukhsiyar

- Practice of Revenue farming or *Ijara* was started.
- *Jizyah* was abolished.
- Jai Singh of Amber was made Governor of Malwa, he was also given the title of '*Mirza Raja Sawai*'.
- Ajit Singh of Marwar was made Governor of Gujarat, and given the title of *Maharaja*.
- Confirmed earlier arrangement that his deputy in Deccan, Daud Khan Panni, had concluded with Maratha King Shahu in 1711 granting them *Chauth* and *Sardesmukhi* of Deccan.

Farrukhsiyar (AD 1713–19)

- Sayyid Brothers Abdullah Khan and Hussain Ali Khan helped to secure throne.
- Chin Quilich Khan or Khan Bahadur better known as Nizamul-Mulk, was made governor of six provinces of Deccan, with headquarters at Aurangabad.
- bdullah Khan (real name Hasan Ali) was made wazir and Hussain Ali, Mir Bakshi.
- Mir Jumla was his trusted noble.
- Banda Bahadur, the Sikh leader was defeated, captured and executed in 1716.
- In 1719, Hussain Ali made settlement with Peshwa Balaji Vishwanath (Treaty of Delhi) whereby granted *Chauth* and *Sardeshmukhi* of Deccan in return for active armed resistance in case struggle for supremacy at Mughal court.
- *Jizya* was finally abolished.
- Farrukhsiyar was deposed and murdered by Sayyid brothers.
- Jat leader Churaman was defeated but pardoned (1717) at the instance of Wazir Sayyid Abdullah Khan.
- In 1717, granted duty free export and import to the English for annual payment of Rs 3000 only. English were also given right to rent additional territory around Calcutta. This *firman was* called the Magna Carta of the East India Company.

Rafi-ud-Darajat (AD 1719)

- Arrangements made with Marathas were ratified.
- Died soon due to heavy consumption of liquor.

Rafi-ud-Daullah (AD 1719)

- Took title of Shah Jahan II.
- Died soon of dysentery in September 1719.

Muhammad Shah (AD 1719–48)

- Original name Raushan Akhtar, took title of Muhammad Shah in Sept. 1719 once placed on throne.

Muhammad Shah

- Ratan Chand, a grain dealer was made diwan and was given the title of Raja, enjoyed great influence in governance.
- Court intrigues led to murder of Hussain Ali by nobles in Deccan. His brother Sayyid Abdullah Khan attempted to raise Muhammad Ibrahim, replacing Muhammad Shah, but failed, and killed in 1720.
- Jai Singh of Amber and Ajit Singh of Jodhpur were supporters of Sayyid and brothers.
- Supported by Turani nobles headed by Nizam-ul-Mulk and Muhammad Amin Khan.
- Nizam-ul-Mulk was made Wazir in 1722. Carried out many administrative reforms, but dissatisfied by the infighting at court, left for Deccan, where he founded state of Hyderabad.
- Bengal acquired virtual independence under Murshid Quli Khan(1717).
- Burhan-ul-Mulk Saadat Khan was made *Subahdar* of Awadh, established his rule over there.
- Marathas became stronger in Deccan under Baji Rao I who defeated even Nizam-ul-Mulk in 1728 and expanded in Malwa, Gujarat and Bundelkhand.
- Jats under Badan Singh established themselves in districts of Agra and Mathura.
- In Gangetic doab, Rohillas of Katehar and Bangash nawabs of Farrukhabad established their independent kingdoms.

Ahmad Shah (AD 1748–54)

- Son of Muhammad Shah from a dancing girl named Udham Bai.

Ahmad Shah

- Safdarjung, the Nawab of Awadh became the Wazir of Mughal Emperor.
- Along with Mir Mannu, the governor of Punjab, defeated Ahmad Shah Abdali at Manpur (1748).
- He was forced by Abdali in (1751) to cede the territory up to Sirhind, that is Punjab, Multan etc.

- Jat Chief Badan Singh was given the title of *Mahendra* and his son Suraj Mal the title '*Rajendra*' by Mughal Wazir Safdarjung.

Alamgir-II (AD 1754–59)

- Formally ceded the territory up to Sirhind annexed by Abdali in 1751.

Alamgir-II

- Abdali entered Delhi in 1757 and plundered as far as Mathura and Agra.
- *Khutba* was read in Abdali's name.
- Abdali's son Timur Shah was married to Alamgir II daughter Zohra Begum, gave empire back to Alamgir II.
- Rohilla chief Najib-ud-Daula was appointed as Abdali's personal 'Supreme Agent' and Mir Bakshi at Mughal Court.
- This led to conflict between Abdali and Marathas which was fought at Panipat in 1761.
- He was murdered by his Wazir Imad-ul-Mulk.

Shahjahan-III (AD 1759–60)

- Crowned by Imad-ul-Mulk but soon deposed by Nana Purandare and Appaji Jadav.

Shahjahan-III

Shah Alam-II (AD 1760–1806)

- Crowned himself Shah Alam II at Patna on 24 Dec. 1759 under protection of Shuja-ud-Daulah.

Shah Alam-II

- Defeated by British along with Awadh and Bengal at the battle of Buxar (1764).
- Signed treaty of Allahabad in 1765 with East India Company.
- Remained in exile for 12 years, brought to Delhi by Marathas in 1772 and declared themselves to be protector of Mughal Court.
- By 1785 Mahadji Scindia dominated Mughal Court.
- Maratha Peshwa was appointed as *Vakil-i-Mutlaq* (Regent) and Scindia as deputy *Vakil*.

- In 1789 Mahadji Scindia defeated and killed Rohilla Chief Ghulam Qadir and liberated Emperor from his control.
- In 1803, imprisoned by British & confined to Red Fort after defeating Marathas by Lord Lake.

Akbar-II (AD 1806–37)

- His grant was fixed to ₹ 11.5 lakhs per annum.

Akbar-II

- He dispatched Raja Ram Mohan Roy to raise his allowance.
- Presentation of *Nazr* or gift by Governor-General, was ended in 1813, however, staffs of East India Company paid *Nazr*.
- Reduced to status of a King rather than Emperor.

Bahadur Shah-II (AD 1837–62)

- All types of *Nazrs* were stopped.
- In 1856, title of King was dropped by Canning for successors of Bahadur Shah II were to leave Red Fort and to live near Qutub Minar.
- His successors were to have title of Prince of Timurid House.
- The leaders of Revolt of 1857 declared him to be the Emperor of India and fought against the British in his name.

Bahadur Shah-II

- All sons except one Mirza Jiwan Bakht were slot by Hudson.
- After suppression of Revolt, he was deported to Rangoon where he died in 1862.

Causes for the Decline of the Mughal Empire

- Worthless and negligent late Mughal Emperors.
- Absence of definite law of succession, leading to unstability of government and growth of partisanship at cost of patriotism.
- A heterogeneous and non-hereditary nobilitiy.
- Degeneration of nobility with factious feuds and intrigues.
- Jagirdari crisis and vast expansion of territory which made it difficult for the weak rulers to control it.
- Revolt of Rajputs, Sikhs, Jats and Maratha's due to Aurangzeb's religious policy.
- Failure of Aurangzeb's Deccan Policy.
- Invasions of Nadir Shah and Ahmed Shah gave a death blow to Mughal Empire.

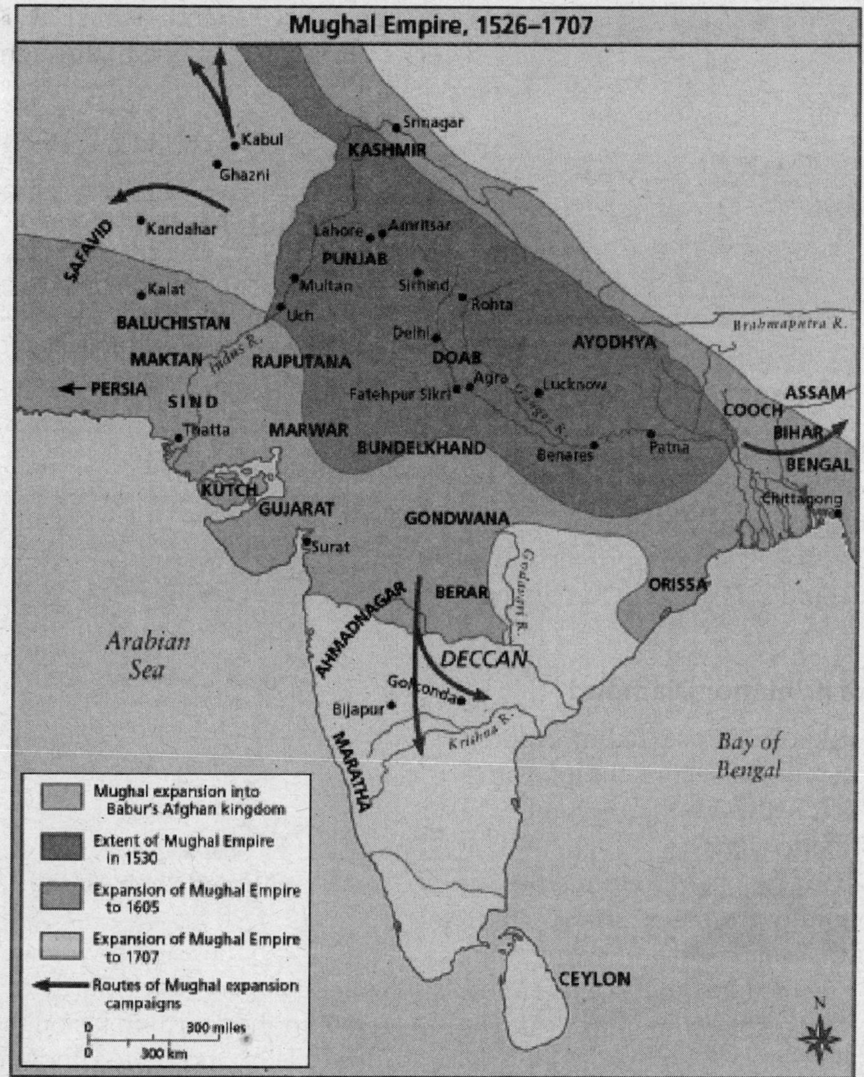

Mughal Empire, 1526–1707

Foreign Invasions

Nadir Shah

- Nadir Shah of Persia captured Qandhar and eyed the Afghanistan territory on the Mughal border. The Mughal Subedar Nasir Khan without posing any resistance, he fied from Afghanistan.
- Nadir Shah entered Punjab Through Peshawar. He met the royal Mughal army at Karnal on 13th February in 1739.
- The royal army's main contingent under the emperor Mohammed Shah and Mizam-ul-Mulk did and join the battle. As a result, the army under Sadat Khan, Khan-Dauran and Nasir Mohammed signed the treaty with Nadir Shah accepting to give Nadir Rs. 2 crore in lieu of protecting their territory.

Nadir Shah

- During his invasion, Nadir Shah entered Delhi on 20th March and ordered a general massacre, in which about 20,000 citizens were killed. The property was ransacked and every part of the city was looted.

The Story of Kohinoor Diamond

After the battle of Panipat, Babur ordered his son Humayun to secure the treasures at Agra, which had been the capital of the Lodi dynasty since 1502.

When Babur joined Humayun at Agra, Humayun presented him with a magnificent diamond. It has always been a matter of some dispute, but it seems almost certain that this splendid gem was the ***Kohinoor*** (mountain of light), making its first appearance in history. The ***Kohinoor*** was given to Humayun by the family of the ***Raja*** of ***Gwalior,*** whom he had given protection. Humayun later gave the diamond to Shah Tahmasp of Persia. The Shah sent it as a present to Nizam Shah in the Deccan. Somehow, the gem returned during the 17th century into the treasury of the Mughal emperor, Shah Jahan. When Nadir Shah plundered Delhi in 1739, he seized the diamond along with the other Mughal jewels and named it Kohinoor. The Kohinoor passed through several hands before finally resting in the Tower of London, where it remains on display even today.

Ahmed Shah Abdali

- Ahmed Shah Abdali, the successor of Nadir Shah launched his first invasion at Punjab in AD 1748, it was followed by another invasion in AD 1749, in which he defeated Mon-ul-Mulk, the Governor of Punjab.

Ahmed Shah Abdali

- In AD 1752, Abdali invaded Punjab for the third time and fourth time in AD 1756. In the fourth invasion, he reached upto Delhi and looted Indian territory as far as Mathura and Agra. In course of all these invasions, he did not meet with any resistance.
- He invaded India for the sixth time in AD 1760 and regained Punjab. A fierce battle was fought on 14th January, 1761 between the Ahmed Shah Abdali and Marathas at Panipat. After initial success in what is known as the Third Battle of Panipat, the Marathas suffered a crushing defeat.

IMPORTANT FACTS TO REMEMBER

Key term/Concept		Meaning
(a)	Mir Bakshi	Head of military, pay, and accounts office
(b)	Khani-i-Saman	Head of imperial household
(c)	Chief Qazi	Head of judiciary department
(d)	Mir Maal	Lord privy seal
(e)	Mustaufi	Auditor general
(f)	Mushriff	Revenue secretary
(g)	Waqa-i-Navis	News reporter
(h)	Mir Arz	In-charge of petitions
(i)	Mir Tozak	Master of ceremonies
(j)	Amul Guzar	Head of revenue administration in parganas
(k)	Bitakchi	Writer/record keeper
(l)	Shiqdar/Shikdar	In-charge of law and order
(m)	Nasq/Kankut	Wherein estimate was made of the produce by government officials
(n)	Muqtai	Fixed revenue demand leased in cash
(o)	Dahsala/Zabti system	Average produce per bigha of each category of land was ascertained based on past 10 years produce. One third of the average produce per bigha of land in respect to various crops in various categories of land, fixed as state demand. Adopted by East India Company in the Ryotwari system.

Chapter at a Glance

- After the death of Aurangzeb, Muaazam emerged victorious in the war of succession.
- Muazzam ascended the throne with the name of Bahadur Shah-I in 1707 at the age of 67.
- During Bahadur Shah's reign Jizya was abolished.
- Bahadur Shah gave a high Mansab to Guru Govind Singh.
- Bahadur Shah released the Maratha Prince Sahu.
- Jahandar Shah came to the throne in 1712 A.D.
- He was dominated by his mistress Lal Kunwar. She imitated the style of Nur Jahan.
- Administration was virtually in the hands of Zulfiqar Khan.
- Jahandar Shah was the first later Mughal ruler to get the throne with the help of nobles.

- The policies of Aurangzeb were reversed.
- Jai Singh of Amber was given the title of Mirza Raja Sawai and appointed Governor of Malwa.
- Ajit Singh of Marwar was awarded the title of Maharaja and appointed Governor of Gujarat.
- Sahu was granted Chauth and Sardeshmukhi of Deccan.
- Farrukh Siyar came to the throne in 1713 A.D. with the help of Sayyid brothers.
- Sayyid brothers were known as King makers.
- Sayyid brothers dominated Mughal court and empire from 1713 to 1719. The elder brother Abdullah Khan was Wazir and younger. Hussain Ali Khan was Mir Bakshi.
- Sayyid brothers belonged to Hindustani group of Mughal nobility.
- In 1719, the Sayyid brothers deposed Farrukh Siyar and killed him.
- After Farrukh Siyar, Sayyid brothers placed Rafi-ud-darajat on the throne but he died soon.
- Muhammad Shah came to the throne in 1719 A.D.
- Muhammad Shah was known as 'Rangila'.
- Nadir Shah, the Napoleon of Iran invaded India and inflicted a crushing defeat on Mughal army at Karnal on Feb. 13, 1739.
- Nadir Shah captured Delhi and Muhammad Shah was imprisoned. He plundered Delhi.
- Nadir Shah's total plunder has been estimated at Rs. 70 crores. He also carried away the famous Kohinoor diamond and the jewel studded Peacock Throne of Shah Jahan.
- Various provinces became independent (Bengal, Hyderabad, Awadh, Carnatic etc.)
- The Jats under Badan Singh established themselves in the districts of Agra and Mathura and founded the Jat state of Bharatpur.
- Sayyid brothers were murdered in 1720 A.D.
- Ahmad Shah came to the throne in 1748 A.D.
- Safdarjung, the Nawab of Awadh became the Wazir of the Empire.
- His Wazir (after Safdarjung), Imad-ul-Mulk blinded him and placed Alamgir-Il on the throne.
- Ahmad Shah Abdali invaded India thrice during his reign.
- Alamgir-II came to the throne in 1754 A.D.
- Ahmad Shah Abdali invaded fourth time in his reign in 1755.
- The Marathas were invited by his Wazir to save guard the empire against Abdali.
- In 1759 he was murdered by his wazir, Imad-ul-Mulk.
- Real name of Shah Alam II was Ali Gauhar.
- Along with Mir Qasim and Shuja-ud-daulah, he was defeated by English at the battle of Buxar in 1764.
- He lived for several years at Allahabad as a pensioner of the East India Company.
- He regained the throne of Delhi with the help of Maratha sardar Mahadji Scindhia in 1772.

- British under Lord Lake captured Delhi and Agra in 1803.
- He was killed by Ghulam Qadir in 1806.
- English concluded Treaty of Allahabad (1765).
- Bahadur Shah Zafar was the last Mughal Emperor.

Questions for Self Assessment

1. Compare the Peshwas' bureaucratic management with that of the Imperial Mughal administration.
2. Explain the reasons for the decline of Mughals.

Previous Year Question Paper (1998-2017)

1. Who among the following Indian rulers established embassies in foreign countries on modern lines ? **(2015)**
   (a) Haider Ali (b) Mir Qasim
   (c) Shah Alam II (d) Tipu Sultan
2. What was the immediate reason for Ahmad Shah Abdali to invade India and fight the Third Battle of Panipat? **(2010)**
   (a) He wanted to avenge the explusion by Marathas of his viceroy Timur Shah from Lahore.
   (b) The frustrated Governor of Jullundhar Adina Beg Khan invited him to invade Punjab.
   (c) He wanted to punish Mughal administration for non-payment of the revenues of the Chahar Mahal (Gujarat, Aurangabad, Sialkot and Pasrur).
   (d) He wanted to annex all the fertile plains of Punjab upto the borders of Delhi to his kingdom.
3. Consider the following statements.
   1. In the Third Battle of Panipat, Ahmed Shah Abdali defeated Ibrahim Lodi.
   2. Tipu Sultan was killed in the Third Anglo-Mysore War.
   3. Mir Jafar entered in a conspiracy with the English for the defeat of Nawab Siraj-ud-daulah in the Battle of Plassey.

   Which of the statements given above is/are correct ?
   (a) 1, 2, and 3 (b) 3 only
   (c) 2 and 3 (d) None **(2004)**
4. Which one of the following statements is NOT correct? **(2003)**
   (a) Ali Mardan Khan introduced the system of revenue farming in Bengal.
   (b) Maharaja Ranjit Singh set up modern foundries to manufacture cannons at Lahore.
   (c) Sawai Jai Singh of Amber had Euclid's 'Elements of Geometry' translated into Sanskrit.
   (d) Sultan Tipu of Mysore gave money for the construction of the idol of Goddess Sarda in the Shringeri temple.
5. *A:* Shah Alam II spent the initial years as an Emperor outside Delhi.
   R: There was always a lurking danger of foreign invasion from the north-west frontier. **(2003)**
   (a) Both A and R are true and R is the correct explanation of A
   (b) Both A and R are true but R is not a correct explanation of A
   (c) A is true but R is false
   (d) A is false but R is true
6. How did the Mughal emperor Jahandar Shah's reign come to an early end?
   (a) He was deposed by his Wazir.
   (b) He died due to slip while climbing down steps.

(c) He was defeated by his nephew in a battle.
(d) He died of sickness due to too much consumption of wine. **(2003)**

7. Match List-I with List-II and select the correct answer using the code given below the lists: **(1998)**

List-I	List-II
A. 1556	1. Battle of Haldi Ghati
B. 1600	2. Nadir Shah's capture of Delhi
C. 1686	3. Death of Shivaji
D. 1739	4. Grant of Charter to East India Company
	5. Accession of Akbar

Codes:	A	B	C	D
(a)	3	4	2	1
(b)	5	4	3	2
(c)	5	2	1	4
(d)	1	5	3	2

Answers with Explanation

1. (d) Tipu Sultan established embassies in Egypt, France and Turkey on modern lines.
2. (a) In March 1758 Raghunath Rao, the Maratha leader, crossed into the Punjab and drove away prince Timur, Ahmad Shah Abdali's son and agent out of the Punjab. The following months saw the Maratha authority extending up to Attack. The Marathas appointed Adina Beg Khan as Governor of the Punjab on his agreeing to pay an annual tribute of 75 lakhs of rupees. On Adina's death, Sabaji Sindhia assumed charge as Governor of the Punjab. Perhaps, it was Raghunath Rao's mistake to advance into Punjab without crushing Najib-ud-Daula or befriending Shuja-ud-Daula of Oudh or befriending the Jats and the Rajputs.
3. (b) The Third Battle of Panipat was fought between Ahmad Shah Abdali and Marathas in 1761. Marathas were defeated by Ahmad Shah Abdali.
4. (a) Murshid Quli Khan introduced revenue farming.
5. (c) Ali Gauhar, the son of Alamgir II, ascended the throne under the name Shah Alam II (1758-1806). He was a nominal ruler. The real power was in the hands of Ghaziuddin Feroz Jang. A group of Muslims in Delhi came together against him and sought the support of Marathas. The third Battle of Panipat was fought during his time. Famine in south and the Buxar war with the English in 1764 were the main events of his reign. After defeat in the Buxar war, he conducted a treaty with the Engilsh. He conferred the Eiwani of Bengal and return in Bihar upon the British, receiving a pension of 26 lakhs from the British along with the Subas of Kara and Allahabad. Later, his pension was also stopped as he went over to Marathas.
6. (c) Jahandar Shah (1712-1713) or Umizuddin was the victorious son of Bahadur Shah I (1707-1712) in the war of succession after him. After killing his three brothers, he occupied the thorne with the help of Zulfiqar. He was a greedy and unworthy ruler. He was killed by his nephew Farrukhsiyar with the cooperation of Sayyid brothers.
7. (b)

Practice Paper

1. Who founded the city Hyderabad and built Charminar in it?
   (a) Ahmed Quli Qutub Shah
   (b) Mohammed Quli Qutub Shah
   (c) Ibrahim Qutub Shah
   (d) Quli Qutub Shah
2. Consider the following statements about later Mughals.
   1. Shuja-ud-din was first appointed Diwan and Deputy Governor of Bengal.
   2. Murshid Quli Khan was appointed as Diwan of Bengal in 1707.
   3. Siraj-ud-Daulah ascended the throne of Bengal with the help of his cousin Shaukat Jang.

   Which of the above statements is/are correct?
   (a) Only 1 (b) Only 2
   (c) Both 1 and 3 (d) None of these
3. Consider the following statements:
   1. Maharaja Ranjit Singh was the founder of Punjab.
   2. He was not very liberal in religious matters.
   3. He was forced to sign the Tripartite Treaty (1838) allowing East India Company to pass freely through Punjab.

   Which of the above statements is/are correct?
   (a) 1 and 2 (b) 2 and 3
   (c) 1 and 3 (d) All of these
4. From whom did Ranjit Singh acquire the world famous diamond Kohinoor?
   (a) Nadir Shah
   (b) Zaman Shah
   (c) Shah Shuja
   (d) Dost Mohammed
5. The Nawab of Bengal who shifted the capital from Daca to Murshidabad was:
   (a) Murshid Quli Khan
   (b) Shaja-ud-din
   (c) Alivardi Khan
   (d) Siraj-ud-daulah
6. Sayyad brothers' effort to contain rebellions and to save the empire from administrative disintegration failed because:
   (a) The feelings of the rebels had become too strong to be controlled.
   (b) A stage had been reached when nothing could work.
   (c) They were faced with constant political rivalry, quarrels and conspiracies at the court.
   (d) The fabric of the empire had been destroyed by the niblings of the rebels and the English.
7. Which one of the following pairs is not correctly matched?

Rulers	Major Autonomous States
(a) Murshid Quli Khan	Bengal
(b) Asaf jah Nizam-ul-Mulk	Hyderabad
(c) Saadat Khan	Mysore
(d) Sawai Jai Singh	Amber

8. During the reign which of the following Mughal Emperors was the Sikh leader Banda Bahadur captured and executed?
   (a) Aurangzeb
   (b) Bahadur Singh
   (c) Jahandar Singh
   (d) Farrukh Siyar

9. The Maratha kingdom was founded by Shivaji during the reign of
   (a) Mohammed-bin-Tughlaq
   (b) Akbar
   (c) Shah Jahan
   (d) Aurangzeb
10. Which one of the following indicates the correct chronological order of the later Mughal emperors?
   (a) Bahadur Shah-I, Farrukh Siyar, Jahandar Shah, Mohammed Shah
   (b) Farrukh Siyar, Bahadur Shah-I, Jahandar Shah, Mohammed Shah
   (c) Bahadur Shah-I, Jahandar Shah, Farrukh Siyar, Mohammed Shah
   (d) Jahandar Shah, Bahadur Shah-I, Mohammed Shah, Farrukh Siyar
11. Consider the following statements about later Mughals
   1. The seeds of the disintegration of Mughal empire were sown during the time of Aurangzeb
   2. He has 3 living sons viz Muazzam, Azam and and Kam Baksha
   3. Muazzam proceeded fast from Kabul to Agra

   Which of the above statements is/are correct?
   (a) 1 and 2 (b) 2 and 3
   (c) 1 and 3 (d) All of these
12. Match List-I with List-II and select the correct answer using the code given below the lists:

List-I	List-II
A. Shah-e-Bekhabar	1. Saiyyad Brothers
B. Kalusha	2. Bahadur Shah
C. Thorale	3. Sambhaji
D. King Makers	4. Baji Rao I

Code:	A	B	C	D
(a)	2	4	3	1
(b)	2	3	4	1
(c)	1	4	3	2
(d)	1	3	4	2

13. Consider the following:
   1. Jahandar Shah introduced the evil practice of Ijarah, i.e., Revenue farming.
   2. Farrukh Siyar came to the throne with the help of Zulfikar Khan.

   Select the correct answer using the codes given below:
   (a) 1 and 2 only (b) 1 only
   (c) 2 only (d) None
14. Match List-I with List-II and select the correct answer using the code given below the lists:

List-I	List-II
A. Mir Bakshi	1. Head of Military
B. Mushriff	2. Master of Ceremonies
C. Shiqdar	3. In-charge of law and order
D. Mir Tozak	4. Revenue Secretary

Code:	A	B	C	D
(a)	2	4	3	1
(b)	2	3	4	1
(c)	1	4	3	2
(d)	1	3	4	2

Answers

1. (d)	2. (d)	3. (c)	10. (c)	11. (d)	12. (b)
4. (c)	5. (a)	6. (c)	13. (b)	14. (d)	
7. (c)	8. (d)	9. (d)			

CHAPTER 3

The Rise of Regional States

The Bengal

- With the decline of Mughal Empire after the death of Aurangzeb, Bengal became an independent viceroyalty for all practical purposes under Murshid Quli Khan.
- He was appointed as Bengal's Diwan in AD 1700, as Naib Subahdar (Deputy Governor) in AD 1713 and later as Subahdar (Governor) in AD 1717 by Farrukhsiyar.
- His de facto rule from AD 1700 was, thus, made de jure in AD 1717 (between AD 1700-07 Prince Azim, son of Bahadur Shah, was the Governor and between AD 1707-13 Farrukhsiyar, son of Azim was the Governor).
- Murshid justified the confidence reposed in him by the efficient management, which raised Bengal to the highest degree of prosperity.
- A few months before his accession to the throne, Farrukhsiyar made an attempt to replace Murshid.
- But, it proved futile as Murshid repulsed the troops sent against him and killed the commander Rashid Khan (May AD 1712).

Murshid Quli Khan

- He was granted the governorship of Orissa by the Emperor Farrukhsiyar in AD 1719.
- He transferred his capital from Dacca to Murshidabad.

Murshid Quli Khan

- He gradually assumed autonomy, though continuing to profess theoretical allegiance to the Mughal emperor and to pay tribute as well as presents.

- He improved the financial position of the region by measures, such as, transfer of large parts of Jagir lands into Khalisa (crown) lands, introduced the system of revenue-farming etc.
- He regulated the prices of articles and forbade the hording of grains.
- He introduced reforms in agriculture, such as, grant of Takkavi loans to peasants for personal use.
- He brought about reorganization of administration and establishment of law and order by suppressing the rebellious zamindars.
- He maintained strict control over foreign trading company's activities; prevented the servants of the East India Company from abusing the privileges granted to the company by the Mughal Farman of 1691 (Aurangzeb) and 1717 (Farukhsiyar).

Zamindari Uprisings

- 1st by Sitaram Ray, Uday Narayan and Ghulam Muhammad.
- 2nd by Sujat Khan.
- 3rd by Nijat Khan.
- After defeating them, Murshid Kuli gave their zamindaris to Ramjivan.

Shuja-ud-din (AD 1727–1739)

- He was the son-in-law of Murshid.
- He continued the policies and reforms of Murshid. His principal advisers in the matter of administration were **Rai-i-rayan Alamchand** (an able financer) and **Jagat Seth** (the famous banker).
- He was also granted the governorship of Bihar by the Emperor Muhammad Shah in AD 1733 (from this time onwards the nawbas of Bengal ruled over Bengal, Bihar and Orissa). He appointed Alivardi Khan as the Naib Subahdar of Bihar.

Sarfaraz Khan (AD 1739–1740)

- He was the son of Shuja.
- He took the title of **Alam-ud-Daula Haider Jung.**
- He lacked administrative ability and was incapable of discharging the duties of government.
- He got more involved in enjoying the royal pleasures.
- He was defeated by Alivardi Khan governor of Bhiar, in the **Battle of Giriya (AD 1740)** and was murdered.

Alivardi Khan (AD 1740–1756)

- He legalized his usurpation by receiving a Farman from Emperor Muhammad Shah after paying him ₹ 2 crore.
- Faced the continuous incursions of Marathas in Bengal finally bought peace with them by ceding the revenues of a part of Orissa to Raghuji Bhonsle and an annual payment of ₹ 12 Lakh as the Chauth of Bengal (AD 1757).
- He was opposed to the attempts of the English and French to strengthen their fortifications in **Calcutta** and **Chandernagore** respectively.
- He refused to pay any tribute to the Mughal emperor when the latter demanded it (AD 1746).
- He favored and nominated **Siraj-ud-daula**, the son of his youngest daughter, as his successor.

Siraj-ud-Daula (AD 1757–1757)

- He prohibited the English from fortifying their factories at Calcutta but on their refusal to comply with his orders, he seized the English factory at **Kasimbazar** (June 4, 1756) and then **Calcutta** (June 15, 1756).
- Fought the **Battle of Plassey** with English forces on June 23, 1757, this battle saw the treachery of Mir Jafar and Rai Durlabh; bravery of small force under Mohanlal and Mir Madan; desertion of the Nawabs forces and escape of Siraj and his capture and execution by Miran (Son of Mir Jafar).

Mir Jafar (AD 1757–1760)

- He granted the right to free trade in Bengal, Bihar and Orissa and the Zamindar of the 24 Paraganas to the British, besides paying them a sum of ₹ 17.7 million as compensation for the attack on Calcutta.
- His reign saw the beginning of the drain of wealth from India to Britain.
- He is also known as the Jackal of Clive.
- He made futile efforts to replace the English by the Dutch, but the Dutch were defeated by the English at Bedara in AD 1759.

Mir Qasim (AD 1760–1763)

- He granted the Zamindari of Burdwan, Midnapore and Chittagong to the British.
- He introduced several revenue and military reforms to strengthen his position.
- He transferred his capital from Murshidabad to Monghyr (AD 1762).
- There was conflict between the Nawab and the British for sovereign power.
- He stopped the misuse for the **dastaks** (free passes allowed to the company).
- He abolished all duties on internal trade against British wishes in order to protect the Indian traders (1763).
- He appointed a German official **Walter Rin Hard** (Samru) for modernization of army.
- Mir Qasim murderded Subahdar Ramnarayan of Bihar and occupied the factory at Patna by defeating English officer, Ellius.
- Hence, in 1763 AD, English announced Mir Jafar as the Nawab of Bengal and declared war against Mir Qasim.

Mir Jafar (AD 1763–1765)

- His reinstatement in 1763 by the British took place after the outbreak of the war with Mir Qasim. He died in AD 1765.
- **Battle of Buxar** (October 22,1764) was fought between the British and three allies (Mir Qasim, Shuja-ud-daula of Awadha and Shah Alam II). This battle resulted in the defeat of the allies by the British forces under major Hector Munro.

Najam-ud-Daula (AD 1765–1772)

- He was the son of Mir Jafar.
- He was made the Nawab in AD 1765 and remained a puppet in the hands of the British during the period of 'Dual System of Government'.
- In AD 1772, he was pensioned off when the company took over the direct charge of Bengal.

The Awadh: Saadat Khan Burhan-ul-Mulk (AD 1722–1739)

- He founded the autonomous Awadh state in AD 1722.

Saadat Khan Burhan-ul-Mulk

- He was appointed as the governor of Awadh by Emperor Muhammad Shah.
- He was the leading member of the Irani party in the imperial court.
- Through his military reforms, he made Awadh economically and politically strong.
- He treated Hindus and Muslims equally in the matter of employment. The highest post of his government was held by Maharaja Nawab Rai.
- Asafzah Nizam-ul-Mulk (the leader of Turani party) was his rival in the Mughal court.
- He played a crucial role in the imperial affairs during the invasion of Nadir Shah and committed suicide in AD 1739, to save his name and honour.

Safdarjung/Abdul Mansur (AD 1739–1754)

- He was the nephew and son-in-law of Saadat Khan.
- He led an expedition to Bihar and occupied Patna in AD 1742.
- He took part in the **Battle of Manpur** against Ahmad Shah Abdali (AD 1748).
- He was appointed as the Wazir of the Mughal Empire and was granted the province of Allahabad as well, by the Mughal emperor Ahamd Shah in AD 1748.
- From AD 1748, the Nawab of Awadh came to be known as the Nawab Wazir, since Safdar and his successors held both the "Nawabship" of Awadh and the "Wajirship" of the Mughal Empire.
- He entered into an alliance with the Marathas, resulted in the extension of his territories.

Shuja-ud-daula (AD 1754–1775)

- He was the son of Safdarjung.
- **Ali Gauhar** (Shah Alam) the heir apparent of the puppet Mughal Emperor Alamgir II was provided protection at his court.
- He was deriven out of Delhi by Turani Wazir, Imad-ul-Mulk.
- He was an ally of the Afghan invader Ahmed Shah Abdali.
- He was involved in the Battle of Buxar (AD 1764) in which he lost Allahabad and Kara; paid off huge indemnity to the British and had to enter a defensive alliance with the British.
- He concluded the **Treaty of Banaras (AD 1773)**, with Warren Hastings whereby Kara and Allahabad were sold to the Nawab and British troops were stationed at Awadh to protect the Nawab, for which he had to pay a subsidy to the British.

- He defeated the Rohillas with the help of the British and annexed Rohilkhand to Awadh in AD 1774.

Asaf-ud-daula (AD 1775–1797)

- He signed the **treaty of Faizabad (AD 1775)** with the British.
- The treaty proved to be an expensive arrangement, for while it increased his liabilities, it sharply decreased his revenues.
- He transferred his capital from Faizabad to Lucknow in AD 1775.
- He is also known for promoting Lucknow culture and built important monuments like Imambara and Rumi Darwaza.

Wajir Ali (AD 1797–1798)

- The period of Wajir Ali (son of Asaf) was too brief and historically insignificant.

Saadat Khan

- He was elder brother of Asaf.
- He ascended the throne in AD 1798 with the help of the British.
- He signed a subsidiary treaty with Lord Wellesley in November AD 1801, by which the Nawab was deprived of about half of his territory for the maintenance of the subsidiary troops.

Wajid Ali Shah

- He was also known as **Jaan-i-Alam** and **Akhtarpiya.**
- He was the last ruler of Awadh. During his period, Awadh was annexed by Lord Dalhousie in February, AD 1856, on the pretext of mis-governance and he was pensioned off and deported to Calcutta.
- He promoted classical music and dance forms with performs like Kalka-Binda brothers in his court.

The Hyderabad: Nizam-ul-Mulk Asaf Jah (AD 1724–1748)

- He founded the autonomous state of Hyderabad.

Nizam-ul-Mulk Asaf Jah

- His first term as the viceroy of the Deccan was between AD 1713 and AD 1715.
- His original name was Chinquilich Khan, but Emperor Farrukhsiyar conferred on him the tittles of **Khan-i-Duran** and later **'Nizam-ul-Mulk'.**
- His second terms as the viceroy of the Deccan fell between AD 1720 and AD 1722.
- He was appointed as a Wazir of the Mughal Empire (AD 1722–24) by Muhammad Shah.
- Frustrated with the Mughal Court politics, he marched towards Deccan without the Emperors permission and laid the foundation of an independent state of Hyderabad in AD 1724.

- Muhammad Shah confirmed his viceroyalty of Deccan and granted him the title of **"Asaf Jah"** in AD 1725.
- Though virtually independent in Deccan, he continued to recognize the Mughal Emperor as sovereign.
- He established peace and security in the region by suppressing all disaffected nobles and putting stop to theft and robbery.
- He made an effort to stop the plundering raids of the Marathas (though partially successful) and to revive agriculture and industry by giving incentives to farmers and craftsmen.
- He adopted tolerant policy towards the Hindus. Puran Chandra was appointed as his Dewan.
- He signed **Treaty of Bhopal** in 1738 with the Peshwas and acted as peace maker in the **Battle o Karnal** in 1739.

Nasir Jung (AD 1748–1750)

- He was defeated and murdered by Muzaffar Jung (son of Nasir's sister and grandson of Nizam-ul-Mulk).

Muzaffar Jung (AD 1750–1751)

- He acceded to the throne with the help of the French.
- His rule came to an abrupt end with his accidental death.

Salabat Jung (AD 1751–1760)

- He was the third son of Nizam-ul-Mulk.
- He came to the thorne with the help of the French. Other Niizam's of Hyderabad were Nizam Ali (AD 1760–1803), Sikandar Jah (AD 1803–29), Nasir-ud-Daula (AD 1829–57), Afjal-ud-Daula (AD 1857–69), Mahabat Ali Khan (AD 1869–1911) and Osman Ali Khan (AD 1911–49).
- Nizam Ali concluded **Subsidiary treaty** with the English in AD 1798, thus becoming the first state to do so.
- Hyderabad remained independent until it became a part of independent India. The relation of the Nizam's with the British remained one of friendship and they helped the British, time and again, in suppressing the revolts.
- The Nizam also provided assistance to the British during the AD 1857 Revolt.
- Nizams were great patron of art, culture and literature. They built **Salarjung Museum** in Hyderabad and **Chow Mahalla Palace.**
- It was in September 1948, with the efforts of SBV Patel that by **Operation Polo,** Indian Military was successful in merger of Hyderabad into the Indian Union.

The Mysore

- Mysore became independent under the Hindu *Wodeyar* Dynasty in 1565 after the fall of Vijayanagar Empire. Between AD 1731 and 1734 the two brothers, **Devaraja** (Dalwai or commander in chief) and **Nanaraja** (Sarvadhikari or controller of revenue and finance) usurped the power in the state and became the de facto rulers. The state became a bone of contention between the Peshwa and Nizam.
- During the Second Carnatic war Nanarja allied with the English, to capture Tiruchirapalli (Tamil Nadu), but later on he shifted his allegiance from the English to the French.

Haider Ali (AD 1760–1782)

- He started his career as a soldier in the service of the Mysore state but was later promoted to the position of **Commander in Chief.**

Haider Ali

- He had a meritorious record as the **Faujdar of Dindigul.**
- He trained his troops on western lines and established a modern arsenal (AD 1755) at Dindigul with French help.
- He played a very important role during the Tiruchirapalli Campaigns.
- He defended Srirangapatnam (capital of Mysore) against the Marathas in AD 1759 and was rewarded by conferring the title of **Fateh Haider Bahadur** (Brave victorious lion) on him by Nanaraja (the prime Minister) who was the de facto ruler though **Chikka Krishna Raja** continued to be the dejure ruler of Mysore.
- After pensioning off Nanaraja, Haider became the de facto ruler of Mysore in AD 1760, but continued to recognize Krishna Raja as the lawful ruler.
- He had to fight several wars with Marathas, for consolidating his position.
- His administrative reforms made Mysore one of the leading Indian powers.
- He allied with the French and the Nizam and gave in the **First Anglo-Mysore War** (AD 1767–69) and forced them to conclude a humiliating treaty, **Treaty of Madras,** in April 1769.
- In 1781, he was defeated by Eyrecoote in the **Battle of Portonovo.**
- He allied with the Marathas and the Nizam in the **Second Anglo-Mysore War** (AD 1780–84) and captured Arcot during the course of war and inflicted a very humiliating defeat on the English again in AD 1782.
- He died on December 7, 1782 during the course of the second Anglo-Mysore war.

Tipu Sultan (AD 1782–1799)

Capital: Srirangapatnam

- He succeeded Haider Ali and in contrast of his father, he dethroned the Raja of Mysore and openly assumed the **title of Sultan** in AD 1786.
- He continued the **Second war with British** till AD 1784, when both the sides got tired and concluded peace by the **Treaty of Mangalore** (March 1784) on the basis of mutual restitution of conquests.
- He fought the **Third Anglo-Mysore war** (AD 1790–92) in which the Marathas and Nizam allied with the British. He signed the **Treaty of Srirangapatnam (March 1792)**, which led to the surrender of nearly half of the Mysorean territory to the victories' allies.

- The fourth **Anglo-Mysore war (AD 1799)** ended in complete collapse of Tipu's power and he died fighting.
- After the war, a titular ruler belonging to the Mysore Hindu Ruler family was placed on the throne and subsidiary alliance was imposed. The territory was divided among the British, Marathas and the Nizam of Hyderabad.
- Tipu organized the infantry on the Uproar lines and made attempts to build a modern navy-establishment of two dockyards.
- He appreciated the importance of economic strength as the foundation of military strength of his Empire.
- He made attempts to introduce modern industries by extending state support.
- He sent ambassadors to France, Turkey, Iran, Peru and to Zaman Shah of Afghanistan to develop foreign trade.
- He attempted to set up a trading company on the European lines.
- His introduced a **new System of Coinage,** new scales of weights and measures and a new calendar.
- Like his father he also issued coins with the images of Hindu deities. He had great regards for **Jagadguru Shankaracharya** of Sringeri and offered him funds for the repairs of temples.
- He tried to increase the state income by the abolition of the Jagir System and also by reducing the hereditary possessions of the Poligars (feudal chiefs).
- He stopped the collection of illegal taxes and granted remission, whenever the need arose, so as to improve the position of the peasantry.

Important Facts related to Tipu

- He was great admirer of Jagadguru Sankracharya of Sringeri and offered him funds for the establishment of image of Goddess Sharda which was vandalized by Marathas.
- **Tarikh-i-Khudai** is his autobiography.
- He wrote a military manual **Fatahul Mujahidin,** in which rocket technology and rocket bridges was mentioned.
- He completed Lal Bagh Project (Bangalore) started by Haider and also laid foundation of Krishnaraj Sagar Dam on Cauvery River.
- Took keen interests in the French revolution and planted the tree of liberty at Srirangapatnam and became the member of the Jacobin Club. He also called himself "Citizen Tipu".
- The famous temple of Sri Rangnath was situated barely a hundred yards from his place. He assumed the title of Padshah in 1979.

The Punjab: Sikhism and Sikh Gurus

- Guru Nanak established the Sikh religion in Punjab. There were ten sikh gurus.

Guru Nanak (AD 1469 to 1539)

- 1st sikh guru and he established the Nanak Panth.
- He was contemporary to Ibrahim Lodi and Babur.

Personal Details

Brith	Talwandi
Death	Kartarpur (Derababa)

Father's Name	Kaluji
Mother's Name	Tirpta
Wife's Name	Sulakshni
Title	Hajrat Rabbul Majij

Guru Angad (Lehna) (AD 1539–52)

- He shifted the seat of guru of Khadur.
- He discovered the Gurumukhi script and regularized the langar system.

Guru Amardas (AD 1552–74)

- He shifted the seat of guru to Goindwal.
- Mughal emperor Akbar visited Goindwal to meet him. Akbar gave land grants to Bibibhani, daughter of Amaradas.
- He divided his spiritual empire into 22 parts called Manjis and each Manjis was put under the charge of Sikha.

Guru Ramdas (AD 1574–81)

- Mughal emperor Akbar granted him 500 bigha land on which be established the city of **Amritsar** (earlier known as Ramdaspur).
- He is made the post of Guru hereditary.

Guru Arjan Dev (AD 1581–1606)

- He is also known as "Saccha Badshah".
- He constructed a lake at Amritsar and also Santoshsar lake at Ramdaspur. In AD 1589, he constructed the Harimandir Saheb in the mid of Amritsar lake.
- He founded the city of Tarantarn, Kartarpur and Govindpur.
- He levied a compulsory religious tax (1/10th of one's income).
- In AD 1604, he wrote the **Adigranth.**
- He was executed by Mughal emperor Jahangir in AD 1606.

Guru Arjan Dev

Guru Hargovind (AD 1606–45)

- He transformed the Sikhs into a warrior caste.
- He fortified the city of Amritsar and built a 12 feet high "Aakaal Takhaqt" in the Harmandir Saheb complex at Amritsar.
- He permitted his followers to take non-vegetarian food.
- He founded the city of Kiratpur in Kashmir.

Guru Harraya (AD 1645–61)

- He met Darashikov, son of Aurangzeb.
- His son Ramraya visited Aurangzeb's court.

Guru Harkishan (AD 1664–75)

- During his period, Ramraya established a separate seat at Dehradun. His followers were known as Ramrayi.

Guru Teg Bahadur (AD 1664–75)

- He shifted the seat of guru to Makhovali.
- He was executed by Aurangzeb. Sis Ganj Gurudwara at Delhi marks the site of his Martyrdom.

Guru Govind Singh (AD 1675–1708)

- 10th and last guru of the Sikhs.
- He was bron in AD 1666 at Patna.
- He founded the city of Anandpur and established his seat there.
- He founded the city of Paonta in Himachal Pradesh and gave Military training to his followers.
- He defeated Fatehshah, ruler of Srinagar and then established four forts at Anandgarh, Keshgarh, Lauchgarh and Fatehgarh.
- He established the Khalsa Panth in AD 1699. (on Baisakhi day)
- **War with the Mughals** Battle of Nandon (AD 1690), two Battles of Anandpur, Battle of Chankmaur and Battle of Khirdana (AD 1705).
- Adigranth was lost in the Battle of Khiradana but he complied it again.
- He summoned the assembly of Sikhs at Anantpur and selected 5 persons (Panj Piaras) who took the water of immortality. The Sikhs were now required to keep 5 k's viz, Kesh, Kripan, Kach, Kanga and Kara.
- He wrote Krishna Avtar, Chindi diwar, his Autobiography– Vichitra Natak and Dasvan Padshah ka Granth.
- The Sikh Khalsa (army of the pure) rose up against the economic and political represented in Punjab towards the end Aurangzeb's rule.
- After the formation of the Khalsa, the political and military power of the Sikhs grew tremendously and by the early 1800's, the Sikhs managed to carve out an independent kingdom in the Mughal Empire, which they retained until the British annexations in the 1850's.
- An additional factor in this context being the Afghan defeat of the Maratha armies which accelerated the breakaway of Punjab from Delhi and helped in founding the Sikh overlandship in the North-West.

Banda Bahadur (AD 1708–16)

- Guru Gobind Singh died In AD 1708 and after him Banda Bahadur took the leadership of the Sikhs in the first decade of the 18th century and began the Sikh war of independence against the Mughal imperial authority. He defeated Wazir Khan, the governor of Sirhind and established himself in a strong hill fort which he named Lohgarh.

Banda Bahadur

- His disciples called him **"Sachha Padashah"** or veritable sovereign and coins were struck in his name. Under Banda, the Sikhs became a formidable force in Punjab between AD 1707 and AD 1715 and the Mughal's had not put in immense efforts to control him.
- Abdus Samad Khan, the Mughal Governor of Lahore, ultimately succeeded in defeating and capturing Banda Bahadur and his followers. He and his son were tortured to death

at Delhi during the reign of Emperor Farrukhsiyar on 19th June 1716.

- After Banda, the Sikhs organized themselves under the leadership of Ranjit Singh, who formed Dal Khalsa or the army sof theocracy of Sikhs. The invasions of Nadir Shah in AD 1739 and Ahmed Shah Abdali, between AD 1748 to AD 1767, provided opportunities for the further assertion of Siksh influcnece and power in Punjab.
- In AD 1764, the Sikhs assembled at Amritsar and struck the first coin of pure silver with the legned **"Degh, Tegh, Fateh".** This is regarded as the first proclamation of the Sikh sovereignty in Punjab.
- In AD 1770's, they organized themselves into 12 "misls" (Military brotherhood with democratic setup) or confederacies. The leaders of these misls exercised control over different areas in the Punjab.
- Thus Maha Singh, the father of Ranjit Singh, was the leader of Sukarchakiya misl and controlled the territory between the Ravi and the Chenab.

Name of the Misl	Name of the Founder or leader
Singhpuria Misl	Nawab Kapur Singh
Ahluwalia Misl	Jassa Singh Ahluwalia
The Ramgurhia Misl	Jassa Singh Ramgarhia
The Phulkian Misl	Phul Singh
Kanhiva Misl	Jai Singh
Bhagi Misl	Hari Singh
Sukarchakya Misl	Charat Singh
Nishanwalia Misl	Sardar Sangat Singh
Karor Singhia Misl	Bhagel Singh
Dallewalia Misl	Gulab Singh
Nakai Misl	Hira Singh
Shahidi Misl	Baba Deep Singh

Ranjit Singh (AD 1792–1839)

- The leader of the Sikhs with a modern vision and under him the Sikh power reached its Zenith.

Ranjit Singh

- He was the son of Maha Singh, a head of Sukarchakiya misl (a Small Jagir or regency of Punjab). Punjab was divided into twelve such Jagirs at that time.
- He ascended the throne in AD 1792, at the age of 12, but during the initial five years of his reign he ruled through a Regency Council, headed by his mother.
- He took the complete charge of the government, in AD 1797, at the early age of 17 years.
- In AD 1798, Zaman Shah (Son of Ahmed Shah Abdali) who considered himself to be the rightful ruler of Punjab, authorized Ranjit Singh to occupy Lahore and rule it on his behalf.
- He captured Lahore and Amritsar from the Sardars of Bhagi Misl.

- He made Lahore his political capital and assumed the title of Maharaja of Lahore in AD 1799.
- He achieved supremacy over the other misls and established his kingdom in which Sikhs, Hindus and Muslims lived together in harmony and increasing prosperity.
- He employed European officers and introduced strict military discipline into his army before expanding into Afghanistan, Kashmir and Ladakh.
- He established his authority over the entire territory from Sutlej to Jhelum.
- He defeated the confederacy of Sikh misls formed under Gulab Singh, thus emerging a powerful leader of the whole Sikh community.
- He signed the **Treaty of Amritsar** in AD 1809 with the East India Company (Lord Metcalf) regarding rights over the Sutlej area.
- He helped Shah Shuja, grandson of Ahmed Shah Abdali, during the succession war in Afghanistan and in return, took the famous Kohinoor diamond form him Later the throne was occupied by **Dost Mohammad.**
- Sikh forces, under the commandership of **Hari Singh Naula,** defeated the Afghan invader, Dost Muhammad.
- East India Company removed Dost Mohammad from the throne of Kabul and place Shah Shuja in his place.
- He signed **Tripartite Treaty, in AD 1838**, with Shah Shuja and the EIC (Lord Auckland), which gave freedom to the British troops to pass through the Punjab. Thus, the English rest cited the advance of Russian forces in India through Punjab, with the help of Ranjit Singh.
- He was an able administrator who not only maintained but also expanded his empire through battle and well thought out strategic treaties with the Afghans and the English.
- He renovated the Sikh Shrine decorating the lower half with marble and the entire upper portion was inlaid with copper surmounted with thin plate of gold and gave it the modern name of the **Golden Temple.**
- He died in AD 1839.
- After the death of Ranjit Singh, the line of weak Successors followed—Kharak Singh; Nao Nihal Singh; Sher Singh and Dalip Singh, which led the Sikh empire to its downfall.

First Anglo-Sikh War

- During the reign of Dalip Singh the English invaded Punjab (the first Anglo Sikh War, AD 1845-46), occupied Lahore and dictated a peace treaty, known as the Teraty of Lahore, on March 9,1846.
- Since the Lahore Durbar was unable to pay the war indemnity, it agreed to transfer to the company the hill countries situated between the river Beas and Indus, including the province of Kashmir. **Gulab Singh** who was instrumental in these negotiations, was given Kashmir by the company.

Second Anglo-Sikh War

- However the things did not improved in Punjab which soon led to the **Second Anglo-Sikh War (AD 1848–1849)** after which Punjab was annexed to the company by Lord Dalhousie. **Raja Dalip Singh** and **Rani Jindal** (the queen of Ranjit Singh) were sent away to London on fixed annual pensions.

- Lawrence became the first commissioner of Punjab.

The Jats

- Spread mainly in the rural regions of Haryana, Punjab, western parts of the Ganga Doab and eastern Rajputana, the Jats were recognized as a group practicing agriculture, during the ancient and medieval periods. Being strong warriors, they were also employed as soldiers by Hindu as Well as Muslim kings.
- However in the second half of the 17th century the ambition of some of the Jat Zamindars of the Agra region to establish an independent principality brought them in conflict with the Mughal government, the Rajputs and the Afghans.
- Finally it was **Suraj Mal** who successfully welded the scattered Jat Zamindars near Agra into one powerful state. Though internally, it remained a tribal confederacy, the rise of a Jat state had a definite impact on the political system of North India. Some important leaders of the community were as follows:

Gokla

- He was the Zamindar of Tilpat.
- He provided leadership to the Jat uprisings in AD 1669.
- It was suppressed by the Mughal governor, Hasan Ali khan.

Rajarama

- He was the Zamindar of Sinsani.
- He provided leadership to the Jat uprising in AD 1685.
- It was suppressed by Raja Bishan Singh Kachwaha of Amber.

Churaman (AD 1690–1721)

- He was the nephew of Rajarma.
- He defeated Mughals in AD 1704 and captured Sinsani.
- He obtained Mansab from the Mughal ruler Bahadu Shah I and established the state of Bharatpur.
- He served in Bahadur Shah's campaign against Banda Bahadur.
- He became influential in the region after Bahadur Shah's death in AD 1712.
- He was suppressed by Raja Jai Singh Sawai of Amber.

Badan Singh (AD 1722–1756)

- He was the nephew of Churaman.
- Ahmad Shah Abdali gave him the title of "Raja".
- He may be regarded as the real founder of the Jat states of Bharatpur.

Suraj Mal (AD 1756–1765)

- He was the adopted son and successor of Badan Singh.
- Under him the Jat kingdom reached its zenith. He had remarkable talents for war and diplomacy.
- He is remembered as "The Plato of Jat Tribe" and as "Jat Ulysses."
- He led expeditions in the regions of Agra, Mewar and Delhi agreed to help the Marathas in the 3rd Battle of Panipat. His expansionist activities resulted in a clash with Najib-ud-daula, the vice-regent of Delhi.
- He was killed by Pathans near Delhi.

Rajputs

- Rajputs were unhappy with the policies of emperor Aurangzeb and declared their independence. In AD 1708, Bahadur Shah invaded Jodhpur, followed by the Mughal commander Hussain Ali in AD 1714.
- In AD 1721, Sayyid brothers appointed Maharaja Jai Singh as the Subahdar of Agra and emperor Muhammad Shah further gave him the area of Gujarat.

Sawai Jai Singh II (AD 1688–1747)

- He was a distinguished statesman and an astronomer. He went on to construct observatories also known as **Jantar Mantar** in stone so as to calculate planetary positions at Varanasi, Delhi, Ujjain, Mathura and Jaipur which is a world heritage site.

Sawai Jai Singh II

- He also compiled a table of observation known as Ziz-i-Jadid-Muhammad Shahi, also translated important works into Sanskrit including Euclid's Geometry.
- He was a social reformer who tried to curb the practice of female infanticide. He went on to perform Ashwamedha sacrifice (Vedic ritual).
- He was also given the title **of Sarmad-i-Raja-i-Hind.**

City of Jaipur

Foudations of the city was laid in AD 1727 by Sawai Jai Singh II. It was one of the first planned cities based on the principles of Vastu Shastra with help of town planner Vidhyadhar Bhattacharya. The king shifted his capital from Amber to Jaipur.

Chapter at a Glance

- The foundations of Hyderabad was laid down by the Mughal wazir Chinklich Khan alias Nizam-ul-Mulk in 1724. He had played major role in the donwfall of Saiyyad brothers and in place of his work, he got the Subahdari of Decean.
- The profit from the weak central government was taken by the affluent province of Bengal, Murshidkuli Khan and Alivardi Khan were two very brave and efficient rulers in Bengal. With their efforts, Bengal became independent. Murshidkuli Khan was the Dewan of Bengal since 1700. In 1717 when he was made the Subadar of Bengal, he established law and order and made Bengal free from internal dissensions and external dangers. Bengal became free from external dangers. Bengal became free from revolts. Sita Ram Roy, Udai Narain, Ghulam Mohammad and Shujat Khan revolted but they were all defeated and their Jagirs were given to Ram Jeewan.
- The founder of the independent kingdom of Awadh was Sadaat Khan popularly known as Burhan-ul-mulk. In 1772 he became the Subahdar of Awadh. He had to face the revolt of Zamindars.

Majority of the Jagirdars had become rebellious and they rebelled whenever they found the opportunity. All the energy of Sadaat Khan was wasted in crushing these revolts. Had he used this energy in developing his state, things could have been different. His successor Safdarjung wrote "The chiefs of Awadh rebelled in a minute. They were more dangerous than the Marathas."

- After the downfall of Vijaynagar, the state of Mysore had its separate existence. It was ruled by the Wadiyar Dynasty. During the time of Chikka Krishna Raj the influence of his two ministers, Nanja Raj and Dev Raj increased their power and the king remianed just a puppet in his hands. At the same time Hyder Ali emerged as the ruler. He made Mysore a very powerful and prestigious state. The British began to consider him as their dangerous rival.
- In 18th century, there were numberous small feudal lords in Kerala but four of them were important—Calicut, Chirakkal, Kochin and Travancore. Martanda Verma was very influential there. In 1766 Hyder Ali subjugated Kerala.

Previous Year Question Paper (1998–2017)

1. The Vijay Satambha (Tower of Victory) at Chittor was built by
   (a) Rana Pratap (b) Rana Kumbha
   (c) Rana Sanga (d) Bappa Raval
   (IAS 1998)
2. Who is considered the father of Sahtara (Sitar)?
   (a) Mian Tansen
   (b) Baiju Bawara
   (c) Khurshro Khan
   (d) Bade Ghulam Ali Khan **(IAS 1999)**
3. Match List-I with List-II and select the correct answer using the codes given below the Lists

List-I (Place)	List-II (Associated with)
A. Tughlaqabad	1. Alauddin Khilji
B. Red Fort, Delhi	2. Shahjahan
C. Hauj Khas	3. Firoz Shah Tughlaq
D. The City of Siri	4. Ghiyasuddin Tughlaq

Codes:	A	B	C	D
(a)	1	2	3	4
(b)	4	2	3	1
(c)	4	3	2	1
(d)	3	1	4	2

(UPPCS 1998)

4. In which of the following cities is Charminar situated?
   (a) Mysore (b) Rajkot
   (c) Hyderabad (d) Lucknow
   (UPPCS 1998)
5. Match the following

Temple/Heritage Site	State
A. Brihadeswara Temple	1. Orissa
B. Dilwara Temple	2. Tamil Nadu
C. Lingaraja Temple	3. Karnataka
D. Hampi Group of Monuments	4. Rajasthan
	5. Kerala

Codes:	A	B	C	D
(a)	1	3	5	4
(b)	2	4	1	3
(c)	2	3	1	4
(d)	1	4	5	3

(IAS-2001)

6. Match List-I with List-II and select the correct answer using the codes given below the Lists

List-I	List-II
A. Iltutmish	1. Mausoleum at Sasaram
B. Quli Qutub Shah	2. Agra Fort
C. Sher Shah	3. Charminar
D. Akbar	4. Qutub Minar

Codes:	A	B	C	D
(a)	3	4	2	1
(b)	4	3	1	2
(c)	4	3	2	1
(d)	3	4	1	2

(IAS-2002)

7. Which one of the following pairs of History landmark and the associated person is NOT correctly matched
   (a) Slave Dynasty : Qutubuddin Aibak
   (b) Tughlaq Dynasty : Ghiyasuddin
   (c) Second Anglo -Mysore War : Hyder Ali
   (d) Battle of Buxar : Sirajuddaulah

(IAS-2003)

8. Match List-I (Events) with List-II (Years) and select the correct answer using the codes given below the Lists

List-I	List-II
A. Alauddin Bahman Shah proclaimed king of Deccan	1. 1298
B. Governor of Malwa made himself independent of Delhi Sultanate	2. 1336
C. Alauddin Khilji conquered Gujarat	3. 1347
D. Foundation of Vijaynagar on the banks of Tungabhadra	4. 1401

Codes:	A	B	C	D
(a)	3	4	1	2
(b)	4	3	2	1
(c)	3	4	2	1
(d)	4	3	1	2

(IAS-2004)

9. Dhrupad Dhamar style of singing was started by
   (a) Amir Khusrau
   (b) Raja Man Singh Tomar
   (c) Tansen
   (d) Vishnu Digambar Paluskar

(IAS-2005)

10. Match List-I with List-II and select the correct answer using the codes given below the Lists

List-I	List-II
A. Ibadatkhana	1. Qutubuddin Aibak
B. Jama Masjid, Delhi	2. Rana Kumbha
C. Adhai Din Ka Jhonpada	3. Shahjahan
D. Vijay Stambha, Chittor	4. Mehmud Begada
	5. Akbar

Codes:	A	B	C	D
(a)	5	3	1	2
(b)	5	3	4	2
(c)	2	4	5	1
(d)	3	5	1	4

(IAS-2006)

11. Match List-I with List-II and select the correct answer using the codes given below the Lists

List-I (Dynasty)	List-II (State)
A. Kadamba	1. Orissa
B. Kharvela	2. Karnataka
C. Chalukya	3. Bengal
D. Pala	4. Gujarat

Codes:	A	B	C	D
(a)	1	2	4	3
(b)	1	2	3	4
(c)	2	1	3	4
(d)	2	1	4	3

(IAS-2007)

12. Consider the following statements:
    1. Mirabai was a contemporary of Guru Nanak
    2. Ramdas was a contemporary of Shivaji

    Which of the statements given above is/are correct?
    (a) 1 only (b) 2 only
    (c) Both 1 and 2 (d) Neither 1 nor 2
    (IAS-2008)

13. Consider the following statements
    1. Muhammad Shah (1719 - 48) was the first Mughal ruler to patronize Urdu.
    2. Malik Muhammad Jayasi wrote the famous epic 'Padmavat' in Hindi.

    Which of the statements given above is/are correct?
    (a) 1 only (b) 2 only
    (c) Both 1 and 2 (d) Neither 1 nor 2
    (IAS-2009)

14. Who of the following built the temple of the Sun God at Konark?
    (a) Avantvarman (b) Narasimha I
    (c) Kapilendra (d) Purushottama
    (IAS-2010)

Answers

1. (b)	2. (c)	3. (b)
4. (c)	5. (b)	6. (b)
7. (d)	8. (a)	9. (b)
10. (a)	11. (d)	12. (c)
13. (c)	14. (b)	

Practice Paper

1. Khalsa was founded by
   (a) Guru Gobind Singh
   (b) Guru Ramdas
   (c) Guru Nanak
   (d) Guru Arjun Dev **(SSC 2005)**
2. Which was the birth place of Guru Nanak?
   (a) Gurdaspur (b) Amritsar
   (c) Lahore (d) Talwandi
   (SSC 2006)
3. Which Governor General had entertained Ranjit Singh with great honour at Ropar?
   (a) Minto I (b) William Bentick
   (c) Hastings (d) Auckland
   (SSC 2007)
4. Which Governor General is associated with Doctrine of Lapse?
   (a) Lord Ripon (b) Lord Dalhousie
   (c) Lord Bentick (d) Lord Curzon
   (SSC 2010)
5. Tipu Sultan took support of which one of the following powers to fight the English?
   (a) Portuguese
   (b) French

(c) Spanish
(d) Dutch **(SCRA 2005)**

6. In which of the following years, the Battle of Buxar was fought?
(a) 1764 (b) 1766
(c) 1767 (d) 1761
(RRB 2006)

7. Which one of the following places was famous as capital of Tipu Sultan?
(a) Srirangpattam (b) Gulbarga
(c) Hampi (d) None of these
(RRB 2008)

8. Tipu Sultan died fighting the English forces under
(a) Lord Cornwallis
(b) Lord Wellesley
(c) Lord Dalhousie
(d) Lord Hastings
(CRPF Assit. Commt. 2008)

9. When did the British Government start ruling India directly?
(a) After the Battle of Plassey
(b) After the Battle of Panipat
(c) After the War of Mysore
(d) After Sepoy Mutiny
(RAS/RTS 2003)

10. Consider the following statements
1. The Sikh leader Banda Bahadur was captured and killed during the reign of Emperor Farrukhsiyar.
2. The Marathas fought with Ahmed Shah Abdali at Panipat during the reign of Emperor Shah Alam II.

Which of the above statements is/are correct?
(a) 1 only (b) 2 only
(c) Both 1 and 2 (d) neither 1 nor 2
(NDA 2004)

11. **Assertion (A):** The state of Hyderabad was founded by Nizam-ul-Mulk, as wazir of Mughal Emperor.
Reason (R): The Mughal Emperor frustrated all the attempts of Nizam-ul-ulk at reforming the administration of the empire.
Code:
(a) Both A and R are true and R is the correct explanation of A
(b) Both A and R are true but R is not a correct explanation of A
(c) A is true but R is false
(d) A is false but R is true **(NDA 2004)**

12. Who issued *Firman* granting Diwani of Bengal, Bihar and Orissa to the English?
(a) Ahmed Shah (b) Bahadur Shah
(c) Furrukhsiyar (d) Shah Alam II
(NDA 2006)

13. Who was the first Indian native ruler to accept the system of Subsidiary Alliance?
(a) Scindia of Gwalior
(b) Nizam of Hyderabad
(c) Dalip Singh of Punjab
(d) Gaikwad of Baroda
(NDA 2007, CDS 2003, MP PCS (P) 2009)

14. The state of Jhansi was made a part of the British Empire in India through
(a) The policy of Doctrine of Lapse
(b) The policy of Subsidiary Alliance
(c) Mayo's Provincial settlement
(d) War against Gangadhar Rao
(CDS 2001)

15. With reference to the colonical rule of India, which one of the following was NOT the feature of subsidiary Alliance System?
(a) A subsidiary British army was to be maintained in the Indian State.
(b) The determination of expenses incurred on the subsidiary British army was the duty of Indian State.
(c) The Indian State had to keep a British resident in her capital.

(d) Indian soldier could be used by the company commanders. **(CDS 2002)**

16. The founder of the autonomous kingdom of Awadh was
(a) Shujauddaula
(b) Saadat Khan Burhan-ul-Mulk
(c) Safdarjang
(d) Sher Shah **(CDS 2004)**

17. Who of the following joined Mir Qasim and Shujauddaula in declaring war upon the English East India Company and was later defeated by the British at the Battle of Buxar?
(a) Jahandar Shah
(b) Farrukhsiyar
(c) Muhammad Shah
(d) Shah Alam II **(CDS 2004, 2006)**

18. The main cause of the conflict between Nawab Sirajuddaula and the East India Company was that–
(a) The British opposed the succession of Sirajuddaula
(b) The British misused the Dustaq (free duty passes)
(c) The British attacked the French settlement of Chandranagar in Bengal
(d) The incident of black hole had occured **(CDS 2004)**

19. Consider the following statements
1. The treaty of Lahore was concluded between Sikhs and English Company during the tenure of Lord Ellenborough.
2. Lord Dalhousie made the annexation of Punjab to the British dominion.

Which of the statements given above is/are correct?
(a) 1 only (b) 2 only
(c) Both 1 and 2 (d) Neither 1 nor 2 **(CDS 2005)**

20. Who among the following was the first Governor General of Bengal?
(a) Robert Clive
(b) William Bentick
(c) Marquess Wellesley
(d) Waren Hastings **(CDS 2006)**

21. By which one of the following Acts did the Governor General of Bengal became the Governor General of India?
(a) The Regulating Act
(b) The Pitt's India Act
(c) The Charter Act of 1793
(d) The Charter Act of 1833 **(CDS 2006)**

22. With reference to the treaties made by the English with native rulers of India in the 18th century, which one of the following pairs is NOT correctly matched ?
(a) Treaty of Allahabad : Shujauddaulah
(b) Treaty of Purandar : Marathas
(c) Treaty of Mangalore : Anwaruddin
(d) Treaty of Srirangapatnam : Tipu Sultan
(CDS 2006)

23. What was the reason of ground for the British Empire to annex Sambalpur in 1850?
(a) Lack of proper governance
(b) Death of its ruler without an heir
(c) Subsidiary Alliance
(d) Its involvement in a conspiracy against British Rule **(CDS 2008)**

24. Who among the following was NOT a party to the league that was defeated by the British in the Battle of Buxar?
(a) Shujauddaulah
(b) Shah Alam

(c) Mir Jafar
(d) Mir Kasim **(CDS 2009)**

25. The Dual Governent recommended by Lord Clive provided that the
(a) Criminal justice would be left to the Nawabi officials, while civil and fiscal matters would be controlled by the company.
(b) Company will look after fiscal matters and all the rest would be dealt by the India rulers.
(c) Indian rulers will deal with all the matters of administration under the supervision of a company official.
(d) Indian rulers will only titular head and all the powers shall be directly dealt by the Company. **(CDS 2010)**

26. Which of the following Indians was appointed as Deputy Diwan of Bihar by Robert Clive?
(a) Omi Chand (b) Manik Chand
(c) Rai Durlabh (d) Raja Shaitab Rai
(44th BPSC 2001)

27. Who was appointed Deputy Diwan of Murshidabad (Bengal) by Robert Clive after the Allahabad Treaty?
(a) Mohd. Reza Khan
(b) Raja Shitab Rai
(c) Rai Durlabh
(d) Syed Ghulam Hussain
(45th BPSC 2002)

28. Emperor Shah Alam II gave the diwani of Bengal, Bihar and Orissa to East India Company on
(a) 12 August, 1765
(b) 18 August, 1765
(c) 29 August, 1765
(d) 21 August, 1765
(48th-52nd BPSC 2008)

29. Hyder Ali was defeated at Porto Novo by which British General?
(a) Captain Pophem
(b) Sir Eyrecoot
(c) Captain Hector Munro
(d) General Gedard **(JPSC 2003)**

30. The successor of Maharja Ranjit Singh was
(a) Kharaq Singh
(b) Harihar Singh Nalwa
(c) Sher Singh
(d) Naunihal Singh **(JPSC 2003)**

31. Which Sikh Guru helped the rebel prince Khusro with money and blessings?
(a) Guru Hargovind
(b) Guru Govind Singh
(c) Guru Aruju Dev
(d) Guru Tegh Bahadur
(UP PCS (P) 2003)

32. A group of eunuches and ladies dominated in the Government under:
(a) Muhammad Shah (1719-48)
(b) Ahmed Shah (1948-54)
(c) Alamgir II (1754-59)
(d) Shah Alam II (1759-1806)
(UP PCS (M) 2004)

33. Sirajuddaulah was defeated by Lord Clive in the battle of:
(a) Plassey (b) Buxar
(c) Munger (d) Wandiwash
(UPPCS 2005)

34. In whose reign, Guru Nanak Dev established Sikhism?
(a) Firoz Shah Tughlaq
(b) Sikandar Lodi
(c) Humayun
(d) Akbar **(UPPSC 2008)**

35. Who of the following compiled 'Adigranth' or 'Guru Granth Saheb'?
(a) Guru Nanak Dev
(b) Guru Teg Bahadur
(c) Guru Govind Singh
(d) Guru Arjun Dev **(Utt. PSC 2005)**

36. The first Governor General of India was appointed in
(a) 1774 (b) 1833
(c) 1858 (d) 1911
(Utt. PSC 2007)

37. Which of the following was capital of Raja Ranit Singh of Punjab?
(a) Amritsar (b) Lahore
(c) Rawalpindi (d) Peshawar
(Utt. PSC 2005)

38. When was the Battle of Plassey fought?
(a) 1757 (b) 1789
(c) 1848 (d) 1857
(MPPSC 2004)

39. First decisive military success of English East India Company in India is marked by
(a) Battle of Buxar
(b) Battle of Plassey
(c) Battle of Panipat
(d) Battle of Haldi Ghati
(MPPSC 2008)

40. The book 'Jiz Muhammad Shahi' related to knowledge of Astrology produced in 1733 is written by-
(a) Jaswant Singh of Jodhpur
(b) Raja Bharmall of Amber
(c) Sawai Jai Singh of Jaipur
(d) Maharana Amar Singh of Udaipur
(RAS/RTS 2007)

41. Who converted Sikhs into a martial race?
(a) Arjun Dev (b) Gobind Singh
(c) Hargobind (d) Teg Bahadur
(WBPSC 2007)

42. Who founded independent sultanate of Bengal?
(a) Ilias Shah
(b) Murshid Quli Khan
(c) Hussain Shah
(d) Alivardi Khan **(WBPSC 2007)**

43. Who founded Sikhism?
(a) Gobind Singh (b) Ramdas
(c) Nanak (d) Hargobind
(WBPSC 2007)

44. Which Sikh Guru assumed the title 'Sachcha Padshaha'?
(a) Guru Nanak
(b) GuruTeg Bahadur
(c) Guru Hargovind
(d) Guru Gobind Singh **(WBPSC 2007)**

45. The first Governor General of India was
(a) Lord Clive
(b) Lord Canning
(c) Lord William Bentick
(d) Lord Lytton **(WBPSC 2007)**

46. Who among the following was not involved in the conspiracy against Sirajuddaulah?
(a) Manikchand (b) Omichand
(c) Mohanlal (d) Clive
(WBPSC 2008)

47. The East India Company secured the Diwani from
(a) Sujauddaulah (b) Aurangzeb
(c) Bahadur Shah (d) Shah Alam II
(WBPSC 2008)

48. The Gurumukhi script was introduced by
(a) Guru Amardas(b) Guru Ramdas
(c) Guru Angad (d) Guru Nanak
(WBPSC 2008)

49. Who was the Governor General when the first Anglo-Burmese war started?
(a) George Barlow
(b) Lord Hastings
(c) Lord Minto
(d) Lord Amherst **(WBPSC 2008)**

50. Who was the last independent Nawab of Bengal?
(a) Sirajuddaulah (b) Najmuddaulah
(c) Mir Kasim (d) Mir Jafar
(WBPSC 2008)

51. The last major extension of British Indian territory took place during the time of
(a) Dufferin (b) Lytton
(c) Curzon (d) Minto I
(UPSC 2000)

52. Who among the following Indian rulers established embassies in foreign countries on modern lines?
(a) Haider Ali (b) Mir Qasim
(c) Shah Alam II (d) Tipu Sultan
(UPSC 2001)

Answers

1. (a)	2. (d)	3. (b)	28. (a)	29. (b)	30. (a)
4. (b)	5. (b)	6. (a)	31. (c)	32. (b)	33. (a)
7. (a)	8. (b)	9. (d)	34. (b)	35. (d)	36. (b)
10. (c)	11. (a)	12. (d)	37. (b)	38. (a)	39. (a)
13. (b)	14. (a)	15. (d)	40. (c)	41. (b)	42. (b)
16. (b)	17. (d)	18. (b)	43. (c)	44. (b)	45. (c)
19. (b)	20. (d)	21. (d)	46. (c)	47. (d)	48. (c)
22. (c)	23. (b)	24. (c)	49. (d)	50. (c)	51. (a)
25. (a)	26. (d)	27. (a)	52. (d)		

CHAPTER

4

Emergence of European Powers in India

The Portuguese

- It was in AD 1492 that Christopher Columbus, who wanted to reach India but discovered America instead leading to exploration and colonization of these continents.
- Prince Henry of Portugal encouraged voyages for the discovery of sea-routes to India following which Bartholomew Diaz reached Cape of Good Hope in AD 1948.
- Vasco da Gama (colonial Man) from Lisbon, discovered a new sea route from Europe to Asia via Cape of Good Hope. He was helped by Gujarati Navigator Ibn Majid.
- He landed at Calicut on May 21, 1498. Calicut, then under the Zamorins, enjoyed a high degree of prosperity. The Zamorin was kind to all classes of merchants who came to his kingdom, tolerated all creeds and allowed perfect freedom to all in commercial affairs.
- He gave the newcomers a friendly reception. Vasco da Gama returned to Portugal in AD 1499.
- A second expedition, under Pedro Alvarez Cabral and Gama reached Calicut in AD 1500.
- Cabral, founder of the Brazil forced Calicut to submit and persecuted Arabian traders, in the interest of Portuguese commerce in India.
- A fresh expedition under Vasco da Gama which started in AD 1501 demanded from the Zamorin the banishment of every Muslim resident from Calicut. He strengthened the factories at Cochin and Cannanore and left a squadron to supervise the Malabar Coast and to destroy all Arab vessels coming to it from the Red Sea.
- On his departure, the Arab merchants and the Zamorin attacked the raja of Cochin who bravely held out until relieved by arrival of the next Portuguese fleet in AD 1503.
- The next Portuguese expedition under Lopo Soares destroyed all the ports in which Arab influence prevailed and prevented any ships from coming to or leaving Cochin except their own.

Portuguese Trade

- The Portuguese maritime empire acquired the name of Estado ha India which intended to monopolies the pepper and spice trade of the East.
- Besides controlling the whole of the export trade to Europe, the Portuguese monopolized the port-to-port trade on the Malabar Coast and the trade from the Indian to the Persian coast on the one side and to Malacca on the other.
- Portugal's initial objective was to seize the spice trade, but after Cabral's voyage she decided to divert to herself all the trade of the East with Europe. It was not realized in Portugal that command over the Eastern trade could not be established by sending an annual fleet and establishing a few isolated factories.

Power Establishment

- Thus, a new policy was adopted in AD 1505; a Governor was to be appointed for a three year term.

Francisco de Almeida (AD 1505–09)

- First Governor of Portuguese territory who also fortified Fort Manual in Cochin and built a fort at Anjadiva.

Franciso de Almeida

Battle with Egypt, Turkey and Gujarat

- The systematic assault of the Portuguese on the Muslim (Mainly Arab) monopoly to trade in the Indian Ocean and the Red Sea deprived Egypt and Turkey of the duties on Indian goods passing through the sea route and across Egypt to Alexandria. Similarly, the Sultans of Bijapur and Gujarat feared that the Portuguese would extend their control from the southern (Malabar) ports to the northern ports and encroach upon their interest. This brought about an alliance between Egypt, Turkey and Gujarat against the Portuguese intruders.
- In a Naval battle fought near haul, the combined Muslim fleet won a victory over the Portuguese fleet under Almeida's son who was killed in the battle (January 1508). A year later, Almeida defeated the combined Muslim fleet in a naval **battle near Diu** (February 1509). This victory provided to Portuguese naval supremacy in Asia and "turned the Indian Ocean for the next century into a Portuguese sea."

Alfonso de Albuquerque (AD 1509–15)

- Albuquerque, the next governor built up a great territorial power in India. The plan of Albuquerque consisted of three series of operations.
    - The control of the Persian Gulf and the Red Sea.
    - The establishment of the headquarters of the Portuguese power at central port in the West Coast of India.

- The destruction of Arab trade in the Malaya Peninsula and the Far East.

- The **Conquest of Goa from the Adilshahi Sultan of Bijapur** was Albuquerque's first achievement (February 1510). But as the city was quickly recaptured by the Sultan of Bijapur, he had to undertake second expedition. He recaptured the place and fortified it against any surprise attack. The conquest of Goa Put "The seal on Portuguese naval supremacy along the south-west coast".
- Albuquerque thus extended and fulfilled the aims of Almeida. He gave the Portuguese power a territorial base in India. In view of the paucity of manpower in Portugal, Albuquerque encouraged the lower class of the Portuguese settler to marry Indian women.
- He maintained friendly relations with Vijaynagar and even tried to secure the goodwill of Bijapur. He created regular bodies of trained troops from among Indians. He died in AD 1515 leaving the Portuguese as the strongest naval power in India.

Nino da Cunha (AD 1529—38)

- Established settlements at San Thome near Madras and at Hughli in Bengal and thus developed commerce on the eastern coast.
- In AD 1534, the Portuguese secured permission to build factories at **Satgaon** (Porto Piqueno, little port) from the Sultan of Bengal.
- Chittagong continued to be the 'great port' but Satgaon, the little port lost its prosperity in the second half of the sixteenth century and Hughli became the Porto Piqueno.
- Both Akbar and Jahangir left the Portuguese in undisturbed enjoyment of their rights and privileges at Hughli. In AD 1535, Cunha got possession of **Diu** and **Bassein** from Bahadur Shah of Gujarat.
- By AD 1571 the Asiatic empire of Portugal was divided into three independent commands, namely (i) a **Governership at Mozambique** Controlling the settlements on the African coast; (ii) a viceroyalty at Goa in charge of the Indian and Persian territories coast; and (iii) a governership at Malacca to control the trade of Java and the Spice Archipelago.
- Gradually almost all of their territories were lost to Marathas (Salsette and Bassein in AD 1739)
- Only Goa, Diu and Daman remained with them until AD 1961.

Factual Aspects Associated with Portuguese Control

- The Portuguese brought to India the **Cultivation of tobacco.**
- The Portuguese spread **Catholicism** in certain regions on India's western and eastern coasts. Institution of inquisition was established at Goa in AD 1560.
- The first printing press in India was set up by the Portuguese at Goa in AD 1556; the first scientific work on Indian medicinal plants by a European writer was printed at Goa in AD 1563.
- The Portuguese established their trading stations at Calicut, Cochin, Cannanore, Daman, Salsette, Chaul,

Bombay, San Thome near Madras and Hughli in Bengal.

- Cochin was the early capital of the Portuguese in India. Later the capital was transferred to Goa by Nino da Cunha.
- In AD 1661, the king of Portugal gave Bombay to Charles II of England as dowry when Charles II married the former's sister.
- **Faitories:** It was unfortified trading outposts established by Portuguese on land which could also serve strategic purposes included fleets.
- Gama visited India three times and was buried at **Fort Kochi.**
- **Francisco Xavier,** a famous saint came to India in the period of **Martin Dsousa** to spread Christianity in India and Asia.
- He converted the fisherman tribe on coromandel coast (Paravars) and Malabar coast (Mukkuvas) into Christianity.
- **Cartaze System:** Under this system, all ships passing through Portuguese territories were forced to buy permits or passes, otherwise ships were captured.

The Dutch

- Vereenigde Oos Indische Companie (VOC), popularly known as, Dutch United East India Company was formed in AD **1602.** It was a national undertaking and was granted an exclusive right to trade with India and the East Indies for twenty-one years.

Jan Huygens Linschoten

- It was Corneliess Houtman, a Dutch who first identified all sea routes for them but the real founder of Dutch company in India was Jan Huygens Linschoten, that's why Dutch company is popularly known as Jan or Van company, also wrote a detail account of his experience in India in his work ltinerairo.

Jan Huygens Linschoten

- The company was vested with ample power of attack and conquest by the state. It was the first multinational company to issue stock. The skilful administrative system and the enthusiastic national support which the company enjoyed enabled it to monopolies the entire Spice trade to Europe.

Dutch Settlements in India

- What brought Dutch to India, in the first instance, was rather the requirements of the **archipelago** then of the European market; in other words, it was a distinctly subsidiary interest. The spices of the archipelago were exchanged for cotton goods from Gujarat and the Coromandel Coast.

Settlements at Coromandel Coast

- After an earlier abortive attempt to start trade at Surat and on the Malabar Coast, Admiral Van der Hagen opened up trade with the Coromandel Coast and set up a permanent factory at Masulipatnam (Early in 1605).

- Soon another factory was founded at Devanampatnam (Tegnapatam) or **Fort St David** as it came to be called later (Under English occupation).
- In AD 1610, upon negotiating with the king of Chandragiri, the Dutch found another factory at Pulicut, named **Fort Geldira** in honour of the home province of Van Berchaem, the Director–General of the Coromandel factories.
- Till AD 1689, Pulicut was the chief centre of Dutch on the Coromandel Coast, when it was superseded by Negapatam, acquired from the Portuguese in 1659 AD.
- **Exports:** Textile, woven according to special patterns constituted the chief export of the Coromandel ports.
- As early as AD 1612, the Coromandel trade was described as the left arm of the Malaccas and neighbouring islands by Hendrik Brower, since without the cottons from thence, trade would be dead in the Malaccas.
- Other commodities exported by the Dutch were indigo and saltpeter. Opium, the most important export was consumed in Java and China and yielded enormous profits.
- **Imports:** As regarding imports, apart from species the chief articles of import to the Coromandel were sandalwood and pepper from the archipelago, copper from Japan and textiles from China.
- **Trade from Bengal:** In Bengal the Dutch first established a factory at Pipli, but soon abandoned it for Balasore which was in turn neglected when a firm footing was obtained at Chinsura on the Hughli in AD 1653.
- The Dutch constructed Fort Gustavus at Chinsura. Subsequently, they established factories at Kasimbazar and Patna.

Settlements at Malabar Coast

- Since the pepper trade of Malabar was considered to be less valuable than the Coromandel cloth trade, the Dutch ignored the Malabar Coast.
- The only port belonging to them on this side was **Vengurla** to the North of Goa.
- After a bitter struggle for power, Dutch were finally defeated by English in the **Battle of Bedara, 1759.**

The Significance of the Dutch Trade

- The Dutch on the one hand, dislodged the Portuguese from India's maritime trade, and on the other, they gave a new direction and commodity structure to India's foreign trade. The credit for making Indian textiles the premier export from India goes to the Dutch. The Dutch instead of the spices greatly promoted the export of textiles, which they considered more lucrative. Gradually the Indian textiles found wide acceptance in far flung parts of the world.

The English

- Before the East India Company established trade in India, **John Mildenhall,** a English merchant came to India over land route to trade with Indian merchant in 1599.
- By the end of the seventieth century the merchants of England were jealous of

the prospects of their Dutch rivals and began preparations for a commercial voyage to the East.

- Finally through the charter granted by Queen Elizabeth I on 31 December, 1600 AD under the title of 'The Governor and Company of Merchants of London trading into the East Indies' was formed.
- It was having joint stock structure, independent fleets and court of directors (24 in number) annually elected by Shareholders with profit making as main motive.
- The immediate aim of the company was the acquisition of the spices and pepper of the Eastern Archipelago and therefore the First two voyages of the company, between AD 1601–1606, were made, not to India, but to Achin (In Sumatra), Bantam (in Java) and the Malaccas.
- Finally with the third voyage in AD 1608, the English initiated the process of the company's trade with India and Captain William Hawkins who had experience in such ventures and could speak Turkish, was provided with a letter from King James I to Akbar.

English Settlements at Western Coast

- The English beginning in India was not very promising on account of Portuguese rivalry. **William Hawkins** journeyed from Surat and arrived at the **Jahangir's Court**, in AD 1609, but failed to get permission to erect a factory at Surat.
- Jahangir though initially willing to grant permission later refused due to Portuguese pressure.
- However the victory of English under Captain Best over Portuguese fleet at Swally (near Surat) in AD 1612 broke the tradition of Portuguese naval supremacy and a Farman was issued by Jahangir permitting the English to establish a factory at Surat (AD 1613).
- **Sir Thomas Roe,** the royal ambassador from King James I to the Mughal emperor, succeeded in getting two *Farmans* by 1618, one of the Mughal Emperor Jahangir, and the other of the Prince (Khurram) granting the permission to trade and erect factories in different parts of the Empire.
- **Surat** was one of the Chief centers of maritime trade and caravans started from it for all the inland parts of India. Indeed, it is from Surat that the English extended their inland trading operations and by 1616 built subordinate factories at **Ahmedabad, Baroda, Broach and Agra.**
- By AD 1630, the trade of Surat had grown to such dimensions, that the directors continued it into the headquarters of the company on the West Coast.
- It was finally replaced by **Bombay as headquarter** of the company on the West Coast in AD 1687.

Bombay

- In AD 1661, the Portuguese gave Bombay as a part of dowry to their princess, Catherine of Braganza, on her marriage with Charles II. The Company acquired Bombay from Charles II on lease at an annual rent of ten pounds in AD 1668.
- The English secured Bombay at a very crucial moment when Surat was being repeatedly attacked by the Marathas.

Governors of Bombay

- **Gerald Aungier**, who was the first governor of Bombay (AD 1669 to 1677), was the true founder of Bombay's greatness. He resolved to make Bombay completely safe for shipping and trade, free from danger on the land-side from the Marathas and on the sea-side from the Portuguese and the pirates of the coast.
- Under Aungier, Bombay became a safe asylum for all merchants and manufacturers. He established vigorous and strict discipline over all the inhabitants of the city and allowed every community to enjoy the free exercise of their religion.
- During his governorship the old Panchayat system was revived, so that justice was actually brought to the door of the people even in minor cases. He saved English lives and Properties during Shivaji's second sack of Surat in AD 1670.
- However under the successors of Aungier, began the general decline of Bombay which continued till the close of the first quarter of the eighteenth century.
- The peaceful and orderly government of Aungier was in striking contrast with terror which prevailed under **Sir John Child.**

John Child

- During this period, interlopers (the individual English merchants independent of the Company's control) created problems. At the close of the seventeenth century, these interlopers took to open piracy.
- In AD 1686, two pirate ships captured several Mughal vessels in the Red Sea, upon which the Mughal governor of Surat violently reacted against the English, particularly at Sir John Child, President of Surat and Governor of Bombay.
- Though John Child punished the interlopers savagely whenever they were caught, the evil grew more rampant. These pirates and interlopers were the principal cause of the disastrous war which the English subsequently waged with the Mughals.
- John Child got really frightened and hastened to assure the **Emperor Aurangzeb,** who was then in the Deccan, that he had really no hostile intention. But Aurangzeb was not deceived by Child's intention of friendship; he issued orders that the Englsih should be treated as enemies. At last, John Child supplicated the emperor for peace, whereupon the latter imposed the following humiliating terms upon the English.
    - All sums due from the Company to the Mughal subjects should be immediately paid.
    - Recompensation should be given for such losses as the Mughals had suffered.
    - The hated Sir John Child should leave India within nine months.

English Settlements in Eastern Coast

- The Englsih were permitted to trade in Masulipatnam in AD 1611 and in AD 1630 secured the **'Goldent farman'** from the **Sultan of Golcunda** (AD 1632) which ensured safety and prosperity of their trade.

Madras: Fort St George

- In AD 1639, Francis Day obtained the site of Madras from the Raja of Chandaragiri with permission to build a fortified factory, which was named Fort St George.
- It was only with the foundation of Madras by the English in 1639, their arrival at Hughli in AD 1650 and their establishment of a factory at Balasore in north Orissa that the position of the English on the eastern coast became strong and permanent. Madras soon replaced Masulipatnam as the headquarter of English on the Coromandel Coast and in AD 1641 all the English settlements in eastern India (Bengal, Bihar and Orissa) and the Coromandel were placed under the control of the President and council of Fort St George.

English Settlements in Bengal

- In England, there was a growing demand for Bengal goods, especially for silk and saltpeter and the trade of the Bengal factories consequently increased. In AD 1633, the Mughal governor of Orissa gave the English merchants permission to establish factories at Hariharapur (Near the mouth of Mahanadi), Balasore and Pipli. The English also succeeded to establish their factory at Hughli in AD 1651, followed by those at Patna, Dacca and Kasimbazar.
- In AD 1667, Aurangzeb gave the English a *Farman* for trade in Bengal and five years later, in AD 1672, the Mughal governor, Shaista Khan, issued an order confirming all the privileges already acquired by the English.
- In AD 1686, the hostilities broke out between the English and the Mughal government in Bengal.
- In retaliation for the sack of Hughli (October 1886) the English captured the imperial forts on the east of the Midnapore district and at Balasore. But the English were forced to leave Hughli and to retie to an unhealthy place at the mouth of the river.
- After the conclusion of peace between the Company and the Mughal government in February 1690, **Job Charnock** returned to Bengal as agent, where he established an English factory on February 10,1691.
- On the same day, an imperial order was issued permitting the English "to contentedly continue their trade" in Bengal on Payment of Rs 3000 a year in lieu of all dues. This marked the **Foundation of Calcutta** which was destined to develop as one of the greatest Indian cities.
- The rebellion of **Sobha Singh** a Zamindar in the district of Burdwan gave an opportunity to the English to fortify their settlement at Sutanuti in AD 1696. They were permitted by Azimush Shah Governor of Bengal, to purchase the Zamindari of the three villages of Sutauti, Kalikata and Govindpur on Payment of Rs 1200 to the old proprietors.

Fort William

- In AD 1696, a serious rebellion occurred in Bengal under an Afghan named

Rahim Khan who plundered the whole country along the Hughli.

- Alarmed by rebellion and the inability of the Mughal viceroy to put it down, the English at Calcutta as well as the Dutch at Chinsura asked permission to fortify their factories and to raise troops. The viceroy ordered them, in general terms, to defend themselves; so the English began to build walls and bastions round their factory AD 1697. This was the origin of Fort William, named after King William III.
- Next year they got the permission to rent, besides Calcutta, the villages of Sutanati and Govindpur. The security of Calcutta, which began with the building of the fort, was now completely assured.
- In AD 1700, the directors constituted Bengal as a separate presidency independent of Madras and nominated Sir Charles Eyre as its first President. In 1701, Aurangzeb, who had often suspected the English of piratical acts and was now confirmed in his suspicions by the two rival English Companies accusing each other of piracy, ordered the general arrest of all the Europeans in India.
- Aurangzeb's death in AD 1707 made the English at Calcutta fear that their growing trade would be swept away by the coming tide in civil war and anarchy. After protected negotiations, the English got confirmation of their privilege from the new emperor **Shah Alam** and the **de facto ruler of Bengal Murshid Quli Khan.** They looked hopefully to peace and prosperous trade.
- The period from AD 1708 upto the middle of the eighteenth century, saw the expansion of the Company's trade and influence in India.
- The most important event in the history of the Company during these years was the diplomatic mission led by **John Surman** in AD 1715 to the court of the Mughal Emperor **Farruksiyar,** resulting in the grant of three famous *Farmans* addressed to the officials in Bengal, Hyderabad and Gujarat. The *Farmans* gave the company many valuable privileges.
    - In **Bengal,** it exempted the Company's imports and exports from additional customs duties, excepting the annual payment of Rs 3000 as settled earlier. The company was allowed to rent additional lands around Calcutta.
    - In **Hyderabad,** the company's old privilege of freedom from dues in trade was retained and it had to pay only the existing rent for Madras.
    - At **Surat,** the Company was exempted from the levy of all duties for its exports and imports in lieu of an annual payment of Rs. 10000 and the coins of the company minted at Bombay were to have currency throughout the Mughal empire.
- In the subsequent years, the English East India Company began to extend its territorial claims. It defeated Dutch (Battle of Bedara, 1759) and French (Battle of Wandiwash, 1760) and by the end of the eighteenth century, it succeeded in establishing its paramountancy.

The Danes

- The Danes arrived in India in 1616. They established settlement at Tranqueber

(Tamil Nadu) in 1620 and Serampore (Bengal) in 1676. Serampore was their headquarter.

- They were forced to sell their settlements to British in 1854.

The French

- **'Compagnie des Indes Orientales'** popularly known as the French East India Company was formed by **Colbert** (the famous minister of Louis XIV), under state patronage in AD 1664.
- In AD 1667, an expedition was sent under **Francois Caron,** who established the first French factory in India at Surat. In AD 1669, **Marcara** founded another French factory at Masulipatnam by securing patent from the Sultan of Golcunda.
- In July 1672, French squadron under **Da La Haye** occupied **San Thome** near Madras, which the Sultan of Golcunda had conquered from the Portuguese ten years earlier.
- This led to an alliance of the Dutch and the Sultan of Golcunda against the French. Faced with a critical situation, De la Haye had to capitulate (September 6, 1674) and surrender San Thome to the Dutch who allowed the Sultan of Golcunda to reoccupy it.
- Meanwhile, in 1673, **Francois Martin,** director of the Masulipatnam factory, obtained from Sher Khan Lodi, governor of Valikondapuram, a site for a factory, while later developed into Pondicherry and its first government was Francois Martin.
- In Bengal, the French laid the foundation of their famous settlement of Chandranagar in AD 1690 on a site granted to them by **Shayista Khan.**

Contribution of Martin

- In AD 1701, Pondicherry was made the headquarter of all possession of the French in the East and Martin was appointed Director-General of French affairs in India.
- It has been held that Martin foresaw the descendance of the Indian powers planned the acquisition of Indian predominance for the French as the essential condition of free commercial development.
- He completed the building of Fort Louis at Pondicherry, helped to strengthen the Company's position at Chandranagar in Bengal and attempted to revive even the declining French factory at Surat.
- The Death of Martin in December AD 1706 marked the decline of French power in India, which persisted till AD 1719 and to the reconstitution of the company in AD 1720.
- The reconstituted company named the **United Compagnie des Indes** was formed by a royal edict and entrusted with the whole of French colonial trade.
- The French power in India was revived under **Lenoir and Dumas** (governors) between AD 1720 and AD 1742. They occupied Mahe in the Malaba, Yanam in Coromandel (Both in AD 1725) and Karikal in Tamil Nadu (AD 1739).
- The arrival of **Dupleix** as French governor in India in AD 1724 saw the beginning of Anglo-French conflict (Carnatic wars) resulting in their final defeat in India, at the Battle of Wandiswash in AD 1760.

First European Company in India—Portuguese

- Factories of Portuguese Company—First Cochin (AD 1503) Second Connore (AD 1505).
- First Factory of Dutch Company—Masulipatnam (AD 1605).
- First Factory of British Company—Masulipatnam (AD 1611)
- First French Factory—Surat (AD 1668)

The European Commerce

- India had maintained it trade relations with the foreign merchants even during the earlier centuries. But there was a great difference between the foreign merchants who had earlier settled in and conducted brisk trade from India and the Europeans who came to India in the Sixteenth and Seventeenth centuries.

Difference between Earlier Foreign Merchants and Europeans

- The earlier foreign merchants had mere commercial motives and had very little or no support from their native governments.
- But the European merchants who came to Indian during this period had the political and military support of their respective governments.
- They were not individual merchants but represented their respective nations and tried to establish and safeguard their maritime trade on the strength of their superior naval powers.
- Military superiority was the backbone of their commercial enterpris and they established their fortified trading settlements, called factories, on the coastal parts of India, immune from the administrative control of the local power.
- No doubt, due to the participation of the Portuguese, the Dutch, the English and the French India's foreign trade grew phenomenally in the sixteenth and seventeenth centuries, but in course of time the commercial motives turned into territorial ambitions and by the close of the eighteenth century India, from a bulk exporter, transformed into one of the biggest importers of the industrially manufactured goods.

The Structure and Pattern of Trade

- There was adverse balance of trade as the European powers had very few goods to offer back to Asia. Therefore, trade was financed through semiprecious metals extracted from South American colonies.
- Later, intra state trade was practice i.e., bringing spices from spices islands and Japan's cooper to India and exporting Indian textiles from South East Asia to Europe.
- But the problem of trade finance and deficit was over with the conquest of Bengal and export of opium to China.

Economic Colonialism and British Rule

- RP Dutt in his work "India Today" has suggested three phases of economic colonialism and exploitation.

First Phase of Mercantilism (AD 1757–1813)

- In this phase, Company purchased goods at cheap rates and sold commodities at high prices, apart from investment of surplus revenues for purchasing finished goods for export to England. This phase coincided with success of industrial revolution in Britain.

Second Phase of free Trade or Industrial Capitalism (AD 1813–1858)

- This phase is marked by conversion of India as market of finished goods from Britain and a source of raw materials along with gradual decline in Indian industries including exports because of heavy duties. However, this phase continued till AD 1947.

Third Phase of Financial Imperialism

- This phase was reflected by investment of surplus capital by British in India under guarantee system i.e., private British capitals investment in India was guaranteed for safe returns i.e., guarantee of private investment of public cost.
- Single best example was railways and later on plantation, banking, shipping, export-import. The return of such investments constituted single biggest source of drain of wealth to Britain popularly known as 'home charges' and such capital investments were termed as public debt at India.

Drain of Wealth

- Dadabhai Naoroji explained the Drain of Wealth Theory in his book "Poverty and Un-British Rule in India".
- It is that part of national wealth which was not available for consumption of Indians and was being drained away to England without any economic or material return and this drain was continuous in nature.
- Home charges
  - Expenditure by Secretary of State and India office in London.
  - Dividends of shareholders of East India Company.
  - Interest on public debt, war and military expenditure and store purchases in England.
- Interest on foreign capital investments.
- Foreign banking shipping, insurance and managing agencies.

Land Revenue System

Permanent Settlement

- Introduced in Bengal, Bihar–Odisha, districts of Banaras and Northern districts of Madras by Lord Cornwallis in 1793. John Shore planned this settlement.
- It declared zamindars as the owners of the land. Hence, they could keep $1/11^{th}$ of the revenue collected to themselves while the British got a fixed share of $10/11^{th}$ of the revenue collected. The zamindars were free to fix the rate.
- Assured of their ownership, many zamindars stayed in towns and exploited their tenants.

Ryotwari Settlement

- It was introduced in Bombay, Madras and Asom. Munro and Charels Reed recommended it.
- In this system the direct settlement was made between the Government and the Ryots.

- The revenue was based on the basis of the quality of the soil and the nature of the crop.
- The revenue was fixed for a period not exceeding 30 years. It was based on the "Scientific Rent Theory of Ricardo."
- The position of the cultivator became more secure.

Mahalwari System

- It was introduced in the area of Ganga valley **NWFP,** Parts of Central India and Punjab.
- Revenue settlement was to be made by village or estates with landlords.
- In this system, a settlement was made with the village which maintained a form of common ownership known as Bhaichara or with Mahals, which were group of villages. Revenue was periodically revised.

Economic Impacts of British Rule

- Decline of handicraft industries beyond recovery not compensated by rise of modern industries.
- Adverse impact on agriculture because of new land tenure systems.
- Emergence of new social classes, landlords, money lenders and officials.
- Increased rural indebtedness.
- Commercialization of agriculture produce of specialized crops or cash crops not for local use of consumption but for exports, saw its peak in plantation sector i.e., indigo, tea, coffee, rubber and sugarcane.
- It was a forced process where farmers were forced to sell their produce at marginal prices.

Chapter at a Glance

- Vasco da Gama started his voyage from Lisbon in 1497.
- The Portugues allied themselves with the rulers of Honnavar, Bankipur and Bhatkal against Bijapur.
- Cochin was the best of all ports on the Malabar coast.
- The trade was carried on with China, Arabia and other countries from the port of Quilon.
- Portugal's initial objective was to capture the spice trade of the east.
- The Dutch expelled the Portugese from Sri Lanka (1638 to 1658).
- The Dutch occupied Cape of Good Hope in 1652.
- Goa was made the seat of Bishop in 1538.
- The fanatic religious policy of the Portuguese was responsible for their rapid downfall.
- The Portuguese were responsible of crippling the Indian Navy for their benefits.
- Bartholomio Diaz accompanied Cabral to India.
- Christopher Columbus started his voyage in 1492 to explore the route to India.
- Dutch occupied Malacca in 1641.
- The chief of the factory at Golcunda was also the company's agent in the Court of Qutub Shahi ruler.
- The chief articles of import to the Coromandel coast were spices, sandal wood and pepper.
- Alfonso de Albuquerque can be called the real founder of the Portuguese empire in India.

- The Dutch conquered Java Island in 1619 A.D.
- The Englishmen were brutally massacred by the Dutch in the Battle of Amboyna (1623).
- Thomas Roe obtained the right to trade in Gujarat for East India Company.

Previous Year Question Paper (1998-2017)

1. What was/were the object/objects of Queen Victoria's Proclamation (1858) ?
   1. To disclaim any intention to annex Indian States
   2. To place the Indian administration under the British Crown
   3. To regulate East India Company's trade with India.

   Select the correct anwer using the code given below:
   (a) 1 and 2 only (b) 2 only
   (c) 1 and 3 only (d) 1, 2 and 3
   (2015)
2. Which amongst the following provided a common factor for tribal insurrection in India in the 19th Century?
   (a) Introduction of a new system of land revenue and taxation of tribal products.
   (b) Influence of foreign religious missionaries in tribal areas.
   (c) Rise of a large number of money lenders, traders and revenue farmers as middlemen in tribal areas.
   (d) The complete disruption of the old agrarian order of the tribal-communities. **(2011)**
3. With reference to the period of colonial rule in India. "Home Charges" formed an important part of drain of wealth from India. Which of the following funds constituted "Home Charges"?
   1. Funds used to support the India Office in London.
   2. Funds used to pay salaries and pensions of British personnel engaged in India.
   3. Funds used for waging wars outside India by the British.

   Select the correct answer using the codes given below:
   (a) 1 only (b) 1 and 2 only
   (c) 2 and 3 only (d) 1, 2 and 3
   (2011)
4. Karl Marx explained the process of class struggle with the help of which one of the following theories?
   (a) Empirical liberalism
   (b) Existentialism
   (c) Darwin's theory of evolution
   (d) Dialectical materialism **(2011)**
5. With whose permission did the English set up their first factory in Surat?
   (a) Akbar (b) Jahangir
   (c) Shahjahan (d) Aurangzeb
   (2009)
6. The ruler of which one of the following States was removed from power by the British on the pretext of misgovernance?
   (a) Awadh (b) Jhansi
   (c) Nagpur (d) Satara **(2007)**
7. Which one of the following is the correct chronological order of the battles fought in India in the 18th Century?
   (a) Battle of Wandiwash–Battle of Buxar–Battle of Ambur–Battle of Plassey
   (b) Battle of Ambur–Battle of Plassey–Battle of Wandiwash–Battle of Buxar
   (c) Battle of Wandiwash–Battle of Plassey–Battle of Ambur–Battle of Buxar

(d) Battle of Ambur–Battle of Buxar–Battle of Wandiwash–Battle of Plassey **(2005)**

8. Which of the following pairs are corectly matched?

List-I (Period)	(List-II (War)
1. AD 1767-69	First Anglo-Maratha War
2. AD 1790-92	Third Mysore War
3. AD 1824-26	First Anglo-Burmese War
4. AD 1845-46	Second Sikh War

Select the correct answer using the codes given below:

Codes:

(a) 2 and 4 (b) 3 and 4
(c) 1 and 2 (d) 2 and 3 **(2004)**

9. At a time when empires in Europe were crumbling before the might of Napoleon, which one of the following Governor-General kept the British flag flying high in India?
(a) Warren Hastings
(b) Lord Cornwallis
(c) Lord Wellesely
(d) Lord Hastings **(1999)**

Answers

1. (a)	2. (c)	3. (a)
4. (d)	5. (b)	6. (a)
7. (b)	8. (d)	9. (c)

Practice Paper

1. Which one of the following was NOT a French settlement in India?
(a) Pondicherry (b) Mahe
(c) Goa (d) Chandranagar
(SSC Sec. Off. (Aud.) 2006)

2. Where are the traces of Portunguese culture found in India?
(a) Goa (b) Calicut
(c) Cannanore (d) Cochin
(SSC Tax Assit. 2009)

3. Who was the first Governor General of Bengal?
(a) Robert Clive
(b) Warren Hastings
(c) William Bentick
(d) Cornwallis **(SSC Tax Assit. 2009)**

4. Who were the first Europeans to reach India for trade?
(a) Portuguese (b) British
(c) Dutch (d) French
(Bihar SSC LDC 2005)

5. The French East India Company was formed in:
(a) 1600 (b) 1660
(c) 1664 (d) 1668
(SCRA 2000)

6. The English East India Company founded a permanent factory at Surat in the year:
(a) 1611 (b) 1613
(c) 1621 (d) 1626
(UGC NET/JRF (History) 2007)

7. The administration of the English East India Company in India came to an end of:
(a) 1857 (b) 1858
(c) 1862 (d) 1892
(CPF Assit. Commt. 2008)

8. The battle of Wandiwash (1760) was fought between:
(a) Marathas and the Portuguese
(b) The English and the French

(c) The English and the Portuguese
(d) Marathas and the English

(CPF Assis. Commt. 2008)

9. Bombay was acquired by the English from the Portuguese in the year:
(a) 1661 (b) 1612
(c) 1600 (d) 1595

(NDA 2001)

10. During the Mughal period which one of the following traders first came to India?
(a) Portuguese (b) English
(c) Dutch (d) Danish

(NDA 2003)

11. Who granted the permission to establish the French factory at Masulipatnam?
(a) Abdulla Kutub Shah
(b) Nasir Jung
(c) Muzaffar Jung
(d) Salabat Jung **(NDA 2004)**

12. Vasco da Gama dicovered the sea-route to India in which one of the following years?
(a) 1498 (b) 1492
(c) 1494 (d) 1493

(NDA 2004)

13. Match List-I with List-II and select the correct answer by using the codes given below the Lists

List-I (Company)	List-II (Factory)
A. French	1. Calicut
B. English	2. Masulipatnam
C. Dutch	3. Pondicherry
D. Portuguese	4. Hughli

Codes:	A	B	C	D
(a)	3	4	1	2
(b)	3	4	2	1
(c)	4	3	1	2
(d)	4	3	2	1

(CDS 2000)

14. **Assertion (A):** The French were defeated by the British in the Third Carnntic War at the battle of Wandiwash.
Reason (R): The Indian rulers did not support the French.
Code:
(a) Both A and R are true and R is the correct explanation of A
(b) Both A and R are true but R is not a correct explanation of A
(c) A is true but R is false
(d) A is false but R is true **(CDS 2000)**

15. With reference to the colonial period of India, the trade monopoly of the East India Company was ended by:
(a) The Regulating Act of 1773
(b) Pitt's India Act of 1784
(c) The Charter Act of 1813
(d) The Charter Act of 1833

(CDS 2002, 2006)

16. In 1717, who among the following Mughal emperors had issued the royal edict to allow the business privilege to Britain's East India Company?
(a) Shah Alam II (b) Bahudur Shah
(c) Jahandar Shah (d) Farrukhsiyar

(CDS 2004)

17. Why did Dutch East India Company fail to maintain its influence in India?
(a) Portuguese did not allow them to trade in India.
(b) There was a growing interference of Dutch Government in the Company's internal affairs.
(c) Dutch indulged in forcible religious conversion of the people and thus were expelled by local kings.
(d) The English forces made them to leave India. **(CDS 2005)**

18. Who granted the permission to establish the first British factory at Hoogli in Bengal?
(a) Shah Shuja
(b) Murshid Quli Khan

(c) Shujauddin
(d) Alivardi Khan **(CDS 2005)**

19. The first definite step to provide parliamentary control over East India Company was taken by:
(a) The Regulating Act of 1773
(b) ThePitt's India Act of 1784
(c) The Charter Act of 1793
(d) The Charter Act of 1813**(CDS 2005)**

20. Consider the following statements
(1) Dutch opened a factory at Pulicut in 1609.
(2) English built a factory at Masulipatnam in 1611.
Which of the statements given above is/are correct?
(a) 1 only (b) 2 only
(c) Both 1 and 2 (d) Neither 1 nor 2
(CDS 2006)

21. During whose reign did Sir Thomas Roe have regular attendance at the Mughal court to secure commercial privilege?
(a) Akbar (b) Jahangir
(c) Shahjahan (d) Aurangzeb
(CDS 2006)

22. Who was Francisco de Almeida?
(a) Portuguese Viceroy in India
(b) English Viceroy in India
(c) Dutch Viceroy in India
(d) French Viceroy in India**(CDS 2007)**

23. Which of the British Officials defeated Portuguese at Sowlley?
(a) William Hawkins
(b) Thomas Best
(c) Thomas Roe
(d) Josiah child **(44th BPSC 2001)**

24. Which one of the following was the immediate cause of the First Carnatic War?
(a) Anglo - French Rivalry
(b) Austrian War of Succession
(c) Issues of Carnatic Succession
(d) Capture of French ships by the British **(44th BPSC 2001)**

25. Which one of the following Mughal Emperors gave an important *Farman* to the English fo facilitationg their trade in India?
(a) Bahadur Shah I
(b) Farrukhsiyar
(c) Shah Alam II
(d) Bahadur Shah II
(45th BPSC 2002, WB PSC Kolkata Police Exam 2007)

26. Who was the first Portuguese Viceroy in India?
(a) Diaz
(b) Vasco da Gama
(c) Francisco de Almeida
(d) Albuquerque
(45th BPSC 2002, SSC Sec. Off. (Aud.) 2008)

27. One of the following rulers, who had granted Diwani to the East India Company, was
(a) Farrukhsiyar (b) Shah Alam I
(c) Shah Alam II (d) Shujauddaula
(UP PCS (P) 2004)

28. Among the following factories in Bengal, the one established by the Portuguese was
(a) Kasim Bazar (b) Chinsura
(c) Hoogly (d) Srirampur
(UP PCS (P) 2004)

29. Who were the first Europeans to set up sea trade centres in India?
(a) The English
(b) The French
(c) The Portuguese
(d) The Dutch **(UP PSC (P) 2005)**

30. Which English Governor of East India Company in India was expelled by Aurangzeb?
(a) Aungier
(b) Sir John Child
(c) Sir John Gayer
(d) Sir Nicholas Waite
(MP PSC (P) 2008)

31. With reference to the entry of European powers into India, which one of the following statements is NOT correct?
    (a) The Portuguese captured Goa in 1499
    (b) The English opened their first factory in South India at Masulipatnam
    (c) In Eastern India, the English Company opened its first factory in Orissa in 1633
    (d) Under the leadership of Dupleix, the French occupied Madras in 1746. **(UPSC 2003)**
32. In India, among the following locations, the Dutch established their earliest factory at
    (a) Masulipatnam (b) Pulicut
    (c) Chochin (d) Kasim Bazar
    (UPSC 2003)
33. In the year 1611, where was the English East India Company given permission to set up a factory (Trading post)?
    (a) Bangalore
    (b) Madras
    (c) Masulipatnam
    (d) Surat **(UPSC 2006)**
34. Which one of the following was the first fort constructed by the British in India?
    (a) Fort St. George
    (b) Fort St. David
    (c) Fort St. William
    (d) Fort St. Angelo **(UPSC 2007)**
35. Who among the following Europeans, were the last to come to pre-independence India as traders?
    (a) Dutch (b) English
    (c) French (d) Portuguese
    (UPSC 2007)
36. During the time of which Mughal Emperor did the English East India Company establish its first factory in India?
    (a) Akbar (b) Jahangir
    (c) Shahjahan (d) Aurangzeb
    (UPSC 2008, 2009)
37. With reference to Pondicherry (now Puducherry), consider the following statements :
    1. The first European power to occupy Pondicherry were the French.
    2. The second European power to occupy Pondicherry were the Porteguese.
    3. The English never occupied Pondicherry

    Which of the statement (s) given above is/are correct?
    (a) 1 only (b) 2 and 3 only
    (c) 3 only (d) 1, 2 and 3
    (UPSC 2010)

Answers

1. (c)	2. (a)	3. (b)	22. (a)	23. (b)	24. (d)
4. (a)	5. (c)	6. (b)	25. (b)	26. (c)	27. (c)
7. (b)	8. (b)	9. (a)	28. (c)	29. (c)	30. (b)
10. (b)	11. (a)	12. (a)	31. (a)	32. (a)	33. (d)
13. (b)	14. (c)	15. (d)	34. (a)	35. (c)	36. (b)
16. (d)	17. (d)	18. (a)	37. (a)		
19. (b)	20. (b)	21. (b)			

5

Constitutional Development and Acts

The history of constitutional development is a history of raving ambitions and insidious plots hatched by Britishers. Although, it led to the ultimate accomplishment of Indian constitution, but the passage was full of digs and holes. The self esteem was at stake and every effort was made to butcher the pride of Indians. But Indians never looked down. India was blessed with its own constitution. The following milestones can be attributed to the constitutional development.

Regulating Act of 1773

This was the first step taken by the British Government to control and regulate the affairs of the East India Company in India.

- It designated the Governor of Bengal as the Governor-General of Bengal.
- The first Governor-General was Lord Warren Hastings.
- It subordinated the Governors of Bombay and Madras to the Governor-General of Bengal.
- The Supreme Court was established at Fort William (Calcutta) as the Apex Court in 1774.

The Pitts India Act, 1784

- This Act gave the British government the supreme control over Company's affairs and its administration in India.
- Established dual system of governance. Court of directors consisting of 24 members to look after commercial functions.
- Board of control consisting of 6 parliamentary Commissioners appointed to control civil, military and revenue affairs of India.
- Strength of Governor general-incouncil reduced to 3.
- Subordinated the Bombay and Madras presidency to Bengal in all questions of war, diplomacy & revenues.
- First effective substitution of Parliamentary Control over East India Company.

The Charter Act of 1833

- End of company's trade monopoly even in tea and with China. Company was asked to close its business at the earliest.

- Governor-General of Bengal to be Governor-General of India. (Ist Governor-General of lndia- Lord William Bentick).
- Governors of Madras and Bombay deprived of legislative powers.
- A fourth member, law member, added to council of Governor-Generals.
- Government Service was thrown open to the people of India.
- All laws made by Governor-General in-Council henceforth to be known as Acts and not regulations.

Charter Act of 1853

- The legislative and executive functions of the Governor-General's Council were separated.
- It introduced a system of open competition as the basis for the recruitment of civil servants of the Company.
- Inclusion of additional members to the Governor General's Council, which was to act as the Legislative Council (total members-12).

Government of India Act of 1858

- This Act transferred the Government, territories and revenues of India from the East India Company to the British Crown.
- In other words, the rule of Company was replaced by the rule of the Crown in India.
- The powers of the British Crown were to be exercised by the Secretary of State for India.
- The Secretary of State was a member of the British Cabinet.
- He was assisted by the Council of India, having 15 members.
- He was vested with complete authority and control over the Indian administration through the Governor-General as his agent.
- He was responsible ultimately to the British Parliament.
- The Governor-General was made the Viceroy of India.
- Lord Canning was the first Viceroy of India.

Significance

- The Act rang the death-knell of the trading company which was born in 1600 A.D.
- The abolition of Dual Government in England has some good effects.
- The centralization of authority stole away all confusions, uncertainity and red tapism of company's rule in India.
- The establishment of Indian council was unique measure to provide expert advice to the secretary of state.
- The office of secretary of state for India became more responsible and dignified.

Growth of the Central Legislature

Act	Composition	Function
1773	Members of G.G. Council	No distinction between Legislative and Executive functioning
1784	3 Members of G.G. Council	Same
1793	3 Members of the G.G. Council	Same

1833	3 + 1 Law Member	Empowered to make laws for all British territories
1853	10 Members + 4 members of Executive Council, 1 Chief Justice of Supreme Court Plus Judge, 4 representatives of provinces	Legislature became a representative Assembly in miniature
1858	10 Members	Same
1861	17 Members (5 members of Executive Council + not less than six and not more than 12 additional members)	Advisory body, no power to discuss finance
1892	22 Members (6 members of the Executive Council + not less than 10 and not more than 16 additional members)	Empowered to discuss budget, allowed to ask question but no supplementary questions were allowed.
1909	69 Members containing 60 additional members. 60 additional members included: 28 Nominated officials, 32 Non officials (5 nominated and 27 elected), Elected members = 13 General electorate, 2 special electorate, 12 class electorate. 12 class electorate included 6 Landholders, 6 Muslim Jamindars.	Empowered to move resolutions, discuss budget and ask supplementary questions

Queen Victoria's Proclamation (1858)

- It assured the people of India that no discrimination would be made on the basis of caste, colour, race and creed.
- It assured the princes that their rights, dignity and honour would be respected and there shall be no encroachment in their territorial possessions.
- It declared unconditional pardon and general amnesty. The proclamation no doubt laid the foundation of new policy in India.

Indian Councils Act of 1861

- It introduced for the first time the representative institutions in India.
- It provided that the Governor-General's Executive Council should have some Indians as the non-official members while transacting the legislative businesses.
- Initiated the process of decentralisation by restoring the legislative powers to the Bombay and the Madras Presidencies.
- It accorded the statutory recognition to the portfolio system.

Indian Councils Act of 1892

- The additional members in the central as well as the provincial legislative councils were increased but the official members still formed the majority.
- The Act empowered the Governor General in council to frame rules regarding the nomination of members. But he was required to seek the approval of secretary of state for India.
- To elect the members of the councils the system of indirect elections was introduced. Now the District Boards,

Universities, Municipal Committees and Chamber of Commerce were empowered to return their members to these councils.

- The functions of the provincial legislative councils were enlarged and they were empowered to make new laws or repeal the old ones with the prior permission of Governor General.
- The Act empowered the Governor General to fill the seat in the case of Central legislative and by the Governor in the case of provincial legislature.

Indian Councils Act, 1909 (Morley-Minto Act)

The period from 1892 to 1905 was that of great stress and storm in Indian politics. There was much discontent among the Indian masses by the reactionary politics of Lord Curzon. The partition of Bengal was resisted throughout the country. The extremists wanted to offer stiff resistance to the government. The government wanted to weaken the National Movement. She, therefore, determined to suppress the extremists. But at the same time in order to win the favour of moderates, she decided to introduce certain administrative reforms. Efforts were also made to win over the Muslims against the Hindus. All this planning was made jointly by Indian secretary Morely and Indian viceroy Minto.

- Morley was the secretary of state, while Minto was the Indian Viceroy.
- Additional members in central legislative assembly were increased to 60.
- Introduced for the first time indirect elections to the Legislative Councils.
- Separate electorate was introduced for the Muslims.
- 27 non-official seats were to be filled in by elections. They were distributed as follows:
  - By non-official members of the Provincial Legislative councils.
  - By landholders of 6 provinces
  - By Muslims of 5 provinces
  - Alternately by Muslim landholders of UP/Bengal Chambers of commerce of Calcutta and Bombay.
  - Muslims were to be elected by Separate electorates.
- Resolutions could be moved before the budget was taken in its final form. Supplementary questions could be asked.

The Govt. of India Act, 1919

- Popularly known as Montague-Chelmsford Reforms,
- The idea of "Responsible Government" was emphasised upon.
- Devolution Rules: Subjects of administration were divided into two categories – "Central" and "Provincial". Subjects of all India importance (like railways & finance) were brought under the category of Central, while matters relating to the administration of the provinces were classified as provincial.
- Dyarchy system introduced in the Provinces. The Provincial subjects of administration were to be divided into two categories "Transferred" and "Reserved" subjects. The transferred subj ects were to be administered by the Governor with the aid of Ministers responsible to the Legislative Council. The Governor and his Executive Council were to administer the reserved subjects (Rail, Post, Telegraph, Finance, Law &

Order, etc.) without any responsibility to the legislature.

- An office of the High Commissioner of India was created in London.
- Indian legislature became "bicameral" for the first time.
- Communal representation extended to Sikhs.
- Secretary of State for India now to be paid from British revenue.

The Govt. of India Act, 1935

The Government of India Act of 1919 provided for a review of the political situation in India every ten years. In 1927 the process of review was set in motion by the appointment of the all-white Simon Commission. The all parties conference submitted the Indian view point in the famous Nehru Report (1928). The Simon Commission Report was discussed in the Round Table Conferences held in London during 1930-32. The proposals of the British Government were published in a white paper, which provided the basis for the Act of 1935.

The Act was based on two basic principles, federation and parliamentary system.

- Provided for the establishment of an All India federation consisting of the British Provinces and the Princely States. The joining of Princely States was voluntary and as a result the federation did not come into existence.
- Dyarchy was introduced at the Centre (e.g. department of Foreign Affairs and Defence were reserved for the Governor General). Provincial autonomy replaced Dyarchy in Provinces. They were granted separate legal identity.
- It made a three-fold division of powers –Federal, Provincial and concurrent lists. Residuary powers were to be with the Governor General.
- The Indian Council of Secretary of State for India was abolished.
- Principle of separate electorate was extended to include Anglo-Indians, Indian Christians and Europeans.
- A Federal Court was to be constituted with a chief Justice and 10 other judges. This was set up in 1937.
- Sind and Orissa were created.
- Franchise was based on property qualifications.

Provincial Elections under the GOI Act, 1935

The Congress won a massive mandate. It formed ministries in eight provinces–Madras, Bombay, Central Provinces, Orissa, Bihar, UP, NWFP and Assam.

- Haripura Session (Feb. 1938) declared Purna Swaraj ideal to cover Princely States.
- Tripuri Congress (Mar. 1939) favoured active participation in the Princely States because of the federal structure of the 1935 Act and due to assumption of office by the Congress after the 1937 elections.
- The Tripuri Session witnessed Bose vs. Sitaramyya (Gandhi's nominee) conflict. Bose resigned to form the Forward Bloc.

August Offer, 1940

The Viceroy (Linlithgow) put forward a proposal that included:

- Dominion Status in the unspecified future

- A post-war body to enact the constitution
- Expansion of Governor-General's Council with representation of the Indians,
- Establishing a War Advisory Council. In this offer he promised the Muslim League and other minorities that the British Government would never agree to a constitution or government in India, to which did not enjoy their support (the Muslim League had demanded Pakistan in its Lahore session of 1940). The Congress rejected this offer because: There was no suggestion for a national government and because the demand for Dominion Status was already discarded in favour of Purna Swaraj. It encouraged anti-Congress forces like the Muslim League.

The Cripps Mission: March-April 1942

Under the pressure of Allies and the need for gestures to win over Indian public opinion, the British were forced to offer reconciliatory measures. After the fall of Rangoon to the Japanese the British decided to send the Cripps Mission to India for constitutional proposals, which included:

- Dominion status to be granted after the war with the right to secede (Any province could, if it so desired, remain outside the Indian Union and negotiate directly with Britain).
- Consitution making body to be elected from Provincial Assemblies and Princes' nominees after the War.
- Individual prince could sign a separate agreement with the British which in effect accommodated the Pakistan demand.
- British would however, control the defence for war period.

The Congress did not want to rely upon; future promises. It wanted a responsible government with full powers and also a control over the country's defence. Gandhi termed the proposals as a post dated cheque in a crashing bank. Cripps Mission failed to satisfy Indian nationalists and turned out to be merely a propaganda device for US and Chinese consumption.

But above all the Cripps Proposals brought in "Pakistan" through the backdoor via the "local option" clause. Though the Cripps Mission failed, Cripps' proposals provided legitimacy to the Pakistan demand by accommodating it in their provision for provincial autonomy.

Wavell Plan, 1945

- A sign of interim arrangement.
- Reconstitution of Viceroy's Executive Council.
- To advance India towards her goal of full self government.
- Appointment of a High commissioner to look after Britain's commercial interests.
- The Executive Council was to work like a Provisional national Government.
- The provinces were to have ministries, again formed on coalition basis.

Cabinet Mission (March-June 1946)

- Members–Pethwick Lawrence (secretary of State), Stafford Cripps and Alexander.
- The Mission rejected the demand for a full-fledged Pakistan (Comprising the whole of all the Muslim majority areas). The Mission reasoned that the

right of communal self-determination, if conceded to Muslims, also had to be granted to non-Muslims who formed majorities in West Bengal and Eastern Punjab, as well as in Assam. The 'truncated' or smaller Pakistan was unacceptable to the League.

The Plan proposed

- Rejection of the demand for a full fledged Pakistan.
- For a very loose union of all the Indian territories under a centre that would control merely the defence, the Foreign Affairs and the Communications, leaving all other subjects to the existing provincial legislatures.
- Provincial legislatures would elect a Constituent Assembly. The members would divide up into three sections–A, B & C while electing the constitutent Assembly. All these sections would have the authority to draw up provincial constitutions and even group constitutions.

  Section A: Non Muslim Majority provinces (Bombay, United Provinces, Bihar, Central Provinces, Orissa, Madras)

  Section B: Muslim majority provinces in the north-west (Sind, NWFP & Punjab)

  Section C: Muslim majority provinces in North east (Bengal, Assam)
- Communal questions in Central legislature were to be decided by a simple majority in both communities.
- Provinces were to have full autonomy & residual powers.
- Princely states were no longer to be under paramountcy of British Government.
- After the first general elections, a province could come out of a group and after 10 years a province could call for reconsideration of the group or union constitution.
- Each group had powers to set up intermediate level legislature and executive on their own.
- The plan failed on the issue of the nature of grouping–Jinnah was for compulsory while Nehru was for grouping only till the formation of a constituent assembly. On 29th July 1946 Jinnah withdrew his earlier acceptance of the plan and fixed 16 August 1946 as Direct Action Day. Calcutta, Noakhali, Garmukteshwar were the storm centres. Communal massacre weakened the Congress position in the NWFP.

Interim Government (September 1946)

- Came into existence on 2nd September 1946, in accordance with Cabinet Mission's proposal and was headed by J L Nehru. Muslim League refused to join it initially.
- Wavell persuaded the League leaders to join on 26 October 1946.
- 8th December 1946–Constituent Assembly begins its session with Liaqat Ali Khan of Muslim League as the Finance Minister
- The Interim government, obstructed by its League members and bureaucracy was reduced to a figurehead and was unable to control the communal carnage.

Attlee's Announcement (February 1947)

In July 1947, on the basis of Mountbatten plan the bill of Indian Independence was presented in the British Parliament, which was passed on 18th July, 1947. On its basis British rule over India ended and two independent countries viz. India and Pakistan were carved up.

- British Prime Minister Atlee on 20 February 1947 announced that the British would withdraw from India by 30 June, 1948 and that Lord Mountbatten would replace Wavell. British powers and obligations vis-a-vis the princely states would lapse with transfer of power but these would not be transferred to any successor Government in British India. Partition of the country was implicit in the provision that if the constituent assembly was not fully representative then power would be transferred to more than one central govt.

Mountbatten Plan (3rd June Plan)

- His earlier Plan Balkan was abandoned for the 3rd June Plan.
- The Plan declared that power would be handed over by 15 August 1947 on the basis of dominion status to India and Pakistan.
- Mountbatten supported the Congress stand that the princely states must not be given the option of independence. They would either join India or Pakistan.
- Boundary commission was to be headed by Radcliffe and the award was to be announced after Republic day (which was a major cause of massacres).
- Punjab and Bengal Legislative Assemblies would meet in two groups, Hindu's and Muslims, to vote for partition. If a simple majority of either group voted for partition, then these provinces would be partitioned. In case of partition, two dominions and two constituent assemblies would be created.

Jinnah's Fourteen Points

1. Any constitution to be drawn for free India should be Federal.
2. Minorities should adequately represent in all legislatures.
3. A uniform measure of autonomy for every province.
4. One-third seats should be reserved for Muslims.
5. Representation on the basis of separate electorate.
6. Full religious liberty.
7. No territorial redistribution.
8. Not to adopt any bill on the ground that it was injurious to the interest of a particular community.
9. Sindh to be separated from Bombay presidency.
10. Indiscrimination of Baluchistan and NWFP.
11. Adequate share for Muslims.
12. One-third ministers from Muslim community.
13. Adequate safeguards to protect Muslims.
14. Change in constitution can be made only with the concurrence of Indian Federation.

Indian Independence Act of 1947

- Till 1947, the Government of India functioned under the provisions of the 1919 Act only. The provisions of 1935 Act relating to Federation and Dyarchy were never implemented.
- The Executive Council provided by the 1919 Act continued to advice the Governor-General till 1947.
- It declared India as an Independent and Sovereign State.
- Established responsible Governments at both the Centre and the Provinces.

- Designated the Governor-General of India and the Provincial Governors as the Constitutional Heads (nominal heads).
- It assigned dual functions (Constituent and Legislative) to the Constituent Assembly and declared this dominion legislature as a sovereign body.

Historical Background	
1687	The first Municipal Corporation in India was set up in Madras.
1772	Lord Warren Hastings created the office of District Collector.
1829	The office of the Divisional Commissioner was created by Lord William Bentick.
1859	The portfolio system was introduced by Lord Canning.
1860	A system of Budget was introduced.
1870	Lord Mayo's resolution on financial decentralisation visualised the development of local self-government institutions in India.
1872	First census in India was conducted during Lord Mayo's period.
1881	First regular census was conducted during the period of Lord Ripon.
1882	Lord Ripon's resolution was hailed as the 'Magna Carta' of local self-government. He is regarded as the 'Father of local self-government in India'.
1905	The tenure system was introduced by Lord Curzon.
1905	The Railway Board was set up by a resolution of the Government of India.
1921	Public Accounts Committee was created at the Centre.
1921	Railway Budget was separated from the General Budget.
1935	Reserve Bank of India was established by an Act of the Central Legislature.

The Acts and their Basic Features	
1858	The power was transferred from company to crown and establishment of the office of secretary of state and Indian council.
1861	The introduction of portfolio system.
1892	The system of indirect election was introduced.
1909	Introduction of communal electorate.
1919	Introduction of dyarchy in the provinces.
1935	Introduction of provincial autonomy, the dyarchy at central and provision for all India Federation.

Chapter at a Glance

- Lord Canning was the first Governor General to adopet the additional title of Viceroy.
- Queen Victoria's proclaimation was read by Lord Canning at a Darbar held at Allahabad.
- The power was transferred from company to Crown by the Act of 1858.
- The Act of 1858 received the Royal assent on 2 August, 1858.
- By the Act of 1909 Mr. S.P. Sinha was appointed Law member to the Governor General's Executive Council.
- Morely, the secretary of state for India, appointed two Indians Mr. K.G. Gupta

and Syed Hussain Bilgrami to the India Council.

- By the Act of 1909 there were four kind of electroates for Central Legislature: (i) General (ii) Special (iii) Class electrolate and (iv) Muslims. For the provincial legislatures the electorate were of three kinds (i) General (ii) Special (iii) Class electrolate.
- The two Boundary commissions for Punjab and Bengal were set up by the Act of 1947 under the chairmanship of Sir Cyril Radcliffe.
- Burma ceased to be a part of India by the Act of 1935.
- Commenting on the provisions of the Act of 1935, Jawahar Lal Nehru said, "The Act had all brakes but no engine".
- The Federal court was established by the Act of 1935.
- The Act of 1935 vested the control of the Railways in a new authority known as the Federal Railway Authority which and seven members who were kept free from the control of ministers and councillors.
- Under the Meston Awards, the provincial Governments were required to make certain annual contributions to the Government of India.
- The system of Dyarchy was introduced in 1921 in nine Governor's provinces.
- by the Act of 1919 the salary of the secretary of state for India was made a charge on British revenue.
- A fifth member was added to the Executive Council of the Viceroy by the Act of 1861. The member was to be onlinary and to be a financial expert.

Previous Year Question Paper (1998-2017)

1. The Government of India Act of 1919 clearly defined
   (a) The separation of power between the judiciary and the legislature
   (b) The jurisdiction of the central and provincial governments
   (c) The powers of the Secretary of State for India and Viceroy
   (d) None of the above **(1998)**
2. With reference to the Cabinet Mission, which of the following statements is/are correct?
   1. It recommended a federal government.
   2. It enlarged the powers of the Indian courts.
   3. It provided for more Indians in the ICS.

   Select the correct answer using the code given below:
   (a) 1 only (b) 2 and 3
   (c) 1 and 3 (d) None **(1999)**
3. The "Instrument of Instructions" contained in the Government of India Act 1935 have been incorporated in the Constitution of India in the year 1950:
   (a) Fundamental Rights
   (b) Directive Principles of State Policy
   (c) Extent of executive power of State
   (d) Conduct of bussiness of the Government of India **(2010)**
4. Consider the following statements:
   1. The Charter Act 1853 abolished East India Company's monopoly on Indian trade
   2. Under the Government of India Act 1858, the British Parliament

abolished the East India Company altogether and undertook the responsibility of ruling India directly.

Which of the statements given above is/are correct?

(a) 1 only (b) 2 only
(c) Both 1 and 2 (d) Neither 1 nor 2

(2006)

5. Which one of the following Acts of British India strengthened the Viceroy's authority over his executive council by substituting "portfolio" or departmental system for corporate functioning?
   (a) Indian Councils Act, 1861
   (b) Government of India Act, 1885
   (c) Indian Councils Act, 1892
   (d) Indian Councils Act, 1909 **(2002)**
6. Which one of the following provisions was **NOT** made in the Charter Act of 1833?
   (a) The trading activities of the East India Company were to be abolished.
   (b) The designation of the supreme authority was to be changed as the Governor-General of India in Council.
   (c) All law-making powers to be conferred on Governor-General in Council.
   (d) An Indian was to be appointed as a Law Member in the Governor-General's Council. **(2003)**
7. Match List-I (Acts of Colonial Government of India) with List-II (Provisions) and select the correct answer using the codes given below the lists:

   List-I (Acts of Colonial Government of India)
   A. Charter Act, 1813
   B. Regulating Act
   C. Act of 1858
   D. Pitt's India Act **(2002)**

   List-II (Provisions)
   1. Set up a Board of Control in Britain to fully regulate the East India Company's affairs in India.
   2. Company's trade monopoly in India was ended.
   3. The power to govern was transferred from the East India Company to the British Crown.
   4. The Company's directors were asked to present to the British Government all correspondence and documents pertaining to the administration of the company.

   Codes:

	A	B	C	D
(a)	2	4	3	1
(b)	1	3	4	2
(c)	2	3	4	1
(d)	1	4	3	2

8. Which one of the following is not a feature of the Government of India Act of 1935?
   (a) Dyarchy at the Centre as well as in the Provinces
   (b) A bicameral legislature
   (c) Provincial autonomy
   (d) An All-India Federation **(2000)**
9. The most short-lived of all of Britain's constitutional experiments in India was the
   (a) Indian Councils Act of 1861
   (b) Indian Councils Act of 1892
   (c) Indian Councils Act of 1909
   (d) Government of India Act of 1919 **(1999)**
10. BR Ambedkar was elected to the Constituent Assembly from
    (a) West Bengal
    (b) The then Bombay Presidency
    (c) The then Madhya Bharat
    (d) Punjab **(1996)**

Answer

1. (b)	2. (a)	3. (b)
4. (d)	5. (a)	6. (c)
7. (c)	8. (a)	9. (d)
10. (d)		

Answers with Explanation

1. (b) GOI Act, 1919 is also known as the Montague-Chelmsford Reforms, came into force in 1921.
   It relaxed central control over the provinces by demarcating and separating the central and provincial subjects.
   It also separated provincial budgets from central budgets.
2. (a) Cabinet Mission 1946, proposed for a federal scheme, where most of the functions were to be performed at the provincial level.
   By, 1944, most of the ICS officers were Indians.
   The other provisions are not part of Cabinet Mission, as it was mostly related to the Constitutional scheme.
3. (b) The directive principles are like instruments which were issued to the Governor in general and Governors of colonies and to those of India by the British Government under the 1935 Act. and under the draft Constitution. It was proposed to issue such instructions to the president and Governors. The text of these instruments of the instructions is found in Scheduled IV to the Constitution of India.
4. (d)
5. (a) In 1861, Lord Canning introduced portfolio system. The year 1892 was entirely on Legislative Council and 1909 strengthened Viceroy's authority over executive council.
6. (c) The members of the Constituent Assembly were elected by Legislative Assemblies of various provinces on the basis of proportional representation. They were nominated neither by British Parliament nor by Governor General. They represented all parties.
7. (c)
8. (a) By the Act. of 1935 Dyarchy was abolished and Orissa and Sind were created and all provincial subjects were transferred to popular control in view of a federation in centre. Bicameral legislatures were established in Madras, Bombay, Bangal, and United provinces, Bihar and Assam but the Act remained entirely silent about dominion status.
9. (d) India has the system of judicial review. But in UK, the Parliament is Supreme, there is no provision for Judicial review.
10. (d) Dr. B.R. Ambedkar was not elected for Constituent Assembly by the Bombay, Legislative Council of where he was a resident but later on he was nominated by West Bengal Legislative Council.

Practice Paper

1. Consider the following:
   (i) End of dual system of government.
   (ii) Setting up of the Calcutta Madrasa in 1781.
   (iii) Impeachment on charges of murder and bribery
   (iv) Permanent Settlement of Bengal.

Warren Hastings was associated with which of the following?

(a) i, ii and iii (b) ii, iii and iv
(c) i, iii and iv (d) i and ii

2. Which of the following were the highlights of Cornwallis regime?
(i) Permanent Settlement of Bengal
(ii) Reorganization of revenue courts
(iii) Compilation of 'Cornwallis Code'
(iv) Establishment of the Thanas

(a) i and iii (b) i and ii
(c) i, iii and iv (d) i, ii, iii and iv

3. Which of the following did not occur during the Governor Generalship of William Bentinck?
(a) Abolition of sati
(b) Macauly's Reforms
(c) Establishment of a Medical College at Calcutta
(d) Annexation of Sindh to the British empire

4. Match the following lists of Viceroys and events:

List I (Viceroys)	List II (Events)
(A) Lord Canning	1. Kuka movement
(B) John Lawrence	2. Setting up of Department of Agriculture
(C) Lord Mayo	3. Famine Commission under Campbell
(D) Lord Northbrooke	4. Transfer of the government from the company to the British crown

Codes:	A	B	C	D
(a)	4	3	2	1
(b)	3	4	2	1
(c)	1	2	3	4
(d)	2	1	4	3

5. Who was the Viceroy of India when the Indian National Congress was formed?
(a) Lord Ripon
(b) Lord Northbrooke
(c) Lord Dufferin
(d) Lord Lansdowne

6. Lord Ripon was associated with
(a) Removal of Veracular Press Act
(b) Resolution of institution of locol-self government
(c) Enactment of the First Factory Act
(d) All of the above

7. Match the following lists of Viceroys and events:

List I (Viceroys)	List II (Events)
(A) Lord Ripon	1. Introduction of the Ilbert Bill
(B) Lord Lytton	2. Appointment of a Famine Commission under Strachey
(C) Lord Dufferin	3. Annexation of Upper Burma
(D) Lord Hardinge II	4. A coronation Durbar at Delhi

Codes:	A	B	C	D
(a)	1	2	3	4
(b)	2	1	3	4
(c)	3	4	1	2
(d)	4	2	3	1

8. The Indo-Afghan border of the Durand Line was demarcated during the viceroyality of
(a) Lord Elgin I
(b) Lord Lansdowne
(c) Lord Chelmsford
(d) Lord Reading

9. Who was the Viceroy of India when the Muslim League launched the heinous 'Direct Action Day?

(a) Lord Linlithgow
(b) Lord Wavell
(c) Lord Mountbatten
(d) Lord Rajagopalachari

10. Which of the following is/are wrongly matched?
(i) Lytton: Lee Commission
(ii) Mayo: Scholarship scheme
(iii) Ripon: Repeal of Vernacular Press Act
(iv) Canning: Queen Victoria's Proclamation
(a) i, iii and iv (b) i and ii
(c) ii and iv (d) iv only

11. Consider the following statements:
1. The Charter Act 1853 abolished East India Company's monopoly on Indian trade
2. Under the Government of India Act 1858, the British Parliament abolished the East India Company altogether and undertook the responsibility of ruling India directly.
Which of the statements given above is/are correct?
(a) 1 only (b) 2 only
(c) Both 1 and 2 (d) Neither 1 nor 2

12. Which one of the following provisions was **NOT** made in the Charter Act of 1833?
(a) The trading activities of the East India Company were to be abolished.
(b) The designation of the supreme authority was to be changed as the Governor-General of India in Council.
(c) All law-making powers to be conferred on Governor-General in Council.
(d) An Indian was to be appointed as a Law Member in the Governor-General's Council.

13. Which one of the following Acts of British India strengthened the Viceroy's authority over his executive council by substituting "portfolio" or departmental system for corporate functioning?
(a) Indian Councils Act, 1861
(b) Government of India Act, 1885
(c) Indian Councils Act, 1892
(d) Indian Councils Act, 1909

14. Which of the following laid the foundation of central administration in India?
(a) Pitt's India Act of 1784
(b) Regulating Act of 1773
(c) Government of India Act of 1858
(d) Charter Act of 1833

15. Arrange the following events in chronological order:
1. Hindu widow remarriage act
2. Abolition of Sati
3. Woods Despatch
4. Macaulay Minute
Correct code is:
(a) 1, 2, 3, 4 (b) 2, 4, 3, 1
(c) 1, 3, 4, 2 (d) 4, 1, 2, 3

16. Which of the following is not a recommendation of Charles Wood's Despatch?
(a) An education department to be established in every province.
(b) At least one Government school is opened in every district.
(c) The Indian native should be given training in the English language.
(d) Affiliated private schools should be given grant in aid.

17. According to Doctrine of Lapse, when the ruler of a protected state died without a natural heir, his state was not to pass to an adopted heir as sanctioned by the age old tradition of the country. Following states were annexed by applying this doctrine

1. Nagpur 2. Satara
3. Balaghat 4. Jhansi

Arrange the above states of annexation in chronological order.

(a) 2-3-4-5-1 (b) 2-3-1-5-4
(c) 3-1-2-4-5 (d) 3-1-4-5-2

18. The "Instrument of Instructions" contained in the Government of India Act 1935 has been incorporated in the Constitution of India in the year 1950.
(a) Fundamental Rights
(b) Directive Principles of State Policy
(c) Extent of executive power of State
(d) Conduct of bussiness of the Government of India

19. Match the following:

List-I
1. Lord Mountbatten
2. Dr. Rajendra Prasad
3. Dr. B.R. Ambedkar
4. Pandit J.L. Nehru
5. Dr. K.M. Munshi

List-II
A. Chairman of the Drafting Committee
B. First Prime Minister of India
C. Member of the Constituent Assembly
D. Last British Governor-General
E. President of the Constituent Assembly
F. Legal adviser to the Constituent Assembly

Codes:

(a) 1-D,	2-A,	3-E,	4-B,	5-F
(b) 1-D,	2-E,	3-F,	4-B,	5-A
(c) 1-D,	2-E,	3-A,	4-B,	5-C
(d) 1-D,	2-C,	3-F,	4-B,	5-A

20. Which of the following are among the provisions of the Act of 1858?
1. The administration of India and the Indian Territories was transferred to the Crown.
2. The East India Company was abolished.
3. The Governor-General of India was to be known as the Viceroy of India and a Secretary of State for India was also appointed.
4. The administrative power of India was to be shared between the East India Company and the Crown of England.

Codes:

(a) 1, 3 and 4 (b) 1, 2 and 3
(c) 2, 3 and 4 (d) All the above

21. Which of the following are not correctly matched?
1. Government of India Act, 1919–Dyarchy
2. Government of India Act, 1935–Provincial autonomy
3. Minto-Morley Reforms–Separate Electorate
4. Mountbatten Plan–Constituent assembly
5. Cabinet Mission Plan, 1946 – Partition of India

Codes:

(a) 4 and 5
(b) 1 and 4
(c) 1 and 5
(d) 2 and 3

Answers

1. (a)	2. (d)	3. (d)	13. (a)	14. (b)	15. (b)
4. (a)	5. (c)	6. (d)	16. (c)	17. (a)	18. (b)
7. (a)	8. (b)	9. (b)	19. (c)	20. (b)	21. (a)
10. (b)	11. (b)	12. (d)			

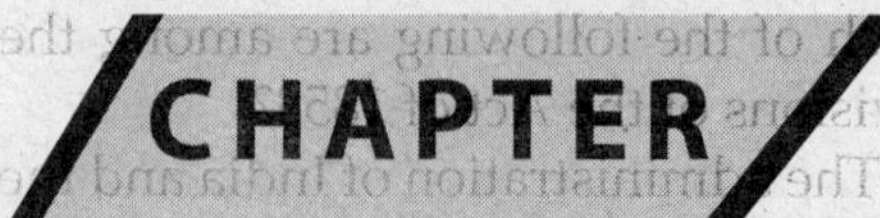

6

Governor-Generals and Viceroys of India

Governors of Bengal (1757-74)

Robert Clive (1757-60 and 1765-67)

- Governor of Bengal from 1757-60 and 1765-67, and the true founder of British political dominion in India.

Robert Clive

- The English defeated Siraj-ud-Daula in the Battle of Plassey (1757), and Mir Jafar became the Nawab of Bengal.
- French were defeated by the East India Company (EIC) in the Battle of Bidar (1759).
- Concluded Treaty of Allahabad (16th August 1765) with Shuja-ud-daula and Shah Alam-II.
- Established Dual Government in Bengal in 1765.
- He forbade the servants of EIC from indulging in private trade and made payment of internal duties obligatory.
- Established Society of Trade (1765) with trade monopoly in salt, betelnut and tobacco. It was abolished in 1767.

Holwell (1760)

- Officiating Governor of Bengal.

Vansittart (1760-65)

- The Battle of Buxar (1764)

Verelst (1767-69)

- Colonial Administrator and the Governor of Bengal.

Cartier (1769-72)

- Bengal famine (1770)

Warren Hastings (1772-74)

- Abolished Dual Government in 1772.

Governor-Generals of Bengal (1774-1833)

(Regulating Act of 1773)

Warren Hastings (1774-85)

- Introduced Quinquennial Settlement of land revenue in 1772, later on he reversed to Annual Settlement (1777) on the basis of open auction to the highest bidder.

Warren Hastings

- Became Governor-General of Bengal in 1774 through the Regulating Act of 1773.
- Transferred the treasury from Murshidabad to Calcutta, and checked the misuse of *Dastaks*.
- Divided Bengal into districts and appointed collectors and other revenue officials.
- Dismissed Deputy Diwans, Mohammed Reza Khan (Bengal)and Raja Shitab Rai (Bihar).
- Appointed Munni Begum as regent of minor Nawab Mubarak-ud-Daula of Bengal.
- Signed treaty of Faizabad (1775) with Asaf-ud-daula of Awadh.
- Stopped annual allowance of Rs 20 lakh to Shah Alam II on charges of seeking protection from the Marathas.
- Took away Allahabad and Kara from Mughal Emperor and sold it to Nawab of Awadh for Rs. 50 Lakh.
- Codified Hindu and Muslim laws, and started Diwani and Faujdari adalats at the district level and Sadar Diwani and Nizamat adalats (appellate courts) at Calcutta.
- Foundation of Asiatic Society of Bengal with Sir William Jones in 1784.
- Associated with the Chait Singh (Raja of Banaras) affair, 1778.
- After his return to England in 1785, impeachment proceedings were initiated against him in the house of Lords but after a long trial of 7 years he was eventually acquitted.
- In 1776 Manu's Law was translated as the *Code of Gentoo Laws*, and *Fatwa-i-Alamgiri* was also translated.
- Wrote an introduction to the first English translation of *Gita* by Charles Wilkins.
- Important wars fought during his tenure were Rohilla War (1774), first Anglo-Maratha War (1776-82), and second Anglo-Mysore war (1780-84).

Sir Macpherson (1785-86)

- Officiating Governor-General of Bengal.

Lord Cornwallis (1786-93)

- Introduced *Cornwallis Code* based in 1793. According to which courts were set up at different levels and revenue administration was separated from judicial administration in order to reform the judiciary.

Lord Cornwallis

- The post of District Judge was created, and the Superintendent of Police was made the head of district police who became the in-charge of an area of 1000 sq. km.
- Besides the English magistrates were also given police powers and divested the Zamindars of all police powers.
- A ten-year settlement was concluded with the Zamindars in 1790 which was made permanent in 1793.
- Raised salaries of the officials with Collectors getting 1% of the revenue collection in addition to their salary of Rs. 1500, and this system of civil, police and judicial administration remained in force till 1858.
- Important war fought during his tenure was the third Anglo-Mysore War (1790-92) which ended with the Treaty of Srirangapatnam (1792) after Tipu Sultan's defeat.

Sir John Shore (1793-98)

- First Charter Act of 1793 was passed.

Sir John Shore

- The Battle of Kharda (1795) was fought between the Nizam and Marathas which resulted the defeat of Nizam.
- Most known for his policy of non-intervention.
- Ahmad Shah Abdali's grandson named Zaman Shah attacked India.

Sir A. Clarke (1798)

- Officiating Governor-General of Bengal.

Lord Richard Wellesley (1798-1805)

- Described himself as Bengal Tiger.

Lord Richard Wellesley

- Created Madras Presidency after the annexation of the Kingdoms of Tanjore and Carnatic.
- Introduced the system of Subsidiary Alliance in 1798 to achieve British Paramountcy in India.
- Signed Treaty of Bassein (1802) with the Peshwa, and fought Second Anglo-Maratha War (1803-05) which led to the defeat of Scindhia, Bhonsle and Holkar.
- In the fourth Anglo-Mysore War (1799) Tipu Sultan was defeated and died.
- Lord Lake captured Delhi and Agra in 1803 and the Mughal Emperor was put under Company's protection.

Lord Cornwallis (1805)

- Europeanisation of administrative services, introduction of civils services and reforms to purify and improve administration. Carnwallis is called the Father of Civil Service in India.

Sir George Barlow (1805-1807)

- He worked in the capacity of an officiating Governor-General of Bengal.

Sir George Barlow

- Followed a policy of non-intervention.
- Sepoy Mutiny at Vellore (1806).
- Third Governor-General who tried to restore peace between Scindhia and Holkar.
- Holkar accepted subsidiary alliance by Treaty of Rajpurghat in 1805.
- End of second Anglo-Maratha War (1803-05).

Lord Minto-I (1807-1813)

- Signed Treaty of Amritsar in 1809 with Ranjit Singh.
- Charter Act of 1813 was passed.
- Sent missions to Persia and Kabul under the leadership of Malcolm and Elphinstone respectively.

Lord Hastings (1813-1823)

- Adopted the policy of intervention and war.

Lord Hastings

- Succeeded in the Anglo-Nepalese War (1813-19), signed the Treaty of Sogauli with Gorkha leader Amar Singh.
- Abolished Peshwaship and annexed all his territories in the Bombay Presidency after the third Anglo-Maratha War (1817-18), and forced humiliating treaties on Peshwa and Scindhia.
- Fought against Pindaris (1817-1818), and appointed *Darogas* and forced zamindars to surrender their police.

- Signed a treaty with the Raja of Sikkim and handed over the territory between Hechi and Tista rivers (1817).
- Introduction of Ryotwari Settlement in Madras Presidency by Governor, Thomas Munro (1820).
- Mahalwari system of land revenue was made in North-West Province by James Thomson.

John Adams (1823)

- Officiating Governor-General of Bengal.

Lord Amherst (1823-1828)

- Received by Emperor Akbar-II on terms of equality in 1827.

Lord Amherst

- The first Burmese War (1824-26) was fought during his tenure. He signed the Treaty of Yandaboo in 1826 with lower Burma (Pegu) by which British merchants were allowed to settle on southern coast of Burma and Rangoon.
- Acquired territories in Malay Peninsula, and captured Bharatpur in 1826.

William Butterworth Bayley (1828)

- Officiating Governor-General of Bengal.

Lord William Bentinck (1828-33)

- Most liberal colonial ruler who is also regarded as the father of modern western education in India.

Lord William Bentinck

- Introduced a number of social reforms including the abolition of the practice of *Sati* in 1829, and suppressed *Thugi* in 1830 (Military operation led by William Sleeman).
- Signed a treaty of perpetual friendship with Ranjit Singh in 1831, and annexed Mysore (1831) and Jaintia (1832).

Governor-Generals of India (1833-58)

(Charter Act of 1833)

Lord William Bentinck (1833-35)

- Became the first Governor-General of India by the Charter Act of 1833. This act provided that no Indian subject of the company will be debarred from holding any office on account of religion, place of birth, descent and color.
- Annexed Coorg and central Kachar on the plea of misgovernance, and created the Province of Agra in 1834.

- Defined the aims and objectives of the educational policy of the British Government.
- Appointed Lord Macaulay (1835) as the President of the Committee of Public Instructions which recommended English as the medium of instruction and introduction of English literature and sciences in the curriculum.
- English was to be court language at higher courts but Persian continued in lower courts.
- Abolished provincial courts of appeal and circuit set up by Lord Cornwallis.
- The Regulation of 1833 on land revenue settlement was introduced by Mertins Bird, the father of land-revenue settlement in North India, and use of fields maps and field registers prescribed for the first time.

Sir Charles Metcalfe (1835-36)

- Officiating Governor-General of India.
- Abolished restrictions on press and came to be known as the liberator of press.

Lord Auckland (1836-42)

- First Anglo-Afghan War (1836-42) gave a great blow to the prestige of British in India.
- Tripartite treaty was signed between the Company, Ranjit Singh and Shah Shuja by which Ranjit Singh accepted Company's mediation in the disputes of the Amirs of Sind.
- Shah Shuja conceded his sovereign right to the Company over Sind on the condition of receiving the arrears of the tribute, the amount of which was to be determined by the Company.
- Mandavi State was annexed in 1839.

Lord Ellenborough (1842-44)

- Annexation of Sindh and War with Gwalior (1843).
- Brought the Afghan war to an end.

Lord Hardinge-I (1844-48)

- Fought the first Anglo-Sikh War (1845-46) and concluded the Treaty of Lahore in 1846.
- Prohibited female infanticide and the practice of human sacrifice among the Khonds of Central India.
- Gave preference to English educated in employment.

Lord Dalhousie (1848-56)

- Fought second Anglo-Sikh War (1848-49) and annexed the whole of Punjab.

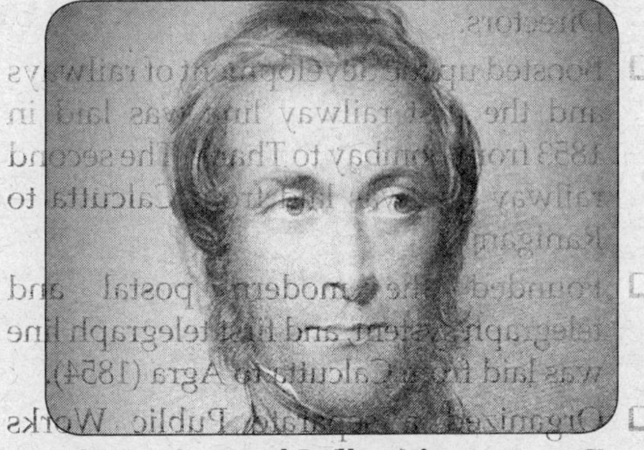

Lord Dalhousie

- Darjeeling and its outlying districts were annexed in 1850.
- The second Anglo-Burmese War was fought in 1852) after which Lower Burma (Pegu) was annexed.

- Used the Doctrine of Lapse and Law of Escheat to annex the Indian princely states of Satara (1848), Jaitpur and Sambalpur (1849), Baghat (1850), Udaipur (1852), Jhansi (1853), and Nagpur (1854).
- Annexed Berar in 1853 from Nizam on account of arrears for auxiliary.
- Annexed Awadh in 1856 on the grounds of maladministration when Nawab Wazid Ali Shah refused to abdicate.
- Introduced Bon-Regulation system, a system of centralized control, in the newly acquired territories.
- Stopped and abolished the pensions and titles of various princes and rulers of native states. For example, he stopped the annual payment of Nana Sahib who was the adopted son of Peshwa Baji Rao II.
- Planned to stop pensions and abolished the regal titles of the Mughal Emperor after the death of Bahadur Shah II, but this was rejected by the Board of Directors.
- Boosted up the development of railways and the first railway line was laid in 1853 from Bombay to Thane. The second railway line was laid from Calcutta to Raniganj.
- Founded the modern postal and telegraph system, and first telegraph line was laid from Calcutta to Agra (1854).
- Organized a separate Public Works Department by divesting the Military Board of this responsibility.
- Started work on the Grand Trunk road and also developed the harbors of Karachi, Bombay and Calcutta.
- Shimla was made summer capital and army headquarter. He also raised Gorkha regiments.
- Hindu Widow Remarriage Act was passed in 1856.
- Recommended the Thomsonian system of vernacular education for the North-western provinces (1853).
- Many Anglo-Vernacular schools and government colleges were established as per the recommendations of Wood's Dispatch (1854). An engineering college was also opened in Roorkee.

Lord Canning (1856-58)

- The Revolt of 1857 occurred during his tenure.
- Bahadur Shah 'Zafar' was sent to Rangoon (Burma).
- The universities of Calcutta, Bombay and Madras were founded in 1857.

Governor-Generals and Viceroys of India (1858-1936)

(The Government of India Act, 1858)

Lord Canning (1858-62)

- Queen Victoria's Proclamation and passage of the Government of India Act, 1858 led to the end of Company's rule in India. The last Governor-General of British India becomes the first Viceroy.

Lord Canning

- The concept of income tax was introduced for the first time in 1858.
- White Mutiny by the European troops of the East India Company in 1859.
- Doctrine of Lapse started by Lord Dalhousie was officially withdrawn in 1859.
- Rajput states of Baghat and Udaipur were returned to their respective rulers.
- The Indian Penal Code was passed in 1858-59. This Code declared slave trade in India as illegal in 1860.
- The Indian High Court Act was enacted in 1861, and the Indian Councils act, 1961 is also passed.
- Indigo Riots in Bengal (1859-60).

Lord Elgin-I (1862-63)

- Suppressed the Wahabi Movement, a Pan-Islamic Movement.

Lord Elgin-I

- Due to his sudden death in 1862, the administration was run by ***Sir Robert Napier*** and ***Sir William T. Denison*** in 1863.

Sir John Lawrence (1864-69)

- Followed a policy of rigid non-interference in Afghanistan called Policy of Masterly Inactivity.
- Telegraphic Communication was opened with Europe (1869-70).
- High Courts were set up at Calcutta, Bombay and Madras in 1865, and reorganized the native judicial service.
- The Anglo-Bhutan War was fought in 1865.
- Expanded the canal works and railways, and advocated state-managed railways.
- Created the Indian Forests Department.

Lord-Mayo (1869-72)

- Started the process of decentralization of finance in India in 1870.
- For the first time in India, a population census is conducted in 1871.
- Established two colleges for education and political training of the Indian princes (Royal College, Kathiawar and Mayo College, Ajmer).
- Organized the Statistical Survey of India.
- Established the Department of Agriculture and Commerce.
- Introduced the system of state Railways.
- The only viceroy to be murdered in office by a Pathan convict in the Andamans in 1872. The administration was look after by ***Sir John Strachey*** and ***Lord Napier Merchistoun*** in 1872.

Lord Northbrook (1872-76)

- Visit of Prince of Wales Edward-VII.
- Kuka Movement in Punjab became rebellious in 1872.
- Bihar famine in 1874, and trial of Gaikwad of Baroda in 1875.
- He resigned over Afghan issue.

Lord Lytton-I (1876-80)

- The most infamous Viceroy, also known as the Viceroy of reverse character.
- The Royal Title Act of 1876 led to the assumption of the title Empress of India (*Kaiser-I-Hind*) by Queen Victoria.
- He organized a Grand Durbar in Delhi in 1877 to decorate Queen Victoria with the above mentioned title when the country was suffering from a severe famine.
- The Vernacular Press was passed in 1878 to curtail the freedom of news-papers published in Indian languages. It empowered a magistrate to call upon the printer and publisher of any vernacular newspaper to enter into an undertaking not to publish any news which would create antipathy against the government.
- The Arms Act of 1878 made it mandatory for the Indians to acquire license for arms.
- Decreased the maximum age limit from 21 years to 19 years for the Civil Services Examination in 1878-79. It was an attempt to prevent Indians from entering Civil Services.
- Appointment of the first Famine Commission under Sir Richard Strachey.
- Policy of Masterly Inactivity towards Afghanistan was replaced by Forward Policy.

Lord Ripon (1880-84)

- Passing of First Factory Act in 1881 to improve labour working conditions.
- Repeal of Vernacular Press Act in 1882.
- The resolution for local Self-Government was passed in 1882. It led to the passing of local self-Government. Acts in various provinces during the Period 1883-85
- First regular census (decennial) was conducted in 1881 which put the total population of India at 254 millions.
- Appointed an Education Commission under Sir William Hunter in 1882 for educational reforms.
- The Illbert Bill controversy erupted during his time in 1883-84. It was related to a bill framed by Sir C.P. Illbert, the law member of Viceroy's Council which recommended abolition of judicial disqualification based on race.

Lord Dufferin (1884-88)

- The Indian national congress was formed in1885 during his viceroyalty.
- Third Anglo-Burmese War led to full and final annexation of Burma in 1885.
- Delimitation of Afghan northern boundary.

Lord Lansdowne (1888-94)

- Passed the Age of Consent Act in 1891 which forbade marriage of girls below 12.
- The second factory Act was passed in 1891 which granted a weekly holiday and stipulated working hours for Children and women.
- Civil Services were categorized into Imperial, provincial, and subordinate.
- Passing of Indian council Act, 1892.
- Appointed Durand Commission to define the boundary between India and Afghanistan in 1893.

Lord Elgin-II (1894-98)

- Munda uprising under the leadership of Birsa Munda (1898-99).

- ❑ Ratification of the convention delimiting the boundary between India and China.
- ❑ The Lyall Commission (1897) was appointed to look into the causes of the great famine of 1896-97.

Lord Curzon (1899-1905)

- ❑ Created a new province called the North-West Frontier Province.
- ❑ Appointed Sir Thomas Raleigh Commission in 1902 to suggest reforms regarding universities, and the Indian Universities Act of 1904 was passed on the basis of its recommendations which increased the official control.
- ❑ A new Department of Commerce and Industry was set up.
- ❑ Ancient Monuments Preservation Act was also passed in 1904 to restore India's rich cultural heritage. The Archaeological Survey of India was also established to serve this purpose.
- ❑ The Pusa Agricultural Research Institute was established in 1903 in Delhi.
- ❑ The Calcutta Corporation Act was passed in 1899 which provided for reduction of elected members.
- ❑ Partition of Bengal (16th October 1905) into two provinces–Bengal proper, and east Bengal and Assam.
- ❑ Appointed a Police Commission in 1902 under Sir Andrew Frazer to inquire into the police administration.
- ❑ Colonel Young Husbands expedition to Tibet in 1904.
- ❑ Set up Irrigation Commission of 1901 and the works on Jhelum canal was completed.
- ❑ The MacDonnell Commission on Famine was appointed in 1900.
- ❑ The Moncrieff Commission on irrigation was appointed in 1902.
- ❑ Official Secrets Act was passed in 1904 which extended the scope of sedition.
- ❑ Passed Indian Coinage and Paper Currency Act in 1899 and put India on a gold standard.
- ❑ He built a greater mileage of railway line than any other viceroy and established the Railway Board.
- ❑ ***Lord Ampthill*** officiated as Viceroy for sometime in 1904.
- ❑ Resigned from his office, because of his controversy with Kitchner (August 1905).
- ❑ Ronatdshay wrote his biography named *"The Life of Lord Curzon"*.

Lord Minto-II (1905-10)

- ❑ Swadeshi Movement was launched in 1905 which continued to garner mass support till 1908.
- ❑ Foundation of Muslim League by Aga Khan, the Nawab of Dacca in 1906.
- ❑ A split occurred in the Congress during the Surat session (1907).
- ❑ Newspapers Act was passed in 1908.
- ❑ Minto-Morley Reforms or the Indian Council Act of 1909 was also passed.
- ❑ Khudiram Bose was hanged on April 30, 1908.
- ❑ Formal adoption of divide and rule policy in 1909, accordingly reservation of seats for Muslims in 1909 reforms.
- ❑ Tilak was sentenced to six years rigorous imprisonment and sent to Mandalay jail.

Lord Hardinge-II (1910-1916)

- ❑ Annulment of partition of Bengal and creation of a Governorship for Bengal like Bombay and Madras in 1911.

Lord Hardinge-II

Lord Chelmsford

- Simultaneous creation of Lieutenant Governorship of Bihar and Orissa and Chief Commissionership for Assam.
- Announcement of transfer of imperial capital from Calcutta to Delhi (1911).
- A separate state of Bihar and Orissa was created in 1911.
- Coronation Durbar of King George-V and Queen Mary was organized at Delhi (December 1911).
- Ghadar Movement started in 1915 in San Francisco
- Bomb thrown on his carriage at Chandni Chowk, Delhi on 23rd December 1912 when he was entering the capital.
- Hindu Mahasabha was founded in 1915 by Madan Mohan Malviya and some Punjabi leaders.
- Passing of the Defense of India Act, 1915.
- Death of Gopal Krishna Gokhale and Pheroz Shah Mehta, and return of Gandhi in 1915.

Lord Chelmsford (1916-21)

- Foundation of Home Rule Leagues by Tilak (April 1916) and Annie Besant (September 1916).
- Moderate-Extremist reunion at the Lucknow Session of Congress (1916), key role played by Annie Besant.
- Lucknow Pact (1916) signed between Congress and Muslim League, Tilak played an important role.
- Sabarmati Ashram was set up by Gandhi in 1916.
- Appointment of Sadler commission in 1917 to envisage a new educational policy.
- Champaran Satyagrah (1917), first time Gandhi experimented his new technique in India, followed by Satyagraha at Ahmedabad (1918) and Kheda Satyagraha (1918).
- August declaration (1917) by Montague, the Secretary of State whereby the control of Indian government will be gradually passed into the hands of Indians.
- A few veteran leaders led by S.N. Banerjee resigns from Congress and set up Indian Liberal Federation (1918).
- Government of India Act, 1919 passed.
- Rowlatt Act (March 1919) and Jallianwala Bagh Massacre (13th April 1919).
- Launching of Khilafat Movement (1919-20) and Non-Cooperation Movement (1920-22).

- Nagpur Session of the Congress (December 1920) leads to changes in constitution of the Congress.
- Foundation of a women's university at Poona (1916).
- Foundation of Banaras Hindu University in 1916, Aligarh Muslim University was also founded.
- Moplah uprising begins in Kerala in 1921.
- Sir S. P. Sinha becomes the first Indian to be appointed a Governor, and second Indian to become a member of British Parliament, the first being Dadabhai Naoroji.

Lord Reading (1921-25)

- Chauri Chaura incident (February 5, 1922) and the withdrawal of Non-cooperation movement by Gandhi.

Lord Reading

- Foundation of Swaraj Party by C.R. Das (Deshbandhu) and Motilal Nehru in December 1922.
- Repeal of Press Act of 1910 and Rowlatt Act of 1919.
- Prince of Wales visits India (November, 1921).
- Foundation of Communist Party of India in 1921-22 by M. N. Roy.
- Establishment of an Inter-University Board.
- Holding of simultaneous examination for the ICS in England and India with effect from 1923.
- Royal Commission on agriculture was established.
- Foundation of Rashtriya Swayamsevak Sangh (RSS) by Hedgewar at Nagpur in 1925.
- Kakori train dacoity (9th August 1925).
- Railway Budget separated from general budget in 1925.
- Skeen Committee on Army reforms appointed in 1925 which submitted its Report in 1926.
- Lee Commission on public services appointed in 1924, submitted report in 1924.

Lord Lytton-II (1925)

- Officiating Viceroy.

Lord Irwin (1926-31)

- Popularly known as the Christian Viceroy.

Lord Irwin

- Young Hilton Committee on currency (1926).

- Swami Shraddhanand, a great nationalist and an Arya Samajist, murdered in 1926 in a communal orgy.
- Appointment of Simon Commission (November 1927) and its visit to India in 1928 boycotted by the Congress.
- Appointment of the Indian States Commission under Harcosurt Butler (1927) to recommend measures for the establishment of better relations between the Indian states and central Government.
- The All India States People's Conference was convened in December 1927 by states people in response.
- Meeting of first All India Youth Congress in 1928.
- Convening of all parties' conference leads to the appointment of a committee under Motilal Nehru to prepare a constitution for India. The committee submits its report known as the Nehru Report in August 1928. It was rejected by Muslim League and Hindu Mahasabha.
- Dipawali Declaration (1929) says that India would be granted Dominion status in due course.
- Purna Swaraj Resolution is passed in the Lahore Session of Congress (Dec. 1929), and 26th January is fixed as the date for first Independence Day.
- Civil Disobedience Movement (CDM) builds up with the *Dandi March* beginning 12th March 1930.
- First Round Table Conference organized in 1930. Congress boycotted it.
- Gandhi-Irwin Pact signed on 5th March 1931 and CDM is withdrawn.
- Murder of superintendent of police, John Saunders.
- Bomb thrown in Central Legislative Assembly, Delhi.
- In 1929 Jatin Das dies after 64 days fast.
- Imperial Council of Agricultural Research was founded.
- Royal Commission on Indian Labour appointed in 1929 which submits its report in 1931.
- Simon Commission submits its report in May 1930.
- Sharda Act passed in 1929 prohibits marriages of girls below 14 years and boys below 18 years of age.
- Jawaharlal Nehru hoists tricolor of Indian Independence on 31st December 1930.

Lord Willingdon (1931-34)

- Gandhi participates in the Second Round Table Conference (September 1931), but the conference fails.

Lord Willingdon

- Gandhi is arrested after his return which results in the resumption of Civil Disobedience Movement in January 1932.
- Third Round Table Conference held in London (1932) without the representation of Congress.
- Announcement of Communal Award (1932) by the British Prime Minister

Ramsay MacDonald, Gandhi goes on fast unto death in the Yervada prison.

- Poona pact is signed between Gandhi and Ambedkar (September 1932).
- Government of India Act of 1935 passed.
- Foundation of Congress Socialist Party by Acharya Narendra Dev and Jai Prakash Narayan (1934).
- Foundation of All India Kisan Sabha (1936).
- Individual Civil Disobedience Movement launched in January 1933.
- Civil Disobedience Movement withdrawn in 1934 from Patna.
- Indian Military Academy was set up at Dehradun in 1932.
- White Paper on political reforms in India published in 1933.
- Burma and Aden separated from British Indian Empire in 1935.
- Orissa, Bihar and Sind were made new states (1935).
- Lee-Moody Pact (October 1933) by Bombay textile group.
- Muslim Conference founded in Kashmir in 1931, and renamed as National Conference in 1938. Important leaders were Sheikh Abdullah and P.N. Bajaj.

Sir George Stanley (1934)

- He served as Governor of Madras from 1929 to 1934 and as acting viceroy of India in 1934.

Governor-Generals and Crown Representatives of India (1936-47)

The Government of India Act, 1935

Lord Linlithgow (1936-43)

- The General Election conducted according to the provisions of the Government of India Act, 1935 results in the formation of Congress Ministries in 8 out of 11 provinces in 1937.

Lord Linlithgow

- *Baron Brabourne* acts as an officiating Crown Representative in 1938.
- Congress Ministries resign in 1939 on the issue of India being dragged into the World War-II and Muslim League observed this day as Deliverance Day (22 Dec. 1939).
- Subhash Chandra Bose resigns from both the presidentship and membership of the Congress in 1939, and forms forward Bloc.
- At the Haripura Session (February 1939) the Congress declares Purna Swaraj ideal to cover native states and British India.
- Muslim League passes the Pakistan Resolution at its Lahore Session (1940).
- Churchill becomes the British Prime minister in May, 1940. He declares that the Atlantic Charter does not apply to India.
- Augsust Offer is made by Linlithgow (1940) and it is rejected by the Congress.
- Gandhi calls for Individual Satyagraha.
- Cripps Mission comes to India in 1942 offering Dominion status and it is also rejected by the Congress.

- The Congress passes Quit India Resolution (8th Aug. 1942) leading to the Quit India Movement.

Lord Wavell (1943-47)

- C.R. Formula (1944) becomes the basis for Gandhi-Jinnah talks, but the talks fail.
- Wavell Plan and Shimla Conference (1945).
- The INA Trials (1945) and Naval Mutiny (1946).
- Cabinet Mission comprising three members—Lawrence, Cripps and Alexander suggests a plan in 1946 which is accepted by both parties, the Congress and Muslim League.
- Launch of the Direct Action Day by the Muslim League on 16th August 1946.
- General elections are organized in 1945-46 along with the elections to the constituent assembly and an Interim Government is formed on September 2, 1946.
- First meeting of the constituent assembly was held on 9th December 1946.

Lord Mountbatten (March-August, 1947)

- Last Viceroy of British India.
- British PM Atlee announces (February 20, 1947) independence of India by June 1948.
- On 3rd June 1947 plan to partition India is announced.
- The Indian Independence Bill is introduced and passed by the British parliament on 4th July 1947.
- On 7 June 1947, Jinnah left for Karachi.
- On August 15, 1947 India is declared independent but with the creation of two entities—India and Pakistan.

C. Rajagopalachari (1948-50)

- The last Governor-General of free India.
- The only Indian Governor-General, remained in office till January 1950.

Important Facts To Remember (Tabular Studies)

Governors of Bengal (1757-74)

- Robert Clive (1757-60 and 1765-67)
- Holwell (1760)
- Vansittart (1760-65)
- Verelst (1767-69)
- Cartier (1769-72)
- Warren Hastings (1772-74)

Governor-Generals of Bengal (1774-1833)

- Warren Hastings (1774-85)
- Sir Macpherson (1785-86)
- Lord Cornwallis (1786-93)
- Sir John Shore (1793-98)
- Sir A. Clarke (1798)
- Lord Rechard Wellesley (1798-1805)
- Lord Cornwallis (1805)
- Sir George Barlow (1805-07)
- Lord Minto-I (1807-13)
- Lord Hastings (1813-23)
- John Adams (1823)
- Lord Amherst (1823-28)
- William Butterworth Bayley (1828)
- Lord William Bentinck (1828-33)

Governor-Generals of India (1833-58)

(Charter Act of 1833)

- Lord William Bentinck (1833-35)
- Sir Charles Metcalfe (1835-36)
- Lord Auckland (1836-42)
- Lord Ellenborough (1842-44)
- Lord Hardinge-I (1844-48)
- Lord Dalhousie (1848-56)
- Lord Canning (1856-58)

Governor-Generals and Viceroys of India (1858-1936)

(Government of India Act, 1858)

- Lord Canning (1858-62)
- Lord Elgin-I (1862-63)
- Sir Robert Napier and Sir William T. Denison (1863)
- Sir John Lawrence (1864-68)
- Lord Mayo (1869-72)
- Sir John Strachey & Lord Napier Merchistoun (1872)
- Lord Northbrook (1872-76)
- Lord Lytton-I (1876-80)
- Lord Ripon (1880-84)
- Lord Dufferin (1884-88)
- Lord Lansdowne (1888-94)
- Lord Elgin-II (1894-98)
- Lord Curzon (1899-1905)
- Lord Ampthill (1904)
- Lord Minto-II (1905-10)
- Lord Hardinge-II (1910-16)
- Lord Chelmsford (1916-21)
- Lord Reading (1921-25)
- Lord Lytton-II (1925)
- Lord Irwin (1926-31)
- Lord Willingdon (1931-34)
- Sir George Stanley (1934)
- Lord Linlithgow (1934-36)

Governor-Generals and Crown Representatives (1936-47)

(Government of India Act, 1935)

- Lord Linlithgow (1936-43)
- Lord Baron Brabourne (1938)
- Lord Wavell (1943-47)
- Lord Mountbatten (March-August 1947)

Governor-Generals of Free India

- Lord Mountbatten (1947-48)
- C. Rajagopalachari (21st June 1948-25th January 1950)

Questions for Self Assessment

- Describe the expansion and consolidation of the British Empire under its various Governor Generals.
- Explain the system of Dual Administration introduced in Bengal. Throw light on its merits and demerits.
- What do you mean by Subsidiary Allince? How did it help to consolidate the British Empire in India?
- Discuss the steps taken by Lord Hastings to extend British power in India.
- What do you mean by the Doctrine of Lapse? Which states were made a part of the British Empire under this Doctrine?

Chapter at a Glance

- The system of portfolio was introduced for the first time by the Act of 1861.
- The Indian Councils Act of 1892 was passed at the instance of Lord Cross, the then secretary of state for India.
- The significant feature of the Indian Council Act of 1892 was the introduction of the Principle of election.
- The word Dyarchy is taken from the Greek words 'di' meaning two and 'archia' meaning rule.
- The royal commission, popularly known as Simon Commission was headed by Sir John Simon, a member of the British Liberal Party.
- **Lord Birken Head** was the secretary of state at the time of the arrival of simon Commission in India.
- Lala Lajpat Rai died by the injuries caused by lathi charge at Lahore while protesting against the Simon Commission.
- The Cripps Mission of 1942 was headed by Sir Stafford Cripps.
- Gandhiji described the Cripps proposals as a Post dated cheque on a failing bank.
- The Wavell plan was published on 4 June, 1945.
- The political conference on Wavell plan began on 29th June, 1945 in Simla. It is popularly known as Simla conference.
- The talks crashed because Mr. Jinnah did not agree to appoint any Muslim in the Executive council of muslims who did not belong to League.
- The Cabinet Mission consisted of three British Cabinet Ministers, (i) Lord Pethic Lawrence (ii) Sir Stafford Cripps and (iii) Mr Alexander.
- The Muslim league rejected the Cabinet Mission Plan and observed 16 August, 1946 as Direct Action Day.
- The constituent Assembly first met on 9 December, 19465.
- The first temporary president of the Constituent Assembly was Dr. Sachchidanand Sinha. On 11 December, 1946. Dr. Rajendra Prasad was elected as the permanent president.

Previous Year Question Paper (2000 to 2017)

1. Which one of the following is the correct chronological order of the battles fought in India in the 18th Century?
   (a) Battle of Wandiwash-Battle of Buxar-Battle of Ambur-Battle of Plassey
   (b) Battle of Ambur-Battle of Plassey-Battle of Wandiwash-Battle of Buxar
   (c) Battle of Wandiwash-Battle of Plassey-Battle of Ambur-Battle of Buxar
   (d) Battle of Ambur-Battle of Buxar-Battle of Wandiwash-Battle of Plassey **(2005)**
2. Which of the following pairs are corectly matched?

List-I (Period)	(List-II (War)
1. AD 1767-69	First Anglo-Maratha War
2. AD 1790-92	Third Mysore War
3. AD 1824-26	First Anglo-Burmese War
4. AD 1845-46	Second Sikh War

Select the correct answer using the codes given below:

Codes:

(a) 2 and 4 (b) 3 and 4
(c) 1 and 2 (d) 2 and 3 **(2004)**

3. At a time when empires in Europe were crumbling before the might of Napoleon, which one of the following Governor-General kept the British flag flying high in India?
(a) Warren Hastings
(b) Lord Cornwallis
(c) Lord Wellesely
(d) Lord Hastings **(1999)**

4. By a regulation in 1793, the District Collector was deprived of his judicial powers and made the collecting agent only. What was the reason for such regulation?
(a) Lord Cornwallis felt that the District Collector's efficiency of revenue collection would enormously increase without the burden of other work.
(b) Lord Cornwallis felt that judicial power should compulsorily be in the hands of Europeans while Indians can be given the job of revenue collection in the districts.
(c) Lord Cornwallis was alarmed at the extent of power concentrated in the District Collector and felt that such absolute power was undesirable in one person.
(d) The judicial work demanded a deep knolwedge of India and a good training in law and Lord Cornwallis felt that District Collector should be only a revenue collector. **(2010)**

5. Who was the Viceroy of India when the Rowlatt Act was passed ?
(a) Lord Irwin
(b) Lord Reading
(c) Lord Chelmsford
(d) Lord Wavell **(2015)**

6. Consider the following statements:
1. Robert Clive was the first Governor-General of Bengal.
2. William Bentinck was the first Governor-General of India.

Which of the statements given above is/are correct? **(2007)**
(a) 1 only (b) 2 only
(c) Both 1 and 2 (d) Neither 1 nor 2

7. The First Factory Act restricting the working hours of women and children and authorizing local government to make necessary rules was adopted during whose time?
(a) Lord Lytton (b) Lord Bentinck
(c) Lord Ripon (d) Lord Canning **(2007)**

8. Consider the following statements:
1. The Charter Act 1853 anolished East India Company's monopoly of Indian trade.
2. Under the Government of India Act 1858, the British Parliament abolished the East India Company altogether and undertook the responsibility of ruling India directly. **(2006)**

Which of the statements given above is/are correct?
(a) 1 only (b) 2 only
(c) Both 1 and 2 (d) Neither 1 nor 2

9. Consider the following statements.
The Government of India Act, 1935 provided for
1. the provincial autonomy
2. the establishment of Federal Court
3. All India Federation at the centre

Which of the statements given above are correct? **(2015)**

(a) 1 and 2 (b) 2 and 3
(c) 1 an 3 (d) 1, 2 and 3

10. Consider the following statements:
1. Warren Hastings was the first Governor General who established a regular police force in India on the British pattern.
2. A Supreme Court was established at Calcutta by the Regulating Act, 1773.
3. The Indian Penal Code came into effect in the year 1860. **(2015)**

Which of the statements given above are correct?
(a) 1 and 2 (b) 2 and 3
(c) 1 and 3 (d) 1, 2 and 3

11. Who among the following repealed the Vernacular Press Act?
(a) Lord Dufferin (b) Lord Ripon
(c) Lord Curzon (d) Lord Hardinge **(2005)**

12. The Montagu-Chelmsford Report formed the basis of:
(a) The Indian Councils Act, 1909
(b) The Government of India Act, 1919
(c) The Government of India Act, 1935
(d) The Indian Independence Act, 1947 **(2004)**

13. Consider the following statements:
Some of the main features of the Government of India Act, 1935 were the:
1. Abolition of diarchy in the Governor's provinces
2. Power of the Governors to veto legislative action and to legislate on their own
3. Abolition of the principle of communal representation.

Which of the statements given above is/are correct? **(2004)**
(a) 1 only (b) 1 and 2
(c) 2 and 3 (d) 1, 2 and 3

14. Which one of the following pairs is not correctly matched?
(a) Pitt's India Act Warren Hastings
(b) Doctrine of Lapse Dalhousie
(c) Vernacular Press Act Curzon
(d) Illbert Bill Ripon **(2004)**

15. Consider the following Viceroys of India during the British rule:
1. Lord Curzon
2. Lord Chelmsford
3. Lord Hardinge
4. Lord Irwin

Which one of the following is the correct chronological order of their tenure ?
(a) 1-3-2-4 (b) 2-4-1-3
(c) 1-4-2-3 (d) 2-3-1-4 **(2004)**

16. During the colonial period in India, what was the purpose of the Whitlay Committe?
(a) To review the fitness of India for further political reforms.
(b) To report on existing conditions of labour and to make recommendations.
(c) To draw up a plan for financial reforms for India.
(d) To develop a comprehensive scheme for Civil Services in India. **(2003)**

17. The aim of education as stated by the Wood's Dispatch of 1854 was:
(a) The creation of employment opportunities for native Indians.
(b) the spread of Western culture in India.
(c) The promotion of literacy among the people using English medium of language.
(d) The introduction of scientific research and rationalism in the traditional Indian education. **(2003)**

18. Which one of the following provisions was **NOT** made in the Charter Act of 1833?
    (a) The trading activities of the East India Company were to be abolished.
    (b) The designation of the supreme authority was to be changed as the Governor-General of India-in-Council.
    (c) All law-making powers to be conferred on Governor-General-in-Council.
    (d) An Indian was to be appointed as a Law Member in the Governor-General's Council. **(2003)**
19. With reference to colonial rule in India what was sought by the Illbert Bill in 1883?
    (a) To bring Indians and Europeans on par as far as the criminal jurisdiction of courts was concerned.
    (b) To impose severe restrictions on the freedom of the native press as it was perceived to be hostile to colonial rulers.
    (c) To encourage the native Indians to appear for civil service examinations by conducting them in India.
    (d) To allow native Indians to possess arms by attending the Arms Act. **(2003)**
20. The real intention of the British to include the princely states in the Federal Union proposed by the India Act of 1935 was to:
    (a) Exercise more and direct political and administrative control over the princely states.
    (b) Involve the princes actively in the administration of the colony.
    (c) Finally effect the complete political and administrative take-over of all the princely states by the British.
    (d) Use the princes to counter-balance the anti-imperialist doctrines of the nationalist leaders. **(2002)**
21. Which one of the following Acts of British India strengthened the Viceroy's authority over his executive council by substituting "portfolio" or departmental system for corporate functioning?
    (a) Indian Council Act, 1861
    (b) Government of India Act, 1858
    (c) Indian Council Act, 1909
    (d) Government of India Act, 1919 **(2002)**
22. With reference to colonial period of Indian history, Match List-I with List-II and select the correct answer:

List-I (Person)	List-II (Event)
A. Macdonald	1. Doctrine of Lapse
B. Linlithgo	2. Communal Award
C. Dalhousie	3. August Offer
D. Chelmsford	4. Dyarchy

Codes:

	A	B	C	D
(a)	3	2	1	4
(b)	3	2	4	1
(c)	2	3	1	4
(d)	2	3	4	1

(2002)

23. Under the Permanent Settlement of 1793, the Zamindars were required to issue *pattas* to the farmers which were not issued by many of the Zamindars. The reason was:
    (a) The Zamindars were trusted by the farmers.
    (b) There was no official check upon the Zamindars.
    (c) It was the responsibility of the British government.

(d) The farmers were not interested in getting *patts*. **(2001)**

24. The last major extension of British Indian territory took place during the time of:
(a) Dufferin (b) Dalhousie
(c) Lytton (d) Curzon **(2015)**

25. Match List-I with List-II and select the correct anwer using the codes given below the lists: **(2015)**

List-I
A. Land allotted to big feudal landlords.
B. Land allotted to revenue farmers or rent collectors.
C. Land allotted to each peasant with the right to sublet, mortgage, transfer, gift or sell.
D. Revenue settlements made at village level.

List-II
1. Jagirdari System
2. Ryotwari System
3. Mahalwari System
4. Zamindari System

Codes:

	A	B	C	D
(a)	1	3	2	4
(b)	1	4	2	3
(c)	3	4	1	2
(d)	2	1	3	4

26. The term 'Imperial Preference' was applied to the
(a) Special privileges on British imports in India.
(b) Racial discrimination by the Britishers.
(c) Subordination of Indian interests to that of the British.
(d) Preference given to British political agents over Indian Princes. **(2015)**

27. The most short-lived of all the Britain's constitutional experiments in India was the:
(a) Indian Council Act of 1861
(b) Indian Council Act of 1892
(c) Indian Council Act of 1909
(d) Government of India Act of 1919 **(2015)**

28. The Governor-General who followed a spirited forward policy towards Afghanistan was:
(a) Minto (b) Dufferin
(c) Elgin (d) Lytton **(1999)**

29. Match List-I with List-II and select the correct answer by using the codes given below the lists: **(2015)**

List-I (Year)	List-II (Event)
A. 1775	1. First Anglo-Burmese War
B. 1780	2. First Anglo-Afghan War
C. 1824	3. First Anglo-Maratha War
D. 1838	4. Second Anglo-Mysore War

Codes:

	A	B	C	D
(a)	4	3	2	1
(b)	4	3	2	1
(c)	3	4	1	2
(d)	3	4	2	1

Answers

1. (b)	2. (d)	3. (c)
4. (c)	5. (c)	6. (b)
7. (c)	8. (b)	9. (d)
10. (b)	11. (b)	12. (b)
13. (a)	14. (c)	15. (a)
16. (b)	17. (c)	18. (d)

19. (a)	20. (d)	21. (a)	25. (b)	26. (a)	27. (c)
22. (c)	23. (b)	24. (a)	28. (d)	29. (c)	

Practice Paper

1. Match the following:

List-I (Governors of Bengal)	List-II (Associated Events)
A. Robert Civie	1. Abolished dual Government of Bengal (1772)
B. Vansittart	2. Bengal Famine (1770)
C. Cartier	3. Battle of Buxar (1764)
D. Warren Hastings	4. Established dual Government in Bengal from (1765-72)

Code:

	A	B	C	D		A	B	C	D
(a)	4	2	3	1	(b)	4	3	2	1
(c)	1	3	2	4	(d)	1	2	3	4

2. Who among the following was the first Governor-General of Bengal?
   (a) Robert Clive
   (b) William Bentinck
   (c) Marquess Wellesley
   (d) Warren Hastings
3. Which of the following statement(s) about Warren Hastings is/are correct?
   1. He was the last Governor of Bengal.
   2. He wrote introduction to the first English translation of 'Gita' by Charles Wilkins.
   3. He started Diwani and Faujdari Adalats at the district level and Sadar Diwani and Nizamat Adalats (appellate courts) at Calcutta.

   Select the correct answer using the codes given below:
   (a) Only 1 (b) 2 and 3
   (c) 1 and 3 (d) All of these
4. Consider the following statements and mark the correct option.
   1. Lord Irwin was popularly known as Christian Viceroy.
   2. A separate State of Bihar and Orissa was created during the Governorship of Lord Hardinge.
   3. During Lord Wellington's Tenure Communal award was propagated in August 1932.

   (a) 1 and 3 (b) Only 1
   (c) 1 and 2 (d) All of these
5. Which one of the following pair is correctly matched?
   (a) Warren Hastings : The Battle of Plassey
   (b) Lord Cornwallis : The Permanent Settlement of Bengal
   (c) Lord Wellesley : The Prohibition of Sati
   (d) Lord Dalhousie : Local Self-Government
6. Which of the following statements about Lord Dhalhousie is correct?
   (a) He abolished titles and pensions and passed widow re-marriage Act.

(b) He recommended the Thomsonian System of Vernacular education for whole of the North Western Provinces.
(c) An engineering college was established at Roorkee during his tenure.
(d) All of the above.

7. Who among the following Governor-General created the Civil Service of India which later came to be known as Indian Civil Service?
(a) Warren Hastings
(b) Wellesley
(c) Cornwallis
(d) Willam Bentinck

8. Consider the following statements:
1. Warren Hastings was the first Governor General who established a regular Police force in India on the British pattern.
2. A Supreme court was established at Calçutta by the Regulating Act, 1773.
3. The Indian Penal Code came into effect in the year 1860.

Which of the statements given above are correct?
(a) 1 and 2 (b) 2 and 3
(c) 1 and 3 (d) All of these

9. At a time when empires in Europe were crumbling before the might of Napoleon, which one of the following Government-Generals kept the British flag flying high in India?
(a) Warren Hastings
(b) Lord Cornwallis
(c) Lord Wellesley
(d) Lord Hastings

10. Who among the following Governor-Generals formed the Triple Alliance against Tipu Sultan?
(a) Warren Hastings
(b) Lord Cornwallis
(c) Lord Wellesley
(d) Lord William Bentinck

11. Match the following Lord William Bentinck

List -I	List - II
(Governor-General)	(Important Policy)
A. Lord Cornwallis	1- Partition of Bengal
B. Lord Wellesley	2- Doctrine of Lapse
C. Lord Dalhousie	3- Permanent Settlement
D. Lord Curzon	4- Subsidiary Alliance

12. Consider the following statements about main features of the Government of India Act, 1935.
1. Abolition of dyarchy in the Governor's provinces.
2. Prower of governors to veto legislative action and to legislate on their own.
3. Aboliton of the principle of communal representation.

Which of the statement (s) given above is/are correct?
(a) Only 1 (b) Both 1 and 2
(c) Both 2 and 3 (d) All of these

13. Which one of the following is not correct about the subsidiary Alliance?
(a) It was formulated by Wellesley.
(b) British army was posted in the subsidary state.
(c) It did not recognise an adopted heir to a subsidiary state.
(d) A British resident was posted in the subsidiary state.

14. Match the following:

List-I	List-II
A. Lord Clive	1. Subsidiary Alliance
B. Lord Wellesley	2. Indian Universities Act
C. Lord Dalhousie	3. Doctrine of Lapse
D. Lord Curzon	4. Dual Government in Bengal

Code:

	A	B	C	D		A	B	C	D
(a)	2	3	4	2	(b)	4	1	3	2
(c)	4	3	2	1	(d)	1	4	2	3

15. Which one of the following pairs is **NOT** correctly matched?
   (a) Lord Wellesley – Subsidiary Alliance
   (b) Lord Dalhousie – Doctrine of Lapse
   (c) Lord Ripon – Vernacular Press Act
   (d) Lord Curzon – Partition of Bengal

16. Which one of the following is NOT correctly matched ?
   (a) Lord Cornwallis – Permanent Settlement
   (b) Lord Wellesley – Subsidiary Alliance System
   (c) Lord Hastings – Second Anglo-Maratha war
   (d) Lord William Bentick – Regulation XVII of 1829

17. Match the following and select the correct answer from the codes given below:

Event	Person
A. Doctrine of Lapse	1. Curzon
B. Partition of Bengal	2. Clive
C. Dual Government in Bengal	3. Dalhousie
D. Social Reforms	4. Bentick

Code:

	A	B	C	D		A	B	C	D
(a)	2	3	1	4	(b)	3	1	4	2
(c)	3	1	2	4	(d)	2	3	4	1

18. Which of the following is wrongly matched?
   (a) The Pitts India Act (1784)–Board of Control to guide and control Company's affairs.
   (b) Charter Actof1817–Company'smonopoly of trade with India ended.
   (c) Charter Act of 1833– Company's debt taken over by the Government of India.
   (d) Charter Act of 1853– To regulate Company's affairs.

19. Which of the following Commissions dealt with the Civil Services?
   (a) Charles Altchison Commission 1886
   (b) Lord Lee Commission, 1923
   (c) Both (a) the (b)
   (d) Neither (a) nor (b)

20. Match the following:

A. Permanent Settlement	1. Parts of Madras and Bombay Presidencies
B. Ryotwati Settlement	2. Gengetic Valley, North West Provinces Punjab
C. Mahalwari Settlement	3. Bengal and Bihar

Code:

	A	B	C		A	B	C
(a)	3	1	2	(b)	1	2	3
(c)	3	2	1	(d)	2	1	3

21. With whom was the Permanent Settlement made?
    (a) With the peasant and cultivators.
    (b) With the muqaddams
    (c) With the zamindars
    (d) With the village communities.
22. What made the British invest their capital in India?
    (a) The British rule was characterised by benevolent despotism. Hence, they believed in the welfare of the people.
    (b) The British wanted India to become an industrial country.
    (c) British capitalism was confronted with the problem of surplus capital
    (d) The British wanted to improve trade with India
23. Which was **NOT** a feature of the new land system under the British?
    (a) Individual land-holder was directly linked with the centralised state.
    (b) The village panchayats retained the power to settle all land disputes.
    (c) The bonds which originally tied the village peasants to the village collectively broke down
    (d) The peasant paid land-rent
24. Which was **NOT** a ruinous feature of Indian agriculture under the British?
    (a) Extreme sub-division of land and its fragmentation.
    (b) Land holdings became more and more un-economic.
    (c) Commercialisation of agriculture.
    (d) Increase in the number and power of zamindars.

Answers

1. (b)	2. (d)	3. (d)	13. (b)	14. (b)	15. (c)
4. (d)	5. (b)	6 (d)	16. (c)	17. (c)	18. (d)
7. (c)	8. (d)	9. (d)	19. (c)	20. (a)	21. (c)
10. (b)	11. (c)	12. (b)	22. (c)	23. (b)	24. (c)

7

The Revolt of 1857

The Great Revolution of 1857

- The Revolt of 1857 was a product of the character and policies of British colonial rule. The causes of revolt emerged from all aspects—socio-cultural, economic and political. Moreover, it was not an isolated rebellion rather a chain of rebellions had already taken place in different areas of their territory, prior to 1857.

Early Precedents

- In 1806, the sepoys at Vellore mutinied, but were crushed with terrible violence.
- In 1824, the 47th Regiment of Sepoys at Barrackpore refused to go to Burma by the sea-route.
- In 1844, seven battalions revolted on the question of *bhatta* and salaries.
- There were mutinies in 1825 (Assam), 1833 (Sholapur), 1844 (Sind) and 1849-59 (Punjab) as well.

The Causes of Revolt

Immediate Cause

- The issue of greased cartridges and military grievances has been over emphasised, as the factor for the Revolt of 1857. The grease was in some instances composed of beef and pig fat. The sepoys, Hindu as well as Muslim, were enraged. The use of the greased cartridges would endanger their religion. However, the recent research has proved that the cartridge was neither the only cause nor even the most important. In fact, the multiple causes i.e. social, religious, political and economic worked together to produce the rebellion.

Social and Religious Causes

- The British had abandoned its policy of non-interference in the socio-religious life of the Indians. Abolition of Sati (1829), Hindu Widow Remarriage Act (1856) were such as direct interference of colonial power into Hindu religious beliefs.
- Christian missionaries were allowed to enter India and carry on with their mission of proselytizing by an act in 1837.

- The Religious Disabilities Act of 1856 modified the traditional Hindu Law. According to it, the change in religion would not debar a son from inheriting the property of his father.

Economic Causes

- British rule led to breakdown of the village self-sufficiency, commercialisation of agriculture, which burdened the peasantry, adoption of free trade imperialism from 1800, de-industrialisation and drain of wealth all of which led to overall decline of economy.

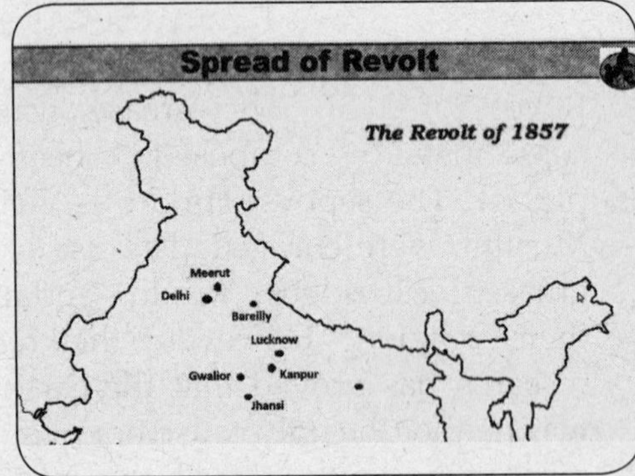

Military Grievances

- The extension of British dominion in India had adversely affected the service conditions of the sepoys. They were required to serve in areas away from their homes without the payment of extra *bhatta*.
- An important cause of military discontent was the General Service Enlistment Act, 1856, which made it compulsory for the sepoys to cross the seas, whenever required. The Post Office Act of 1854, withdrew the free postage facility for them.

Political Causes

- The last major extension of the British Indian territory took place during the time of Dalhousie. Dalhousie announced in 1849, that the successor of Bahadur Shah II would have to leave the Red Fort.

- The annexation of Baghat and Udaipur were however, cancelled and they were restored to their ruling houses.
- When Dalhousie wanted to apply the Doctrine of Lapse to Karauli (Rajputana), it was overruled by the Court of Directors.
- The revolt was basically anti-imperialist and both the sepoys and the civilians wanted to throw out the British imperialists.
- In 1856 the government decided to replace the old fashioned musket 'Brown Bess' by the 'Enfield rifle'. The training for the new weapon was to be imparted at Dum Dum, Ambala and Sialkot.
- On March 29, 1857 the sepoys at Barrackpore refused to use the greased cartridges and, Mangal Pandey, a Brahmin sepoy attacked the Sergeant Major.

- On 10th May, 1857, the sepoys of the 3rd cavalry at Meerut also refused to use the greased cartridges and broke out in open rebellion. They were immediately joined by the 11th and 20th Native infantries.
- On May 12, 1857, Delhi was seized and Bahadur Shah-II of the Mughal dynasty was proclaimed the emperor of India. The real command was in the hands of Bakht Khan who had led the revolt at Bareilly and brought the troops to Delhi.
- In Kanpur the revolt was led by Nana Saheb, who proclaimed himself the Peshwa. He was assisted by Tantia Tope. The rebels defeated General Windham outside Kanpur. Azimullah Khan also led to Kanpur.
- In Lucknow, Begum Hazrat Mahal and Ahmadullah led the revolt. Hazrat Mahal proclaimed Birjis Qadir as the nawab of Awadh against the wishes of the British. Henry Lawrence, the British resident was killed.
- In Jhansi, Rani Laxmibai assumed the leadership of the mutiny.
- In Bareilly, Khan Bahadur proclaimed himself as the Nawab and revolted there.
- In Arrah, Kunwar Singh led the revolt.

Doctrine of Lapse

- According to the policy of Doctrine of Lapse, introduced by Lord Dalhousie, the adopted sons of the deceased kings were de-recognised as heirs to the throne, which subsequently led to the annexation of large number of kingdoms.

Chronology of Dalhousie's Annexation through Doctrine of Lapse

State	Year of Annexation
Satara	1848
Jaitpur (Uttar Pradesh)	1849
Sambhalpur (Orissa)	1850
Baghat	1850
Udaipur	1852
Jhansi	1853
Nagpur	1854

- Dalhousie annexed Awadh in 1856, on the ground of misrule. The annexation of Awadh was also represented by Bengal Army, three-fifth of whom belonged to Awadh. Sir James Outram, who had been the British resident in Awadh since 1854, was appointed as the first Chief Commissioner in 1856, but he was replaced by Sir Henry Lawrence. He was the Chief Commissioner when revolt broke out.
- Dalhousie abolished the titles of the Nawab of Carnatic and the Raja of Travancore and refused to grant the pension to the adopted son (Dhondu Pant, better known as Nana Sahib) of the last Peshwa, (Baji Rao II) after the latter's death in 1851.
- Canning announced in 1856, that the successors of Bahadur Shah were to be known only as princes and not as kings.

Agrarian Causes

- The Summary Settlement of 1856, which was first introudced in the North-Western provinces, was extended to Awadh.

- Heavy over-assessment of land revenue impoverished the peasants.
- The introduction of the institution of private property rights in land by which land became a commodity, which could be bought, sold, rented or leased.

The Course of Revolt

March 1857

- The revolt was sparked on 29th March, 1857. The 19th infantry at Berhampur (Barrackpore), refused to use the newly introudced enfield rifle. The infantry was disbanded. Colonel Mitchell was its Commanding Officer.
- Mangal Pandey, a sepoy of the 34th Native Infantry at Barrackpore attacked and fired at his British officers. The mutiny was suppressed and the leader of the mutiny, Mangal Pandey, was finally trialled and executed.

April-May 1857

- 90 men of the 3rd Native Cavalry stationed at Meerut refused to use the greased cartridge. 85 of them were dismissed and sentenced to 10 years imprisonment on 9th May.
- The next day, on 10th May, the entire Indian garrison revolted. On 11th May, 1857, a band of sepoys from Meerut, who had defied and killed the European officers the previous day, marched to the Red Fort (Delhi).
- Bhadur Shah II was proclaimed the Shahenshah-e-Hindustan. The Sepoy then set out to capture and control the imperial city of Delhi.
- In Faizabad, Maulavi Ahmadullah led the revolt.
- In Delhi the revolt was suppressed by Colonel Nicholson and Hudson.
- In Kanpur and Lucknow the revolt was suppressed by Campbell.
- In Jhansi the revolt was suppressed by Hugh Rose.
- In Allahabad and Banaras the revolt was suppressed by Colonel Neil.
- In Arrah thse revolt was suppressed by William Taylor and Vincent Eyre.
- Bahadur Shah 'Zafar' was arrested and departed to Rangoon where he died in 1862.
- Nana Sahib and Begum Hazrat Mahal escaped to Nepal.
- The revolt was poorly organized and restricted in its scope, and there was no unity among its leaders.
- There was no impact of rebellion beyond Narmada. Even in north India Rajasthan, Punjab and Sind remained quiet.
- The Indian princes such as Schindia of Gwalior, Nizam of Hyderabad, Gulab Singh of Kashmir, and princes of Rajasthan remained loyal to the British.
- The Indian intelligentsia or modern educated class kept away from the revolt.
- The control of the Indian administration was transferred from the East India Company to the Crown by the Government of India Act, 1858.
- The Indian Civil Services Act was passed which provided for an annual competitive examination to be held in London for recruitment to the most coveted civil services in 1861.
- The Army Amalgamation Scheme of 1861 transferred the company's

European troops to the service of crown. The general formula used to reorganize the army was that in Bengal presidency, the proportion between the European and Indian troops should be 1:2 while for Bombay and Madras presidency it should be 1:3.

Areas Affected by the Revolt

- Very soon, the rebellion spread throughout Northern and Central India at Lucknow, Allahabad, Kanpur, Bareilly, Banaras, in some parts of Bihar, Jhansi and other places. However, the Southern India remained quiet. Mutinies took place at a few places in Punjab (Naushera and Hoti Mardan), but Sir John Lawrence (Chief Commissioner of Punjab) easily put them down.

Reasons for Failure of Revolt

- The poor organisation and lack of coordination among the rebels were perhaps the most important causes of its failure. English had better resources, modern weapons and matterials of war.
- Telegraph services kept Supreme Commanders informed about the movement of rebels.
- Lack of unity among Indians, many ruling chiefs and big zamindars, actively helped British to suppress the revolt.
- The modern educated Indians also did not support the revolt.
- Neither the leaders nor sepoys were inspired by any high ideals of patriotism and nationalism.

Participation of Peasants, Zamindars and Weavers in the Revolt of 1857

- Excessive demands of revenue was the major cause of hardships of Indias in general peasants, and zamindars in particular. Peasant participation in the rebellion was provoked first by over-taxation and secondly, by the fact that the sepoys themselves came from the villages.
- Apart from this, the Free Trade Imperialist Policy meant that Indians, particularly spinners and weavers, were thrown out of employment as more than a quarter of the total textile consumption of India was now met by imports from Britain.
- It is not surprising that urban weavers were especially enthusiastic in their support of the revolt, many even joining as armed volunteers.

Chapter at a Glance

- In the Faqir uprising, the leader Chirage Ali was supported by two leaders namely Bhawani Pathak and Devi Chaudhrani.
- The pagal panthis preaced the doctrine of equality, fraternity and truthfulness.
- The real founder of Wahabi movement was Abdul Wahab of Nazd (1703 to 1787).
- Saiyed Ahmad Rae Bareilvi was killed in the battle of Balakot.
- Bhagat Jawahar Mal, the founder of Kuka movement was popularly known as Sian Saheb.
- Ram Singh the other important Leader of the Kuka revolt was deported to Rangoon in 1872.
- Farazi or Faraidi movement was founded by Haji Shariat Ullah of East Bengal.
- Saiyad Ahmed appointed 4 Khalifas namely Maulvi Qasim, Inayet Ali,

Vilayat Ali and Ahmadulla to propogate Wahabi movement.

- 'Diku' were outsiders who settled down in tribal areas.
- *Mariah* was a practice of human sacrifice followed by the Khonds tribe of Orissa.
- Santhals defeated a British army led by Major Burrough.
- Kukis had the peculiar custom of burying their deceased rulers alongwith human heads.
- Singphos killed the British Political agent Colonel White.
- The leaders of the Vishakhapatnam revolt were Birbhadra Rauze and Jagannath Rauze.
- A tribal revolt in Burma brokeout in 1853 which was led by Gaung Gyi.
- In 1842 Bijai Singh, the talukdar of Kunja, near Roorki, revolted. It was suppressed by the British ruthlessly.
- The Sepoy mutiny at Govindgarh was suppressed by Charles Napier.
- Raja of Dhalbhum, Jagannath Dhal revolted in 1867. The revolt was crushed by captain Morgan.
- The cultivators of Savda and Chopada (Khandesh) revolted in 1852.
- The Central Headquarter of the Wahabi movement was Patna.
- The Wahabi movement is also known as Waliullahi movement.
- Stoppage of allowances for active service in a foreign country was the cause of mutiny of the Bengal army in 1844.
- In Saurashtra the revolt of the Wagheras took place against the imposition of British rule.
- Kerala Verma, Raja of Wynoad, raised the banner of revolt against the British.
- The failure of the British Government to withdraw and restore Ahom government after the Burmese war caused the revolt of Assam in 1820's.
- Sikandar Shah, the Nizam of Hyderabad revolted against the imposition of subsidiary alliance on Hyderabad.
- The revolt was sparked off on March 29, 1857.
- Mangal Pandey, a Brahmin Sepoy fired at the Adjutant Surgeant Bath.
- The 3rd cavalry regiment at Meerut refused to use the greased cartridges.
- Dhondu pant, who led the revolt at Kanpur is popularly known as Nand Saheb.
- Rani Laxmi Bai was the widowed queen of Raja Gangadhar Rao.
- Begum Hazrat Mahal at Lucknow declared her II years old son Birjis Qadar as Nawab.
- At the time of great uprising, Lord Canning was the Governor General of India.
- Colonel Ripley was killed at Delhi by his own troops.
- The English bribed Mirza Ilahi Baksh, a close relative of the last Mughal Emperor to get the military secrets.
- Bahadur Shah Jafar was deported to Rangoon.
- Tantiya Tope was betrayed by one of his friends Man Singh.
- In Masulipatnam a green flag and a proclamation, urging the slaughter of the English were seized on 10th July 1858.

- Chiman Sahib, the younger brother of Raja of Kolhapur organised a troop against the English.
- Prominent persons hanged were Tantiya Tope, Abdur Rahim Khan Rohilla, Alauddin Maulvi Syed, Arjun Krishan Patel, Awachit etc.
- Zinat Mahal was the chief queen of Mughal Emperor Bahadur Shah II.
- Bakht Khan was the Commander-in-Chief of the Mughal Emperor.
- At the call of Ali Nazi Khan, the Hindu and Muslim sepoys swore by the Ganges and the Quran that they would lay down their lives to drive the English out of the land.
- The focal points of the revolt included Delhi, Kanpur, Lucknow, Bareilly, Benaras, Jhansi and Arrah.
- 'March to Delhi' was the battle cry for the rebels.
- 'Educated middle class' did not support the revolt of 1857.
- Prince Firoz Shah belonged to the Mughal family who raised the banner of revolt at Mandasour.
- Kunwar Singh of Arrah is regarded as the 'Lion of Bihar'.
- Amar Singh, the brother of Kunwar Singh continued the struggle after his death.
- Sir Hugh Rose described Rani Laxmi Bai as "The best and bravest military leader of the rebels".
- Begum Hazrat Mahal refused to accept the pension offered to her by British and preferred to die unmourn in Nepal.
- Mughal emperor Bahadur Shah II wrote poetries under the Pen name 'Zafar'.

Previous Year Question Paper (1998-2017)

1. Who was the Governor-General of India during the Sepoy Mutiny?
   (a) Lord Canning
   (b) Lord Dalhousie
   (b) Lord Hardinge
   (d) Lord Lytton **(2015)**
2. Which one of the following revolts was made famous by Bankim Chandra Chatterjee in his novel Anand Math?
   (a) Bhil uprising
   (b) Rangpur and Dinapur uprising
   (c) Bishnupur and Birbhum rebellion
   (d) Sanyasi rebellion **(2006)**
3. With reference to the revolt of the year 1857, who of the following was betrayed by a friend; captured and put to death by the British?
   (a) Nana Sahib
   (b) Kunwar Singh
   (c) Khan Bahadur Khan
   (d) Tantia Tope **(2006)**
4. Which one of the following territories was not affected by the Revolt of 1857?
   (a) Jhansi (b) Chittor
   (c) Jagdishpur (d) Lucknow
   (2005)
5. Which one of the following places did Kunwar Singh, a prominent leader of the Revolt of 1857 belong to?
   (a) Bihar
   (b) Madhya Pradesh
   (c) Rajasthan
   (d) Uttar Pradesh **(2015)**
6. Consider the following Princely States of the British rule in India:
   1. Jhansi
   2. Sambalpur
   3. Satara **(2004)**

The correct chronological order in which they were annexed by the British is:
(a) 1-2-3 (b) 1-3-2
(c) 3-2-1 (d) 3-1-2

7. Which one of the following mountain tribes did the British first come into contact with after the grant of Diwani in the year 1765?
(a) Garos (b) Khasis
(c) Kukis (d) Tipperahs
(2002)

8. "In this instance we could not play off the Mohammmedons against the Hindus". To which one of the following events did this remark of Aithison relate?
(a) Revolt of 1857
(b) Champaran Satyagraha (1917)
(c) Khilafat and Non-Cooperation Movement (1919-22)
(d) August Movement of 1942 **(2015)**

9. Consider the following events:
1. Indigo Revolt
2. Santhal Rebellion
3. Deccan Riot
4. Mutiny of the sepoys
The correct chronological sequence of these events is
(a) 4, 2, 1, 3 (b) 4, 2, 3, 1
(c) 2, 4, 3, 1 (d) 2, 4, 1, 3 **(1999)**

10. Match List-I with List-II and select the correct answer by using the codes given below the lists: **(1999)**

List-I (Books)	List-II (Authors)
A. The first Indian War of Independence	1. Rabindranath Tagore
B. Ananda Math	2. Sri Aurobindo
C. Life Divine	3. Bankim Chandra Chatterji
D. Sadhana	4. Vinayak Damodar Savarkar

Codes:

	A	B	C	D
(a)	4	3	2	1
(b)	3	1	2	
(c)	4	3	1	2
(d)	3	4	2	1

11. The educated middle class in India
(a) Opposed the revolt of 1857
(b) Supported the revolt of 1857
(c) Remained neutral to the revolt of 1857
(d) Fought against native rulers **(2015)**

12. As regards, the grievances of the sepoys relating to the conditions of service, which of the following was the most serious?
(a) Question of promotion and pay
(b) Non-observance of caste distinctions
(c) Frequent campaigns in distant lands
(d) Absence of proper and equitable procedure for discipline and control

13. Which of the following classes did not support the rebellion?
(a) The princes
(b) The peasants and artisans
(c) The landed aristocracy and the zamindars
(d) The new middle class

14. Where did the first signs of unrest appear early in 1857?
(a) Awadh
(b) Bengal
(c) Meerut
(d) Upper provinces

15. Who had first opined Revolt of 1857 as the first "Indian War of Independence"?
(a) Karl Marx (b) VD Savarkar
(c) Disraeli (d) Bahadur Shah II

16. Who incited the sepoys in Jhansi, the hurl defiance at their officers and to commit violence and murder?
    (a) Rani Laxmibai (b) Tantia Tope
    (c) Lachman Rao (d) Damodar Rao
17. The leader of the Revolt of 1857 in Assam was
    (a) Diwan Maniram Dutta
    (b) Kandarpesvar Singh
    (c) Purandar Singh
    (d) Piafi Barua
18. What was the approach adopted towards the Indian princes in the Proclamation of queen Victoria?
    (a) It affirmed the treaties made between the British and Indian princes.
    (b) It established feudatroy like relationship between the government and the Indian prince
    (c) Both 'a' and 'b'
    (d) It affirmed the continuation of the Policy of Annexation of Princely States
19. During the Revolt of 1857, the most trusted advisor of Emperor Bahadur Shah was
    (a) Hakim Ahsanullah
    (b) Prince Zawan Bakht
    (c) Queen Zeenat Mahal
    (d) Prince Bakht Khan
20. Rani Laxmibai of Jhansi captured Gwalior with the help of
    (a) Rao Sahib, brother of Nana Sahib
    (b) Tantia Tope
    (c) Both 'a' and 'b'
    (d) Nana Sahib
21. The basic weakness of the Revolt of 1857 was that
    (a) It lacked planning, programme and fund
    (b) Thes rebels failed to understand the significance of contemporary scientific advancements
    (c) Theentire movement lacked a modern, unified and forward looking programme
    (d) There was no understanding of the character of the enemy's political organisation among the rebels
22. Which one of the following pairs is incorrectly matched?

Places of Revolt		Leaders
(a) Allahabad	:	Maulvi Ahmadullah
(b) Banaras	:	Maulvi Liyakat Ali
(c) Farrukhabad	:	Tufzal Hasan Khan
(d) Bijnor	:	Mohammed Khan

23. Which one of the following pairs is incorrectly matched?

Authors		Books
(a) TR Holms	:	Sepoy War
(b) PC Joshi	:	1857 in India
(c) Eric Stokes	:	The Peasant and the Raj
(d) Ashok Mehta	:	1857, The Great Rebellion

24. After the Revolt of 1857, the British recruited the soldiers from the:
    (a) Brahmins of Uttar Pradesh and Bihar.
    (b) Bengalis and Orrias from the East.
    (c) Gurkhas, Sikhs and Punjabis in the North.
    (d) Madras Presidency and Marathas.
25. Which one of the following territories was not affected by the Revolt of 1857?
    (a) Jhansi (b) Chittor
    (c) Jagdishpur (d) Lucknow
26. What was/were the object/objects of Queen Victoria's Proclamation (1858)?

1. To disclaim any intention to annex Indian States.
2. To place the Indian administration under the British Crown.
3. To regulate East India Company's trade with India.

Select the correct answer using the codes given below

(a) 1 and 2 (b) Only 2
(c) 1 and 3 (d) All of the above

Answers with Explanation

1. (a) Charles John Canning (14th December, 1812-17th June 1862), known as the viscount Canning from 1837 to 1859, was an English statesman and Governor-General of India during Sepoy Mutiny (1857-1862).
2. (d) Sanyasi rebellion occurred in 1770 against the ban on visiting the religious places. It was a rebellion that took place in 1773 and continued upto 1800 in North Bengal. Heroic figures like Majanu Saha, Bhawani Pathank, Devi Choudhrani were the leaders of the rebellion.
3. (d) Tantiya Tope was betrayed by Man Singh, a feudatory of Scindhia.
4. (b) Jhansi, Jagdispur and Lucknow were epicenters of Revolt of 1857 under Rani Laxmibai, Kunwar Singh and Begum Hazrat Mahal respectively.
5. (a) Babu Veer Kunwar Singh, one of the leaders of the Indian Rebellion of 1857 belonged to a royal Ujjaini house of Jagdishpur, currently part of Bhojpur district, Bihar state India.
6. (c) A number of princely states were annexed by the British under 'Doctrine of Lapse' introduced by Lord Dalhousie – Satara (1848), Jaipur and Sambhalpur (1849), Baghat (1850), Udaipur (1852) and Nagpur (1854).
7. (b) Khasi is a tribe of Meghalaya.
8. (a) The Hindu-Muslim unity in the Revolt of 1857 was indirectly acknowledged later by Atchison a senior British official bitterly complained and said the above statement.
9. (d) Indigo revolt was a revolt by Indigo cultivators against the indigo producers of Bengal. The English had established the monopoly production of Indigo after seizing land in Bengal and Bihar. They ill-treated the Indian peasants who worked with them. In 1860, the peasants of Pabna and Nadia districts went on strike. In 1860 `Indigo Commission' was set up to review the situation, Degambar and Bishnu Biswas were the leaders of the revolt. The revolt continued upto 1869.
   When the English crushed the Santhals living in the district of Raj Mahal and extracted more revenue, they rebelled under the leadership of Seetu and Kanhu. The government crushed the revolt with difficulty. It had to create a separate Pargana for them. The revolt took place in 1855.
10. (a)
11. (a) The educated middle class in India opposed the revolt of 1857. Broadly speaking, the educated upper and middle classes were critical to muting which they felt to epitomise backwardness. One of the major reasons for the unsuccessful of this mutinity was that only one percent of the ruling chiefs joined to revolt.
12. (a)
13. (d)

14. (b)
15. (b)
16. (c)
17. (a)
18. (c)
19. (a)
20. (c)
21. (c)
22. (a)
23. (b)
24. (c)
25. (b)
26. (a)

Practice Paper

1. The First Governor General and Viceroy of British India was
   (a) Lord Dalhousie
   (b) John Lawrence
   (c) Warren Hastings
   (d) Lord Canning **(SSC 2008)**
2. The administrative consequence of the Revolt of 1857 was the transfer of power from.
   (a) East India Company to the British Crown
   (b) British Crown to the East India Company
   (c) East India Company to the Governor General
   (d) British Crown to the Board of Directors **(SSC 2008)**
3. Mangal Pandey fired the first shot of the Revolt of 1857 at
   (a) Barackpore (b) Meerut
   (c) Kanpur (d) Jhansi
   (SSC 2009)
4. Who, among the following, was **NOT** associated with the Revolt of 1857?
   (a) Maharaja Ranjit Singh
   (b) Nana Sahib
   (c) Begum Hazrat Mahal
   (d) Khan Bahadur **(SCRA 2005)**
5. One of the India's first freedom fighters against British is:
   (a) Mahatma Gandhi
   (b) Kittur Rani Chennamma
   (c) Rani Laxmi Bai
   (d) None of these **(RRB 2005)**
6. The sepoy Mutiny took place in the year
   (a) 1757 (b) 1761
   (c) 1836 (d) 1857
   (Indraprasth Univ. 2007)
7. Consider the following native rulers
   1. Kunwar Singh
   2. Nana Sahib
   3. Scindhia of Gwalior
   4. Nizam of Hyderabad

   Who among these native rulers did **NOT** participate in the Revolt of 1857?
   (a) 1, 2 and 4 (b) 2 and 3
   (c) 3 and 4 (d) 1, 2, 3 and 4
   (NDA 2000)
8. Match List-I with List-II and select the correct answer using the codes given below the Lists

List-I (Leaders)	List-II (Area under their operation)
A. Maulavi Ahmed Shah	1. Barrackpore
B. Mangal Pandey	2. Faizabad
C. Bakht Khan	3. Kanpur
D. Nana Sahib	4. Delhi

Codes:

	A	B	C	D
(a)	3	4	1	3
(b)	3	4	1	2

(c) 2 1 4 3
(d) 3 1 4 2

(NDA 2001)

9. During India's freedom struggle, the Sepoy Mutiny started from which one of the following palces?
(a) Agra (b) Gwalior
(c) Jhansi (d) Meerut
(NDA 2004; Utt. PCS 2007)

10. Who is the author of the book 'The Last Mughal: The fall of a Dynasty, Delhi, 1857'?
(a) John Kirkland
(b) William Dalrymple
(c) Thomas Wilson
(d) Simon Digby **(CDS 2007)**

11. Kunwar Singh led the revolt of 1857 in
(a) Punjab (b) Bengal
(c) Bihar (d) Maharashtra
(BPSC 2002, 2008; UPSC 2005)

12. The Revolt of 1857 was witnessed by the poet
(a) Mir Taqi Mir (b) Zauq
(c) Ghalib (d) Iqbal
(BPSC 2002)

13. Who of the following was the bitterest enemy of the Briish during the Revolt of 1857?
(a) Maulavi Ahmdullah Shah
(b) Maulavi Imadulah
(c) Nawab Liaquat Ali
(d) Maulana Fazi-Haq Khairabadi
(BPSC 2002)

14. Which one of the following commissions is associated with the Army Re-organisation after the suppression of the Revolt of 1857?
(a) Public Service Commission
(b) Peal Commission
(c) Hunter Commission
(d) Simon Commission **(BPSC 2002)**

15. After the revolt of 1857 the British recruited the soldiers from the
(a) Brahmins of UP and Bihar
(b) Bengalis and Orrias from the East
(c) Curkhas, Sikhs and Punjabis in the North
(d) Madras Presidency and Marathas
(BPSC 2008)

16. When did Queen Victoria declared the taking over of Indian Administration under British Crown?
(a) 1 November, 1858
(b) 31 December, 1857
(c) 6 January, 1958
(d) 17 November, 1859
(BPSC 2008, UPPCS 2015)

17. The revolt of 1857 at Lucknow was led by
(a) Begum Hazarat Mahal
(b) Tantia Tope
(c) Rani Laxmi Bai
(d) Nana Sahib **(BPSC 2008)**

18. 'India's war of Independence 1857' is written by
(a) S. N. Sen (b) R.C. Majumdar
(c) V.D. Savarkar (d) S.B. Chaudhari
(UPPSC 2004; SSC 2010)

19. The birth place of Maharani Laxmi Bai, the heroine of the 1857 freedom struggle is
(a) Agra (b) Jhansi
(c) Varanasi (d) Vrindaban
(UPPCS 2008)

20. The modern historian who called the revolt of 1857 as the 'First war of Independence' was
(a) R.C. Majumdar
(b) S.N. Sen
(c) V.D. Savarkar
(d) Ashok Mehta **(MPPCS 2008)**

21. 'In this instance we could not play off the Mohammedans against the Hindus'.

To which one of the following events did this remark of Aitchison relate?
(a) Revolt of 1857
(b) Champaran Satyagraha (1917)
(c) Khilafat and Non-Cooperation Movement
(d) August Movement of 1942

(UPPCS 2000)

22. Which one of the following territories was NOT affected by the Revolt of 1857?
(a) Jhansi (b) Chittor
(c) Jagdishpur (d) Lucknow

(UPPCS 2005)

23. With reference to the 'revolt of the year 1857', who of the following was betrayed by a friend captured and put to death by the British?
(a) Nana Sahib
(b) Kunwar Singh
(c) Khan Bahadur Khan
(d) Tantiya Tope

24. Who was the Governor General of India during the sepoy mutiny?
(a) Lord Canning
(b) Lord Dalhousie
(c) Lord Hardings
(d) Lord Lyttons

Answers

1. (d)	2. (a)	3. (a)	13. (a)	14. (b)	15. (c)
4. (a)	5. (c)	6. (d)	16. (a)	17. (a)	18. (c)
7. (c)	8. (c)	9. (d)	19. (c)	20. (c)	21. (a)
10. (b)	11. (c)	12 (c)	22. (b)	23. (d)	24. (a)

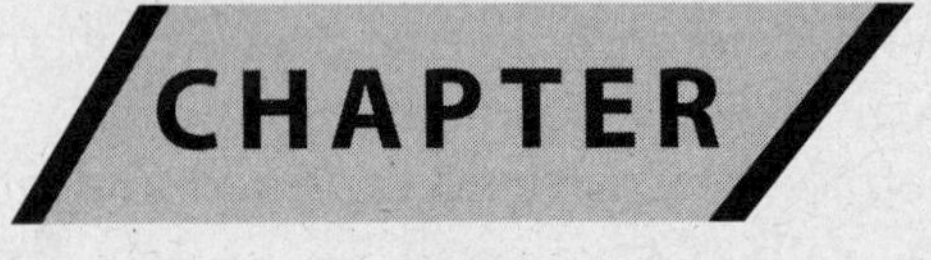

CHAPTER 8

Social and Religious Reform Movements

Causes Behind the Rise of the Movements

Introduction of Western Education and Ideas

- It played an important role in bringing the knowledge of some advanced ideas of the Western world and of modern science to India.
- Educated Indians also became aware to developments in other parts of the world, including movements of nationalism and democracy and later, of socialism, in other courtries.

Knowledge of India's Past

- From the last 18th century, a number of European and Indian scholars began the study of ancient India's philosophy, science, religion and literature.
- This growing knowledge of India's past gave to Indian people a sense of pride for their civilization.
- It also helped the reformers in their work of religious and social reforms. For their struggle against social evils, superstitions and inhuman practices and customs, the reforms used the authority of ancient texts.
- It determined bid of Christian missionary to convert India to Christianity.
- Thus, Indian religious and social reformers made use of their knowledge of western idea as well as of ancient learnings.

Characteristics of Social Reforms

- Base of social reforms was newly emerging middle class. Many of the movements were confined to one religion or caste.
- These movements emerged in different periods of time in different parts of India but having considerable similarities in their objectives.
- Religious reformation was a precondition for social reformation.
- There was cultural ideological struggle against backward element of traditional culture. The movement could not reach

to the masses of peasantry and urban poor.

Major Issues of the Movements

- **Religious Sphere:** It Challenged the idol worship, polytheism, religious superstitions and exploitation by priests.
- **Social Sphere:** It includes the poor position of women (focus on education, eradication of *Sati* practices, child marriages, female infanticide).
- It also focused on regeneration of traditional institutions i.e., cultivation of vernacular languages, creation of alternative system of education, medicine and concern for art, religion, language and philosophy.

Raja Ram Mohan Roy and Brahmo Samaj

- The pioneer and in many respects, the most important figure of the reform movement was Raja Ram Mohan Roy. He was born in a well to do family in Bengal, in 1772.

Raja Ram Mohan Roy

- He received his traditional Sanskrit learning at Banaras and Arabic and Persian learning at Patna.
- Later, he learnt English, Greek, Hebrew, French and Latin.
- He made a deep study of Hinduism, Islam, Christianity and Judaism. He wrote a number of books in Bengali, Hindi, Sanskrit, Persian and English.
- He started two newspapers, one in Bengali (Sambad Kaumudi) and another in Persian (Mirat-ul-Akhbar).
- He was given the **title of Raja** and sent to England by the Mughal Emperor as his envoy.
- He reached England in 1831 and died there in 1833.
- Ram Mohan Roy was convinced that to purify Hindu religion of the evils that had crept into it, it was necessary to bring to the people knowledge of the original texts of their religion. For this purpose, he took up the hard and patient job of publishing the Bengali translation of Vedas and the Upaanishads.
- He advocated belief in a Universal Religion based on the principle of one Supreme God.
- He **condemned idol worship** and the rites and rituals. His greatest achievement in the field of religious reforms was the setting up in 1828 of the Bramho Sabha and in 1830, of the Brahmo Samaj.
- The Brahmo Samaj was the first important organization of religious reforms. It forbade idol worship and discarded meaningless rites and rituals. The Samaj also forbade its members from attacking any religion.
- He gave enthusiastic assistance to David Hare who founded the famous **Hindu College in Calcutta.**

- Established a Vedanta College (1825) in which course both in Indian and Western social and physical sciences were offered.
- He wrote 'A Gift to Monotheisms' or Tuhafat-ul-Muwaihidin' in Persian in 1809 and "Percepts of Jesus" in 1820.
- Ram Mohan Roy's activities were not confined to religious reforms. He supported the introduction of English Education in India, which was necessary to promote enlightenment and knowledge of science.
- He started two newspapers. He was a great believer in the **Freedom of Press** and campaigned for the removal of restrictions on the press.
- The greatest achievement of Ram Mohan Roy in the field of social reforms was the **Abolition of *Sati*** in 1829. Rammohan realized that the practice of Sati was due to extremely low position of Hindu women.
- He, therefore, advocated the abolition of polygamy, e.g., the practice of a man having more than one wife, and wanted women to be educated and given the right to inherit property.
- Ram Mohan Roy and his associates had to face the bitter enmity and ridicule from the orthodox Hindus. The influence of Brahmo Samaj, however, spread, and branches of the Samaj were opened in different parts of the country. The two most prominent leaders of the Brahmo Samaj were Debendranath Tagore and Kesab Chandra Sen. To spread the message of the Brahmo Samaj, Kesab Chandra Sen travelled throughout Madras and Bombay Presidencies and, Later the Northern India.
- In **1866,** there was a **Split in the Brahmo Samaj** Devendranath Tagore founded **Adi Brahmo Samaj** or **Tattva Bodhini Sabha** and **Brahmo Samaj of India** was founded under leadership of Keshab Chandra Sen. Also Anand Mohan Bose started Sadharam Brahmo Samaj and Justice MG Ranade founded the Prarthana Samaj.
- Kesab Chandra Sen and his group held views which were more radical than those of other Brahmo Samajists. They proclaimed freedom from thse bondage of caste and customs, and from the authority of scriptures. They advocated and performed inter caste marriages and widow remarriages, opposed the custom of purdah and condemsned caste divisions.
- While this group rose in prominence, the influence of the other group, which showed little interest in social reforms declined.
- Though the Brahmo Samajists were never large in number, they represented the new spirit of rationalism and reforms.
- They attacked caste rigidity, started taking their food with the people of so called lower castes and those of other religions, opposed restrictions about food and drink, worked for improving the status of women in the society, devoted their lives to the spread of education and condemned the old Hindu opposition of sea voyages.
- The movement started by Ram Mohan Roy, and carried forward by others after him, influenced similar movements of reform in other parts of the country.

Derozio and Young Bengal

- For carrying on the modernizing movements in Bengal, the Hindu College of Calcutta, founded in 1817, played an important role.
- **David Hare,** an associate of Ram Mohan, took keen interest in starting this college.
- He had come from Scotland to sell watches in Calcutta, but later made the spread of modern education in Bengal. In 1826, young man of 17, Henry Lui Vivian Derozio, whose father was of Portuguese origin and mother English woman, joined the Hindu College as a teacher.
- Within on time he drew around him the best boys of the college whom he constantly encouraged to think freely and to question all authority.
- The Young Bengal Movement continued even after Derozio's dismissal and his sudden death in AD 1831.

Ideas and Teachings

- Derozio promoted radical ideas through his teachings and by organizing an association for debate and discussions on Literature, History, Philosophy and Science.
- Through these activities Derozio practically charmed the young students of Calcutta and brought about an intellectual revolution among them.
- His students collectively called the Young Bengal, ridiculed old social traditions and customs, debated the existence of God, defined social and religious conventions and demanded freedom of thought and expression and education for women.
- They cherished the ideals of French revolution and liberal thinking of England.
- The very strong radical views of this group and their unconventional practices like not showing respect to religious idols alarmed the orthodox Hindus of Calcutta.
- They thought the teachings of Derozio were the root cause of the radical views held by the young boys and brought pressure on the authorities of the Hindu College to dismiss him.

Ishwar Chandra Vidyasagar

- He was born in poor Brahmin family in AD 1820, and had a brilliant career as a student in Sanskrit. For his great learning, the Sanskrit College in Calcutta, of which he was the Principal for a few years, conferred on him the title of **Vidyasagar.**

Ishwar Chandra Vidyasagar

- He became a legendary figure for his simple living, fearlessness and spirit of self sacrifice, and his devotion to education and to the cause of downtrodden people.

Ideas and Teachings

- He introduced the study of modern Western thought in the Sanskrit College and admitted students belonging to the so called lower castes to study Sanskrit. Earlier, studies in Sanskrit College were confined to traditional subjects.
- He made a great contribution to the Bengali language, and he is considered the originator of modern Bengali language.
- He was closely associated with many journals and newspapers and wrote powerful; articles advocating social reforms.
- Vidyasagar's greatest contribution was to the cause of widow's upliftment and girl's education.
- He played a great role in the passing of the law which made the marriage of the widows legal. He personally took part in the first widow remarriage that was performed in Calcutta in 1856.
- He was attacked by the orthodox Hindus for his powerful support to the cause of widow remarriage as well as for his efforts at promoting education of girls.
- When, in 1855, he was made special **inspector of schools,** he opened a number of new schools, including girl's school, in the districts under his charge.
- The authorities did not like this and he resigned his post.
- He was closely associated with **John Elliot Drinkwater Bethune** who had started first school for girl's education in Calcutta in 1849.

Reform Movements in Western India

- Beginning in Bengal, the religious and social reform movements spread to other parts of India. In 1867, the **Prarthana Samaj** of Bombay was founded.
- Two of its chief architects were **Mahadev Gobind Ranade and Ramakrishna Bhandarkar.** The leaders of the Prarthana Samaj were influenced by the Brahmo Samaj.
- They condemned the caste system and the practice of untouchability.
- They worked for improving the status of women and advocated widow remarriage.
- **Ranade** (along with Raghunath Rao) who was also one of the founders of the Indian National Congress, founded the **Indian National Social Conference** in 1887 with the aim of working for social reforms effectively all over the country.
- This conference met every year when the session of the Indian National Congress was held, to discuss social problems.
- Ranade believed that without social reforms, it was not possible to achieve any progress in the political and economic fields.
- He was a great advocate of **Hindu-Muslim** unity and declared that in this vast country no progress is possible unless both Hindus and the Muslims join hands together.

Gopal Hari Deshmukh and Jyotiba Phule

- Two other great reformers in Western India were Gopal Hari Deshmukh, popularly known as Lokhitwadi, and

Jyatirao Govindrao Phule, popularly known as Jyotiba.

- Lokhitwadi was associated with a number of social reform organizations. He condemned the caste system and worked for the upliftment of women.
- Mahatma Phule dedicated himself to the cause of oppressed section of society and of women's upliftment.
- In 1848, he started a school for the girls of lower castes and educated his wife so that she could teach in that school. In 1873, he founded the **Satyashodhak Samaj** which was open to everyone without any distinction of caste and religion. Its aim was to work for winning equal rights for the people of the oppressed castes.
- Mahatma Phule opposed the supremacy of the Brahmins and started the practice of arranging marriage ceremonies without Brahmin priests.
- Jyotiba was given the title of Mahatma for his work for the cause of the oppressed.

Reform Movements in Southern India

- Inspired by the Brahmo Samaj, the **Veda Samaj** was established in Madras in 1864. It advocated discarding of caste distinctions and promotion of widow remarriage and girl's education.
- Like the Brahmo Samaj, the Veda Samaj also condemned the superstitions and rituals or orthodox Hinduism and propagated the belief of one supreme God.
- **C Sridharalu Naidu** was the most prominent leader of the Veda Samaj.
- He translated books of Brahmo Samaj in Tamil and Telugu.
- Later, the Brahmo Samaj of South India and its branches were established in some cities of **Tamil Nadu, Karnataka** and **Andhra.**
- Soon after, branches of Prarthana Samaj were also opened and the two Samaj worked together for promoting religious and social reforms.
- **Sree Narayana Dharma Paripalana Yogam or SNDP Movement (1902–03).** A significant movement which was particularly important for the emancipation of the oppressed sections of society was started by **Sree Narayana Guru** in Kerala. Narayana Guru was born in 1854 in an Ezhava family.
- The Ezhavas, along with some others in Kerala, were considered untouchable by Hindus of the so called upper castes.
- Narayana Guru acquired Sanskrit education and devoted himself to uplift the Ezhavas and other oppressed people.
- He started establishing temples in which gods or their images had no place. He founded first temple by installing a stone from the nearby stream.
- **Narayana Guru,** in 1903, founded the Sri Narayan Dharma Paripalana Yogam, which became an important organization for social reform.
- Narayana Guru considered differences based on caste and religion as meaningless and advocated what he called "One Caste, One Religion and One God " for all.

Kandukuri Veeresalingam

- An outstanding leader of the reform movements in Southern India was Kandukuri Veeresalingam.

- He was born in 1848 in an orthodox Brahmin family in Andhra. He was influenced by the ideas of the Brahmo Samaj, Particularly those of Kesab Chandra Sen, and dedicated himself to the cause of social reform. In 1876, he started a Telugu journal which was almost exclusively devoted to social reforms.
- He worked for the enlightenment of the people and many areas of social reforms, but his greatest contribution was to the cause of the emancipation of women.
- This included promoting girls' education and widow remarriages.
- An entire generation of social reformers and nationalist leaders of Andhra was inspired by the writings and the reform activities of Veeresalingam.

Issues Related to Temple Reforms

- Many reformers in Southern India concerned themselves with the reform of certain practices connected with Hindu temples.
- They advocated the ending of **Devadasis** who were attached to the temples. They also wanted that the wealth of the temples, some of which were very rich, should not be amassed by the priests but that the public should exercise control over it.
- In many temples, people of the so called lower castes were not allowed to enter and sometimes even some roads adjoining the temples were barred to them.
- The reformers launched powerful movements for temple entry and against other evil practices which had become associated with temples.
- Unfortunately, in spite of the work done by reformers since the 19th century, even now there are instances in some parts of the country when some people are debarred entry into the temples on grounds of caste.

Dayanand Saraswati and Arya Samaj

- Another influential movement of religious and social reform in Northern India was started by Dayanand Saraswati. Dayanand, whose original name was **Mul Shankara,** was born in Kathiawad in AD 1824.

Dayanand Saraswati

- At the age of 14, he become a rebel by rejecting idol worship. Soon after, he left home and led the life of wandering scholar in search of knowledge. During this period, he acquired mastery over Sanskrit language and literature.
- In AD 1863 Dayanand Saraswati started preaching his doctrine–there is only one God and he should be worshipped not in the form of images but as a spirit. He held that the Vedas contained all the knowledge imparted to man by God and essential so modern science could also be traced there.

- He looked on the Vedas as "India's Rock and Ages". The true original seed of Hinduism. His motto was "Go Back To Vedas" and "India for the Indians".
- With this message, he went about all over the country and in 1875 founded the **Arya Samaj in Bombay**. Dayanand preached and wrote in Hindi.
- The **Satyarth Prakash** was his most important book. The use of Hindi made his ideas accessible to the common people of Northern India. The Arya Samaj made rapid progress in Uttar Pradesh, Rajasthan, Gujarat and particularly in Punjab where it became a very important social and political force.
- He wrote three Books—Satyarth Prakash, Rigvedadi Bhashya Bhumika and Rigveda Bhashya.
- The members of Arya Samaj were guided by **"Ten Principles"** of which the first one was studying the Vedas. The rest were tenets on virtue and morality.
- Dayanand framed for them a code of social conduct, in which there was no room for caste distinction and social inequality. The Arya Samjists opposed child marriages and encouraged remarriage of widows.
- A network of schools and colleges for boys and girls was established throughout Northern India to promote the spread of education.
- In 1886, Lala Hardayal instituted the **Dayanand Anglo Vedic School** of Lahore, which soon developed into a premier college of Punjab, set the pattern for such institutions.
- Here instructions were given through English and Hindi on modern lines.
- Those among his disciples who wanted to maintain the original spirit of Dayanand founded the **Gurukul** at **Haridwar.** This was set up on the pattern of ancient Ashrams.
- Dayanand, asserted the infallibility of Vedas. The influence of Dayanand and Arya Samaj, however, in the promotion of education, uplift of the position of women and weakening the hold of the caste system was deeper than that of many other reform movements.

Suddhi Movement

- Dayanand preached that Vedas were infallible. This was because of his ardent desire to give the Hindus a definite set of religious beliefs, which would give them a militant character.
- Similar in nature was his move for reconversion of those Hindus who had been converted into other religions like Islam and Christianity.
- For this purpose a purificatory ceremony called Shudhi was prescribed.

Ramakrishna Mission and Vivekananda

- Another important reformer of the latter half of the 19th century was **Ramakrishna Paramahansa** (1836–1886) who was a priest in a temple at Dakshineswar near Calcutta. His original name was Gadadhar Chattopadhyay.
- After coming in contact with the leaders of other religions, he accepted the sanctity of all faiths.
- By simplicity of character and homely wisdom, he won the heart of all who gathered around him.

Vivekananda

- Almost all religious reformers of his time, including Kesab Chandra Sen and Dayanand, called on him for religious discussion and guidance.
- The contemporary Indian intellectuals, whose faith in their own culture had been shaken by the challenges from the West, found reassurance from his teachings.
- In order to propagate the teachings of Ramakrishna and put them into practice, Ramakrishna mission was founded in 1897, by his favorite disciple Vivekananda. The mission stood for social service. "The best way to serve God is to serve mankind" was its motto.
- **Ramakrishna Mission,** since its beginning, has grown into a very powerful centre of numerous public activities. These include organizing relief during floods, famines and epidemics, establishing hospitals and running education institutions.
- **Vivekananda** (1863–1902) (Original name—Narendranath Dutta) had a character altogether different from that of his master. He studied deeply Indian and Western philosophies but could not find peace of mind until he met Ramakrishna. He was, however, not content just with spirituality. The question that constantly agitated him was the degenerated condition of his motherland.
- After an all India tour he found everywhere "poverty, loss of mental vigor and no hope for future." He frankly stated, "It is we who are responsible for all our misery and all our degeneration." He urged his countrymen to work for their own salvation.
- For this purpose Vivekananda took upon himself the task of awakening his countrymen and reminding them of their weaknesses.
- He inspired them "to struggle unto life and death to bring about a new state of things–sympathy for the poor, and bread to their hungry mouths, enlightenment to the people at large". A band of workers devoted to this cause were trained through the Ramakrishna Mission.
- Vivekananda's activities outside India helped in promoting an understanding of Indian culture aboard.
- In 1893, he participated in the All World Religious Conference (Parliament of Religions) at Chicago in the USA. His address there made a deep impression on the people of other countries and thus helped to raise the prestige of Indian culture in the eyes of the world.

Muslim Reform Movements

- Among the Muslims the first signs of awakening appeared in the early 19th century, under the leadership of people like **Syed Ahmad of Bareilly** in Uttar Pradesh and **Shariatullah of**

Bengal. They held that because of the degeneration of Islam in India it had fallen into the hands of British. They set themselves to the task of purifying and strengthening Islam and purifying Islamic learnings.

- Shariatullah was the leader of Faraizi movement in Bengal. He condemned the civil influence of the caste system among Muslims.
- The influence of Western ideas and modern education spared among the Muslims later than among some sections of Hindus. During the first half of the 19th century only a handful of Muslims of Delhi and Calcutta had taken to English education.
- Most of them kept themselves away from it because of the attitude of the **Ulema,** who were traditional custodians of Islamic learning, and the unwillingness of the upper class Muslims to reconcile themselves to British rule. The British had gradually robbed both these groups of their influence and rendered them powerless. Deprived of English education and its social and economic advantages, a middle class did not grow among the Indian Muslims for a long time.
- The ill feeling between the British and the Muslims greatly increased as a result of the Revolt of 1857 in which, Muslims had actively participated. At this stage a few enlightened Muslims felt the need for adopting a cooperative policy towards the rulers and improving their social condition with the help of the latter.
- A few movements were also launched aiming at the spread of modern education and removing social abuses like **Purdah** and **Polygamy.** The Mohammadan Literacy society of Calcutta, founded in 1863 by Nawab Abdul Latif, was one of the earliest organizations to take steps in this direction. It played an important role in the spread of education, particularly among the Muslims in Bengal. Abdul Latif also played an important role in Promoting Hindu–Muslim unity.

Wahhabi Movement

- The earliest organized Muslim response to Western influences appeared in the form of the Wahhabi Movement, which was popularly known as **Walliuallah Movement.**
- It was essentially a revivalist movement and was inspired by the teachings of **Shah Walliullah**. Shah Walliullah (1702–62) was the first Indian Muslim leader of the 18th century who expressed concern at the degeneration which had set in among Indian Muslims. He tried to organize the Indian Muslims around the two fold ideals of this movement.
- **Firstly,** the desirability of creating harmony among the four schools of Muslims Jurisprudence which had divided the Indian Muslims. He sought to integrate the best elements of the four schools.
- **Secondly,** the recognition of the role of individual conscience in religion. He held that in cases where the **Quran** and the **Hadis** Provide conflicting interpretations, the individual could make a decision on the basis of his own judgment and conscience. Initially, the movement was directed against the

Sikhs in annexation of Punjab but later (1849), the movement was directed against the British. The movement was suppressed by the superior military force of the British in the 1870s.

Titu Mir's Movement

- **Syed Mir Nisar Ali,** popularly known as Titu Mir, was a disciple of **Sayyid Ahmed Barelvi,** the founder of Wahhabi Movement. Titu Mir organized the Muslim peasants against the Hindu landlords and the British indigo planters.
- The movement was not as militant as the British records made it out to be; only in the last year of Titu Mir's life was there a confrontation between him and the British police. He was killed in action in AD 1831.

Faraizi Movement

- The movement, also called the Fara'idi Movement because of its emphasis on the Islamic faith was founded by **Haji Shariat-Ullah.**
- The movement was popular in East Bengal, and aimed at eradication of social evils prevalent among the Muslims of the region. Under the leadership of Haji's son **Dudu Miyan,** the movement became revolutionary from AD 1840 onwards.
- Dudu Miyan gave the movement and organizational system from village to the provincial level with a Khalifa or authorized deputy at every level.
- The Fara'idis also organized the forces to fight the Hindu landlords and even the police. The death of Dudu Miyan in 1862, finally weakened the movement, and later it survived merely as religious struggle without political overtones.

Sir Syed Ahmed Khan and Aligarh Movement

- The most important movement for the spread of modern education and social reform among Muslims was started by **Sir Syed Ahmed Khan.**

Sir Syed Ahmed Khan

- Syed Ahmed Khan (1817–1898) came from a family of nobles of the Mughal Court. He joined the service of the company as a judicial officer and remained loyal to them during the Revolt of 1857.
- Syed Ahmed Khan was deeply concerned at the depressed position of the Muslims and raising them from their backwardness became his lifelong passion. He strove hard to remove the hostility of the British rulers towards the Muslim and to persuade the Muslims to accept the religious and educational reforms.
- He appealed to the Muslims to return to the original Islamic principle of purity and simplicity.
- He advocated English education for the regeneration of Muslims in India.

For this Syed Ahmed Khan had to face opposition from the orthodox section of Muslim. However, with courage and wisdom, he overcame these obstacles.

- In 1864, he founded the Translation Society which was later renamed as **Scientific Society.** The Society was located at Aligarh. It published Urdu translation of English books on scientific and other subject, alon with an English Urdu journal for spreading liberal ideas on social reforms.
- His greatest achievement was the establishment of the **Mohammedan Anglo Oriental College** at Aligarh in 1875. In course of time, this college became the most important educational institution of Indian Muslims. It provided for education in humanities and science through English medium and many of its staff members came from England. The Muslims throughout India and the British showed much interest, both officially and otherwise in its development.
- The Mohammedan Anglo Oriental (MAO) College, which later on became the **Aligarh Muslim University**, fostered a modern outlook among the generations of students that studied there.
- The college and later when it became a university, attracted students from all communities. It, however, played a particularly important role in the awakening of Muslims in India. The movement of Muslim awakening associated with Syed Ahmed Khan and MAO College came to be known as the Aligarh Movement.
- Though Syed Ahmed Khan opposed the Indian National Congress, he emphasized the unity between Hindus and Muslims.
- Besides introducing modern education among Muslims, Syed Ahmed Khan advocated the removal of many social prejudices that kept the community backwards. His emphasis on science particularly offended the orthodox Muslims.

Opposition to Congress

- Syed Ahmed Khan opposed the activities of the Indian National Congress.
- He believed, like many other leaders at that time, that Indians were not yet ready to govern themselves and that their interest would be best served by remaining loyal to the British Rule.
- He founded the Indian Patriotic Association with the support of some Hindu and Muslim leaders to oppose the Congress and tried to dissuade the Muslim from joining the congress.
- He wanted more time for the Indian Muslims to organize and consolidate their position and thought that this could be best done by maintaining good relations with the British rulers.

Ahrar Movement

- It was a religious Muslim political party founded under the leadership of Syed Ata Ullah Shah Bukhari in 1929.

Ahmadiya Movement

- This Movement was founded by **Mirza Ghulam Ahmed** in 1889. The movement was based on liberal principles.

- It described itself as the standard bearer of **Mohammedan Renaissance** and based itself, like the Brahmo Samaj, on the principle of universal religion of all humanity, opposing jihad (sacred war against non-Muslims). The movement spread Western Liberal education among the Indian Muslims.

The Deoband School

- The Deoband movement was organized by the orthodox section among the Muslim Ulema. It was a revivalist movement whose twin objectives were
  - To propagate among the Mulsim the pure teachings of the Quran and the Hadis.
  - To keep alive the spirit of Jihad against the foreign rulers.
- The Ulema under the leadership of **Muhammad Qasim Nanotvi (1832–80)** and **Rasheed Ahmed Gangohi** (1828—1905) founded the school at Deoband in the Saharanpur district in UP in 1866. The objective was to train religious leaders for the Muslim Community.
- In the school the instruction was imparted in original Islamic religion. The aim was moral and religious regeneration of the Muslim community. The School curriculum did not include English education and Western culture.
- Thus, in contrast to the Aligarh movement which aimed at welfare of the Muslim Community through Western education and support of the British Government, the **Deoband School** preached Islamic faith.
- Similarly, on the political front the Deoband School welcomed the formation of Indian National Congress in 1885.
- In 1888, the Deoband Ulema issued a religious decree (fatwa) against Syed Ahmed Khan's organizations, 'The United Patriotic Association' and 'The Mohammedan Anglo Oriental Association'.
- Muhammad-ul-Hassan (1851–1920), the new Deoband leader, imparted a political and intellectual colour to the religious ideas of the school. He worked out a synthesis of Islamic principles and nationalist aspirations.
- The Jamiat-ul-Ulema gave a concrete shape to Hassan's ideas of protection of the religious and the political rights of the Muslims in the overall context of Indian unity and national objectives.
- **Shibli Nomani,** a supporter of Deoband School favoured the inclusion of English Language and European sciences in the system of education. He founded the **Darul Uloom Nadwatul Ulama** in Lucknow in 1894–96. He believed in the idealism of congress and cooperation between the Hindus and Muslims of India to create a state in which both could live peacefully.

Reform Movements Between Parsis and Sikhs

- Reform movements aiming at eradication of social evils, some of which had became associated with religious practices, emancipation of women and spread to other communities. **Dadabahi Naoroji** (1825–1917) and **Naoroji Furdoonji (1817–1885)** were among the pioneers of religious and social reform in Parsi Community.
- Among the Sikhs, the movement for reform was started by the Singh Sabhas

which were formed at Amritsar and Lahore in the 1870's.

- The two Sabhas played an important role in the spread of education. Through the efforts of the Singh Sabhas and with British support, the Khalsa College was founded at Amritsar in 1892. This college and the school was set up as a result of similar efforts, promoted Gurumukhi, Sikh learning and Punjabi literature as a whole.
- Together, they started a journal **Rast Goftar,** for the purpose and played an important role in the spread of education, particularly among girls. Another important social reformer in the Parsi Community was Sorabji Bengali.
- Later, in the early decades of the 20th century, a powerful movement was launched for the reform of Gurdwaras. The **Gurdwaras,** at that time, were under the control of priests and Mahants who treated them as their private property.
- The movement was led by the **Shiromani Gurdwara Prabandhak Committee** and the **Akali Dal** and aimed at handing over control of the Gurdwaras to representatives of the Sikh Community.
- The movement was led on peaceful lines but those who took part in the movement suffered inhuman cruelties at the hands of people hired by the corrupt Mahants as well as the British police. By this time, the people all over the country had awakened and the struggle for freedom under Gandhiji's leadership had became mass movement.
- The leaders of the freedom movement supported the cause for which the Sikh masses were fighting. In 1925, a law was passed which gave the right of managing Gurdwaras to the Shiromani Gurdwara Prabandhak Committee.

Theosophical Movement

- The Theosophical society was founded by Westerners who drew inspiration from Indian thought and culture. **Madame HP Blavatsky (1830–1891)** of Russo-German Birth laid the foundation of the movement in the United States in 1875. Later **Colonel HS Olcott** (1832–1907) of the US Army joined her.
- In 1882, they shifted their headquarters to India at **Adyar** in Madras. The members of this society believed that a special relationship could be established between a person's soul and God by contemplation, prayer, revelation etc.
- The society accepts the Hindu beliefs in reincarnation, Karma and draws inspiration from the Philosophy of the Upansids and Samkhya, Yoga and Vedanta school of thought. It aims to work for universal brotherhood of humanity without distinction of race, creed, sex, caste or colour.
- The society also seeks to investigate the unexplained laws of nature and the powers latent in man.

Mrs Annie Besant

- In India the movement became somewhat popular with the election of Mrs Annie Besant (1847–1933) as its President after the death of col. Olcott in 1907.
- Early in her life, Mrs Besant lost all faith in Christianity, and came in contact with Theosophy (1882). In 1889, she formally

joined the Theosophical Society. Mrs Besant was well acquainted with Indian thought and culture and her approach was Vedantic as is very evident from her remarkable translation of the Bhagvat Gita.

- Besant laid the foundation of the **Central Hindu College in Banaras in 1898** where both the Hindu religion and the Western scientific subjects were taught. The college became the nucleus for the formation of Banaras Hindu University in 1916. Mrs Besant also did much for the cause of female education. She also formed the Home Rule League on the Pattern of Irish Home Rule Movement.

Other Reform Movements

- **Mahima Movement:** it was founded in Orissa by Mahima Goswami, who laid sufficient stress on disciplined hebits to control the body and mind. It did not recognize any caste, creed, colour or any narrowness that divided human beings.
- **The Deva Samaj:** This Sect was founded in 1887 at **Lahore by Shiv Narain Agnihotri,** who was earlier a follower of Brahmo Samaj. The teachings of the Samaj were complied in a book called Deva Shastra, which emphasizes on the Supreme beings, eternity of soul, the Supremacy of the Guru and emphasis on good action.
- **The Bharat Dharma Mahamandala:** This was an all India Organization of the orthodox educated Hindus who rose in defence or orthodox Hinduism against the teachings of the Arya Samaj, the Theosophists and the Ram Krishna Mission.
- The beginning of this organization was made in 1890 in Punjab by **Pandit Din Dayal Sharma** to counter the teachings of the Arya Samaj.
- In 1895, the Sanatan Dharma Sabha was founded in Haridwar, the Dharma Maha Parishad in South India and Dharma Mahamandali in Bengal to defend orthodox Hinduism.
- In 1902, these various bodies united under a single organization called Bharat Dharma Mahamandala, with headquarters at Varanasi.
- The only progressive reforms proposed by this orthodox organization were to introduce useful reforms into Hindu Society, proper management of Hindu religious institution, to establish Hindu educational institutions etc.
- With the emergence of this movement got divided into two broad sects—the Santana Dharam (which believed in the idol worship and authority of Hindu scriptures) and Arya Samaj.
- **The Madras Hindu Association:** Two such reform associations were founded in Madras. In 1892, the Madras Hindu Social (1848–1919), whose efforts were concerned with the plight of widows, and movement advocating temperance and combating the Devadasi custom.
- **Dharma Sabha:** It was an orthodox society founded by **Radhakant Deb (1794–1876)** in 1830. They opposed the abolition of sati but they played very active role in promotion Western education, even among girls.
- **The Radhaswami Movement:** This movement was founded in 1861 by a banker of Agra, **Tulshi Ram,** popualry known as Shiv Dayal Sabeb of Swamiji Maharaj. The Radhaswamis believe in one Supreme. The sect recognizes

no temples or sacred places. Works of faith and charity, the spirit of service and prayer, are laid down as necessary duties.

- **The Seva Sadan:** This social reform and humanitarian organization was founded in 1885 by the famous Parsi social reformer **Behramji M Malabari,** who relentlessly fought throughout his life against child marriages and 'enforced widowhood'. The Seva Sadan founded by him specialized in the care of socially discarded and exploited women of all castes, providing educational, welfare and medical services.
- **The Servant of India Society:** It was founded in 1915 by **Gopal Krishna Gokhale** to build a dedicated group of people for social service and reforms. In the field of famine relief, union organization, cooperation's and uplift of tribal's and depressed, the society did a very commendable work.
- **The Social Service League:** Narayan Malhar Joshi one of the leading members of the servants of Indian Society, founded the Social Service League in 1911, "to collect and study social facts and discuss social problems with a view to form public opinion on questions of social services" the league opened a number of day and night schools libraries, dispensaries and started Boy's clubs and Scouts crops.

The Rahanumai Mazdayasanan Sabha or Religious Reform Association

- This was a social-religious reform organisation of the Parsis in India. The Western educated and progressive Parsis in India.
- The Western educated and progressive Parsis like Dadabhai Naoroji, J. B. Wacha, S. S. Bengali and **Naoroji Furdonji** founded in 1851, the Rahanumai Mazdayasanan Sabha or Religious Reform Association,which had for its restoration of the Zoroastrian religion to its pristine purity.
- They insisted on the Western education of the Parsi Priests and made great efforts for the spread of Western education among the Parsis, including girls. The age of marriage was increased and the Parsi women achieved their emancipation.
- **Aravipuram Movement:** This Movement was launched in 1888 by **Shri Narain guru,** a great socio-religious reformer of Kerala. He was opposed to the Brahmin of priestly domination and was of the view that even a person of the lower caste could consecrate an image an act as priest in the temple.
- On the Shivratri festival of 1888, shri Narain Guru, in spite of belonging to a lower caste, installed an idol of Shiva at Aravipuram, which was the beginning of this movement.
- **Self Respect Movement:** It was radical movement founded in Tamil Nadu in 1925 by **EV Ramaswami Naicker** popularly known as "Periyar', who opposed Brahman domination and advocated simple Marriages without Brahman Priests and rituals, forcible temple entry, burring of Manusmriti etc. under the British encouragement, this movement emerged as a kind of 'Dravidian Tamil Separatism."

Swami Narayan Sampradaya

- Founded by **Swami Sahiananda** in Gujarat.

- It was a protest against luxurious practices of Vaishnavism.

Namdhari/Kuka Movement

- Founded by Bahi Balak Singh and Baba Ram Singh, in North West frontier province, Ludhiana, in 1841.
- Spread the true sprit of Sikkim, opposed to all caste distinctions.

Indian Reform Association

- Founded by Keshab Chandra Sen in Calcutta in 1870.
- Objective was to create public opinion against Child marriages and for legalizing the Brahma form of marriage and promote intellectual and social status of women.

Paramhansa Mandali

- Founded by Dadoba Pandurang and Bal Shastri Jambhekar in 1849.
- Members took food cooked by low caste people.
- Believed in permitting widow remarriage and in education of women.

Indian National Social Conference

- Founded by MG Ranade and Raghunath Rao in Bombay in 1887.
- Focus was to abolish polygamy and kulinism and promote inter-caste marriages. The conference is also referred as Social reform cell of INC.

Deo Samaj

- Started by Shiv Narain Agnihotri in 1887.
- It preached high moral and social conduct.
- Deva Shastra tells us about the ideals of Deva Samaj.

Depressed Classes Welfare Institute (Bahiskrit Hitkarini Sabha) 1929, Bombay

- Founded by BR Ambedkar.
- To propagate social equality among high caste Hindus and untouchables.
- Demanded constitutional safeguard for the depressed classes.

Bahujan Samaj (1910)

- By Mukundrao Patil in Satara, Maharashtra.
- Opposed to exploitation of the lower castes by the upper caste Brahmin, Landlords, merchants.

Justice Party Movement (1915–16)

- By TM Noor, P Tyagraj Chettiar and CN Mudaliar in Chennai (Tamil Nadu).
- Protest against the domination of Brahmin in government service, education and in the political field.
- The newspaper, "Justice," was their main organ for expressing views and opinions.

Lokhitwadi

- Satarted by Gopal Hari Deshmukh.
- He advocated western education and free education for upliftment of women.
- As a votary of national self reliance, he attended Delhi durbar in 1876, wearing hand spun Khadi cloth.

Poona Seva Sadan (1909)

- Founded by GK Devadhar and Ramabai Pande in Pune.
- Objectives were the economic upliftment and employment of women.

Niskam Karma Math (1910)

- Established by Dhondo Keshav Karpve-pune.
- Maen objectives were social reform, selfless service to mankind, educational progress in women.
- Founded India's 1st women university in Pune, 1916.

The Bharata Stri Mandal (1910)

- Founded by Saralabala Dave Choudharani in Calcutta.
- Ist all Indian women organization.

Seva Samiti (1914)

- Founded at Allahabad by Pandit Hridaynath Kunzru for promoting education and reform.

The Indian Women's Association (1917)

- Started By Annie Besant in Madras for the upliftment of women.

Deccan Education Society

- Founded by MG Ranade, VG Chibdonkar, GG Agarkar in the Pune 1884.
- Objective was to contribute to the cause of education and culture in Western India.
- The society founded the Ferguson College.

Harijan Sevak Sangh (1932)

- Started by Mahatma Gandhi at Pune.
- Organization for removal of un-touchability and social discrimination against untouchables.

Official Social Reform Measures

- Since the beginning of the 19th century the attitude and the policies of the British, towards India were slowly but progressively moved in the direction of cautious intervention in Indian social institutions.
- Orientalism which was the characteristic feature of Hastings period now came to be criticized by a variety of ideological streams which shared the belief that Indian society needed urgent modernization and westernization.
- The **Evangelical Challenge** led by William Wilberforce and Charles Grant (who later became the president of the Company's Board of Control) asserted that Hinduism was based on superstition, idolatry and the tyranny of the priests. Their avowed objectives were to modernize Indians through Christian missionary proselytisation.
- The Radicals headed by Jeremy Bentham, James Mill and John Sturat Mill based their ideas on utilitarian notions of reason and science. They advocated happiness of the greatest number rather than liberty as the aim of the government. The protection of individual life and property were seen as a means to achieve this goal.
- These contending ideologies and the indefatigable efforts of the reformers led to several changes introduced by the British in Indian social practices.

Female Infanticide

- The Practice of killing female infants immediately after their birth was common among upper class Bengalis and Rajputs who considered females to be an economic burden.

- The **Bengal Regulations XXI of 1795 and III of 1804** declared infanticide illegal and equivalent to murder. Similarly, an Act was passed in 1870 which made it compulsory for parents to register the birth of all babies. The **Act of 1870** also provided for verification of female children for some years after birth, particularly in areas where the custom was prevalent.

Abolition of *Sati*

- The term *Sati* literally means a pure and virtuous woman. It was applied in the case of a devoted wife who contemplated perpetual and uninterrupted conjugal union with her husband, after death, and as proof there of burnt herself with the dead body of her husband.
- Some enlightened Indian princes had taken steps to abolish cruel practice in their dominions. Emperor Akbar had attempted to restrict it. The Marathas had forbidden it in their dominions.
- The Portuguese at Goa and the French at Chandernagore had also taken some steps towards its abolition. Early British Governor Generals like Cornwallis, Minto and Lord Hastings had taken some steps to restrict the practice of sati by discouraging compulsion, forbidding administration of intoxicating drugs to the sorrow stricken widows, putting a ban on the burning of pregnant women or widows below 16 years of age and, above all, making compulsory the presence of police officials at the time of sacrifice, who were to see that no compulsion was used. These restrictions, however, proved inadequate and unsuccessful.
- Enlightened Indian reforms led by Raja **Rammohan Roy** urged William Bentinck to take necessary steps and declare the practice of *Sati* illegal. The loss of his sister in law by *Sati* had stirred Rammohan Roy to action and he had published a number of articles condemning the practice.
- Finally, **Regulation XVII of December 1829** declared the practice of *Sati* or of burning or burying alive of widows illegal and punishable by the criminal courts as culpable homicide.
- The Regulation of 1829 was applicable in the first place to Bengal presidency alone, but in 1830 was extended in slightly modified forms to Madras and Bombay Presidencies.

Suppression of *Thugi*

- Another great reform to the credit of **William Bentinck** is the suppression of thugs. The **Thugs, i.e.,** cheats were a sect of hereditary assassins and robbers who lived by preying upon innocent and defenseless travellers.
- A more appropriate name for thugs was **Pansigar,** derived from the scarf and noose used by the thugs to strangle their victims.
- These thugs belonged to both the Hindu and Muslim religions and worshipped the Hindu goddess like Kali, Durga or Bhawani, to whom they offered the heads of their victims as sacrifice. The thugs were hardened criminals and were particularly active in the entire area from Awadh, Hyderabad and Rajputana and Bundelkhand.

- The thugs believed that Thugi was ordained means of livelihood for them and their victims were ordained to die at their hands.
- The public opinion solidly supported the Government measures to suppress Thugi in 1830.
- The operations against thugs were put in charge of **Colonel William Sleeman.** Colonel Sleeman arrested as many as 1500, thugs and sentenced them to death or imprisonment for life.
- Thugi on an organized scale ceased to exist after 1837, although individual bad characters continued their nefarious activities.

Abolition of Slavery

- Slavery was another institution which came under attack in British India. As early as 1774 the government was concerned about this practice.
- Evangelical propaganda against slavery led by **Wilberforce** helped in focusing public attention in Britain on the evils of slavery in India.
- Though Britain abolished slave trade in her dominions in 1820, the company in India acknowledged the legality of slavery on the grounds that it was a traditional practice with religious sanction.
- However, later a clause was inserted in the **Charter Act of 1833** required the Governor-General-in-Council to abolish slavery in India.
- Finally, the **Act V of 1843** declared slavery illegal in India and all existing slaves were emancipated without any compensation to slave owners.
- The **Penal Code of 1860** also declared trade in slavery illegal.

Widow Remarriage and Prohibition of Child Marriage

- The Brahmo Samaj had the issue of widow remarriage high on its agenda and did much to popularise it. Later the efforts were made by **Vishnu Shastri Pandit,** who founded the **Widow Remarriage Association** in the 1850s.
- Another prominent worker in this field was **Karsandas Mulji** who started the Satya Prakash in Gujarati in 1852 to advocate widow remarriage. But it was mainly due to the efforts of Pandit **Ishwar Chandra Vidyasagar (1829–91),** the principal of Sanskrit College, Calcutta, that the Hindu Widow's Remarriage Act, 1856, which legalized marriage of Widows and declared issues from such marriages as legitimate, was passed by the government.
- Vidyasagar cited references from Vedic texts to prove that the Hindu religion sanctioned widow remarriage.
- Though the issue of widow remarriage got the legal sanction by the Act, it still needed the social acceptance. Thus the **Social reformers** continued their task of popularising the issue.
- In western India, **Professor DK Karve** took up the cause of widow remarriage and in Madras Veeresalingam Pantulu made efforts in the same direction.
- Professor Karve started his career as a teacher in the Girl's College at Bombay and in 1891 became a professor at Fergusson college.
- Karve devoted his life to the cause of upliftment of Hindu Widows and became the Secretary of Widow Remarriage Association.

- He himself married a widow in 1893, and in 1899, he opened a widow's home in Poona to provide vocational training to the high caste widows. He crowned his work by setting up an **Indian Women's University at Bombay** in 1916.
- The right of widows to remarriage was also advocated by **BM Malabari,** Justice Govind Mahadeo Ranade and K Natrajan among others.

Child Marriage

- Legislative action in prohibiting child marriage came in 1872 when by the Native Marriage Act, the marriage of girls below the age of 14 and boys below 18 years were forbidden.
- The Act was popularly known as Civil marriage Act. This Act, however, had a limited impact. Later, the relentless efforts of a Parsi reformer, BM Malabari, were rewarded by the enhancement of the age of Consent Act (1891) which forbade the marriage of girls below the age of 12.
- The Sharda Act (1930) further pushed up the marriage age and provided for penal action in marriages of boys below 18 and girls less than 14 years of age.
- In free India, the Child Marriage Restrain (Amendment) Act, 1978 raised the age of marriage for girls to 18 years and for boys to 21.

Beginning of Modern Education

- The first educational institutions supported by the Company's Government were the Calcutta Madrassa and Banaras Sanskrit College established in 1781 and 1791 respectively. The purpose of opening them was to study the Hindu and Muslim law and litersature.
- Later, the Fort William College was set up by **Wellesley** in 1800, for the training of civil servants of the company in languages and customs of Indians. The college published an English-Urdu dictionary, a grammar of Hindi and some other books.
- However, the court of directors ordered the closure of the college in 1802.
- These early attempts for the education of people in oriental languages met with little success.
- Later, the **Christian Missionaries** made an attempt to revive the system of education and advocated the teaching of western literature and Christian religion through the medium of English.
- The **Serampore Missionaries,** in particular, were very enthusiastic for the spread of education on these lines. In this context, a few new types of schools giving instructions in English language and other branches of western learning were opened in the Madras region and then in Bengal and Bombay.
- These were mostly run by Christian Missionaries, who thought that modern education would destroy the faith of Indians in their own religion and they would take to Christianity.
- The first concrete step towards the educational development of India by the British rulers was taken after the **Charter Act of 1813**. This Act sanctioned one lakh of rupees for the purpose of education in India. It, however, took the company another twenty years to have an educational policy for India.

- The British administrators as well as some Indians debated over the type of educational in India. There were two groups, one favouring the traditional learning (Orientalists) and other western learnings (Anglicists). Some Indians such as Ram Mohan Roy advocated western learnings India could make progress.
- In 1835, the government decided in favour of the promotion of European literature and sciences among the natives of India. Following this decision, English was made the medium of instructions in the few school and colleges that were opended by the government. Later, the government's declaration in 1844 that English knowing Indians would be given preference in government jobs made English education popular.

Limitations

- However, the **Resources** allocated to education were extremely meagre, which shows the British rulers, lack of interest in the education of Indian people.
- The New educational system was also criticized on the grounds that it was meant only to produce clerks for the British administration. The education of masses was neglected.
- With the decline of the old system and the neglect of elementary education by the British, about 90 per cent on the Indian population remained illiterate. The stress on English also tended to create a gulf between the English knowing educated Indians and the rest of Indian population. The British rulers also thought the English educated Indians would be the supporters of the British rule.

Positive Impacts

- In spite of its serious limitations, English education had some **Positive features.** It brought Indians, though in very small numbers, into contact with modern knowledge as well as with modern ideas of liberty, equality, democracy and nationalism.
- They became aware of the developments in other parts of the world. They began to think of ways and means to modernize India. Some of them became pioneers of movements for social reforms and, later, of nationalism in India.
- Thus, the expectations of the British rulers that the English educated India's would be supporters of British rule were belied.

Various Social Legislations Under British Rule

- **1795:** Abolition of infanticide by British Regulation.
- **1820:** Abolition of infanticide by Lord Wellesley.
- **1811:** Abolition of Slavery (Under regulation) by Bengal Government.
- **1829:** Abolition of *Sati* by Lord William Bentinck (Under regulation of XVII). Pioneering efforts in this direction were made by Rajaram Mohan Roy.
- **1831–37:** Abolition of *Thugi* by William Bentinck, operation by William Sleeman.
- **1832:** Abolition of slavery (under Regulation of III.)
- **1843:** Abolition of slavery by Lord Ellenborough.

- 1844–48: Lord Hardinge suppressed the practice of making Human Sacrifice that had prevailed among the tribes of Gonds.
- **1856:** Approval of widow remarriage by Hindu widows' remmrriage Act by the efforts of Ishwar Chandra Vidyasagar.
- **1872:** Banning of the child marriage by Native Marriage Act.
- **1891:** Age of marriage for girls was increased to 12 years by age of Consent Act, by the efforts of B. Malabari.
- **1929:** The age of marriage was increased to 18 years in the case of Boys and 14 years in the case of Girls by the Child Marriage Restrain Act, commonly known as Sharda Act.
- **1931:** Banning of child marriage by Infant Marriage Prevention Act.
- **1937:** Right to property given to women.

Chapter at a Glance

- 43rd section of the Charter Act of 1813 spoke of "Revival and improvement of literature (Sanskrit and Arabic literature) and encouragement of learned natives in India."
- The christian missionaries adopted 'service to humanity' as the most attractive way of approaching the people.
- The number of non christian students raised in missionary schools since the time of William Bentick who changed the policy of Cornwallis of excluding Indians from Government services.
- Duff and Alexander Duff were two noted educationists, of the mission.
- Calcutta Female Juvenile School and Serampore Female Society made noted contributions for promotion education among women.
- Ram Mohan Roy helped David Home and Alexander Duff to open colleges.
- The printing press was first brought to India by a portugure jesuits in the 16th century for printing propaganda literature on Roman catholicism in portuguese language.
- By the efforts of Dr. Carry the Agricultural and Horticultural Society of India was formed under government patronage.
- Raja Ram Mohan Roy's Mother name was Tarini Devi, but she was popularly known as Phool Thakurani.
- Ram Mohan Roy is regarded as the Father of Modern Indian Renaissance.
- Prarthana Samaj (Prayer Society) was founded in 1867 in Maharashtra. Its chief architect was M.G. Ranade. Other prominent leaders were Dr. Atma Ram Pandurang and R.G. Bhandarkar.
- Mahadev Govind Ranade is popularly known as "The Prophet of Cultural Renaissance in Western India".
- The turning point in Ram Mohan Roy's life was the performance of Sati by his elder brother's wife in 1811.
- Tattva Bhoomi sabha was founded by Devendra Nath Tagore in 1838.
- Devendra Nath Tagore was the secretary of the British Indian Association which was founded in 1851.
- A fortnightly Journal 'Indian Mirror' was started by Keshav Chandra Sena in 1861.
- The main cause of Schism in Brahmo Samaj was the early marriage of the daughter of Keshav Chandra Sena to the Maharaja of Cooch Bihar.

- The first Arya Samaj was established on 10 April, 1875 at Bombay.
- Shyamji Verma the great nationalist was a pupil and friend of Swami Dayanand.

Previous Year Question Paper (1998-2017)

1. Consider the following statements:
   1. 'Bijaks is a composition of the teachings of Saint Dadu Dayal.
   2. The Philosophy of Pushti Marg was propounded by Madhvacharya.

   Which of the statements given above is/are correct? **(2014)**
   (a) 1 only (b) 2 only
   (c) Both 1 and 2 (d) Neither 1 nor 2
2. Which one of the following pairs does not form part of the six system of Indian Philosophy?
   (a) Mimamsa and Vedanta
   (b) Nyaya and Vaisheshika
   (c) Lokayata and Kapalika
   (d) Sankhya and Yoga **(2014)**
3. Annie Besant was: **(2013)**
   1. Responsible for starting the Home Rule Movement
   2. The founder of the Theosophical Society
   3. Once the President of the Indian National Congress

   Select the correct statement/statements using the codes given below:
   (a) 1 only (b) 2 and 3 only
   (c) 1 and 3 only (d) 1, 2 and 3
4. Which of the following statements is/are correct regarding Brahmo Samaj?
   1. It opposed idolatry.
   2. It denied the need for a priestly class for interpreting the religious texts.
   3. It popularised the doctrine that the Vedas are infallible

   Select the correct answer using the codes given below: **(2012)**
   (a) 1 only (b) 1 and 2 only
   (c) 3 only (d) 1, 2, and 3
5. In collaboration with David Hare and Alexander Duff, who of the following established Hindu College at Calcutta?
   (a) Henry Louis Vivian Derozio
   (b) Ishwar Chandra Vidyasagar
   (c) Keshab Chandra Sen
   (d) Rajaram Mohan Roy **(2015)**
6. Who among the following started the newspaper Shome Prakash?
   (a) Dayanand Saraswati
   (b) Ishwar Chandra Vidyasagar
   (c) Rajaram Mohan Roy
   (d) Surendranath Banerjee **(2007)**
7. Who among the following wrote the book Bahubivah?
   (a) Rajaram Mohan Roy
   (b) Ishwar Chandra Vidyasagar
   (c) Pandita Rambai
   (d) Rabindranath Tagore **(2007)**
8. "Lectures from Colombo to Almora" is based on the experiences of which one of the following?
   (a) Veer Savarkar
   (b) Annie Besant
   (c) Ramkrishna Paramhansa
   (d) Swami Vivekanand **(2006)**
9. Consider the following statements:
   1. Ishwar Chandra Vidyasagar founded the Bethune School at Calcutta with the main aim of encouraging education for women.
   2. Bankim Chandra Chattopadhyay was the first graduate of the Calcutta University.

3. Keshav Chandra Sen's campaign against *Sati* led to the enactment of a law to ban *Sati* by the then Governor General.

Which of the statements given above is/are correct? **(2001)**

(a) 1 only (b) 1 and 2
(c) 2 and 3 (d) 1, 2 and 3

10. Consider the following statement: **(2001)**
   1. Arya Samaj was founded in 1835.
   2. Lala Lajpat Rai opposed the appeal of Arya Samaj to the authority of Vedas in support of its social reform programmes.
   3. Under Keshab Chandra Sen, the Brahmo Samaj campaigned for women's education.
   4. Vinoba Bhave founded the Sarvodaya Samaj to work among refugees.

   Which of these statements are correct?

   (a) 1 and 2 (b) 2 and 3
   (c) 2 and 4 (d) 3 and 4

Answers

1. (d)	2. (c)	3. ()
4. (b)	5. (d)	6. (b)
7. (b)	8. (d)	9. (b)
10. (d)		

Practice Paper

1. The Mohammedan Anglo-Oriental College of Aligarh was founded by:
   (a) Md. Ali Jinnah
   (b) Mohammad Ali
   (c) Shukat Ali
   (d) Sir Syed Ahmed Khan
   (SSC Sec.Off.(Aud.) 2006; WB PSC (P) 2007)

2. The Arya Samaj was founded by
   (a) Swami Dayananda Saraswati
   (b) Swami Vivekanand
   (c) Keshav Chandra Sen
   (d) Ishwar Chandra Vidyasagar
   (SSC Sec.Off.(Aud.) 2007)

3. Which of the following reform movements was the first to be started in the 19th century?
   (a) Prarthana Samaj
   (b) Vragni Samaj
   (c) Arya Samaj
   (d) Ram Krishna Mission
   (SSC Sec.Off.(Aud.) 2007)

4. Who was the founder of Aligarh Movement?
   (a) Sir Agha Khan
   (b) Maulana Altaf Hussain Hali
   (c) Maulana Shibli Nomani
   (d) Sir Syed Ahmed Khan
   (SSC Mat. 2008; NDA 2000)

5. When was the All India Women's Conference founded?
   (a) 1924 (b) 1925
   (c) 1926 (d) 1927
   (SSC Sec.Off.(Aud.) 2008)

6. Which religious reformer of Western India was known as 'Lokhitwadi'?
   (a) Gopal Hari Deshmukh
   (b) R.G.. Bhandarkar
   (c) Mahadev Govind Ranade
   (d) B.G. Tilak
   (NDA 2003; SSC Tax Assit. 2009; CPF Assit. 2008)

7. Match List-I with List-II and select the correct answer using the codes given below the lists

List-I (Institution)	List-II (Associated Person)
A. Atmiya Sabha	1. Ishwar Chandra Vidyasagar
B. Sanskrit College	2. Aurobindo Ghosh
C. National Council of Education	3. Rajaram Mohan Roy
D. Dayanand Anglo Vedic School	4. Lala Hardayal

Codes:	A	B	C	D
(a)	2	4	3	1
(b)	3	1	2	4
(c)	2	1	3	4
(d)	3	4	2	1

(SCRA 2005)

8. Who founded the Bethune College in Calcutta?
   (a) Ishwar Chandra Vidyasagar
   (b) Rajaram Mohan Roy
   (c) Rabindranath Tagore
   (d) Surendranath Banerji

   (UGC NET/JRF (Hist.) 2007)

9. The original name of Swami Dayanand Saraswati was
   (a) Mula Shankar (b) Abhi Shankar
   (c) Gauri Shankar (d) Daya Shankar

   (CPO SI 2003)

10. The 19th century reawakening in India was confined to the
    (a) Priestly class
    (b) Upper middle class
    (c) Rich peasantry
    (d) urban landlords **(CPO SI 2003)**

11. Consider the following statements related to Raja Ram Mohan Roy:
    1. He advocated widow remarriage.
    2. He strongly advocated for the abolition of Sati system.
    3. He advocated for the promotion of English Education

    (a) Only 1 (b) 1 and 2
    (c) 2 and 3 (d) 1, 2 and 3

    (CPO 2003)

12. Match List-I with List-II and select the correct answer using the codes given below the Lists

List-I (Society)	List-II (Founder)
A. Theosophical Society	1. Dadabhai Naoroji
B. London Indian Society	2. Lala Lajpat Rai
C. Servants of India Society	3. Annie Besant
D. Servants of People Society	4. Gopal Krishna Gokhle

Codes:	A	B	C	D
(a)	1	3	4	2
(b)	3	1	2	4
(c)	3	1	4	2
(d)	1	3	2	4

(NDA 2002)

13. Who samong the following set up the Atmiya Sabha in Calcutta in the first half of the nineteenth century?
    (a) Radhakant Dev
    (b) Ram Mohan Roy
    (c) Ishwar Chandra Vidyasagar
    (d) Debendranath Tagore

    (NDA 2002; WB PCS 2004)

14. During the colonial period of India, Asiatic Society of Bengal was founded–
    (a) For carrying on researches into the past history and antiquities of India
    (b) To examine the policy of colonial discrimination against the Indians

(c) For developing English education in India
(d) For carrying out social reforms

(NDA 2003)

15. Who founded the Brahmo Samaj?
(a) Debendranath Tagore
(b) Keshavchandra Sen
(c) Raja Ram Mohan Roy
(d) Ishwar Chandra Vidyasagar

(NDA 2004; MP PSC (P) 2004; Utt. PSC (P) 2005; Utt. PCS (M) 2007)

16. Select the correct chronological sequence of the formation of the given organisations-
(a) Brahma Sabha-Arya Samaj-Madras Mahajan Sabha
(b) Brahma Sabha-Madras Mahajan Sabha-Arya Samaj
(c) Madras Mahajan Sabha-Brahma Sabha-Arya Samaj
(d) Madras Mahajan Sabha-Arya Samaj-Brahma Sabha **(NDA 2004)**

17. Who among the following was the founder of the Servants of India Society?
(a) Bal Gangadhar Tilak
(b) Dadabhai Naroji
(c) Gopal Krishna Gokhle
(d) Lala Lajpat Rai **(NDA 2005)**

18. Who founded the Fort William College at Calcutta?
(a) Lord Cornwallis
(b) Lord Ellenborough
(c) Lord Macalay
(d) Lord Wellesely **(NDA 2006)**

19. Sati was declared illegal and punishable by the Regulation XVII during the Governor Generalship of
(a) Lord William Bentick
(b) Lord Canning
(c) Lord Ripon
(d) Lord Dalhousie **(NDA 2009)**

20. Match List-I with List-II and select the correct answer using the codes given below the Lists

List-I (Movement)	List-II (Personality)
A. Satya Shodhaka	1. Bal Shastri Javekar Mandal
B. Manav Dharma Sabha	2. Jyotiba Phule
C. Darpan	3. Henry Vivian Derozio
D. Young Bengal Movement	4. Mehtaji Durgaram Mancharam

Codes:	A	B	C	D
(a)	1	2	3	4
(b)	2	4	1	3
(c)	4	2	1	3
(d)	2	1	3	4

(CDS 2000)

21. Match List-I with List-II and select the correct answer using the codes given below the Lists

List-I (Year)	List-II (Event)
A. 1764	1. Wood's Despatch
B. 1829	2. Widow Remarriage Act
C. 1854	3. Abolition of Sati
D. 1856	4. Battle of Buxar
	5. Assumption of Diwani

Codes:	A	B	C	D
(a)	4	1	2	5
(b)	5	4	1	2
(c)	4	3	1	2
(d)	1	3	2	5

(CDS 2001)

22. Who among the following founded the Theosophical Society in India in 1879?
    (a) Madam Blavatsky and H.S. Olcott
    (b) Madam Blavatsky and Annie Besant
    (c) H. S. Olcott and Annie Besant
    (d) A.O. Hume and Annie Besant
    (CDS 2003, 2006)
23. **Assertion (A):** The Vernacular Press Act was repealed in 1882 by Lord Ripon.
    Reason (R): The act did not discriminate between English Press and the Vernacular Press.
    (a) Both A and R are true and R is the correct explanation of A
    (b) Both A and R are true but R is not a correct explanation of A
    (c) A is true but R is false
    (d) A is false but R is true **(CDS 2005)**
24. During the period of the Indian freedom struggle, who among the following started the Central Hindu School?
    (a) Annie Besant
    (b) Bhikaji Cama
    (c) M. G. Ranade
    (d) Madan Mohan Malviya
    (CDS 2006)
25. Among the following, who cooperated with Raja Ram Mohan Roy in the implementation of his educational programmes?
    (a) Dwarkanath Tagore
    (b) David Hare
    (c) Henri Vivian Derozio
    (d) William Jones **(CDS 2008)**
26. After the death of Rajaram Mohan Roy, the Brahmo Samaj split into two sections; the Brahmo Samaj of India and the Adi Brahmo Samaj. Who were the leaders of the two sections respectively?
    (a) Keshab Chandra Sen and Debendranath Tagore
    (b) Radhakant Deb and Debendranath Tagore
    (c) Keshab Chandra Sen and Radhakant Deb
    (d) Debendranath Tagore and Radhakant Deb **(CDS 2006)**
27. Kuka Movement was organised by
    (a) Guru Ram Das
    (b) Guru Nanak
    (c) Guru Ram Singh
    (d) Guru Gobind Singh
    (45th BPSC 2002)
28. Who was Shardamani?
    (a) Wife of Raja Rammohan Roy
    (b) Wife of Ramakrishna Paramahansa
    (c) Mother of Vivekanand
    (d) Daughter of Keshab Chandra Sen
    (47th BPSC 2005)
29. Rajaram Mohan Roy established Brahmo Samaj in
    (a) 1816 AD. (b) 1820 AD.
    (c) 1828 AD. (d) 1830 AD.
    (47 BPSC 2005)
30. 'Satyartha Prakash' was written by
    (a) Raja Ram Mohan Roy
    (b) Mahatma Gandhi
    (c) Swami Vivekananda
    (d) Swami Dyanand Saraswati
    (47th BPSC 2005)
31. Who was the founder of the Radha Swami Satsang?
    (a) Haridas Swami
    (b) Siva Dayal Saheb
    (c) Siva Narayan Agnihotri
    (d) Swami Sraddhananda
    (UP PCS (P)2002)
32. Who among the following was the founder of Dev Samaj?
    (a) Vallabhbhai Patel
    (b) Dadabhai Naoroji
    (c) Siva Narayan Agnihotri
    (d) Ram Krishna Paramahansa
    (UP PCS (P) 2002)

33. Who was the founder of Ram Krishna Mission?
 (a) Swami Vivekananda
 (b) Rajaram Mohan Roy
 (c) Swami Dayanand Saraswati
 (d) Ram Krishna Paramahansa

(UP PCS (M) 2004)

34. The leading light of the renaissance movement in India was:
 (a) DebendranathTagore
 (b) Keshav Chandra Sen
 (c) Ishwar Chandra Vidyasagar
 (d) Ram Mohan Roy

(UP PCS (M) 2005)

35. Who one of the following had vigorously advocated for religious education in the Indian Universities?
 (a) Bal Gangadhar Tilak
 (b) Swami Vivekanand
 (c) Mahatma Gandhi
 (d) Madan Mohan Malviya

(UP PCS (M) 2005)

36. Who among the following is known as 'Martin Luthar of India'?
 (a) Swami Dayanand Saraswati
 (b) Rajaram Mohan Roy
 (c) Swami Vivekanand
 (d) Swami Sraddhanand

(UP PCS (M) 2005)

37. Where was first Madarasa set up by the British in India?
 (a) Madras (b) Bombay
 (c) Aligarh (d) Calcutta

(UP PCS (M) 2006)

38. Lord Macaulay is associated with
 (a) Reforms in Army
 (b) Abolitionof Sati System
 (c) English Education
 (d) Permanent Settlement

(UP PCS (P) 2007)

39. Which Governor General had abolished slavery?
 (a) Sir John Shore
 (b) Lord William Bentick
 (c) Lord Ellenhborough
 (d) Lord Cornwallis

(UP PCS Special (P) 2008)

40. Who of the following said 'Good Government is no substitute for self-Government'?
 (a) Lokmanya Tilak
 (b) Swami Vivekanand
 (c) Swami Dayanand
 (d) Rabindra Nath Tagore

(Utt. PCS (P) 2005)

41. Who among the following pioneered the social and religious movement of the 19th Centuryin India?
 (a) Rajaram Mohan Roy
 (b) Dayanand Saraswati
 (c) Vivekanand
 (d) Aurobindo Ghosh

(Utt. PCS (M) 2007)

42. From which area the social and religious reform movements started?
 (a) Bihar (b) Bengal
 (c) Orissa (d) Madras

(Utt. PCS (M) 2007)

43. In which year did Swami Vivekanand participate the World Parliament of Religous at Chicago?
 (a) 1893 (b) 1895
 (c) 1897 (d) 1899

(Utt. PCS (M) 2007; RAS/RTS 2007; UP PCS Special (P) 2008)

44. The Scientific Society was founded by
 (a) Wilton Company
 (b) Lord Cornwallis
 (c) Sir Syed Ahmed Khan
 (d) None of these

45. Who among the following Mughal Kings had sent Raja Ram Mohan Roy as his envoy to London?

(a) Alamgir II (b) Shah Alam II
(c) Akbar II (d) Bahadur Shah II
(MP PCS (P) 2009)

46. Read the following statements carefully
   1. Brahmo Samaj supported Mono-theism
   2. Arya Samaj contributed for the development of education.
   3. Swami Vivekanand founded Ram Krishna Mission.

   Answers on the basis of following codes
   (a) 1, 2 and 3 are true
   (b) 1 and 2 are true
   (c) 1and 3 are true
   (d) 2 and 3 are true **(C PSC (P) 2008)**

47. Which was common among Brahmo Samaj, Ram Krishna Mission and Arya Samaj?
   (a) None of these three had a political mission, but they helped to develop a spirit of patriotism.
   (b) All the three originated from Bengal.
   (c) Founders of all the three were educated in England.
   (d) Founders of all the three took active part in politics **(RAS/RTS 2008)**

48. Who was the founder of Prarthana Samaj?
   (a) Rajaram Mohan Roy
   (b) Debendranath Tagore
   (c) Atmarab Pandurag
   (d) Dayanand Saraswati
   (WB PSC 2004; CDS 2006)

49. When did the Akali Movement start?
   (a) 1901 (b) 1911
   (c) 1921 (d) 1931
   (WB PCS (P) 2007)

50. Who was the inspirator behind the Young Bengal Movement?
   (a) Madhusudan Dutt
   (b) Henry Vivian Derozio
   (c) Krishna Mohan Banerjee
   (d) Ram Gopal Ghosh
   (WB PCS (P) 2007)

51. Who is known as the 'Father of Modern India'?
   (a) Ram Mohan Roy
   (b) Jawahar Lal Nehru
   (c) Mahatma Gandhi
   (d) W. C. Bannerjee **(WB PCS (P) 2008)**

52. The Academic Association was founded by
   (a) Ram Mohan Roy
   (b) Henry Vivian Derozio
   (c) Ishwar Chandra Vidyasagar
   (d) Ishwar Chandra Gupta
   (WB PCS (P) 2008)

53. Who initiated regeneration of Indian Muslims in the 19th Century?
   (a) Syed Ahmed Khan
   (b) Nawab Salimullah
   (c) Badshah Khan
   (d) Abul Kalam Azad
   (WB PCS (P) 2008)

54. Who was Titu Mir?
   (a) Leader of Wahhabi Movement
   (b) Leader of Fairazi Movement
   (c) Leader of Sepoy Mutiny
   (d) Leader of the Indigo Revolt
   (WB PCS (P) 2008)

55. Who among the following was a proponent of Fabianism as a movement?
   (a) Annie Besant
   (b) A.O. Hume
   (c) Michael Madhusudan Dutt
   (d) R. Palme Dutt **(UPCS 2005)**

56. Consider the following statements:
   1. Ishwar Chandra Vidyasagar founded the Bethune School at Calcutta with the main aim of encouraging education for women.
   2. Bankim Chandra Chattopadhyaya was the first graduate of the Calcutta University.

3. Keshab Chandra Sen's compaign against Sati led to the enactment of a law to ban *Sati* by the then Governor General.

Which of the statement given above is/are correct?

(a) 1 only (b) 1 and 2
(c) 2 and 3 (d) 1, 2 and 3

(UPSC 2005)

57. Who among the following, started the newspapwer Shome Prakash?
(a) Dayanand Saraswati
(b) Ishwar Chandra Vidyasagar
(c) Raja Ram Mohan Roy
(d) Surendranath Banerjee

(UPSC 2007)

58. Who, among the following, wrote the book 'Bahuvivah'?
(a) Rajaram Mohan Roy
(b) Pandita Ramabai
(c) Ishwar Chandra Vidyasagar
(d) Rabindranath Tagore **(UPSC 2007)**

59. In collaboration with David Hare and Alexander Dutt, who of the following established Hindu College at Calcutta?
(a) Henry Louis Vivian Derozio
(b) Ishwar Chandra Vidyasagar
(c) Keshav Chandra sen
(d) Rajaram Mohan Roy **(UPPCS 2009)**

60. During Indian freedom struggle, the National Social Conference was formed. What was the reason for its formation?
(a) Different social reform groups or organizations of Bengal region united to form a single body to discuss the issues of larger interest and to prepare appropriate petitions/representations to the government
(b) Indian National Congress did not want to include social reforms in its deliberations and decided to form a separate body for such a purpose
(c) B. Malabari and M.G. Ranade decided to bring together all the social reform groups of the country under one organization
(d) None of the statements 'a', 'b' and 'c' given above is correct in this context **(UPPCS 2012)**

61. Which of the following statements is/are correct regarding Brahmo Samaj?
   1. It opposed idolatry.
   2. It denied the need for a priestly class for interpreting the religious texts.
   3. It popularized the doctrine that Vedas are infalliable.

Select the correct answer using that Vedas are infalliable.

(a) 1 only (b) 1 and 2 only
(c) 3 only (d) 1, 2 and 3

(UPSC 2012)

Answers

1. (d)	2. (a)	3. (b)	16. (a)	17. (c)	18. (d)
4. (d)	5. (d)	6. (a)	19. (a)	20. (b)	21. (c)
7. (b)	8. (a)	9. (a)	22. (a)	23. (c)	24. (a)
10. (b)	11. (d)	12. (c)	25. (b)	26. (a)	27. (c)
13. (b)	14. (a)	15. (c)	28. (b)	29. (c)	30. (d)

31. (b) 32. (c) 33. (a)
34. (d) 35. (b) 36. (a)
37. (d) 38. (c) 39. (c)
40. (c) 41. (a) 42. (b)
43. (a) 44. (c) 45. (c)
46. (a) 47. (a) 48. (c)
49. (c) 50. (b) 51. (a)
52. (b) 53. (a) 54. (b)
55. (a) 56. (b) 57. (b)
58. (c) 59. (d) 60. (b)
61. (b)

CHAPTER 9

Development of Modern Education and Press

Modern Education

The British stressed upon educating Indian on Western lines to get cheaper clerks and spreading western culture. But Western education proved very useful for Indians. Through it, Indians studied the literature of Rouseau, Paine, Mill, Burke, Spencer etc. and they adopted modern, rational, secular, democratic and national political view point. Dr. Bipin Chandra hold the opinion, "Western education did not give birth to National Movement but it was the result of the clash of British and Indian interests. Western education system helped the Indians to acquire thought, so that they might give a lead to National Movement and give it a democratic and modernised direction."

The so called modern system of education came into being, rather late, by replacing the traditional system of education. The process started by the Charater Act of 1813. In between 1600 and 1813, the mode of education was traditional with indigenous means and ideology.

1791 : Warren Hastings set up the Calcutta Madrasa for the learning of Arabic and Persian.

1791 : Jonathan Duncan opened a Sanskrit college at Benaras for the learning of literature, law and religion of the Hindus.

1800 : Fort William College was set up by Lord Wellesely for training civil servants in vernacular languages and customs of India.

Sir Charles Wood Despatch (1854)

- His scheme became the Magna Carta of English education in India.
- The universities of Calcutta, Madras and Bombay were set up in 1857.
- It was Bethune's contribution, which helped a setting up of a number of girls schools.

The Hunter Education Commission (1882-83)

- Its main recommendations were basically for Secondary Education.

- Secondary Education should be in two sectors-literary Education leading to the university entrance examination and commercial and vocational training.

The Raleigh Commission (1902)

- The only Indian member of the commission Gurudas Banerji appointed by Lord Curzon, strongly disagreed with its recommendations, which were adopted in the Indian Universities Act of 1904.

The Indian Universities Act (1904)

- It was enacted to ensure greater government controls over the Universities.
- It transferred the power of ultimate decision in matters of college affiliation and schools recognition to government officials and sought to fix minimum college fees.

Sadler Commission (1917-19)

The two Indian members were Sir Ashutosh Mukherji and Dr. Ziauddin Ahmed. It was mainly for higher education.

- It recommended a twelve year course of Matriculation, then intermediate followed by University.
- University course was limited to three years and divided into Pass Course and Honours.
- Each University should be a Centralized system.
- A Board of women's education was also suggested.

The Hartog Committee 1929

- Financial difficulties due to world economic depression.
- Ideological conflicts, one school of thought advocated quality while the other school advocated rapid expansion of education.
- A determined and planned attempt to eradicate mass illiteracy.

Recommendations

- Condemmed the policy of hasty expansion of education.
- Emphasised on the importance of primary education for the development of nation.
- It recommended a selective system of admission for higher education.
- Emphasis on diversified courses after matriculation, leading to industrial and commercial careers.
- To improve quality rather than to expand the education.

Wardha Scheme

- Wardha scheme of Basic Education (1937), worked out by the Zakir Hussain Committee after Mahatma Gandhi published a series of articles in the Harijan.
- It centred around 'manual productive work' which would cover the remuneration of teachers.
- There was to be a seven year course through the mother tongue of the students. It was to be centred around crafts.

Sargeant Plan of Education (1944)

It envisaged:

- The establishment of elementary schools and high schools
- Universal and compulsory education for all children between the age of six and eleven
- A school course of six years was to be provided for children between age eleven and seventeen.

Radhakrishnan Commission, 1948

The Commission was appointed to report on university education in the country and to suggest improvements.

Recommendations

- Recommended higher salaries and better service conditions.
- Pre-university should be of 12 years duration.
- No college should admit more than 1000 students.
- Working days should not be less than 180 (Exclusive of examination days.)
- Working days should be divided in three terms each of 11 week's duration.

University Grants Commission, 1953

In 1956, the Parliament passed the University Grants Commission Act.

Duties

- To take all steps fit for the promotion and coordination of University education.
- To take steps for the determination and maintenance of standards of techning, research, examination in the universities.
- To ascertain the financial needs of the university.
- Right of inspection of any Department of the University.
- Powers to withhold its grants if and University does not comply with the recommendation of the Commission.

Kothari Commission, 1964

The Commission was appointed in July 1964, by the Government under the chairmanship of Dr. D.S. Kothari to "advise Government on the national pattern of education and on the General principles and policies for the development of educations at all stages and in all aspects".

Recommendations

- Tuition fee at the primary stage should be abolished.
- Attention to the education of women, children, handicapped backward class.
- Introduction of work experience.
- Stress on moral and spiritual values.
- Stress on achieving social and national integration.
- Vocationalisation of secondary education.
- Development of quality of teachers.
- Increasing and strengthening the centres of advanced study.

Development of Press in British India

Introduction

- This first attempts of publish newspaper in India were made by the disgruntled employees of the East India Company who sought to expose the malpractices of private trade.
- **William Bolts,** an ex-employee of the British East India Company attempted to start the first newspaper in India in 1776.
- The first newspaper in India entitled **Hickey's Bengal Gazette** or **The Calcutta General Advertiser** was started by James Augustus Hickey (an employee of the EIC) in 1780.
- After a bitter attack on the Governor-General and the Chief Justice, its circulation was halted by government.

- Hickey protested against this arbitrary harassment without avail, and was imprisoned. He was sentenced to one year in prison and fined Rs. 5000, which finally drove him to penury. Hickey's press was seized in 1782.
- During the first half of 19th century, several newspapers were in operation in the country. Many of these like **Bangadoot** of Ram Mohan Roy, **Rastgoftar** of Dadabhai Naoroji etc advocated social reforms and thus helped to arouse national awakening.
- In 1857, **Payam-e-Azadi** was started in Hindi to fight against the British. The paper was soon confiscated and anyone found with a copy of the paper was persecuted for sedition.
- Again, the first Hindi daily, **Samachar Sudhavarashan,** and two newspapers in Urdu and Persian respectively, **Doorbeen** and **Sultan-ul-Akhar**, faced trial in 1857, for having published a 'Fireman' by Bahadur Shah Zafar, urging the people to drive the British out of India.
- The history of press in India is coloured by the colonial experience. It begins with the coming of the Europeans. The Portuguese were the first European nation who brought a printing press to India.
- The first book published in India was by the Jesuits of Goa in 1557. In 1684, the EIC set up a printing press in Bombay. However, for about a century after this no newspaper was published in the country because the Company's servants in India wished to withhold the news of their malpractices and abuses of private trading; from reaching London.
- Thus, the newspaper history of India came to be inextricably tangled with its political history.
- This was followed by the notorious **Gagging Act** of Lord Canning, under which restrictions imposed on the newspaper and periodicals.

Press Laws and Regulation in British India

- The earliest regulatory measures can be traced back to 1788, when Lord Wellesley promulgated the **Press Regulations,** which had the effect of imposing pre-censorship on an infant newspaper published industry.
- The onset of 1835 saw the promulgation of the **Press Act**, which undid most of, the repressive features of earlier legislation on the subject.

Licensing Regulations, 1823

- Promulgated by Johan Adams (acting Governor-General) Press Regulation of 1823, proved more stringent than any that had been in force earlier.
- The new regulations required. The act was particularly aimed at India language newspaper or those edited by Indians.
  - Every Printer and publisher to obtain a license for starting a press or using it.
  - The penalty for printing and publishing any literature without the requisite license was Rs. 400 for each such publication or imprisonment in default thereof. Magistrates were authorized to attach unlicensed presses.
  - The Governor-General had the right to revoke a license or call for a fresh application.

- As the consequence of the Act, Raja Ram Mohan Roy's Mirat-ul-Akhbar had to stop publication.
- JS Buckingham (James Buckingham), the editor of the Calcutta journal was deported to England.
  - Lord William Bentinck adopted a liberal attitude towards the Press Although Adams' press regulations were not revoked; considerable freedom/relaxation was given to the press Indian as well as Anglo-Indian.
  - Charles Metcalfe, officiating Governor-General (1835-36), finally repealed the 1823 Regulation, with the Press Act of 1835, or Metcalfe Act. For his liberal press policy Metcalfe is often referred to as the "Liberator of Indian press" Lord Macaulay also supported the case for a free press in India.

Important Newspapers/Journals and their Founders

Newspaper/ Magazine	Founder/Editor
Bengal Gazette (India's first newspaper)	James Augustus Hickey
Dighadarshan	Marshmen
Calcutta Journal	J S Buckingham
Samvad-kaumadi	Ram Mohan Roy
Mirat-ul-Akhbar (First newspaper in Persian)	Ram Mohan Roy
Bangdoot	Ram Mohan Roy
Brahmanical Magazine	Ram Mohan Roy
Rast Goftar (first newspaper in Gujarati)	Dada

Chapter at a Glance

- Wood's despatch of 1854 is known as the Magna Carta of English education in India.
- The Punjab University was founded in 1882.
- The Allahabad University was set up in 1887.
- In 1906 the state of Baroda introduced compulsory primary education throughout its territories.
- From 1910 to 1913 G.K. Gohakle made tremendous efforts in the Legislative Council, urging the Government to bear the Responsibility for compulsory primary education.
- Dr. M.E. Sadler was the Vice chancellor of the university of Leads.
- Sadler commission included two Indians namely Dr. Zia-ud-din Ahmad and Sir Asutosh Mukherji.
- The Sadler Commission was of the opinion that the improvement of secondary education was a necessry condition for the improvement of university education.
- The committee under the leadership of Zakir Hussain prepared the syllabus of Wardha Scheme.
- Sir John Sargeant was the Educational Adviser to the Government of India.
- Sargeant Scheme of 1944 is popularly known as Sargeant Plan.

- The Sargeant Plan which was envisaged for 40 years was reduced to 6 years by the Kher committee.
- Universities of Aligarh, Patna, Mysore, Banaras, Dacca, Lucknow and Osmania were established on the recommendation of Sadler Commission.
- Mr. J.F. Mc Dougall served as Associate Secretary of the Kothari Commission.
- Kothari Commission included distinguished educationists and scientists from U.S.A., U.K. and U.S.S.R.
- Kothari Commission is regarded as the first step towards an educational revolution in the country.
- The aim of New Education Policy (1986) is to transform static society into a developed society.
- University Grants Commission was constituted in 1953 on the recommendations of Radha-Krishnan Commission.
- In 1956, U.G.C. was given an autonomous status.
- In 1684, the first printing press of the company was set up in Bombay.
- "The Bengal Gazette' of Hickey was sacked up in 1782 for his outspoken criticism of Government officials and Governor General.
- The first newspaper was published during the Governor Generalship of Warren Hastings.
- Lord Hastings is also known as Earl of Moira.
- Rajaram Mohan Roy and Dwarka Nath Tagore professed against the recommendations of Munroe.
- Charles Metcalfe, the acting Governor General, is known as the 'Liberator of the Indian Press'.
- Act XI of 1835 was replaced by Act of XXV of 1867.
- Act XXVII of 1870 was passed which contained a sedition section.
- The Vernacular Press Act was introduced by Lord Lytton in 1878.
- The Yugantar, the Sandhya and the Bandematram stopped their publication on account of the stringent provisions of the Act of 1908.
- Under the Act of 1908 the Government confiscated seven presses and prosecuted nine newspapers.
- Under the Indian Press Act of 1910, action was taken against 991 printing presses and newspapers.
- A press committee was appointed in 1921 under the chairmanship of Sir Tej Bahadur Sapru (Law member of Governor General's executive) to review the working of the press laws. The press acts of 1908 and 1910 were repealed on the recommendation of this committee.
- Under the Press Act of 1931, the action was taken against Bombay Chronicals, Anand Bazar Patrika, the Liberty and the Free Press Journal.
- The Press laws inquiry committee was set up in 1948 under the chairmanship of Shri Ganganath Jha.
- The Press (objectionable matters) Act 1951 was more comprehensive than any earlier legislation effecting the press.
- The Press (objectionable matters) Act 1951 remained in force up to 1956.
- The chairman of the press commission appointed in 1952 were Justice G.S. Rajadhyaksha.
- The Bengali newspaper 'Somprakash' was founded in 1858 under the joint efforts of Ishwar Chand Vidyabhushan.

- Bengal was pioneer in the field of Indian Journalism. The first newspaper written in an Indian language was started in Bengal.
- Sadhavani edited by Akhay Kumar Sarkar was the most powerful organ of educated opinion in Bengal.
- The first Tamil newspaper was 'Swades Mitram' started in 1882 by G. Subramania Aiyar.
- Sir William Jones was a judge of Supreme court who came to India in 1783.
- Max Muellar the German scholar was known as 'Moksha Muellar' for his contribution in rediscoveing the Indian Glorious past.
- The Anand Math of Bankim Chandra has rightly been called as "The Bible of Modern Bengali Patriotism".
- Warren Hastings set up the Calcutta Madrasa in 1781 for the study of Arabic and Persian.
- The Asiatic Society of Bengal was founded by Sir William Jones in Calcutta in 1784.
- Jonathan Duncan, the resident at Banaras started the Sanskrit College in 1791.
- Lord Welleslley started the Fort William College in 1800 for the training of Civil Servants, which the court of Directors closed in 1802.
- The Charter Act of 1813, was the first to provide an annual expenditure of one lakh rupees "for the revival and promotion of literature."
- David Hare and Rajaram Mohan Roy were instrumental in setting up the Calcutta Hindu College in 1817. Which later developed into the Presidency College. Lord William Bentick, in the Resolution of 7th March 1835, accepted Macualays viewpoint which led to the promotion of European science and literature.

Previous Year Question Paper (1998-2017)

1. Match List-I with List-II and select the correct answer using the codes given below the Lists

List-I (Author)	List-II (Book)
A. Abul Fazl	1. Tabqat - i - Akbari
B. Nizamuddin Ahmed	2. Akbarnama
C. Krishnadeva Raya	3. Rajtarangini
D. Kalhana	4. Amuktamalyada

Codes:

	A	B	C	D
(a)	2	4	1	3
(b)	3	1	4	2
(c)	2	1	4	3
(d)	3	4	1	2

(IAS-2011)

2. Which one of the following pairs is **NOT** correctly matched?

(a)	Sheikh Shihabuddin Suhrawardi	Sufi Saint
(b)	Chaitanya Mahaprabhu	Bhakti Saint
(c)	Minhas-al-Siraj	Founder of Sufi Order
(d)	Lalleshwari	Bhakti Saint

(IAS-2012)

3. The meaning of word Bantai during medieval period was?

(a) Religion Tax
(b) System of calculating revenue
(c) Wealth Tax
(d) Property Tax

(48th - 52nd BPSC 2008)

4. Match List-I with List-II and select the correct answer using the codes given below:

List-I (Place)	List-II (Monument)
A. Elephanta	1. Stupa
B. Shravanbelgola	2. Temple
C. Khajuraho	3. Cave
D. Sanchi	4. Statue

Codes:

	A	B	C	D
(a)	2	4	3	1
(b)	3	4	2	1
(c)	2	4	1	3
(d)	3	2	4	1

(UP PCS(P) 2003)

5. Arrange the following in chronological order and find the correct answer with the help of the codes given below
   1. Ahalya Bai   2. Durgawati
   3. Padmini   4. Tarabai

Codes:
(a) 1 – 2 – 3 – 4   (b) 3 – 2 – 4 – 1
(c) 3 – 4 – 1 – 2   (d) 2 – 1 – 3 – 4

(UP PCS (P) 2003)

6. The poet king who wrote verses in praise of Krishna under the name of Nagari Das was:
(a) Raja Ummed Singh
(b) Raja Ram Singh
(c) Raja Chhatrasal
(d) Raja Savant Singh

(UP PCS (M) 2004)

7. Match the following

A. 1192   1. Third Battle of Panipat
B. 1707   2. Second Battle of Tarain
C. 1761   3. Death of Akbar
D. 1605   4. Death of Aurangzeb

Select the correct answer from the codes given below
Codes:

	A	B	C	D
(a)	1	2	3	4
(b)	4	3	2	1
(c)	2	4	1	3
(d)	2	4	3	1

(UP PCS (M) 2005)

8. Match List-I with List-II on the basis of codes

List-I (Dynasty)	List-II (Capital)
A. Pratihara	1. Tanjore
B. Chola	2. Anhilwada
C. Parmara	3. Dhara
D. Solanki	4. Kannauj

Codes:

	A	B	C	D
(a)	4	1	2	3
(b)	4	3	2	1
(c)	4	2	1	3
(d)	4	1	3	2

(CPSC (P) 2008)

9. The clan of Rajputs who ruled the princely state of Jaipur was
(a) Sisodiyas   (b) Kachhawahas
(c) Rathors   (d) Hadas

(RAS/RTS 2003)

10. In which school of painting Bani Thani was related?
(a) Bundi School
(b) Kishangarh School
(c) Chawand School
(d) Jaipur School

(RAS/RTS 2008)

11. Consider the following events:
    1. Reign of Krishnadeva Raya of Vijayanagar
    2. Consturction of Qutub Minar
    3. Arrival of Portuguese in India
    4. Death of Firoz Tughlaq

    The correct chronological sequence of these events is:
    (a) 2 – 4 – 3 – 1 (b) 2 – 4 – 1 – 3
    (c) 4 – 2 – 1 – 3 (d) 4 – 2 – 3 – 1

    (UPSC 2000)

12. Match List-I with List-II and select the correct answer using the codes given below the Lists

List-I	List-II
A. Iqta	1. Marathas
B. Jagir	2. Delhi Sultans
C. Amaram	3. Mughals
D. Mokasa	4. Vijaynagar

Codes:

	A	B	C	D
(a)	3	2	1	4
(b)	2	3	4	1
(c)	2	3	1	4
(d)	3	2	4	1

(UPSC 2000)

13. The intial design and construction of which massive temple took place during the reign of Suryavarman II?
    (a) Sri Mariamman Temple
    (b) Angkorvat Temple
    (c) Batu Cave Temple
    (d) Kamakhya Temple **(UPSC 2006)**

14. The Nagara, the Dravida and the Vesara are the
    (a) Three main racial groups of the Indian subcontinent
    (b) Three main linguistic divisions into which the languages of India can be classified
    (c) Three main styles of Indian temple architecture
    (d) Three main musical Gharanas prevalent in India **(UPSC 2012)**

15. Who was the author of 'Shahnama'?
    (a) Utbi (b) Firdausi
    (c) Alberuni (d) Barni

    (MPPSC (P) 2015)

Answers

1. (c)	2. (c)	3. (b)
4. (b)	5. (b)	6. (d)
7. (c)	8. (d)	9. (b)
10. (b)	11. (a)	12. (b)
13. (b)	14. (c)	15. (b)

Practice Paper

1. According to Dadabhai Naoroji Swaraj meant
   (a) Complete independence
   (b) Self government
   (c) Economic independence
   (d) Political independence
2. Which book was written by Dadabhai Naoroji on Indian poverty and economy under British rule?
   (a) Indian Economy under British Raj
   (b) British Rule and Economic Drain of India
   (c) Poverty and Un-British Rule in India
   (d) Economic Drain and Poverty of India
3. The partition of Bengal (1905) was annualled by the-

(a) Indian Councils Act
(b) Chelmsford-Montague Report' 1919
(c) Proclamation of Delhi Durbar in 1911
(d) Government of India Act, 1935

(UGC/RF/NET 2007)

4. Who of the following founded the East India Association?
(a) C.R. Das
(b) Dadabhai Naoroji
(c) Debendranath Tagore
(d) V.D. Savarkar

(CPF Assit. Commt. 2008)

5. Consider the following statements:
1. The Indian National Congress was founded during the viceroyalty of Lord Dufferin.
2. The first President of Indian National Congress was W. C. Banerji.
3. The first session of the Indian National Congress was held in Calcutta.
4. In the first session of the Indian National Congress some government officials were also present.

Which of the statements given above are correct?
(a) 1, 2 and 3 only (b) 1, 2 and 4 only
(c) 3 and 4 only (d) 1, 2, 3 and 4

(NDA 2006)

6. At which congress session did Dadabhai Naoroji announce that swaraj was the goal of India's political efforts?
(a) 1886 Calcutta session
(b) 1893 Lahore session
(c) 1905 Benaras session
(d) 1906 Calcutta session **(CDS 2003)**

7. The first session of the Indian National Congress was shifted from Poona to Bombay almost at the eleventh hour because
(a) The leaders of the Bombay Presidency Association were against holding the first meeting of the Congress at Poona.
(b) The Bombay Governor agreed to A.O. Hume's proposal to act as First President of the Congress.
(c) Bombay as the capital of the presidency would help the conference attract more attention if it was held there.
(d) An outbreak of the cholera in Poona forced the organizers of the Congress to shift its venue from poona to Bombay **(CDS 2004)**

8. With reference to Indian freedom struggle, who among the following was labelled as 'Moderate' leader in the Congress?
(a) Gopal Krishna Gokhle
(b) Bipin Chandra Pal
(c) Lala Lajpat Rai
(d) Aurobindo Ghosh **(CDS 2008)**

9. Who among the following was thrice elected president of the Indian National Congress?
(a) Gopal Krishna Gokhle
(b) Surendranath Banerji
(c) Gopal Krishna Gokhle
(d) Sankaran Nair **(CDS 2009)**

10. Consider the following statements and identify the person
During his stay in England, he endeavoured to educate the British people about their responsibilities as rulers of India. He delivered speeches and published articles to support his opposition to the unjust and oppressive regime of the British Raj. In 1867, he helped to establish the East India Association of which he became the Honorary Secretary.

(a) Feroz Shah Mehta
(b) Mary Carpenter
(c) Dadabhai Naoroji
(d) Anand Mohan Bose **(CDS 2010)**

11. Where was the first session of Indian National Congress held?
(a) Calcutta (b) Bombay
(c) Ahmedabad (d) Allahabad
(BPSC 2001, UPSC 2008)

12. Indian National Congress was founded by?
(a) Womesh Chandra Banerjee
(b) Michal Hume
(c) Allon Octavian Hume
(d) Mahatma Gandhi
(BPSC 2001, Indraprastha Univ.2007)

13. Who was the founder of the Indian Association?
(a) Dadabhai Naoroji
(b) Bal Gangadhar Tilak
(c) A.O. Hume
(d) Surendranath Banerjee
(BPSC 2002, WBPCS 2007, 2008)

14. The second session of Indian National Congress was presided over by
(a) Ganesh Agarkar
(b) Surendranath Banerjee
(c) Dadabhai Naoroji
(d) Feroz Shah Mehta **(BPSC 2002)**

15. The partition of Bengal came into effect on
(a) 15th August' 1905
(b) 15th September, 1905
(c) 15th October, 1905
(d) 15th November, 1905 **(BPSC 2002)**

16. Who among the following was **NOT** known as a moderate in the National movement?
(a) Bal Gangadhar Tilak
(b) Dadabhai Naoroji
(c) M.G. Ranade
(d) Gopal Krishna Gokhle **(BPSC 2002)**

17. Which of the following papers was essentially the mouthpiece of the policies of liberals
(a) New India
(b) Leader
(c) Free Press Journal
(d) Young India **(BPSC 2005)**

18. The method of moderate leaders of the Congress was?
(a) Non Co-operation
(b) Constitutional Legitations
(c) Passive Resistance
(d) Civil Disobedience **(BPSC 2008)**

19. The most important organisation of the pre-congress nationalist organisations was the
(a) Bengal British India Society
(b) East India Association
(c) Young Bengal Association
(d) Indian Association of Calcutta
(48th-52nd BPSC 2008)

20. The correct chronological order of following organisations is
1 Bombay Association
2 Madras Mahajan Sabha
3 Indian Association
4 Indian League
(a) 1–2–3–4
(b) 2–3–1–4
(c) 3–4–2–1
(d) 1–4–3–2 **(UPSC 2003)**

21. Who said, 'The Congress is tottering to its fall and one of my greatest ambition while in India is to assist it to a peaceful demise'?
(a) George Hamilton
(b) Lord Curzon
(c) Lord Dufferin
(d) Lord Minto **(UPSC 2002)**

22. Who of the following was the first Muslim President of Indian National Congess'?

(a) Badaruddin Tayabji
(b) Abdul Kalam Azad
(c) Rafi Ahmed Kidwai
(d) M.A. Ansari

(UPPCS 2002, UP Comb.2004, SSC 2008)

23. Who is the exponent of the theory of 'economic drain' of India during the British rule?
(a) Dadabhai Naoroji
(b) M.N. Roy
(c) Jai Prakash Narayan
(d) Ram Manohar Lohiya

(UPPCS 2004)

24. The first Indian to contest an election to the British House of Commons was?
(a) Dadabhai Naoroji
(b) Gopal Krishna Gokhle
(c) Feroz Shah Mehta
(d) W.C. Banerji

(UPPCS 2004, Utt. PSC 2005)

25. Given below a list of persons who became Presidents of Indian National Congress. Arrange them in chronological order. Select your answer using the codes given below the list?
1 Mahatma Gandhi
2 Jawaharlal Nehru
3 Vallabhbhai Patel
4 Smt. Sarojini Naidu

Codes:
(a) 1–2–3–4 (b) 1–3–4–2
(c) 1–4–2–3 (d) 4–3–1–2

(UPPCS 2004)

26. The President of Indian National Congress in 1885 was:
(a) George Yule
(b) Dadabhai Naoroji
(c) W.C. Banerji
(d) W. Wedderburn

(UPPCS 2004, WBPSC 2007)

27. Who, among the following, was **NOT** present in the founding session of Indian National Congress?
(a) Dadabhai Naoroji
(b) G. Subramaniya Lyer
(c) Justice Ranade
(d) Surendranath Bannerjee

(Utt. PCS 2007)

28. Who was the first Indian to become member of the British Parliament?
(a) Badaruddin Tyabji
(b) W.C. Bannerjee
(c) D.N. Wacha
(d) Dadabhai Naoroji

(UPtt. PCS 2007)

29. In which year the Indian National Congress was established?
(a) 1888 (b) 1887
(c) 1886 (d) 1885

(UPtt. PCS 2007)

30. Who was the Viceroy of India at the time of the formation of the Indian National Congress?
(a) Curzon (b) Canning
(c) Lawrence (d) Dufferin

(WBPSC 2008)

31. Who wanted Indian National Congress to be a 'Safety Valve'?
(a) A.O. Hume
(b) Lord Lytton
(c) W.C. Bannerjee
(d) Surendranth Bannerjee

(WBPSC 2008)

32. Who among the following was **NOT** a moderate?
(a) Bipin Chandra Pal
(b) Feroz Shah Mehta
(c) Surrendranath Bannerjee
(d) Gopal Krishna Gokhle

(WBPSC 2008)

33. When was the Indian Association founded ?
(a) 1876 (b) 1884
(c) 1887 (d) 1890

(WBPSC 2008)

34. Who was called 'Grand Old Man of India'?
(a) Dadabhai Naoroji
(b) Jamshedji Tata
(c) Surendranath Bannerjee
(d) C. Rajagopalachari **(WBPCS 2008)**

35. **Assertion (A)**: The basic weakness of the early nationalist movement lay in its narrow social base.
Reason (R): It fought for the narrow interests of the social group who joined it.
(a) Both A and R are true and R is the correct explanation of A.
(b) Both A and R are true but R is not a correct explanation of A.
(c) A is true but R is false.
(d) A is false but R is true.**(UPSC 2007)**

36. Consider the following statements about Madam Bhikaji Cama:
1. Madam Cama unferled the National Flag at the International Socialist Conference in Paris in the year of 1907.
2. Madam Cama served as private secretry to Dadabhai Naoroji.
3. Madam cama was born to Parsi.
Which of the statement (s) given above is/are correct
(a) 1, 2 and 3
(b) 2 and 3 only
(c) 1 and 2 only
(d) 3 only **(WBPSC 2008)**

37. Who among the following, rejected the title of 'Knight hood' and refused to accept a position in the council of the Secretary of State for India?
(a) Motilal Nehru
(b) M.G. Ranade
(c) G.K. Gokhle
(d) B.G. Tilak **(UPSC 2008)**

38. The first President of Indian National Congress was
(a) Dadabhai Naoroji
(b) A.O. Hume
(c) Womesh Chandra Banerjee
(d) Surendra Nath Banerjee
(UPPCS (M)2014)

39. 'Kings are made for public, Public is not made for the King.' Who among the following made this statement during the national movement?
(a) Surendra Nath Banerjee
(b) R.C. Pant
(c) Dadabhai Naoroji
(d) Gokhle **(UPSC 2008)**

40. The theme of Bankim Chandra Chatterjee's famous novel 'Anand Math' is based on
(a) Chunar revolt
(b) Rangpur and Dinajpur revolt
(c) Vishnupur and Veerbhumi revolt
(d) Sannyasi's revolt
(UPPCS (M)2014)

Answers

1. (b)	2. (c)	3. (c)	22. (a)	23. (a)	24. (a)
4. (b)	5. (b)	6. (d)	25. (c)	26. (c)	27. (d)
7. (d)	8. (a)	9. (a)	28. (d)	29. (d)	30. (d)
10. (c)	11. (b)	12. (c)	31. (a)	32. (a)	33. (a)
13. (d)	14. (c)	15. (c)	34. (a)	35. (a)	36. (b)
16. (a)	17. (b)	18. (b)	37. (c)	38. (c)	39. (c)
19. (d)	20. (c)	21. (b)	40. (d)		

CHAPTER

10

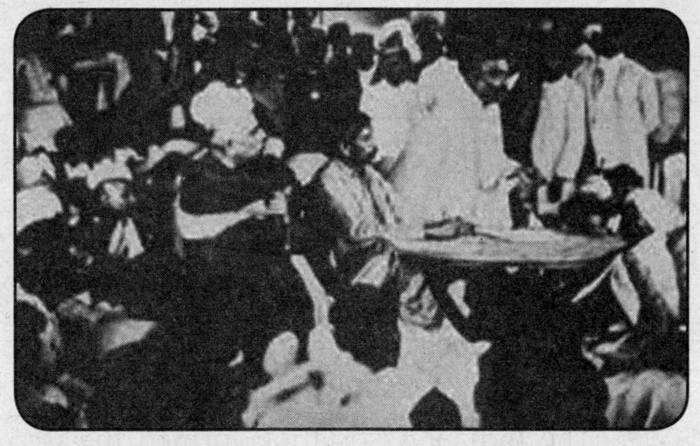

Pre-Congress Political Associations and Development of ICS

Political Associations in Bengal

1. **Bangabhasha Prakasika Sabha** (Associations of Raja Ram Mohan Roy, 1836)
   - It is said to be the first organized political association of India. It was mainly founded to safeguard the interests of the landlords.
   - The organization worked in cooperation with the **British Indian Society in London** and appointed a committee to supply it with regular information about Indian grievances and demands. **Dwarkanath Tagore** was responsible in founding Bengal British India Society in 1843.
2. **Landholders' Society** (Landholders of Calcutta, 1838) also known as **Zamindari Association**, was founded to safeguard the interest of landlords through constitutional agitation.
3. **British India Society** (Mr William Adams, 1839)
4. **British India Association** (George Thompson, 1851) was founded by merging Landholders Society and the Bengal British India Society. It sent a petition to the Parliament praying for expansion of legislature and giving it more popular character, separation of judicial from executive functions, reduction in the Salaries of higher officers, abolition of salt duty and stamp duties etc.
   - The Result was the provision of additional six members to the Governor General's council for legislature purposes by **Indian Council Act 1861**.
   - During the years following the Revolt of 1857, the British Indian Association was the most important political body in India and its organ, the **Hindu Patriot** was the most influential newspaper in the country.
5. **East India Association** (Dadabhai Naoroji, the Grand Old Man of India, 1866) the aim of the East India Association was popularization of Indian grievances so as to influence British public opinion.

6. **Indian Society** (Anand Mohan Bose, 1872)
7. **Indian League** (Sisir Kumar Ghose the founder Editor of 'Amrita Bazar Parika', 1875)
8. **Indian Association** (Anand Mohan Bose, SN Bannerjee, 1876)
   - The Indian Association formed the centre of an all India movement by providing the leadership for agitation on issues such as the age limit for the Indian Civil Services Examination, the **Illbert Bill Agitation.**
   - It is considered to be the most important Pre-Congress Political Organization. It was the only Pre-Congress Organization, which seriously tried to become all India body, and in this context it sponsored an **All Indian National Conference** in 1883 and 1885 at Calcutta.
9. **London Indian Society** (Badaruddin Tyabji, WC Bannerjee and Firoz Shah Mehta, 1865)

Political Associations in Deccan

1. **Bombay Association** (Jaganath Shakerseth, 1852).
2. **Deccan Association (1852)**
3. **Poona Sarvajanik Sabha** (MG Ranade and GV Joshi, 1870): In 1872, the members of the Poona Sarvajanik Sabha submitted a petition to the House of Commons demanding India's direct representation in British Parliament.
4. **Indian National Union** (AO Hume, 1883)
5. Bombay Presidency Association (Ferozshah Mehta, KT Telang, Badruddin Tayyabji, 1885)

Political Associations in South India

1. **Madras Native Association** (1852): The Madras Native Association sent a petition to the British Parliament on the eve of the passing of the Charter Act of 1853, making demands similar to that of the British Indian Association.
2. **Madras Mahajan Sabha** (M Vira-raghavachari, G Subramanya Iyer, Ananda Charlu, 1884)

Popular Campaigns

Pre-Congress political associations organized various campaigns in reaction to British policies, these were:

- For imposition of import duty on cotton (1875)
- For right to join volunteer corps
- For an All India Fund for political Agitation
- For Indianization of government service (1978-79)
- Campaign in Britain to vote for Pro-India Party
- Against Lytton's Afghan Campaign
- Against Vernacular Press Act (1878)
- Against Arms Act (1878)
- Against lowering the maximum age for appearing in Indian Civil Service
- Against plantation labour
- Against inland Emigration Act.
- In Support of Illbert Bill
- Mehta, Telang and Tyabji were known as **Bombay Trimvirate.**
- **Raja Ram Mohan Roy** sowed the seed of political associations in India. He was the first Indian to popularize the grievance of Indians before the British authorities. The trend was followed by Derozians (named after their famous Anglo-Indian teacher, Henry Vivian Derozio) in 1830s. Derozio was a teacher in the Hindu College Calcutta.

He established a daily paper named **The East Indian**.

- In 1883, following Surendranath Banerjee's imprisonment for two months, for contempt of court, it was proposed to raise a **National Fund** so, as to secure the political advancement of the country by means of constitutional agitation in India and England.
- Mahatma Gandhi Suggested the Winding up of Indian National Congress after India achieved independence as the main aim of the party i.e., Freedom was achieved.
- **National Indian Association** was founded by Mary Carpenter (Biographer of Ram Mohan Roy) with the help of Keshav Chandra Sen in Bristol in 1867.

Indian Civil Services

Background

- Under the East India Company administrators of their controlled territories were engaged. These became the HEICS **Honorable East India Company Civil Servants**.
- There were two exclusive groups of civil servants during the formative stage of British rule in India. The higher employees who entered into **"Covenants"** with the company came to be known as "Covenanted" servants, whereas those not singning such agreements came to be known as "Un-covenanted". The latter group generally filled the lower positions.
- This distinction between the covenanted and the un-covenanted virtually came to an end with Constitution of the **Imperial Civil Service of India** based on the recommendations of the public Service Commission, 1886–87, though the phrase "Covenanted" continued to be used of anyone in a salaried position with a long term contract.

Indian Civil Servants

- **Satyendranath Tagore** was the first Indian to compete in Civil Services (1863).
- There were more Indians in 1871. **RC Dutt** (wrote economic history of India), **Bihari Lal Gupta** (wrote an important official note which prepared the gained for Illbert Bill) and **SN Bannerjee** (he was later disqualified).
- **Subhash Chandra Bose** joined Civil Services in 1921 and resigned in the same year. He ranked fourth in the first of Civil Services.
- **Gurusaday Dutt** was the first Indian who secured the first rank in the ICS examination, in 1905.

Satyendranath Tagore

- Satyendranath Tagore was the first Indian to join the Indian Civil Service. He was the elder brother of Guru Dev Rabindranath Tagore. Before 1861, only British officers were appointed to all covenanted posts. The ICS Act of 1861, established the Indian Civil Service. But, it was not an easy task for the Indians to go England and compete with the British for a position.
- Satyendranath Tagore went to England in 1862, to prepare for and compete in the Civil Service Examinations. Satyendranath was selected for the Indian Civil Service in June, 1863. He completed his probationary training and returned to India in November

1864. His first posting was at Bombay Presidency.

- During the course of his service, Satyendranath Tagore travelled throughout the country. His posting outside Bengal helped him to learn several Indian languages. Satyendranath Tagore took keen interest in the activities of Brahmo Samaj and Prathrana Samaj. He retired from ICS in 1897.

Development of ICS in India

- The Civil Services in India during British Rule went through constant experimentation and innovation. It has evolved over a period of two centuries and has been crafted very meticulously by way of a series of legislations by the British authorities. The best way to trace the evolution is through these enactments of Colonial British Government.
- The first move came in the form of **Regulating Act of 1773**, this move abolished diarchy established by Lord Robert Clive.
- This Act made Governor of Bengal the Governor-General for all the British territories in India and also appointed an Executive Council of four members to assist him.
- He was supposed to take decisions with the majority of the Council.
- Warren Hastings was the first Governor-General thus appointed under this act.
- He tried to control the corruption in the company's bureaucracy but had limited success only.
- **The Pitt's India Act of 1784,** established a Board of Commissioners to supervise the civil and military government of the company also called the "Board of Control".
- The Act placed the civil and military government of the company in due subordination of the Government in England.
- Lord Cornwallis was appointed the Governor-General in 1786.
- In 800, Lord Wellesley founded the **College of Fort William** at Calcutta for the purpose of training of new recruits to the covenanted services. But, the watershed in the evolution of Civil Services in India was the introduction of Competitive Entrance Examination for getting selected in the much coveted services. This totally eliminated the element of company's patronage in the system, thereby infusing more professionalism into it.
- As per **Charter Act of 1853**, the services were thrown open to all the citizens of British kingdom, including Indians. But, for all practical purposes the selection process remained highly biased against the entry of Indians. The main reasons for low representation of Indians in the services were the very low maximum age of eligibility for taking the entrance exam and the location of examination centre in England.
- In fact, after successive reductions the maximum age was reduced to 19 years during the tenure of **Lord Lytton**.
- Facilitation of entry of Indians in the elite Civil Services remained one of the strongest demand of the early political agitations, so much so that the first all India political association the "Indian Association" headed by Surendra Nath

Bannerjee Started the "Civil Services Agitation" all over India.

- The major development of Civil Services under British Rule can be tracked along the recommendations of some major **Enquiry commissions** which were established at regular interval to look into the grievances and demands of Indian Nationalists.
- Cornwallis introduced first major reforms in Civil Services. He was the one who introduced the category of covenanted and non-covenanted service in the company's bureaucracy.
- The covenanted was exclusive preserve of firstly the British then the European. This was the precursor of much famous Indian Civil Service. Cornwallis introduced very attractive pay scales for the covenanted civil servants who entered into a convent with the company's government. This disciplined and raised the standard of integrity of the services. Due to extreme prestige these services carried, they are also called 'Heaven born services' and became aspiration of many of talented white European men. Thus, Cornwallis succeeded in removing corruption at least from the higher echelons of the bureaucracy. He also established an elaborate police system.

Commissions Related to ICS

Sir Charles Aitchison Commission, 1886

- Appointed by **Lord Dufferin** to consider the demand for simultaneous examination and the lowering of maximum age. It recommended that the term "Covenanted" and "Uncovenanted" be dropped.
- He suggested that services be divided into three classes—(i) Imperial Indian Civil services, (ii) the Provincial and (iii) the Subordinate Services.
- The first was to recruit in England and the latter in India exclusively out of Indians.
- He recommended that the minimum and maximum age limits be fixed at 19 years and 23 years respectively.
- It rejected the idea of simultaneous holding of examination in both India and England and recommended the abolition of statutory civil services.

Montague-Chelmsford Commission, 1918

- Conceded to the demand of holding of examination simultaneously in India as well as England.
- The commission recommended that one-third of the superior posts in the Indian Civil Services were to be recruited in India and this proportion is to be increased by 1.5% annually.
- Further, it recommended that there should be no racial discrimination in the matter of appointments.

Lee Commission, 1923

- It recommended that the Secretary of State should continue to recruit the Indian Civil Service, the Irrigation Branch of the Services of Engineers and the Indian Forest Services.
- On the basis of **Government of India Act, 1919,** it recommended the establishment of a **Public Service Commission**. It stipulated that 20% of the officers should be recruited

by promotion from Provincial Civil Services and of the remaining 80% half should be Indian and half British.

Government of India Act, 1935

- The Provision was made for establishment of a **Federal Public Service Commission**. Despite all these reforms the Indian Civil Services remained essentially a colonial apparatus which proved to be the provincial **"Steel Frame of British Rule"** in India.
- But, with the ushering of the independent India's Constitution some ground braking changes were made to the existing set up of Civil Services to make it useful in meeting the lofty goals of freedom struggle.

Chapter at a Glance

- The Ryotwari system was first introduced in Tamil Nadu by Thomas Munroe and Captain Read.
- A system of peasants proprietorship was introduced by the Ryotwari System.
- The Regulation of 1822 was based on the recommendations of Mr. Holt Mackenzie, the secretary to the board of Commissioners.
- Merttins Bird is regarded as the Father of Land settlements in Northern India.
- Opium was grown in British territories of Banaras and Patna and also in some Indian States.
- The East India Company had the monopoly of trade in salt and opium.
- Salt was manufactured by solar evaporation along the Coromandel and Malabar Coast.
- The theory of 'Drain of Wealth' was propagated by Dadabhai Naoroji.
- The Idea was forwarded by the first time on 2nd May, 1867, before a meeting of East India Association in London.
- R.C. Dutta Propagated this theory in his book 'The Economic History under Early British rule'.
- The Drain of Wealth was officially adopted by the Indian National Congress in 1896 at Calcutta session.
- The English Scholars discredited the theory of Drain of Wealth on the ground that India's foreign trade had greatly increased in value and volume.
- The growth of modern industries in India was greatly hampered on account of the lack of Indian capital and technical education.
- Before 19th century India was known as 'Sink of precious metals' because India was the pool of manufacture and distribution of diverse commodities all over the world.
- India became a classic British Economy when she was thrown open to British capital investment.
- Karl Marx was the first to formulate the theory of three successive phases of British Colonisation in India, i.e., Mercantilist, Free Trade Mercantile Capitalism and Finance imperialism.
- Dadabhai Naoroji said that "The British rule was a bleeding drain from India."
- In 1875 even Salisbury, the secretary of state for India, remarked 'India must be bled, but the bleeding should be done indiciously.

- In 1865, Dadabhai Naoroji founded the 'London Indian Society' in colloboration with W.C. Bannerjee with the objective of publicising Indian grievances.
- Dadabhai was the first Indian to be elected to the British House of Commons.

Previous Year Question Paper (1998-2017)

1 Consider the following: **(2015)**
   1. Assessment of land revenue on the basis of nature of the soil and the quality of crops
   2. Use of mobile cannons in warfare
   3. Cultivation of tobacco and red chillies

   Which of the above was/were introduced in India by the English ?
   (a) 1 only (b) 1 and 2
   (c) 2 and 3 (d) None

2. The distribution of powers between the Centre and the States in the Indian Constitution is based on the scheme provided in the **(2015)**
   (a) Morley-Minto Reforms, 1909
   (b) Montagu-Chelmsford Act, 1919
   (c) Government of India Act, 1935
   (d) Indian Independence Act, 1947

3. What was the purpose with which Sir William Wedderburn and W.S. Caine had set up the Indian Parliamentary Committee in 1893? **(2015)**
   (a) To agitate for Indian political reforms in the House of Commons
   (b) To campaign for the entry of Indians into the Imperial Judiciary
   (c) To facilitate a discussion on India's Independence in the British Parliament.
   (d) To agitate for the entry of eminent Indians into the British Parliament

4. That the per capita income in India was Rs. 20 in 1867-68, was ascertained for the first time by **(2015)**
   (a) M.G. Ranade
   (b) Sir W. Hunter
   (c) R.C. Dutta
   (d) Dadabhai Naoroji

5. Which one of the following statements is **not** correct? **(1999)**
   (a) Neel Darpan was a play based on the exploitation of the indigo farmers
   (b) The author of the play 'Ghashiram Kotwal' is Vijay Tendulkar
   (c) The play 'Navanna' by Nabin Chandra Das was based on the famine of Bengal
   (d) Urdu theatre used to depend heavily on Parsi theatre.

6. Which of the following pairs are correctly matched ? **(1998)**

1.	Theodore	Mohammedan Anglo-Oriental College, Aligarh
2.	Illbert Bill	Ripon
3.	Feroz Shah Mehta	Congress
4.	Badruddin Tyabji	Muslim League

   Select the correct answer using the codes given below:
   Codes:
   (a) 1, 2, 3 and 4 (b) 2 and 4
   (c) 1, 3 and 4 (d) 1, 2 and 3

Answers

1. (d)	2. (c)	3. (a)
4. (d)	5. (d)	6. (d)

Practice Paper

1. Maulana Abdul Kalam Azad started an Urdu weekly, the Al-Hilal in 1912, but on its being banned by the Governent, he founded the Al-Balagh in
(a) 1913 (b) 1914
(c) 1915 (d) 1916
(SSC 2007)

2. Who was the first women president of Indian National Congress?
(a) Sarojini Naidu
(b) Sucheta Kripalani
(c) Rajkumari Amrit Kaur
(d) Annie Besant
(SSC 2007, SSC CGL 2014)

3. In which session of the Indian National Congress did the historic union of Congress and Muslim League take place?
(a) Surat (b) Bombay
(c) Calcutta (d) Lucknow
(SSC 2008)

4. Who was the founder-editor of the famous newspaper Kesari during the National struggle?
(a) Mahatma Gandhi
(b) Jawaharlal Nehru
(c) Lokmanya Tilak
(d) Muhammad Iqbal
(SSC 2008, WBPCS 2008)

5. The split between the Extremists and Moderates came up in the open at the Surat Congress session in the year
(a) 1905 (b) 1906
(c) 1907 (d) 1910
(SSC 2008)

6. All India Muslim League was formed at
(a) Lahore (b) Aligarh
(c) Lucknow (d) Dhaka
(SCRA 2008)

7. With reference to the colonial rule in India, consider the following events
I. Morley-Minto Reforms Act
II. Transfer of the capital from Calcutta to Delhi
III. First World War
IV. Lucknow Pact
The correct chronological order of these events is:
(a) II-I-III-IV (b) I-II-III-IV
(c) II-I-IV-III (d) I-II-IV-III
(SCRA 2001)

8. Consider the following statements regarding Freedom Movement:
I. The Congress was split into two factions in Surat Session 1907
II. Bal Gangadhar Tilak revived the festivals of Ganpati and Shivaji in Maharashtra to arouse a new spirit among the youth of the country.
III. Aurobindo Ghosh was arrested in connection with Alipore bomb case. Which of these statements (s) is/are correct?
(a) III only (b) I and II only
(c) II and III (d) I, II and III
(SCRA 2003)

9. Consider the following nationalists
1 Bal Gangadhar Tilak
2 Gopalkrishna Gokhle
3 Bipin Chandra Pal
4 Lala Lajpat Rai
Who among these were referred to as militant nationalist of the freedom movemets?
(a) 1, 2 and 3
(b) 2 and 4
(c) 1, 3 and 4
(d) 1, 2, 3 and 4 **(NDA 2000)**

10. Who of the following was a founder of the Bharat Naujawan Sabha in 1926?
   (a) Lala Lajpat Rai
   (b) Sardar Bhagat Singh
   (c) Lala Hardayal
   (d) Sohan Singh Bhakhna **(NDA 2006)**
11. With reference to the Indian freedom struggle, which one of the following is the correct chronological order of the given events?
   (a) Partition of Bengal-Surat Split of Congress- Lucknow Pact
   (b) Partition of Bengal- Lucknow Pact-Surat Split of Congress
   (c) Surat Split of Congress-Partition of Bengal-Lucknow Pact
   (d) Surat Split of Congress-Lucknow Pact-Partition of Bengal

   (NDA 2007)
12. Other than Annie Besant, who among the following also launched Home Rule Movement in India?
   (a) Aurobindo Ghosh
   (b) Bal Gangadhar Tilak
   (c) Gopal Krishna Gokhle
   (d) Moti Lal Nehru **(NDA 2008)**
13. **Assertion (A):** Bhagat Singh and Batukeshwar Dutt threw bombs in the Legislative Assembly in 1929.

   Reason (R): They wanted to kill some members of the Legislative Assembly as a revenge of the Death of Lala Lajpat Rai.
   (a) Both A and R are true and R is the correct explanation of A.
   (b) Both A and R are true but R is not a correct explanation of A.
   (c) A is true but R is false.
   (d) A is false but R is true.
14. Consider the following statements:
   (1) Prior to the establishment of Home Rule League by Annie Besant, it was Lokmanya Tilak who had set up a Home Rule League at Poona.
   (2) The Congress in its Bombay Session in 1915, passed a resolution demanding Home Rule for India.

   Which of the statements given above is/are correct?
   (a) 1 only (b) 2 only
   (c) Both 1 and 2 (d) Neither 1 nor 2

   (CDS 2005, UPPCS 2015)
15. Which one of the following pairs is not correctly matched?
   (a) Partition of Bengal –1905
   (b) Foundation of Muslim League –1906
   (c) Surat Split –1907
   (d) Transfer of India's Capital from Calcutta to Delhi –1909

   (CDS 2006)
16. Who among the following leaders dominated the Lucknow Pact in December, 1915?
   (a) Jawahar Lal Nehru
   (b) Bal Gangadhar Tilak
   (c) Moti Lal Nehru
   (d) Madan Mohan Malviya

   (CDS 2007)
17. Who of the following revolutionaries set up the United India House in the USA?
   (a) Ramnath Puri and Vir Savarkar
   (b) Taraknath Das and G.D. Kumar
   (c) Lala Hardayal and Bhagat Singh
   (d) Harnam Singh and Bhagwan Singh

   (CDS 2008)
18. Consider the following paragraph

   He was the seriously injured in police lathi charge in Lahore during domonstrations against Simon Commission for which he subsequently died in November 1928. Later on the British Officer, who was responsible for the

Lathi charge on him, was shot dead by Bhagat Singh and Rajguru.
The revolutionary referred to in the above paragraph is:
(a) Pandit Gobind Ballabh Pant
(b) Mangal Singh
(c) Moti Lal Nehru
(d) Lala Lajpat Rai **(CDS 2010)**

19. Which of the following leaders presided over the Congress Session at Calcutta in 1906?
(a) Bal Gangadhar Tilak
(b) Gopal Krishna Gokhle
(c) Aurobindo Ghosh
(d) Dadabhai Naoroji **(BPSC 2001)**

20. Which one of the following was not an extremist?
(a) Bal Gangadhar Tilak
(b) Madan Lal Dhingra
(c) Udham Singh
(d) Gopal Krishna Gokhle **(BPSC 2001)**

21. Who gave the 'Inquilab Zindabad' slogan?
(a) Iqbal (b) M.K. Gandhi
(c) Bhagat Singh (d) S.C. Bose
(BPSC 2002, PGDTM 2006)

22. Which one of the following leaders belonged to the Extremist wing of the Congress?
(a) Aurobindo Ghosh
(b) Dadabhai Naoroji
(c) G.K. Gokhle
(d) S.N. Banerjee **(BPSC 2002)**

23. Who said, 'Swaraj is my birthright and I will have it?
(a) Mahatma Gandhi
(b) Bipin Chandra Pal
(c) Gopal Krishna Gokhle
(d) Bal Gangadhar Tilak
(BPSC 2004, WBPSC 2007, SSC 2009)

24. The Muslim deputation (Under the leadership of Aga Khan) mets Lord Minto in 1906 at Shimla and pleaded for?
(a) Separate electorate for Muslims
(b) A composite electorate
(c) Special representation to Muslim by nomination
(d) Higher representation to the Hindus **(BPSC 2004)**

25. The Anushilan Samiti was:
(a) Dedicated to the upliftment of women
(b) Promoting widow remarriage
(c) Special representation to Muslim by nomination
(d) A revolutionary organisation
(BPSC 2005)

26. Who said that 'Congress Movement was neither inspired by the people nor devised or planned by them?
(a) Lord Dufferin
(b) Sir Syed Ahmed Khan
(c) Lord Curzon
(d) Lala Lajpat Rai **(BPSC 2005)**

27. When did the attempt of murder of Kingsford was made at Muzaffarpur?
(a) 1908 (b) 1909
(c) 1907 (d) 1911
(BPSC 2008)

28. In which year did Lord Hardinge cancel the partition of Bengal?
(a) 1911 (b) 1904
(c) 1906 (d) 1907
(BPSC 2008)

29. Brinda Kumar Ghosh was a member of which revolutionary organisation of Bengal?
(a) Anushilan Samiti
(b) Varti Samiti
(c) Swadesh Bandhav Samiti
(d) Shadhana Samaj **(JPSC 2003)**

30. In which of the following movements Bande Mataram was adopted slogan for agitation?
    (a) Revolt of 1857
    (b) Partition of Bengal in 1905
    (c) Non-Cooperation Movement in 1922
    (d) Quit India Movement in 1942

(UPPSC 2002)

31. Of the following who was called the 'father of Indian Unrest'?
    (a) A.O. Hume
    (b) Dadabhai Naoroji
    (c) Lokmanya Tilak
    (d) Mahatma Gandhi

(UPPCS 2003, UPPCS 2004)

32. Two Home Rule League were started in 1915-16 under the leadership of:
    (a) Tilak and Annie Besant
    (b) Tilak and Aurobindo Ghosh
    (c) Tilak and Lala Lajpat Rai
    (d) Tilak and Bipin Chandra Pal

(UPPCS 2003, SCRA 2007)

33. The Ghadar Movement was founded by?
    (a) Ajit Singh
    (b) Lala Hansraj
    (c) Lala Hardayal
    (d) Sohan Singh Bhakhna

(UPPCS 2004,CDS 2006,UPPCS 2008, WBPCS 2008)

34. Given below is a list of organisations. Select those engaged in revolutionary activities, using the code given below the list:
    1. Abhinav Bharat
    2. Anushilan Simiti
    3. New Nationalist party
    4. Indian Patriot Association

    (a) 1, 2 and 3 (b) 2, 3 and 4
    (c) 1 and 2 (d) 1, 2 and 4

(UPPCS 2004)

35. Who among the following was the chief architect of reconciliation between the Extremists and the Moderates?
    (a) Annie Besant
    (b) M.A. Jinnah
    (c) Madam Cama
    (d) Firoz Shah Mehta **(UPPCS 2004)**

36. Who of the following had called Mohammad Ali Jinnah as 'Ambassador of Hindu-Muslim Unity?
    (a) Annie Besant
    (b) Sarojini Naidu
    (c) Bal Gangadhar Tilak
    (d) None of these **(UPPCS 2004)**

37. Shyamji Krishna Verma established Indian Home Rule Society in
    (a) London (b) San Francisco
    (c) Berlin (d) Paris

(UPPCS 2004)

38. Who was the founder of All India Muslim League?
    (a) Syed Ahmed Khan
    (b) Mohammad Iqbal
    (c) Agha Khan
    (d) Nawab Salimullah Khan

(UPPCS 2007, WBPSC 2008, Utt.PSC 2008, CDS 2009)

39. Shri Aurobindo Ashram is situated in:
    (a) Tamil Nadu
    (b) Karnataka
    (c) Rameshwaram
    (d) Pondicherry **(UPPCS 2007)**

40. Who among the following established a Republican Government in abroad?
    (a) Raja Mahendra Pratap
    (b) Subhash Chandra Bose
    (c) Ras Behari Bose
    (d) None of these **(UPPCS 2008)**

Answers

1. (a)
2. (d)
3. (d)
4. (c)
5. (c)
6. (d)
7. (b)
8. (d)
9. (c)
10. (b)
11. (a)
12. (b)
13. (c)
14. (a)
15. (d)
16. (b)
17. (b)
18. (d)
19. (d)
20. (d)
21. (c)
22. (a)
23. (d)
24. (a)
25. (d)
26. (d)
27. (a)
28. (a)
29. (a)
30. (b)
31. (c)
32. (a)
33. (c)
34. (a)
35. (b)
36. (b)
37. (a)
38. (d)
39. (d)
40. (a)

CHAPTER 11

Birth of Indian National Congress

Introduction

- In 1883, the government held an international exhibition in Calcutta and invited people from across the country. Indian Association decided to hold its first Indian conference in Calcutta at the same time so that it can reach to the masses but the plan failed.
- In 1884, at the annual convention of the Theosophical Society at Adyar in Madras, AO Hume proposed formation of a committee so as to make necessary preparation for a session at Pune to be held in 1885.
- Members of the Committee included AO Hume, SN Bannerjee, Narendra Nath Sen, Subramanya Aiyar, P Ananda Charlu, Sardar Dayal Singh, Lala Sriram, KT Talang and VN Mandalik.

AO Hume

- AO Hume was retired British Member of Indian Civil Services. He played an important role in the foundation of the Indian National Congress in 1885.
- Earlier, he founded the Indian National Union in 1884, which is considered to be the forerunner of the Indian National Congress.
- He Served as the general secretary of INC from 1885 to 1906.

AO Hume

- In April 1985, National Telegraph Union was formed to keep the English Press informed about India.
- Before the formation of Indian National Congress, two sessions of the Indian National Conference had been held in 1883 and 1885 under the guidance of SN Bannerjee and Anand Mohan Bose.

Formation of the Congress

- Indian National Congress was finally formed on December 28, 1985.
- The first session of the Indian National Congress was held on December 28, 1885 at Tejpal Sanskrit Pathshala, Bombay under the Presidentship of W C Bannerjee.

  Note: The venue of 1st meeting was changed from Pune to Bombay due to the outbreak of Cholera in Pune.
- The word "Congress" was borrowed from North American History.
- The first session of the Congress was attended by 72 delegates.

Representation in the Congress

- As regard the representation among the classes; the educated middle class had the largest share. The legal profession was most heavily represented among the professions. The Brahmins among the castes were comparatively larger in number.
- Among the province Bombay, Calcutta and Madras took the leading part. The masses were conspicuous by their absence.

- In 1886, the delegates to congress became 436.
- Moderate leaders dominated the Congress in its early phase.
- Early congressmen had an implicit faith in the efficacy of peaceful and constitutional agitation.
- The Moderate belief in the essential sense of justice and goodness of the British.
- To inform British public about the problems faced by Indians they sent deputation of leading Indians to Britain.
- In 1889, British Committee of Indian National Congress was founded under the chairmanship of Wedderburn (Biographer of AO Hume) in London and a journal "India" was also started.
- First President, WC Bannerjee, defined Congress's objective as promotion of personal intimacy and friendship among all Indians and removal of prejudices based on caste, creed and regional differences, for fuller development of India as a Nation.

Opposition to Congress

- From Indians Syed Ahmed Khan and Raja Sheo Prasad of Banaras founded United Indian Patriotic Association to oppose the Congress.
- It had the blessing of British Government. Sir Syed Ahmed Khan was loyal to the British for the cause of Muslim Movement.
- He even rejected the Drain Theory of Dadabhai Naoroji.

- AO Hume published a pamphlet, "An old men's hope" in the Madras Session in 1887.
- 1889 session is Bombay under William Wedderburn, was also attended by Charles Baradlaugh.
- Dadabhai Naoroji was the first Indian and Asian to become member of the British Parliament in 1892.
- In 1890, Kadambini Ganguly, the first woman graduate of Calcutta university, addressed the Congress Session.

- From Bruisers the British first provided patronage to the Congress however soon found it outgrew their plans, therefore, patronage was withdrawn and Congress was termed as factory of sedition.

- Lord Dufferin was the viceroy of India during the formation of Congress and Lord Cross the Secretary of State for India.
- Dufferin described the Congress as the "mouthpiece of Microscopic Minority". On 1888, Viceroy warned the Princely States, not to support the Congress.

Safety Valve Theory

- According to British historians, Hume formed the Congress with the idea that is would prove a "Safety Valve" for releasing the growing discontent of the Indians.
- However, the Modern Indian historians disagree to this theory. In their opinion, Indian intelligentsia established Indian National Congress as a national body to express the political and economic demands of the Indians.
- Bipin Chandra observes that the early leaders used AO Hume as "lighting conductor" (Catalyst) to bring together the naionalistic forces.

- **1st President of INC:** WC Bannerjee
- **1st Woman President:** Annie Besant (1917)
- **1st Muslim President:** Bardruddin Tyabji
- **1st English President:** George Yule
- **Gandhi became President:** 1924, Belguam
- **Jawaharlal Nehru became President:** 1929, Lahore
- **Subhash Chandra Bose became President:** 1938, Haripura

The Sessions of Congress			
December, 1885	Bombay	WC Bannerjee	• Held at Gokaldas Tejpal Sanskrit Paathshala, Bombay. Earlier the session was to be held at Poona, but the Venue was shifted due to the outbreak of Cholera at Poona. Attended by 72 delegates.
December, 1886	Calcutta	Dadabhai Naoroji	
December, 1887	Madras	Badruddin Tayabji	• First session to be presided over by a Muslim President.
December, 1888	Allahabad	George Yule	• First session to be presided over by an Englishmen.
December, 1889	Bombay	William Wedderburn	• A Committee on Indian National Congress was endorsed.
December, 1890	Calcutta	Ferozshah Mehta	• Kadambini Ganguly, the First Women graduate of Calcutta University addressed to session.

December, 1891	Nagpur	A Ananda Charlu	
December, 1892	Allahabad	WC Bannerjee	
December, 1893	Lahore	Dadabhai Naoroji	
December, 1894	Madras	Alfred Webb	• Mr Webb was an Irish member of the British Parliament.
December, 1895	Poona	Surendranath Bannerjee	
December, 1896	Calcutta	MR Sayani	
December, 1897	Amraoti	C Sankaran Nair	
December, 1898	Madras	A M Bose	
December, 1899	Lucknow	RC Dutt	
December, 1900	Lahore	NG Chandavarkar	
December, 1901	Calcutta	Dinshaw E Wacha	
December, 1902	Ahmedabad	Surendranath Bannerjee	
December, 1903	Madras	Lal Mohan Ghosh	
December, 1904	Bombay	Sir Henry Cotton	
December, 1905	Varanasi	Gopal Krishna Gokhale	
December, 1906	Calcutta	Dadabhai Naoroji	• Expounded Swaraj. Boycott resolution passed. Swadeshi resolution passed. National Education Policy endorsed.
December, 1907	Surat	Ras Behari Ghosh	• The session witnessed the split between the Moderates and the Extremists. The candidates of extremists at this session who lost the presidential election was Lala Lajpat Rai.
December, 1908	Madras	Ras Behari Ghosh	• In Madras session Constitution for the Congress Ratified.
December, 1909	Lahore	Madan Mohan Malaviya	
December, 1910	Allahabad	Sir William Wedderburn	
December,1911	Calcutta	Bishan Narayan Dhar	
December, 1912	Bankipur	RN Mudhalkar	

December, 1913	Karachi	Nawab Syed Mohammad	
December, 1914	Madras	Bupendranath Bose	
December, 1915	Bombay	S P Sinha	
December, 1916	Lucknow	Ambika Charan Mazumdar	• Reunion of Moderates and Extremists. Lucknow pact signed betwen Congress and Muslim League.
December,1917	Calcutta	Annie Besant	• First Woman President. She gave first flag to Congress Green and Red.
December, 1918	Delhi	Madan Mohan Malaviya	• Resignation of moderates like SN Bannerjee.
December, 1919	Amritsar	Motilal Nehru	
September, 1920	Calcutta (Special Session)	Lala Lajpat Rai	• Non-cooperation resolution passed by Congess
December, 1920	Nagpur	C Vijaya Raghavachariya	• Change in the Constitution of Congress. Non-Cooperation resolution ratified.
December, 1921	Ahmedabad	C R Das	• Formation of Swaraj Party
December, 1922	Gaya Delhi (Spcial Session)	Abul Kalam Azad	• The Youngest President
December, 1923	Kakinada	Maulana Muhammad Ali	
December, 1924	Belgaum	Mahatma Gandhi	• The Only session where Gandhiji was the President
December, 1925	Cawnpore	Sarojini Naidu	• First Indian woman President
December, 1926	Guwahati	S Srinivas Iyengar	
December, 1927	Madras	MA Ansari	• Independence resolution passed for the first time on the insistence of JL Nehru. This was a snap resolution. A resolution for the boycott of Simon Commission was passed.
December, 1928	Calcutta	Motilal Nehru	• First All India Youth Congress came into existence. Return of Gandhi to active politics after 6 years.
December, 1929	Lahore	Jawaharlal Nehru	• Poona Swaraj Resolution; Congress working commitee authorized to launch CDM. Nehru Report got a decent burial.

December, 1930			• On account of the Civil Disobedience Movement no congress session could be held in 1930, but JL Nehru continued as President.
March, 1931	Karachi	Vallabhbhai Patel	• Resolution on Fundamental Rights and National Economic policy Pt Jawaharlal Nehru drafted the Resolution on FR.
April, 1932	Delhi	R D Amritlal	
April, 1933	Calcutta	Mrs Nellie Sengupta	
October, 1934, 1937	Bombay	Dr. Rajendra Prasad	• Formation of Congress Socialist Party • No session, but Rajendra Prasad continued as President.
April, 1936, 1937	Lucknow Faizpur	Jawaharlal Nehru Jawaharlal Nehru	• First Session to be held in village • Demanded the formation of a Constituent Assembly • Adoption of an agrarian programme.
February, 1938	Haripura	Subhash Chandra Bose	• National Planning Committee was set up under the Chairmanship of JL Nehru.
March, 1939	Tripuri	Subhash Chandra Bose, After defeating Dr. Pattabhi Sitaramayya	• Resignation of SC Bose (Rajendra Prasad took over) and formation of forward block.
March, 1940	Ramgarh	Maulana Abul Kalam Azad	• Acted as the President of Congress for six consecutive years • The annual session of the Congress could not be held for 5 years on account of the launching of the Quit India Movement. When the Congress was declared illegal organization and all congress leaders put behind the bars. Azad contined to be the President.
November, 1946 1947	Meerut Delhi	Acharya JB Kriplani Rajendra Prasad	• He was the President of Congress when India achieved Independence.

Chapter at a Glance

- Dada Bhai Naoroji is known as 'the grand old man of India'.
- The first Factory Act was passed in 1881 during the Governor Generalship of Lord Ripon.
- The second Factory Act was passed in 1891 during the Governor Generalship of Lord Lansdowne.
- In 1908, the textile workers of Bombay went on strike over the imprisonment of Bal Gangadhar Tilak.
- The Madras Labour Union was the first modern Trade Union Organisation of India.
- The Madras Labour Union mainly comprised of the labours of Buckingham and Carnatic Mills.
- The All India Trade Union Congress in 1920 was a direct outcome of the esablishment of the International Labour Organisation in 1919.
- The Gaya Session of the Congress (1922) decided to assist the AITUC (All India Trade Union Congress) in organising workers.
- The term 'Left' and 'Right' were used for the first time as political terms in France.
- The Communist Party of India was formed by M.N. Roy.
- Philip Spratt came to India in December 1926 and organised a number of unions.
- The communist movement involved in three conspiracy trials: (i) Peshawar conspiracy trial (1922-23), (ii) The Kanpur conspiracy trial (1924) and (iii) the Meerut conspiracy trial (1920-33).
- In July 1934 the Communist Party of India was declared an illegal organisation.
- R.P. Dutta and Ben Bradley, published their thesis entitled 'The Anti-Imperialist People's Front in India' in March 1936.
- The communists, the Congress Socialist Party and the trade unionists planned to organise a common front on the basis of a common minimum programme.
- In 1946 the communists put forward before the Cabinet Mission a plan of dividing India into 17 separate sovereign states on the model of U.S.S.R.
- The communists branded the Congress socialists as 'Fake Socialists'.
- The Congress Socialists branded the communists as 'Social Chauvinists'.
- The Bihar Socialist Party was formed in 1931 by Jai Prakash Narayan, Phulan Prasad Verma etc.
- The Congress Socialists described Jinnah as a tool in the hands of imperialists.
- Prof. Einstein, Harold Laski, H.G. Wells and American president Roosevelt sympathetically commented on Meerut conspiracy trials.
- The Meerut trail dealt a heavy blow to the working class movement.
- The Nationalists leaders who were in close touch with AITUC included Lala Lajpat Rai, V.V. Giri, C.R. Das, Subhash Chandra Bose, Sarojini Naidu etc.

Previous Year Question Paper (1998-2017)

1. The Ghadr (Ghadar) was a:
   (a) Revolutionary association of Indians with headquarters at San Francisco.

(b) Nationalist organization operating from Singapore.
(c) Militant organization with head-quarters at Berlin.
(d) Communist movement for India's freedom with headquarters at Tashkent. **(2015)**

2. Who among the following gave a systematic critique of the moderate politics of the Indian National Congress in a series of articles entitled New Lamps for Old?
(a) Aurobindo Ghosh
(b) R.C. Dutt
(c) Syed Ahmad Khan
(d) Viraraghavachari **(2015)**

3. Who among the following used the phrase 'Un-British' to criticize the English colonial control of India?
(a) Anandmohan Bose
(b) Badruddin Tyabji
(c) Dadabhai Naoroji
(d) Ferozshah Mehta **(2015)**

4. Where were the Ghadar revolutionaries, who became active during the outbreak of the World War I based?
(a) Central America
(b) North America
(c) West America
(d) South America **(2005)**

5. What was Komagata Maru?
(a) A political party based in Taiwan
(b) Peasant communist leader of China
(c) A naval ship on voyage to Canada
(d) A Chinese village where Mao Tse Tung began his long march **(2015)**

6. Who among the following was a proponent of Fabianism as a movemnt?
(a) Annie Beasant
(b) A.O. Hume
(c) Michael Madhusudan Dutt
(d) R. Palme Dutt **(2005)**

7. Match List-I with List-II and select the correct answer using the codes given below the lists:

List-I	List-II
A. Chittagong Armoury	1. Kalpana-Dutt Rao
B. Abhinav Bharat	2. Guru Ram Singh
C. Anushilan Samiti	3. Vinayaka Damodar Savarkar
D. Kuka Movement	4. Aurobindo Ghosh

Codes:

	A	B	C	D
(a)	1	3	4	2
(b)	1	3	2	4
(c)	3	1	2	4
(d)	3	1	4	2

(2015)

8. The native state of Tripura became involved in the Freedom movement early in the 20th century because:
(a) The Kings of Tripura were always anti British.
(b) The Bengal revolutionaries took shelter in Tripura.
(c) The tribes of the state were fiercely freedom loving.
(d) There were already some groups fighting against the kingship and its protector, the British. **(2015)**

9. 'Abhinava Bharat' a secret society of revolutionaries was organised by:
(a) Khudiram Bose
(b) V.D. Savarkar
(c) Prafulla Chaki
(d) Bhagat Singh **(2015)**

10. Which one of the following defines extremist ideology during the early phase of Indian freedom movement?

(a) Stimulating the production of indigenous articles by giving them preference over imported commodities
(b) Obtaining self-government by aggressive means in place of petitions and constitutional ways
(c) Providing national dedication according to the requirements of the country
(d) Organising coups against the British empire through military revolt. **(2015)**

11. The Indian Muslims in general, were not attracted to the Extremist movement because of the:
(a) Influence of Sir Sayyid Ahmad Khan
(b) Anti-Muslim attitude of Extremist leaders
(c) Indifference shown to Muslim aspirations
(d) Extremists policy of harping on Hindu past **(2015)**

12. Who was the leader of the Ghadar party?
(a) Bhagat Singh
(b) Lala Hardayal
(c) Bal Gangadhar Tilak
(d) V.D. Savarkar **(1998)**

Answers

1. (a)	2. (a)	3. (c)
4. (b)	5. (c)	6. (a)
7. (a)	8. (b)	9. (b)
10. (b)	11. (d)	12. (b)

Practice Paper

1. Who let the salt Satyagrha Movement with Mahatma Gandhi?
(a) Annie Besant
(b) Mridula Sarabhai
(c) Muthu Lakshmi
(d) Sarojini Naidu **(SSC Grad. 2000)**

2. In which of the following movements did Mahatma Gandhi make the first use of Hunger Strike as a weapon?
(a) Ahmedabad Strike, 1918
(b) Rowlatt Satyagraha, 1919
(c) Non-Cooperation Movement, 1920-22
(d) Bardoli Satyagraha, 1928
(SSC Grad. 2000)

3. From where did Acharya Vinoba Bhava start the individual Satyagraha in 1940?
(a) Nadiad in Gujarat
(b) Paunar in Maharashtra
(c) Adyar in Tamil Nadu
(d) Guntur in Andhra Pradesh
(SSC Grad. 2000)

4. Which one of the following writings is **NOT** related to Mahatma Gandhi?
(a) My Experiments with Truth
(b) Harijan
(c) The Holy Family
(d) Hind Swaraj **(SSC Grad. 2006)**

5. The book 'Unto this Last' which influenced Gandhi was authored by:
(a) Boris Yeltsin
(b) John Ruskin
(c) Pushkin
(d) Ruskin Bond
(SSC Sec. Off.(Aud.) 2006)

6. Moti Lal Nehru and Chitta Ranjan (C.R.) Das were the founder-members of the:
(a) Communist Party of India
(b) Forword Block
(c) Socialist-Swarajist Party
(d) Swarajya Party
(SSC Sec. Off. (Aud.) 2006)

7. Gandhi considered Khadi as a symbol of:
   (a) Industrialisation
   (b) Economic Independence
   (c) Economic growth
   (d) Moral Purity
   (SSC Sec. Off. (Aud.) 2006)
8. 'India wins Freedom' is the autobiography of:
   (a) Abul Kalam Azad
   (b) Muhammad Ali
   (c) Zakir Hussain
   (d) Syed Ahmed Khan
   (SSC Sec. Off (Aud.) 2006, SSC Data Entry Operator 2009)
9. The Round Table Conference at London met for the decision of:
   (a) A future constitution of India
   (b) Provision of Provincial Autonomy
   (c) Gandhi's demands for calling off Civil Disobedience Movement
   (d) Congress claim to be the sole representative of Indians
   (SSC Sec. Off. (Aud.) 2006)
10. Sarvodaya stands for:
   (a) Total revolution
   (b) Non Co-operation
   (c) Upliftment of all
   (d) Non-Violence
   (SSC Sec. Off. (Aud.) 2007)
11. In which city of South Africa was Mahatma Gandhi beatien up and thrown off the pavement by the white people?
   (a) Cape Town (b) Durban
   (c) Johannesburg (d) Pretoria
   (SSC Sec. Off. (Aud.) 2007)
12. Who attend the Congress of Oppressed Nationalist at Brussels in 1927, on behalf of the National Congress?
   (a) Jawahar Lal Nehru
   (b) Mahatma Gandhi
   (c) Dr. Ansari
   (d) Moti Lal Nehru
   (SSC Sec. Off. (Aud.) 2006)
13. Which of the following are the most important teachings of Gandhiji?
   1. Truth
   2. Non-Violence
   3. Religion
   4. Satyagraha
   Select the correct code:
   (a) 1 and 3 only (b) 2 and 4 only
   (c) 1 and 2 pm;u (d) 1, 2 and 3 only
   (SSC Mat. 2008)
14. Gandhiji was the staunch supporter of:
   (a) Big industries
   (b) Cottage industries
   (c) Both a and b
   (d) None of these
15. Who was the last British Viceroy of India?
   (a) Lord Lintithgow
   (b) Lord Wavell
   (c) Clement Atlee
   (d) Lord Mountbatten **(SSC Mat. 2008)**
16. The Swarajya party was formesd following failure of:
   (a) Non Cooperation Movement
   (b) Civil Disobedience Movement
   (c) Quit India Movement
   (d) Champaran Satyagraha
   (SSC Mat. 2008)
17. Who was the President of Indian National Congress when the Mountbatten Plan was accepted?
   (a) Jawahar Lal Nehru
   (b) Sardar Patel
   (c) Maulana Azad
   (d) J.B. Kripalani **(SSC Grad. 2008)**
18. Who developed the idea that 'means justify the ends'?
   (a) Kautilya
   (b) Raja Ram Mohan Roy

CHAPTER

12

Struggle for Independence: Early Phase (1885 to 1918)

Introduction

According to WC Bannerjee, the Congress was mainly a forum to represent its views to the British authorities, in whose sense of justice it had tremendous faith and the educated Indians in general and the congress in particular were thoroughly loyal, well wishers of the government. Every year the congress passed resolution expressing loyalty to the British crown.

Moderate Phase (1885-1905)

- During this period (1885-1905) congress was dominated by such leaders who by their method of functioning were termed moderates or liberals. They appealed through petitions, speeches and articles loudly professing loyalty to the Raj. The methods of the moderates can best be described as 'Constitutional Agitation'.
- However, the greatest limitation of the moderate leaders was that, they failed to realize the important nature of the British rule. They even failed to achieve, anything substantial by their methods.

Demands of Moderates

- The political demand of congress were moderate while its economic demands were radical and anti imperialist. Expansion and reform of legislative council, leading to popular control of administration.

- Greater opportunities for Indians in the public services by holding ICS examination simultaneously in England and India, this was achieved finally in 1923.
- Removal of restriction on freedom of the press and the speech.

- Abolition of discriminatory laws, which restricted the freedom of the people (e.g., Arms Act).
- Separations of the Judiciary from the Executive.
- A strong point made by the nationalists during this phase was about the economic drain of India. In this context, they demanded the end of India's economic drain.
- The reduction of land revenue in order to lighten the burden of taxation on the peasants.
- Improvement in the condition of work of the plantation laborers.
- Abolition of the Salt tax.
- The reduction of the high military expenditure in the Government of India.
- Reimposition of import duties on cotton goods.
- Other demands were raising of an Indian volunteer force; Higher jobs for Indians in the army; Protection for Indians settled abroad; Reduction of land revenue along with extension of irrigation and development of agricultural banks in order to make the agriculturist less dependent on moneylenders; Modification of forest laws; More funds for technical education which would promote Indian Industries.

Self Government of Moderates

- By the beginning of the 20th century, the moderates' nationalists put forward the claim of self-government within the British Empire as in the colonies of Australia, New Zealand and Canada. Gokhle first made this demand from the Congress Platform in 1905.
- Dadabhai Naoroji made this demand in 1906, in his presidential address at Calcutta Session of Congress.

Important Moderate Leaders

- Dadabhai Naoroji, Grand old man of India.
- Gopal Krishna Gokhale (Tilak Called him the diamond of India)
- Ferozshah Mehta
- MG Ranade
- Surendranath Bannerji
- Badruddin Tyabji
- WC Bannerji
- Dinsha Wacha
- Anand Mohan Bose
- RC Dutt
- Rash Behari Ghosh
- Dwarkanath Ganguli
- GV Joshi
- Viraraghavachari
- Anand Charlu
- Lala Lajpat Rai, (During his initial years of political activities).

Achievements of Moderates

- Creation of a wide national awakening.
- Popularization of the ideas of Democracy and Nationalism.
- Exposed the exploitative character of British imperialism.
- In this context the Theory of Drain of Wealth, popularized by the Moderates, played the most important role.
- Their concrete achievements were the appointment of a public service commission in 1856 ; the enactment of the Indian Council Act of 1892, which provided, some powers to elected local bodies.

- Their efforts resulted in a resolution of the Houses of Commons (1893) for simultaneous examination of the ICS in London and India appointment of the Welby Commission on Indian expenditure (1895).

> The greatest limitation of the Moderate Leadership was that it failed to realize the true nature of British rule and the importance of mass struggle.
> They confined their movement to the educated middle classes.

The Revolutionaries (1905-1918)

- The moderate policies of the early Congress disillusioned many of its younger leaders known as neo-nationalists or extremists.
- The extremists advocated Boycott of foreign goods, use of Swadeshi goods, National Education, Passive Resistance Swaraj. For some extremists Swaraj referred to complete autonomy or independence and not just self Government as was declared by moderates.
- The Boycott of British made goods and use of Swadeshi or home made products was designed to encourage Indian Industries. The idea of a National scheme of education was to encourage the boycott of Government-controlled universities and colleges.
- Bengal National College was established at Calcutta and a large number of national schools sprang up in East Bengal. Guroodas Bannerji headed the Bengal Council of National Education. In Madras the Pachiappa National College was set up. In Punjab the DAV movement made considerable headway.
- The extremists well understood and heighted the negative role of Britain in Indian. They talked of democracy, constitutionalism and progress and talked of broadening the social base of the national movement. They also realized that these objectives could not be realized without pressure tactics and some sort direct action. The policy of the extremists yielded good dividends. The partition of Bengal was annulled in 1911, which gave a new self-confidence and self-assurance to Indian nationalists.

Causes for the Rise of Revolutionaries

- There was a growing consciousness among the Indians of the exploitative character of the British colonial rule in India. The writings of early nationalist leaders had exposed the true nature of British Rule in India e.g., Ranade's Eassay on Indian Economy, Dadabhai Naoroji's Poverty and un-British Rule in India (1901), RC Dutt, Economic History of India (1901) etc.
- Some of the repressive policies of the British government which led to the discontent among the people and resulted in the growth of extremism were:
    - Welvy Commission on expenditure was set up.
    - The withdrawal of cotton excise duties in 1986.
    - The imprisonment of Tilak and some other leaders/editors for preaching nationalism, 1897.
    - The deportation of Natu brothers without trial 1897.

- The enactment of law, making it an offence to preach nationalism (1809).
- The enactment of the Indian Official Secretes Act, to restrict the freedom of the press (1904).
- The controversial partion of Bengal in 1905.
- The Three pillars of Extremism were Lal, Bal and Pal (Lala Lajpat Rai, Bal Gangadhar Tilak and Bipin Chandra Pal).
- All of them though their newspapers Tilak's Kesari, Pal's New India and Lala's Punjabi launched vehement attacks on the British Government.

❑ The immediate cause for the rise of extremism was the reactionary rule of Lord Curzon (1889-1905), considered the congress as an unclean thing and seditious organization.

❑ The Calcutta Corporation Act (1899), the Official Secrets Act and the Indian Universities Act created great resentment in India.

❑ The Delhi Durbar held in 1903, to mark the accession of king Edward VII, coming at a time, when India had not fully recovered from devastating effects of the famine of 1899–1900 was interpreted as a 'Pompous pageant' to a starving population. Curzon wrote to the Secretary of State in 1900, The Congress is tottering to its fall, and one of my greatest ambitions, while in India, is to assist it to a peaceful demise.

❑ The worst and most hated aspect of Curzon's administration was the Partition of Bengal in 1905. Curzon partitioned Bengal, ostensibly for administrative convenience, but in reality for curbing the growing nationalism. It is said that partition aided rather than deterred the forces undermining the British position in India.

Some Prominent Revolutionaries

Bal Gangadhar Tilak (1856-1920)

❑ Known as Lokmanya to the Indians and as the 'Father of Indian Unrest' to the British, he was regarded as 'One of the most dangerous pioneers of disaffection'. He began his political career as a moderate but by the beginning of the 20th century became an extremist.

❑ Tilak said Indians could not achieve any success if we croak once in a year like a frog. Tilak the greatest pillar of extremism indentified nationalism with the feeling of Hindutva. He wrote, "the Hindu of the Punjab, Maharashtra, Telengna and Dravida are one and the reason for this is the only Hindu Dharma."

❑ He used religious orthodoxy as a method of mass contact through his organization of the Ganapati Festival (1893) and Shivaji Festival from 1896 onwards.

❑ He was the first to give the slogan of Swarajya, Swadeshi and Boycott and wrote in his paper Kesari, "Our nation is like a tree", of which the original trunk was Swarajya and branches were Swadeshi and Boycott. He initiated a kind of no revenue campaign among the famine stricken peasants of Maharashtra in 1896-97.

Conservative Nature of Tilak

❑ Though a radical in politics, he was a conservative in social reforms. Tilak opposed the British Government initiative in the matter of social reforms. Hes did not consider social and political reforms to be interlinked and was of the opinion that political freedom should precede social reforms.

- He quarreled with the reformers over the Age of Consent Bill in 1891. The efforts of Parsi reformers BM Malabari led to the enactment of Age of Consent Act, 1891, which forbade the marriage of girls below the age of 12. Tilak threw a challenge to the National Social Conference in 1895, by not allowing it to hold its session in the Congress pavilion in Poona.
- The National Social Conference was under the influence of Moderate wing. Same year in July, Tilak and his group ousted Ranade and Gokhale from the control of poona Sarvajanik Sabha.
- He was a distinguished member of the Deccan Education Society and he was instrumental in founding the New English School, which later became the Fergusson college. In 1916 Tilak organized his own Home Rule League at Poona and declared "Swaraj is my Birthright and will have it".
- He was imprisoned several times by the British for his nationalist activities.
- As early as 1882, for criticizing in strong language the treatment meted out to the Maharaja of Kolhapur, the government tried and sentenced Tilak to four months' imprisonment.
- Again in 1897 Tilak was charged with spreading feelings of disaffection against the British Government and sent jail for 18 month's rigorous imprisonment and again in 1908 for 6 years (In the Mandalay Jail in Burma).
- At the Lucknow Session of the Congress (December 1899), Tilak attempted to move a resolution condemning Governor Sandhrust's administration of Bombay.
- He played a prominent role in anti-partition movement of 1905-08 and was responsible in making it an All India Movement. During Swadeshi Movement he declared, Swaraj is essential for the exercise of Swadharma, without Swaraj there could be no social reform, no industrial progress, no useful education and no fulfillment of national life.

Lala Lajpat Rai (1865-1928)

- Populary known, as Punjab Kesari, he was the leader of the 'College faction' of the Arya Samaj. The Gurukul fassction was led by Lala Munshi Ram. Lajpat Rai became an extremist leader in the beginning of the 20th century and played an important role in anti-partition movement.
- He was the editor of the 'Punjabee' and the author of a book 'Unhappy India'. He had declared that political rights could not be won by an organization which could not distinguish between begging rights and claiming them.
- Lala Lajpat Rai was also wedded to the idea of Hindu Nationality; however in this context he was not as rigid as Tilak.
- In Punjab, the cult of Swadeshi was propagated by Lala Lajpat Rai. While leading an anti Simon procession he was wounded and later died of injuries.

Bipin Chandra Pal (1858-1932)

- Known as the Father of Revolutionary Thought in India, B C Pal began his career as a Journalist and started the Paridarsak (a weekly); and later became the Assistant Editor of Bengal Public Opinion and the Tribune. He started New India in 1901 to propagate his brand of nationalism revolving around the ideals Swaraj, Swadeshi, Boycott and National education.

- He began his political career as a moderate, but later drifted towards the extremism. In 1902, he wrote, The Congress here and its British committee in London are both begging institutions.

Last Years of Pal

- Bipin Chandra Pal, in association with Aurobindo Ghosh edited the Bande Mataram in 1906.
- In the same year Bipin Chandra was sentenced to six months imprisonment on account of his refusal to tender evidence against Aurodbindo Ghosh during the latter's trail in the Bande Mataram's sedition case.
- After his imprisonment (March-August) 1908 his political thinking took on a different shape and form precipitating during his self-imposes exile (1908-11) in England.

Aurobindo Ghosh (1872-1950)

- Aurobindo Ghosh published "New Lamps for Old" in 1893-94 (While serving as a lecturer in Baroda) in which he criticized the Moderate politics of the Congress. He described the Congress leaders pleas to the government on issues like Legislative Councils and simultaneous civil services examination in London and India as playing with bubbles. He advocated the Doctrine of Passive Resistance in series of articles in 1907 in Bande Matram.
- Aurobindo played an important role in anti-partition movement and propounded the theory of organized an relentless boycott of British goods, British system of education, Judiciary and Executive.
- He became the principal of the Bengal National College started in Calcutta in 1906. He declared Swaraj as the fulfilment of the Ancient life of India under modern conditions, the return of Satyuga of National greatness. He was arrested by the British in 1908 due to his involvement in the Kennedy murders.
- After his release from the jail, in 1910, he went to Pondicherry and thereafter concentrated on philosophical, spiritual and literary activities. Some of his books were, Savitri (The longest epic poem in English), The Life Divine etc.
  - Aurobindo Ghosh raised patriotism to the Pedestal of mother worship and said; 'I know my country as my mother'. I adore her. I worship her.
  - In his work, Bhavani Mandir he wrote, 'Our mother country is not a piece of earth, neither a figure of speech nor a fiction of mind. It is mighty Shakti composed of the Shaktis of all the millions of units that make up the nation'.

Partition of Bengal and the Swadeshi Movement

- Among the Lord Curzon's administrative measures, the one that elicited the strongest opposition was the Partition of Bengal in 1905.

- The Province of Bengal, which was the most popular province of British India, comprised of Bengal proper (both West and East Bengal), Assam, Bihar and Orissa with its capital at Calcutta.
- In 1874, the British speared Assam from Bengal by making it a Chief Commissioners province and adding to it, the predominantly Bengali-Speaking area of Sylhet.
- Assam was further extended in 1897 by the transfer for the time being of South Lushai hill tract from Bengal.
- Real attack on Bengal came as early as 1899 when Curzon reduced the number of elected members in the Calcutta corporation primarily to satisfy the European business interests in the city, who often complained of delay in the grant of licenses and similar other facilities.
- After this Curzon launched an assault on the autonomous character of Calcutta University. Armed with the recommendation of Indian Universities Commission, whose sole Indian member (Gurudas Banerjee) disagreed wholly with, others, Curzon passed the Universities Act (1904).
- The objective used as a pretext was to raise the standard of education all round.
- The Universities Act cut down the number of elected senate members (mostly Indians) and transferred the ultimate power of affiliating colleges and schools, as well as giving them grant-in-aid, to the Government Officials.
- Another objective behind the partition was to Split up the Hindus and Muslims. Explaining the Political purpose behind partition to his superiors in London Curzon said he wanted to split up and thereby weaken a solid body of opponents to British Rule.

Idea Behind Partition of Bengal

- The idea of partition was first given by William Ward in 1896 (Chief Commissioner of Assam).
- Later, to meet the growing nationalist challenge in Eastern India, Curzon and his advisor, Sir A Fraser, (the lieutenant Governor of Bengal), and HH Risley, (Secretary, Home Department, Government of India) searched for an effective answers and eventually found it in the division of Bengali-speaking people.
- The official statement made by Risley was, Bengal united is a power, Bengal divided will pull several different ways. Similarly, Curzon also said, an Indian's only business was to be governed and it was a sacrilege on his part to have any other aspiration.

Roads to Partition

- The Curzon scheme to partition Bengal came to be publicly known from the time the Viceroy wrote his minute on Territorial Redistribution on 1 June, 1903.
- On 4 July, 1905 the Governemnt of India officially announced its decision to form the new province of East Bengal and Assam with its capital at Dacca comprising the Chittagong, Dacca and Rajshanhi division, Hill Tippera (Tripura), Malda and Assam (The Muslim majority province).

- The province came into existence on 16 October, 1905, by breaking up Bengal and its 41.5 million Bengali speaking people. After the partition of Bengal the two new Provinces that came into existence were East Bengal and Bengal.
- The truncated new province of Bengal with its capital at Calcutta was to comprise 11 districts of West Bengal, the district of Darjeeling, as also the whole of Bihar and Orissa (Majority of the population being Hindu).
- Sir Bamfylde Fuller, who described Muslims as his favorite wife, was the first Lieutenant Governor of East Bengal and Assam succeeded by Sir Lancelot Haze.
- The Congress called the plan of Partition of Bengal (1905) Preposterous (Completely unreasonable, absurd or shocking).

Anti-Partition Movement

- The initial objective of the movement was the annulment of Partition of Bengal. However, it was soon superseded by the greater objective of attainment of Swaraj.
- There were sharp press campaigns against the partition scheme, numerous public meeting were held in opposition to it and the petition were drafted and sent to the government for its annulment. Big conferences were held at the Town Hall Calcutta. However, all these methods failed, leading to a search for new techniques from the middle of 1905 and resulted in the discovery of the boycott of British goods as an effective weapon.
- The Boycott suggestion, during the Swadeshi Movement, first came from Krishna Kumar Mitra's Journal Sanjivani on 3 July, 1905. The suggestion was accepted by prominent public men at the Calcutta Town Hall/Federal Hall meeting of 7 August, 1905. It was here that the resolution to launch Swadeshi Movement was passed and the slogan of 'Bande Mataram' was adopted.
- Rabindranath Tagore composed 'Amar Sonar Bangla' for the occasion which was sung by huge crowds parading the streets (This song was adopted as its national anthem by Bangladesh in 1971 after liberation). Bipin Chandra Pal emphasized on the idea of Passive Resistance or refusal to render any voluntary or honorary service to the Government. Savarkar founded the Mitra Mela.

Day of Partition

- The Partition officially came into effect on 16 October, 1905. The leader of the protest movement declared it to be a day of National mourning throughout Bengal.
- No cooking was done and the shops and market places were kept closed.
- SN Banerjee and Ananda Mohan Bose addressed huge gathering of people (The largest till then under the nationalist banner).
- Rabindranath Tagore and Ramendra Sunder Trivedi called for the observance of Raksha-Bandhan (The tying of thread on each other's hand as a symbol of brotherhood) and Ramendra Sunder Trivedi, called for Arandhan on the day the partition was put into effect.

- The National Song, Vande Mataram composed in Sanskrit by Bankim Chandra overnight, became the national song for whole country. (it was sung for the first time at the 1896 session of INC.)
- Aurobindo Ghosh came out with the theory of organized and relentless boycott of British goods, British system of education, judiciary and executive and the Social boycott of the loyalists and civil disobedience of unjust laws. The boycott of British product was followed by the advocacy of Swadeshi and holding of Swadeshi meals. Charka came to signify the popular concern for the country's economic self-sufficiency.
- An important aspect of the Swadeshi movement was the emphasis placed on self-reliance or Atmaskti (Advocated by Rabindranath Tagore). Several exclusive Indian Industrial ventures such as the Calcutta Potteries, Bengal Chemical Swadeshi Stores (Opened by Acharya PC Ray), Lakshmi Cotton Mills, Mohini Mills and National Tannery were started.
- Even Rabindranath Tagore helped to open a Swadeshi store. The Swadeshi movement also led to boycott of the officially controlled educational institutions. In this context the concept of National education was propounded and the leader of Swadeshi movement decided to run a parallel system of education.
- The University of Calcutta, which supervised education in school and college, was denounced as a Gulam Khana (House for slaves) and Bengal Council of National Education headed by Guroodas Banerjee was established with a view to organizing a system of education on national lines and under national management.
- The government made attempt to suppress the students by threatening to withdraw grants, scholarships and affiliations of the institutions to which belonged, through the infamous circular of 22 October, 1905 issued by Carlyle, the Chief Secretary of the Government of Bengal (the circular is also known otherwise as the Carlyle Circular).
- This led to the establishment of Bengal Technical Institute (Started on 25 July, 1906 and which later turned into the College of Engineering and Technology, Jadavpur).
- The Bengal National College and School was set up on 15th August, 1906 with Aurobindo Ghosh as its Principal. Panchaiyapp's National College was founded at Madras.
- The Congress supported the Boycott movement only for Bengal at its Banaras Session in 1905. Extremists wanted to extend the movement to the other parts of the country, but the moderates refused to accept this. In 1906 Session of Congress at Calcutta, Dadabhai Naoroji declared the aim of Congress to be Swaraj like that of UK and other Colonies.
- The four compromise resolutions passed at this session were—Swadeshi, Boycott, National Education and Self Government. Here the demand for Swaraj was raised for the first time from the Congress platform.
- Indian Society of Oriental Art was set up in 1907. Nand Lal Bose became the first recipient of scholarship offered by

the Society. A large number of national volunteer bodies or samities Sprang up in.

- Some of the distinguished society among them were:
  - Dawn society (Named after the Journal—Dawn) by Sachindra Mukherjee.
  - The Anti-Circular Society
  - The Swadeshbhandhav
  - The Anushilan by Promtha Mitter.
  - The Dacca Anushilan Samiti by Pulin Das.
- These Samitis preached the essential of Swadeshi and Boycott, took up social work during famines and epidemics, imparted physical and moral training, organized crafts and national schools and set up arbitration committees and village societies.
- Many prominent Muslims joined the Swadeshi Movement including Abdur Rasul (the famous barrister), Liaquat Hussain (the popular agitator) and Guznavi (the businessmen). Maulana Abul Kalam Azad joined one of the revolutionary terrorist groups.

End of the Movement

- With the split of Congress at Surat the Swadeshi Movement lost its major strength and force and was finally suppressed by the British through repressive measures like imprisonment and deportation of many of its leaders in 1908.
- However, the Swadeshi movement was the beginning of the organized movement in India. The significant of the movement can be assessed from the fact that Mahatma Gandhi wrote, the real awakening in India took place after partition of Bengal.

Annulment of Partition of Bengal (December 1911)

- In December 1911 King George V and the Queen visited India (He was the only British king visited India). On December 12, 1911 a magnificent coronation Durbar was held in Delhi, which was chosen as the seat of the imperial function.
- The official proclamation regarding the annulment of the Partition of Bengal and the transfer of British capital from Calcutta to Delhi was made in Delhi Darbar.
- After the annulment of partition the West and East Bengal were integrated and three separate states created—(i) Bengal (Comprising East and West Bengal) (ii) Assam (of same status it had in 1874) (iii) Bihar and Orissa (finally separated in 1935).

Hardinge Bomb Case

- December 23, 1912 was fixed as the date for the Viceroy's state entry into the new Capital, Delhi.
- On that day, when the Viceroy and Vicerine, the ruling princes and senior officials were being taken in long procession through Chandni Chowk in Delhi, a bomb was thrown at the elephant carrying the Viceroy.
- Harding was badly wounded. Ras Behari threw the bomb. Bhai Bal Mukund was sentenced to death in the Hardinge Bomb case.

Surat Split

Cause behind the Split

- The difference between the Moderates and the Extremists widened during the Swadeshi movement.
- The issues being spread of Boycott outside Bengal, choice of the method for struggle, conflict of ideologies and clash of personalities.
- The Extremists wanted to extend the idea of boycott and Swadeshi to the regions outside Bengal and also to include the government services, law courts, Legislative Council and all other forms of associations with the British in their programme. The Moderates on other hand were not in favour of this.
- There was controversy over the issue of Presidentship in Calcutta Congress session (1906). Pal and Aurobindo wanted Tilak to be the president, but the Moderates were in no mood to accept him. Finally both the groups accepted Dadabhai Naoroji as the President.
- Having failed in their attempt to get Tilak installed at President the extremists—Tilak, Aurobindo, Pal, Ashwini Kumar Dutt, GS Khaparde etc. formed themselves into a pressure group.
- At Calcutta it had been decided to hold the next session of the congress at Nagpur but later Ferozshah Mehta changed the venue to Surat, so as to exclude Tilak from standing as a candidate for presidentship (Surat was in Tilak's home province of Bombay).
- The growing difference between the moderates and the extremists came to the fore at the Surat session of the Congress in 1907, when against the wishes of the Extremists who preferred Lala Lajpat Rai; Ras Behari Ghosh was chosen as president.
- Finally, the moderates who were in majority gained complete control over the congress organization and the extremists were suspended from the INC.
- The Moderates met after the split on December 28, 1907 and formed a Convention Committee for drawing up the new constitution of the INC. This Committee met at Allahabad in April 1908 and drew up a Constitution and the INC finally ratified it at its Madras session in 1908.
- The provision of the new Constitution closed the door of the INC to the extremists. It was only after 1916, with the entry of the extremists in the congress, that the congress could be reactivated.

Foundation of All-India Muslim League

- **Simla Deputation:** The Partition of Bengal created a communal divide. On October 1, 1906 a Muslim deputation led by the Agha Khan, met Lord Minto at Simla. The address presented by the deputation claimed a privileged position for Indian Muslims on the grounds of political importance, military service and the historical memories of their lost political glory.
- Minto gave a categorical assurance that the political rights and interests of the Muslims as a community would be safeguarded.

- The Simla Deputation was followed in Eastern Bengal by Muslim in Eastern Bengal by Muslim meetings in support of the Partition of Bengal. Nawab Habibulla (or Salimullah) of Dacca, favored by Lord Curzon, took the leadership of the pro-partition movement.
- A meeting was held at Dacca on December 30, 1906, where it was decided to form a political association, called the All India Muslim League, with three objectives:
  - To promote among Muslim loyalty to the British Government.
  - To protect and advance the political rights of the Muslims; and
  - To prevent the rise among the Muslims of any feeling of hostility towards other communities without prejudice to other objects of the League.
- To propagate his Anti League views, Maulana Muhammad Ali started an English Journal 'Comrade' and an Urdu Paper 'Hamdard'. He also started Al-Hilal, which served as mouthpiece of his Nationalist view.
  - The Amritsar session of the League, held in 1908, under the Presidentship of Sir Syed Ali Imam, demanded a separate electorate for the Muslims, which was conceded to them by the Morley-Minto reforms 1909.
  - Jinnah for many years opposed the League. In 1910, at the Allahabad session of the Congress, he moved a resolution condemning the system of communal electorates.

Home Rule Movement

- The Home Rule Movement was the Indian response to the first World War and represented the emergence of a new trend of aggressive politics. Annie Besant and Bal Gangadhar Tilak proved to be the pioneers of this new trend. However, the idea of starting a Home Rule League in India originated with Annie Besant.
- On 16th June, 1914, Bal Gangadhar Tilak was released after serving a long term in prison and he concentrated all his attention on securing the re-admission of himself and other extremists into the Indian National Congress.
- Mrs Annie Besant who had just jointed the Indian National Congress pressurised the Congress to admit the extremists. Consistent efforts secured them their re-entry in December 1915. However, she failed to get the Congress approve her Scheme of Home Rule League.
- The definite campaign for Home Rule, began with the publication of weekly, The Commonweal, on January 2nd 1914. Tilak started the Indian Home Rule League in April 1916 and 5 months later in September 1916 Mrs Annie Besant started the Home Rule League.
- Tilak's league was to work in Maharashtra (Excluding Bombay City), Karnataka, the Central province and Berar and Annie Besant League was given charge of rest of India.
- The Home Rule Movement had borrowed the term 'Home Rule' from a similar movement in Ireland. The main

objective of Home Rule League was to attain Home-rule for India within the British Empire, on the lines of the automous colonies of Australia, New Zealand etc.

Tilak's Home Rule League

- Tilak's Home Rule League, launched at the Bombay Provincial Conference held at Belgaum in April 1916, was organized into 6 branches; Tilak launched propaganda in favour of Home Rule through Maharatta and Kesari.
- It published pamphlets in Kannada, Gujarati, Marathi and English.
- The demands included Swaraj formation of Linguistic states and education in vernaculars.
- According to Tilak, India was like a son who had grown up and attained maturity and it was right now that the trustee or the father should give him what his was due.
- It was during the Home Rule Movement that Bal Gangadhar Tilak was given title of Lokmanya.
- On 23rd July, 1916 (Tilak's sixtieth birthday), British served him notice asking him to show cause why he should not be bound over for good behavior and demanded securities of Rs. 60000. Tilak was defended by a team of lawyers led by Muhammad Ali Jinnah.
- Tilak lost the case in the lower court but the High Court exonerated him in November 1916. This gave fillip to the Movement and Tilak pushed home the advantage by declaring that Home Rule now had legal sanction.

Annie Besant's Home Rule League

- Annie Besant had come to India from England in 1893 to work for the Theosophical Society. She had set up her headquarter at Adyar near Madras. Annie Besant's Home Rule League was formally inaugurated in September 1916, in Madras, with George Arundale, as the organizing secretary.
- Most of league's works carried on by Annie Besant and her lieutenants—Arundale, CP Ramaswamy Aiyer, and BP Wadia.
- Annie Besant also brought out the papers New India and Commonweal. The Commonweal adopted as its Cardinal Programme, Religious Liberty, National Education, Social Reform and Political Reform aiming at self-government for India within the British Commonwealth.
- The definite campaign for home rule began with the publication of a weekly journal 'The Commonweal', the main aim was to popularize the idea of and achieving self government for India within the British common wealth Jawaharlal Nehru in Allahabad and B Chakravarti and J Banerjee in Calcutta joined the league.
- The Government of Madras in June 1917 came with the decision to place Mrs Besant and her associate BP Wadia and George Arundale under arrest. This led to nationwide protest. Sir S Subramaniya Aiyer renounced his knighthood in protest.
- The repression of the government only served to harden the attitude of the agitators.

- Montague, the secretary of state, commented that Shiva cut his wife into fifty-two pieces only to discover that he had fifty-two wives.
- That is what happened to the Government of India when it interned Mrs Besant.
- Some leaders who stayed away from the League like Madan Mohan Malaviya, Surendranath Banerjee and MA Jinnah now enlisted as members of the Home Rule League.
- Tilak advocated passive resistance to the AICC meeting in July 1917, and Gandhiji suggested the collection of signatures of one thousand men willing to defy the interment orders and march to Besant place of detention.
- After Montague's declaration (August 1917) also known as August Declaration. Mrs Besant finally dropped her league but Tilak continued his movement.
    - Facing with this growing agitation, the government in Britain decided to adopt a soft line. Annie Besant was released in September 1917.
    - She, at Tilak's instance, was elected President of the annual session of the Congress in December 1917 where she declared India is no longer on her knees for boons; she is on her feet for Rights.

Lucknow Pact (1916)

The Lucknow Session (1916) is rememberable for two important developments.

(i) The first was the re-admission of the extremists.

(ii) The second was the bond of alliance between the Congress and the Muslim League.

- During the First World War, a Muslim organization Ehrar League proposed that Muslims should participate and try reach an accord with the Congress.
- The League at its annual session of 1915 in Bombay which was also attended by many Congress leaders (Gandhi, Malviya and Sarojini Naidu) appointed a committee to draw up a scheme of political reforms in consultation with other communities.
- During simultaneous annual sessions of the League and Congress held at Lucknow in December 1916 both passed resolution separately for a joint and reached an agreement to cooperate in the political filed on the basis of a common programme. Tilak and Annie Besant agreed on a common programme. Tilak and Annie Besant dominated the Lucknow session.
- This agreement is generally known as the Lucknow Pact or the Congress-League Scheme. The pact had resulted largely due to Tilak's effort.
- The Lucknow Pact exhorted the British Government to confer self-Government to India as early as possible, to expand Provincial Legislative Council and the Governor Generals Legislative Council and to provide for greater representation of the elected members on the expanded council.
- If further demanded that the powers of making appointments to the Indian Civil Services should vest in the government of India and that the commissioned and non-commissioned ranks in the military and naval services should be thrown open to Indians. The pact also marked the formal acceptance of separate electorates for Muslims.

- The pact succeeded in getting the reforms through Montague Chelmsford reforms of 1919.
- However, the All-India Hindu Mahasabha led the crusade against the Lucknow Pact, at its conference held in Lucknow, VP Madhav Rao, in this presidential address, and attacked the principle of separate electorates.
- At the same time, certain conservative Muslims vigorously opposed coorperation with the congress, which they identified as 'Hindu Body'.
- The Congress-League or the Lucknow Pact survived till the suspension of the Non-cooperation Movement in February 1922, after the Chauri-Chaura incident.
- Dr RC Mazumadar who is very critical of the Lucknow Pact, is of the view "For no one can doubt in the light of subsequent events, that the congress action in 1916 well and truly laid the foundation on which Pakistan was built thirty years later".
- The basic defect of the Lucknow Pact was that it was based on the wrong notion that Hindus and Muslims formed separate communities, and therefore the pact proved to be only a temporary truce.
  - Idea of Boycott was first suggested in Sanjibani Magazine by KK Mitra.
  - Organization founded during Swadeshi Movements.
    - Dawn Society by satish Chandra Mukherjee (also a magazine Dawn).
    - Anti circular society with Liaquat Hussain and Abdul Gaffar as members.
    - Anushilan Samiti (Dhaka) by Pulin Das.
    - Swadeshi Bandhav Samiti by Ashwani Kumar Dutt.
    - Swadeshi Samaj by Rabindranath Tagore.
  - Raj Kumar Shukla invited Gandhiji to Champaran.
  - Anasuya Behn (sister of Ambalal Sarabhai) and Sarla Devi (his wife) Supported Gandhiji in Ahmedabad Satyagraha.

Montague Declaration (1917)

- The aftermath of the First World War, the rapid growth of the revolutionary activities and the popularity of the Home Rule Movement pressurised the British to effect a change in its policies and adopt a conciliatory attitude towards the demands of the Indian nationalists. On August 20, 1917, Montague (Secreatary of State of India) Made a historic Declaration in the House of Commons defined the goal of British Policies in India.
- He defined this goal as the Increasing association of Indians in every branch of administration, and the gradual development of self-governing institution with a view to the progressive realization of Responsible Government in India as an integral part of British Empire.
- Shortly, thereafter, Montague visited India in November 1917, to ascertain the views of all shades of political opinion in India. On the basis of these discussions a detailed Report on Indian Constitutional Reforms was prepared, which was published in July 1918. This

report in turn formed the basis of the Montague-Chelmsford Reforms or the Government of India Act, 1919.

Reactions to Montague's Declaration

- Reactions within the Congress sharply varied. The Moderates welcomed it as the Magna Carta of India while others criticized it as falling for short of the legitimate expectation of India.
- Tilak Characterised the Montague Declaration as sunless dawn.

Second Split in INC (1918)

- The division of opinion within the congress on the Montague declaration ultimately resulted in the second split in the party, this time the Moderates walking out. The INC in a special session (August 1918) criticised the August Declaration as disappointing and unsatisfactory and suggested important modification.
- The moderates led by Surendranath Bannerjee, supported the declaration in a separate conference (November 1918).
- This brought about the second split in the Congress. The ultra moderates started a new party called the National Liberal League in 1918, later on known as All-India Liberal Federation.

Revolutionary Activities in India

First Phase

- Vasudev Balwant Phadke, known as father of militant nationalism, gathered backward classes including Kols and Bhils and tried to create rebellion within British Empire. But he was caught and deported to Aden.
- By 1902, four revolutionary groups were set up in Calcutta and Midnapur.
  - Midnapur Society by Sarla Ghosal (edited Bharti Magazine)
  - Anushilan Samiti
  - Atmonnoti Group
  - Yugantar group by Barindra Kumar Ghosh, Raja Subodh Malik and Hemchandra Qanungo.
- First Political robbery was conducted in 1906, known as Rangpur Dacoity.
- A bomb manufacturing unit was set up at Maniktala (Calcutta).
- Kingsford Attempt to Murder Case, 1908 yugantar group planned to kill Kingsford, the magistrate of Mazzafarpur, but failed. Aurobindo Ghosh was arrested and Khudiram Bose was arrested and executed in Hijni jail, Hazaribagh.
- There was an assassination attempt on the life of Governor General, Lord Hardinge (December 1912) by Master Amir Chandra, Awadh Bihari and Basant Kumar Biswas.
- In Madras, revolutionary activities were carried on by Bharat Mata Association under Vanchi lyer and supported by VO Chidambram Pillai.
- Indian Madras, revolutionary outside India were based on the principle of absolute political freedom. Prominent groups were
  - India House By Shyamji Krishna Verma set up in London: He also started the newspaper 'The Indian Sociologist'. VD Savarkar was its member, who later started the secret societies Abinav Bharat and Mitra Mela.

- Other members Lala Hardayal, VN Chatterjee, MPT Acharya, PM Bapat, VSS Iyer and Madan Lal Dhingra (Assassinated British Officer Curzon Wylie in 1909.)

- Paris Indian Society was founded by Madam Bhikaji Cama. She started two newspapers Vande Mataram and Madans Talwar.
- India Independence Committee was set up by Virendranath Chattopadhayaya in Berlin.
- A Provisional Government of Free India was set up in Kabul in 1915 under Presidentship of Raja Mahendra Pratap, Barkatullah (Prime Minister) and Obeidullah Sindhi as Home Minister.
- Ghadar Party Movement (1913): Indian nationalists' including student like Tarak Nath Das who published Free Hindustan Newspaper in North America helped in rising awareness about nationalism.
  - Similarly, Hind Association of Pacific coast was set up in 1913 by Sohan Singh Bhakna and also started a newspaper, Hindustani Ghadar, edited by Lala Hardayal.
  - Soon activities of the association came to be known as Ghadar Party Movement which was first secular, democratic, revolutionary movement.
  - It's headquarter was known as Yugantar Ashram in San Francisco (USA). They published the newspaper Hindustani Ghadar.
  - In Punjab, Bharat Mata Society under Kartar Singh carried the Ghadar Movement. Similarly in Hong Kong a Sikh priest, Bhagwan Singh, carried the movement.
  - The movement ended with the arrest of Lala Hardayal, beginning of World War and Komagata Maru incident (Chartered ship of Gurudith Singh carrying Muslim and Sikh immigrants from Vancouver but the British government did not allow anyone to leave the ship at Calcutta and violent protest broke out).

Second Phase

- ❑ Bhagat Singh founded the Naujawan Bharat Sabha.
- ❑ Kakori Train Dacoity Case, 1925—Ram Prasad Bismil and Ashafqulla were accused.
- ❑ Murder of Saunders (ASP of Lahore), 1929—Bhagat Singh was accused.
- ❑ Assembly Bomb Case (Delhi), 1929—Bhagat Singh, Batukeshwar Dutta and Rajguru.
- ❑ Surya Sen was accused in Chittagong Armoury Dacoity, 1930.
- ❑ Udham Singh murdered General Dyer in London in 1940.

Chapter at a Glance

- The East India Association was founded by Dada Bhai Naoroji in 1866.
- The venue of the first session of Indian National Congress was fixed at Pune. The venue was shifted to Bombay because cholera broke out at Pune.

- At Bombay the session was held at Tejpal Sanskrit Paathshala, Bombay.
- 72 delegates participated in the first session of Indian National Congress.
- At the time of the first session of Indian National Congress in 1885, the secretary of state for India was Kimberely.
- The government servants were forbidden to take any part in the proceedings of the Congress after the Allahabad session (1888).
- The Boycott against the partition of Bengal was suggested by a Bengali weekly 'Sanjivani' and was adopted at a public meeting at Bagerhat.
- The All India Muslim League was established on 3 December, 1906.
- Vasudeo Balwant Phadke created a terror for British authorities in 1878 in Maharashtra.
- The great revolutionary Sri Shyamji Krishna Verma was a great Sanskrit scholar and had also been the *Dewan* of Udaipur and Junagarh States.
- Shyamji Verma, the first man to initiate and fight for India's struggle of independence from outside India started to publish a journal 'Sociologists' from January 1905.
- V.D. Savarkar wrote a book 'Joseph Mazzini–Biography and Politics' in 1906.
- Madam Bhikaji Cama was arrested in 1914 and deported to an island for four years.
- The original name of the Gadar Party was 'Hindi Association of the Pacific Coast'.
- The branches of Gadar Party was established at Manila, Bangkok, Hongkong, Shanghai and Panama.
- In 1915 an Indian Independence Committee was formed with the help of German Government to organise invasion of Burma from Siam and China.
- Tilak set up Indian Home Rule League on 28 April, 1916 with Headquarter at Poona.
- Annie Besant founded the Home Rule League on 1 September, 1916 with Headquarter at Madras.
- In 1910, Baba Gurdit Singh floated a shipping company under the name of 'Guru Nanak Navigation Company' and hired a Japanese Ship 'Kamagata Maru'.
- Vishnu Ganesh Pingle, Ras Behari Bose and Sachin Sanyal arrived at Punjab to organise a final revolt on 21 February, 1915.

Previous Year Question Paper (1998-2017)

1. The Partition of Bengal made by Lord Curzon in 1905 lasted until
   (a) The First World War when Indian troops were needed by the British and the partition was ended.
   (b) King George V abrogated Curzon's Act at the Royal Durbar in Delhi in 1911.
   (c) Gandhiji launched his Civil Disobedience Movement.
   (d) The Partition of India in 1947 when East Bengal became the Pakistan.
   (2015)
2. The 1929 Session of Indian National Congress is of significance in the history of the Freedom Movement because the:
   (a) Attainment of Self-Government was declared as the objective of the Congress.

(b) Attainment of Poorna Swaraj was adopted as the goal of the Congress:
(c) Non-Cooperation Movement was launched.
(d) Decision to participate in the Round Table Conference in London was taken. **(2015)**

3. The people of India agitated against the arrival of Simon Commission because:
(a) Indians never wanted the review of the working of the Act of 1919.
(b) Simon Commission recommended the abolition of Dyarchy (Diarchy) in the Provinces.
(c) There was no Indian member in the Simon Commission.
(d) The Simon Commission suggested the partition of the country. **(2013)**

4. Quit India Movement was launched in response to:
(a) Cabinet Mission Plan
(b) Cripps Proposals
(c) Simon Commission Report
(d) Wavell Plan **(2013)**

5. With reference to Indian History, the Members of the Constituent Assembly from the Provinces were:
(a) Directly elected by the people of those provinces.
(b) Nominated by the Indian National Congress and the Muslim League.
(c) Elected by the Provincial Legislative Assemblies.
(d) Selected by the Government for their expertise in constitutional matters. **(2013)**

6. The demand for the Tabhaga Peasant Movement in Bengal was for:
(a) The reduction of the share of the landlords from one-half of the crop to one-third.
(b) The grant of ownership of land to peasants as they were actual cultivators of the land.
(c) The uprooting of Zamindari system and the end of serfdom.
(d) Writing off all peasant debts. **(2013)**

7. The Ilbert Bill controvercy was related to the:
(a) Imposition of certain restrictions to carry arms by the Indians.
(b) Imposition of restrictions on newspapers and magazines published in Indian languages.
(c) Removal of disqualifications imosed on the Indian magistrates with regard to the trial of the Europeans.
(d) Removal of a duty on imported cotton cloth. **(2013)**

8. The Congress ministries resigned in the seven provinces in 1939 because:
(a) The Congress could not form ministries in the the other four provinces.
(b) Emergence of a 'left wing' in the Congress made the working of the ministries impossible.
(c) There were widespread communal disturbances in their provinces.
(d) None of the statements (a), (b) and (c) given above is correct. **(2012)**

9. During the freedom struggle, the National Social Conference was formed. What was the reason for its formation ?
(a) Different social reform groups or organizations of Bengal region united to form a single body to discuss the issues of larger interest and to prepare appropriate petitions/representations to the government.

(b) Indian National Congress did not want to include social reforms in its deliberations and decided to form a separate body for such a purpose
(c) Behramji Malabari and M.G. Ranade decided to bring together all the social reform groups of the country under one organistion.
(d) None of the statements (a), (b) and (c) given above is correct in this context. **(2015)**

10. Which of the following parties were established by Dr. B.R. Ambedkar?
    1. The Peasants and Workers Party of India
    2. All India Scheduled Castes Federation
    3. The Independent Labour Party

    Select the correct answer using the codes given below:
    (a) 1 and 2 only (b) 2 and 3 only
    (c) 1 and 3 only (d) 1, 2, and 3**(2012)**

11. Mahatma Gandhi undertook fast unto death in 1932, mainly because:
    (a) Round Table Conference failed to satisfy Indian political aspirations.
    (b) Congress and Muslim League had differences of opinion.
    (c) Ramsay MacDonald announced the Communal Award.
    (d) None of the statements (a), (b) and (c) given above is correct in this context. **(2012)**

12. Consider the following statements:
    The most effective contribution made by Dadabhai Naoroji to the cause of Indian National Movement was that he:
    1. Exposed the economic exploitation of India by the British.
    2. Interpreted the ancient Indian texts and restored the self-confidence of Indians.
    3. Stressed the need for eradication of all the social evils before anything else.

    Which of the statements given above is/are correct? **(2015)**
    (a) 1 only (b) 2 and 3 only
    (c) 1 and 3 only (d) 1, 2 and 3

13. The Rowlatt Act aimed at:
    (a) Compulsory economic support to war efforts.
    (b) Imprisonment without trial and summary procedures for trial.
    (c) Suppression of the Khilafat Movement.
    (d) Imposition of restrictions on freedom of the press. **(2015)**

14. The Lahore Session of the Indian National Congress (1929) is very important in history, because
    1. The Congress passed a resolution demanding complete independence
    2. The rift between the extremists and moderates was resolved in that Session
    3. Resoloution was passed rejecting the two-nation theory in that Session

    Which of the statements given above is/are correct?
    (a) 1 only
    (b) 2 and 3
    (c) 1 and 3
    (d) None of the above **(2015)**

15. Mahatma Gandhi said that some of his deepest convictions were reflected in a book titled, "Undo this Last" and the book transformed his life. What was the message from the book that transformed Mahatma Gandhi?

(a) Uplifting the opporessed and poor is the moral responsibility of an educated man
(b) The good of individual is contained in the good of all
(c) The life of celibacy and spiritual pursuit are essential for a noble life
(d) All the statements (a), (b) and (c) are correct in this context **(2011)**

16. With reference to Indian freedom struggle, Usha Mehta is well-known for:
(a) Running the secret Congress Radio in the wake of Quit India Moement
(b) Participating in the Second Round Table Conference
(c) Leading a contingent of Indian National Army
(d) Assisting in the formation of Interim Government under Pandit Jawaharlal Nehru **(2011)**

17. With reference to the period of Indian freedom struggle, which of the following was/were recommended by the Nehru report?
1. Complete Independence for India.
2. Joint electorates for reservation of seats for minorities.
3. Provision of fundamental rights for the people of India in the Constitution.

Select the correct answer using the codes given below:
(a) 1 only (b) 2 and 3 only
(c) 1 and 3 only (d) 1, 2 and 3 **(2011)**

18. Which one of the following observations is not true about the Quit India Movement of 1942?
(a) It was a non-violent movement
(b) It was led by Mahatma Gandhi
(c) It was a spontaneous movement
(d) It did not attract the labour class in general **(2011)**

19. What was the reason for Mahatma Gandhi to organize a satyagraha on behalf of the peasants of Kheda?
1. The Administration did not suspend the land revenue collection in spite of a drought.
2. The administration proposed to introduce Permanent Settlement in Gujarat.

Which of the statements given above is/are correct? **(2011)**
(a) 1 only (b) 2 only
(c) Both 1 and 2 (c) Neither 1 nor 2

20. With reference to Simon Commission's recommendations, which one of the following statements is correct?
(a) It recommended the replacement of diarchy with responsible government in the provinces.
(b) It proposed the setting up of inter-provincial council under the Home Department.
(c) It suggested the abolition of bicameral legislature at the Centre.
(d) It recommended the creation of Indian Police Service with a provision for increased pay and allowances for British recruits as compared to Indian recruits. **(2010)**

21. Four resolutions were passed at the famous Calcutta session of Indian National Congress in 1906. The question of either retention OR rejection of these four resolutions became the cause of a split in Congress at the next Congress session held in Surat in 1907.
Which one of the following was not one of these resolutions ?
(a) Annulment of partition of Bengal
(b) Boycott
(c) National education
(d) Swadeshi **(2010)**

22. After Quit India Movement, C. Rajagopalachari issued a pamphlet entitled "The Way Out". Which one of the following was a proposal in this pamphlet?
    (a) The establishment of a "War Advisory Council" composed of representative of British India and the Indian States.
    (b) Reconstitution of the Central Executive Council in such a way that all its members, except the Governor General and the Commander-in-Chief should be Indian leaders.
    (c) Fresh elections to the Central and Provincial Legislatures to be held at the end of 1945 and the Constitution making body to be convened as soon as possible.
    (d) A solution for the constitutional deadlock. **(2010)**
23. What was the immediate cause for the launch of the Swadeshi movement?
    (a) The partition of Bengal done by Lord Curzon.
    (b) A sentence for 18 months rigorous imprisonment imposed on Lokmanya Tilak.
    (c) The arrest and deportation of Lala Lajpat Rai and Ajit Singh; and passing of the Punjab Colonization Bill.
    (d) Death stentence pronounced on the Chapekar brothers. **(2010)**

Answers

1. (b)	2. (b)	3. (c)
4. (b)	5. (c)	6. (a)
7. (c)	8. (d)	9. (d)
10. (b)	11. (c)	12. (a)
13. (b)	14. (a)	15. (d)
16. (a)	17. (b)	18. (a)
19. (a)	20. (a)	21. (a)
22. (d)	23. (a)	

Practice Paper

1. Who called Gandhiji 'half naked beggar'?
   (a) Mountbatten
   (b) Hastings
   (c) Winston Churchill
   (d) Jinnah **(Bihar SSC LDC 2005)**
2. Arrange the following events with reference to India's Freedom Movement in chronological sequence:
   I. First Round Table Conference
   II. Poona Pact
   III. Simon Commission
   IV. Gandhi-Irwin Pact
   The correct chronological sequence of these events is
   (a) I– III– II–IV (b) III, I, II, IV
   (c) I, III, IV, II (d) III–I–IV–II
   (SCRA 2001)
3. **Assertion (A):** During the India Freedom struggle, the Non-co-operation Movement was called off by the Congress Working Committee in its meeting at Bardoli.
   Reason (R): Mass violence occurred at Chauri- Chaura in 1922.
   (a) Both A and R are true and R is the correct explanation of A
   (b) Both A and R are true but R is not a correct explanation of A

(c) A is true but R is false
(d) A is false but R is true
(SCRA 2001, NDA 2005, Utt. PCS (M) 2007)

4. The final arrangements for the India's independence were worked out by the:
(a) Cabinet Mission
(b) Simon Commission
(c) Gandhi-Irwin Pact
(d) Cripps Mission **(SCRA Grad 2003)**

5. Match List-I with List-II and select the correct answer using the codes given below the Lists:

List-I (Event)	List-II (Year)
A. Khilafat Movement	1. 1930
B. Chauri-Chaura Incident	2. 1917
C. Champaran Movement	3. 1920
D. First Round Table Conference	4. 1922

Codes

	A	B	C	D
(a)	2	3	4	1
(b)	4	1	2	3
(c)	2	1	4	3
(d)	3	4	2	1

(SCRA 2003)

6. **Assertion (A):** Rabindra Nath Tagore relinguished the Knighthood.
Reason (R): The Jallianwala Bagh Massacre caused deep anguish in the heart of Rabindra Nath Tagore and that prompted him to relinguish the Knighthood.
(a) Both A and R are true and R is the correct explanation of A
(b) Both A and R are true but R is not a correct explanation of A
(c) A is true but R is false
(d) A is false but R is true
(SCRA 2005)

7. With which of the following newspapers was JawaharLal Nehru associated?
(a) The Leader
(b) Amrit Bazar Patrika
(c) The Tribune
(d) National Herald
(Indraprastha Univ.(Delhi) Mass Comm. 2007)

8. Which of the following days was declared as the 'International Day of Non-voilence' by the UNO?
(a) August 15 (b) October 2
(c) November 12 (d) October 26
(Dena Bank Special Officers, Corp. Bank PO 2007)

9. 'Dyarchy' in the provincial Government was established by the
(a) Act of 1892 (b) Act of 1909
(c) Act of 1919 (d) Act of 1935
(UGC NET/JRF (Hist) 2007)

10. During India's freedom struggle, which one of the following led to the first 'All India Hartal'?
(a) Protest against Rowlatt Act
(b) Protest against Jallianwala Bagh Massacre
(c) Trial of Mahatma Gandhi
(d) Arrival of Simon Commission
(CPF Assit. Commat. 2008)

11. On which one of the following dates Jawahar Lal Nehru unfurl the tri-colour national flag on the banks of the Ravi as the clock struck the midnight?
(a) 31st December, 1929
(b) 26th January, 1930
(c) 31st December, 1931
(d) 26th January, 1933
(CPF Assit. Commat. 2008)

12. The famous INA trials took place in the Red Fort, Delhi in
(a) 1945 (b) 1946
(c) 1944 (d) 1947
(GIC for lecturer (UP) 2009)

13. Who among the following had headed the group of advocates to argue the case on behalf of the Indian National Army in 1946 in the Red Fort trials?
(a) Bhulabhai Desai
(b) Kailash Nath Katju
(c) Tej Bahadur Sapru
(d) Jawahar Lal Nehru
(GIC for lecturer (UP) 2009)

14. During which one of the following movements did Mahatma Gandhi write: 'Personally I am so sick of slavery that I am even prepared to take the risk of anarchy'?
(a) Home Rule movement
(b) Non-Cooperation movement
(c) Civil Disobedience movement
(d) Quit India Movement [NDA 2000]

15. Consider the following statements:
1. The Lahore Session of the Congress in 1929 adopted the resolution on Purna Swaraj (Complete Independence).
2. The Karanchi Session of the Congress in 1931 passed the resolution on the Fundamental Rights.
3. The Congress Session of Lucknow in 1936 was held under the presidentship of Subhash Chandra Bose.
4. The August, 1942 resolution of the Congress Party adopted the slogan 'Do or Die'.

Which of these statement is/are correct?
(a) 1 and 3
(b) Only 4
(c) 2 and 3
(d) 1, 2 and 4 **(NDA 2001)**

16. Consider the following events:
1. Swadeshi Movement
2. GurudwaraGuru-ka-BaghAgitation.
3. Chittagong Armoury Raid
4. Guruvayur Temple Satyagraha

The correct chronological order of these events is:
(a) 1 – 2 – 3 – 4 (b) 3 – 4 – 2 – 1
(c) 4 – 3 – 2 – 1 (d) 3 – 2 – 4 – 1
(NDA 2001)

17. Who among the following was associated with Kakori Conspiracy Case?
(a) Abul Kalam Azad
(b) Shahnawaz Khan
(c) Khan Abdul Ghaffar Khan
(d) Ashfaqulla **(NDA 2001)**

18. Who among the following wrote the book 'A nation in the making'?
(a) Dinbandhu Mitra
(b) Bal Gangadhar Tilak
(c) Surendra Nath Banerjee
(d) Subhash Chandra Bose
(NDA 2002)

19. At the second Round Table Conference, the Indian National Congress was represented by:
(a) Jawahar Lal Nehru
(b) Rajendra Prasad
(c) Mohandas Karamchand Gandhi
(d) Vallabh Bhai Patel
(NDA 2002, RAS/RTS 2008)

20. **Assertion (A):** The Indian National Congress opposed the Simon Commission and did not co-operate with it.

Reason (R): The Simon Commission had no Indian representative.
(a) Both A and R are true and R is the correct explanation of A.

(b) Both A and R are true but R is not a correct explanation of A
(c) A is true but R is false
(d) A is false but R is true

(NDA 2002)

21. With reference to Indian freedom struggle, consider the following statements:
    1. C.R. Das and Moti Lal Nehru formed the Congress-Khilafat Swaraj Party.
    2. In 1919, Gandhiji was elected President of the Khilafat Conference.
    3. The Communist Party of India was banned by the Government in 1934.

    (a) 1 and 2 (b) 2 only
    (c) 1 and 3 (d) 1, 2 and 3

(NDA 2003)

22. Consider the following events:
    1. Gandhi-Irwin Pact
    2. First Round Table Conference.
    3. Simon Commission
    4. Poona Pact

    The correct chronological order of these events is
    (a) 1 – 4 – 3 – 2 (b) 2 – 1 – 3 – 4
    (c) 3 – 2 – 1 – 4 (d) 2 – 3 – 1 – 4

(NDA 2003, SCRA 2001)

23. Which one of the following pair is not correctly matched?
    (a) Purna Swaraj Resolution : 1929
    (b) Martyrdom of Sardar Bhagat Singh: 1931
    (c) Formation of Congress Socialist: 1938
    (d) Simla Conference :1945

(NDA 2004)

24. Who among the following was regarded by Mahatma Gandhi as his Political Guru?
    (a) Dadabhai Naoroji
    (b) Bal Gngadhar Tilak
    (c) Pheroz Shah Mehta
    (d) Gopal Krishna Gokhle

(NDA 2004, Utt. PSC (M) 2007)

25. Which one of the following chronological orders of the given event is correct?
    (a) The Civil Disobedience Movement-The Cripps Mission-The Cabinet Mission's Plan
    (b) The Cripps Mission-The Civil Disopbedience Movement-The Cabinet Mission's Plan
    (c) The cripps Mission-The Cabinet Mission's Plan-The Civil Disobedience Movement.
    (d) The Civil Disobedience Movement-The Cabinet Mission's Plan-The Cripps Mission. **(NDA 2004)**

26. For which one of the following movements did Mahatma Gandhi give the slogan 'Do or Die"?
    (a) Kheda Satyagraha
    (b) Non-Cooperation Movement
    (c) Civil Disobedience Movement
    (d) Quit India Movement

(NDA 2005, UPSC 2009)

27. Where was the first Peasant Movement launched by Mahatma Gandhi?
    (a) Bardoli (b) Dandi
    (c) Champaran (d) Wardha

(NDA 2006, CDS 2003)

28. Who among the following was a founder of the Swaraj Party?
    (a) Vallabh Bhai Patel
    (b) Rajendra Prasad
    (c) C.R. Das
    (d) Narendra Dev

(NDA 2007, WB PSC (P) 2008)

29. Who among the following national leaders did not opt to defend the case dealing with the trial of the soldiers of the Indian National Army in 1945?
    (a) Tej Bahadur Sapru
    (b) Bhulabhai Desai
    (c) C. Rajgopalachari
    (d) Jawahar Lal Nehru **(NDA 2007)**

30. During the freedom struggle, Aruna Asaf Ali was a major woman organiser of the underground activities in:
    (a) Bardoli Satyagraha
    (b) Quit India Movement
    (c) Civil Disobedience Movement
    (d) Khilafat Movement

(NDA 2007, UPSC 2009)

Answers

1. (c)	2. (d)	3. (a)	16. (a)	17. (d)	18. (c)
4. (a)	5. (d)	6. (a)	19. (c)	20. (a)	21. (d)
7. (d)	8. (b)	9. (c)	22. (c)	23. (c)	24. (d)
10. (a)	11. (a)	12. (b)	25.(a)	26. (d)	27. (c)
13. (a)	14. (d)	15. (d)	28.(c)	29. (c)	30. (b)

CHAPTER

13

The Gandhian Era in India (Second Phase)

Gandhi's Early Life

- Mohandas Karamchand Gandhi was born on October 2, 1869 at Porbandar in Saurashtra (Gujarat) in a well-to-do family. He proceeded to England in 1888, and returned to India as a Barrister-at-law in 1891.
- He failed as a practicing lawyer both at Rajkot and in Bombay.

Gandhiji in Africa

- Gandhiji reached Durban in 1893 to sort out some legal problems of Dada Abdullah, a Gujarati merchant, becoming the first highly educated Indian to have come South Africa.
- There, he was deeply shocked by the political and social disabilities which were imposed by law, administrative and social measures of the Europeans upon the Indian residents.
- He revolted against the racial injustice, discrimination and degradation to which Indians had to submit in the South African colonies.
- Indian labourers in South Africa and the Indian merchants were denied the right to vote. They had to register and pay a poll-tax.
- They could reside only in prescribed locations, which were insanitary and congested. The Asians as also the Africans could not stay out of doors after 9.00 pm nor could they use public footpaths.
- Gandhiji soon assumed the leadership of the struggle against these conditions and during 1893–1914 was engaged in a struggle against the racist authorities of South Africa.
- It was during this struggle that he evolved the technique of Satyagraha based on truth and non-violence.
- He founded a political association known as the Natal Indian Congress and also a newspaper called Indian Opinion with a view to educating Indians in political matters and giving publicity to their grievances.

Satyagrahi

- An ideal Satyagrahi was to be truthful and peaceful, but at the same time he would refuse to submit what he considered wrong.
- He would accept suffering willingly in the course of struggle against the wrong doer. But even while resisting evil, he would love the evil-doer.
- He would be utterly fearless. According to Gandhiji non-violence was not a weapon of the weak and the cowardly.
- Only the strong and brave could practice it.

Gandhi's Success in Africa

- He used passive resistance or civil disobedience or Satyagraha for the first time against a legislation making it compulsory for Indians living in South Africa to take out Certificates of registration which held their finger prints.
- He also protested against restrictions on Indian Migration. The Indians defined the law by crossing over from one province to another without producing the evidences.
- In 1906, he set up the Tolstoy Farm in Transvaal with the help of his German architect friend, Kallenbach, to house the families of the Satyagrahis.
- He led a struggle against a judgment of the South African Supreme Court which invalided all marriages not conducted according to Christian rites and registered by the Registrar of marriages. In 1909, Gandhiji released his book Hind Swaraj. The Gandhian ideas are illustrated in this book.

Ideology and Thought of Gandhi

What is Gandhian Philosophy?

- It is the political, economic religious and social ideas adopted and developed by Gandhi, first during his period in South Africa from 1893 to 1914, and later of course in India.
- The twin cardinal principles of Gandhi's thought are truth and non-violence.
- Although there are elements of unity in Gandhi's thought, they are not reduced to a system. It is not a rigid, inflexible doctrine, but a set of beliefs and principles, which are applied differently according to the historical and social setting.
- Interpretation of the principle underwent much evolution during Gandhi's lifetime, and as a result many inconsistencies can be found in his writings, to which he readily admitted.
- As a guide to action, Gandhian philosophy is a double-edge weapon. Its objective is to transform the individual and society simultaneously in accordance with the principles of truth and non-violence.

Satyagraha of Gandhi

- One of the most important aspects of Gandhi's political ideology is Satyagraha. Satyagraha literally means "holding on the Truth." It may also be described as love-force or soul-force.
- Satyagraha is the hallmark of Gandhian political strategy. This was his philosophy of political action. Two basic components of it were truth and Non-violence.

- To Gandhi, Satyagraha was "the closely tied to the doctrine of ahimsa, as Satyagraha is essentially ahimsa in action. Satyagraha entails non-violence, non-cooperation and self-sacrifice.
- The principles of Satyagraha are opposed to wrongs and injustice. A Satyagrahi was not to compromise with evil, injustice and wrong. In fact he was not to co-operate with them.
- The loving self-sacrifice and suffering of the Satyagrahis intended to generate compassion and awaken ahimsa in the hearts and minds of the contending party.
- The truth was to be established and change of opponent's heart was to be brought about not by any forceful or violent means but by arousing the conscience of the opponent or by inflicting of suffering on oneself.
- Gandhian Satyagraha is the weapon of brave. It was in fact, a struggle without fear and cowardice. According to Gandhi, a Satyagrahi must be fearless. Gandhi therefore talked about the soul force or the inner spiritual stamina and about making efforts to strengthen it.

Role of the Masses

- While ahimsa is the driving force, non-cooperation is the principle action of a Satyagraha campaign. Gandhi expressed the political implication of this principle when he said "the government cannot exercise control over us without our cooperation" in this context Gandhi recognized the basic role of the masses, in any political struggle against British.
- Gandhi had immense faith in the capacity of the masses and he, therefore, based his entire politics on the militancy and self-sacrificing spirit of the masses.

Gandhi and Non-violence

- The doctrine of non-violence is another important aspect of Gandhi's ideology. "My creed is non-violence under all circumstances. My method is conversion, not coercion; it is self-suffering, not the suffering of the tyrant." This statement by Gandhi captures the basic principles of non-violence.
- The Gandhian ideal of "active ahimsa" entails not just abstaining from all violence, but fully embracing an enemy with love. It "requires deliberate self-suffering" and therefore "call forth the greatest courage". Ultimately, the self-suffering of a practitioner of ahimsa is intended to awaken and converts the soul of the enemy, who will then be overpowered by pity and love.

Gandhi on Swadeshi

- Gandhi was a champion of Swadeshi, which he believed was essential to Satyagraha and Swaraj. Swadeshi entailed complete self-sufficiency in the political economic and religious life of the Indian people.
- According to Gandhi , Swadeshi is that spirit in us which restricts us to use the service of our immediate surroundings to the exclusion of the more remote.
- Swadeshi was an integral part of Gandhi's overall vision for an Independent India—one in which self-sufficient, self-governing, village republics were the foundation of the country.

- Gandhi believed that if the Indian masses followed the Swadeshi Doctrine, "then every village of India will... be a self-supporting and self-contained unit, exchanging only such necessary commodities with other villages where they are not locally producible".
- Gandhi was of the Opinion that Swadeshi was "a religious discipline to be undergone in utter disregard of the physical discomfort it may cause to individuals." In following the principles of Swadeshi, people would utilize only indigenous political institutions, ancestral religious and locally manufactured articles.
- If a person should find of these defective, that individual should serve it by purging it of its defects.

Novel Ideas of Gandhi

- The novel value of Gandhi's political method is of great significance. Beside Satyagraha, it includes Civil Disobedience, Non-Cooperation, Court arrest, **Hartal,** Hunger strike, Marches etc.
- These novel methods became an indispensable part of the overall Nationalist programme and strategy. Moreover, they were used effectively and to a great extent successfully in our struggle for independence.

Gandhi and Imperialism

- The ultimate aim of Gandhian struggle was not political freedom alone but a life of dignity for the masses. He believed that the mere removal of the British by the Indian rulers would result in nothing more than "English Rule without Englishmen".
- The exploitation of poor by rich and British rule was just a manifestation of that. He, therefore, directed his political struggle towards those forces.

Socio-Economic Outlook

- Gandhi's ideas and activities transcended political boundaries. They exhibited a deep concern for social transformation. Moreover, even his economic outlook subsumed a deep social content.
- His concerns for Hindu-Muslim unity, for the upliftment of Harijans, for raising the status of women in the society, promotion of khadi, village reconstruction etc are expression of broad social outlook of Gandhi.
- Moreover, the socio-economic programme of Gandhi helped to spread the message of nationalism down to the lowest and most oppressed section of the society. This in one sense developed pan-Indian loyalty towards the congress and national movements.
    - His programme of Harijans welfare included opening of roads, wells and temples for them. Though primarily aimed at improving the lot of untouchables, these programmes naturally brought him close to the heart of these people.
    - Village reconstruction could immediately get him the support of rural folks who formed the overwhelming majority of Indian population. Khadi had a real attraction for the peasants and artisans who suffered heavily due to the process of modernization and industrialization of colonial types.

Religious Outlook

- His Hinduism revolved around a few fundamental beliefs: in the supreme reality of God, the unity of all life, and the value of ahimsa as a means of realizing God. While in South Africa, Gandhi undertook a comparative study of religions, which gave rise to the all-embracing nature of his religious outlook. He had faith that "Religions are different roads converging into the same point".
- Because he saw all religions as essentially the same, he advocated mutual tolerance and respect between different religions. To Gandhi: "The various religions were as so many leaves of a tree; they might seem different but at the trunk they are one".
- Gandhi insisted that the function of religion was to unite rather than divide people. He had faith in "the absolute oneness of God and therefore of humanity". Based on this, he believed, "We have but one soul. The rays of the sun are many through refraction. But they have the same source".
    - Gandhi believed that religion must be applied to everyday life. To him, religion was an ethical framework for the conduct of daily life. For Gandhi, applying religion to daily life necessitated applying religion to policies as well.
    - Many people criticized Gandhi for mixing religions and politics, however, these critics did not fully understand what Gandhi meant by religion: It is not the Hindu religion, but the religion which transcend Hinduism, which changes one's very nature, which binds one indissolubly to the truth within and whichever purifies.
    - It is the permanent element in human nature, which leaves the soul restless until it has found itself.

Constructive Programme

- The constructive work is the significant aspect of Gandhian strategy. It included development of Khadi, Cottage industries, Spinning, Women's upliftment, Hindu-Muslim unity, upliftment of Harijans, National education etc. in the course of time these became symbolic of rendering one's contribution towards his country.
- The most important significance of the constructive programme is that it facilitated the involvement of even those who did not have aptitude and taste for Political and Parliamentary activity and secondly it also helped in sustaining the sense of activism during the passive phase of the mass movement.

External Influences that Shaped Gandhi

- The vaishnavite tradition, in which Gandhi was brought up, taught him the fundamentals like the importance of prayer, and consideration to all forms of life.
- Gandhi drew inspiration from the Bhagavad-Gita, which remained a continuous source of inspiration for him throughout his life.
- The writings of Leo Tolstoy (especially The Kingdom of a God is within you), had also influenced Gandhi. Gandhi translated Tolstoy's, A Letter to a

Hindu, written in 1908 in response to aggressive Indian nationalists. The two corresponded until Tolstoy's death in 1910. The letter by Tolstoy's applies Hindu philosophy from the vedas and the sayings of Krishna to the growing Indian nationalism.

- Gandhi was also inspired by the American writer Henry David Thoreau's who popularized the theory of civil disobedience in his famous essay Civil Disobedience.

Gandhi: Early Political Activities

- It was through involvement in three local disputes in Champaran (In North Bihar), in Kheda (in Gujarat), and in Ahmedabad in 1917–18 that Gandhi emerged as an influential political leader.
- In Champaran, he took up the cause of peasants against landlords, in Kheda that of farmers against revenue-officials and in Ahmadabad that of mill-workers against mill-owners.
- In every case the strategy was Satyagraha. In every case the principles were truth and non-violence. And in every case the real force working under Gandhi was "mass participation".

The Arrival of Mahatma

- On receipt of instructions from GK Gokhale, Gandhi retuned to India from South Africa in January 1915.
- Instead of immediately entering India politics, he spent 1915 and much of 1916 touring India, visiting places as far apart as Sind and Rangoon, Banaras and Madras in order to get to know his homeland and to make himself known to his countrymen.
- His only excursion into politics was his demand (October 1915) for the abolition of the system of indentured labour for manual work outside India. No Satyagraha was started because the Government of India abolished the system before the date fixed by him (31 July, 1917).
- His constructive work began with the foundation of the Sabarmati Ashram at Ahmedabad in May 1915. At that stage he did not lay so much stress by agitation, as by working for the moral, material and economic regeneration of his countrymen.
- He believed that once people made themselves fit by character and capacity the grant of privileges would follow as a matter of course.
- Till the beginning of 1917, Gandhi was more of a freelance preacher and social worker than a recognized politician. Gokhale was his closest ally.
- After his death (February 1915) he was refused admission to the Servants of India Society which Gokhale had founded in 1905, to educated the backward and to organize political work. BG Tilak opposed him because he did not publicly support the Home Rule League.

Champaran Satyagraha (1917)

First Civil Disobedience

- In Champaran—a permanent settlement area there were large zamindaris estates under rich and influential landlords. Most of the villages were leased out by the Zamindars to Thikadars of whom the most influential group was European indigo planters.
- Though the planters were temporary tenure-holders, they not only realized rent from peasants but also excised civil and criminal jurisdiction over them. The result was the reduction of the peasantry, in the words of Gandhi, to an abjectly helpless condition.
- The major problem at Champaran in Bihar was of the Indigo planters. The European planters forced the peasant to grow indigo on 3/20th of the total land area (tin Katie system). Peasants were also forced to sell their produce at the Prices fixed by the Europeans. When the German syntactic dyes replaced indigo, the planters demanded for high rents and illegal dues from the peasants in order to maximize their profit.
- An attempt by the local officials to extern him from the Tirhut Division (in which Champaran was situated) failed because the Bihar Government disapproved of such action; but the incident became a cause célèbre. And there were loud protests against the Government's policy from the leading papers in the Bombay presidency and in Bengal. For the first time in Indira Gandhi was displaying that magnetic personality which was to draw multitudes to him and to earn him the title of Mahatma and the nickname of Bapu. Under pressure from the Government of India, the Government of Bihar appointed a committee of enquiry (June, 1917) the recommendations of the committee were implemented, partly by the Champaran Agrarian Act of 1917 and partly by executive orders.
- These included several concessions and prescription of limits for enhancement of rents.
  - Gandhiji was invited by Rajkumar Shukla to Champaran. He was joined by Rajendra Prasad, Mazhar-ul-Haq Mahadeo Desai, Narhri Parekh, Mahadeo Desai, and J.B. Kripalani at Champaran.
  - Through tours in rural areas, he established direct contact with ordinary people and talked about their concerns in the language which they understood. This was a novel political technique; it had never been practiced by the educated leaders of the Congress.
  - For the first time the peasants were drawn into political agitation under a new type of leadership.

Ahmedabad Textile Mill Issue (1918)

First Hunger Strike

- While Gandhiji was still engaged to his task in Bihar, he received a letter from Sharmati Anasuyabai. She informed him about the condition of workers in Ahmedabad mills and requested him to take up their cause with the mill owners.
- The terrible plague of 1917-18, led to a heavy decline in the number of workers in the major industrial city of Ahmedabad. In order to attract the workers, the mill owners started paying

them 75 percent of their wages as plague bonus.

- The mill-owners declaration of locking out the mills on February 22, 1918 made the situation even more serious. At least the issue was resolved with the intervention of Mahatma Gandhi.
- The mill owners agreed to give 35 percent of wages as bonus. This offer was accepted by the workers.
    - With the normalization of the situation, the mill owners decided to withdraw the plague bonus but the workers opposed their decision. The mill owners were prepared to give 20% increase but the workers were demanding a 50% raise in the wages in view of the price hike. Consequently, the relations between the mill-owners and the workers became quite tense.

Kheda Satyagrah

First Non-Cooperation Movement

- In 1917 most of the Kharif Crops of the farmers of Kheda district in Gujarat were destroyed due to heavy rains thus incapacitating them to pay the land revenue to the government.
- When the government refused to comply with the peasant's demand to remit land revenues, Gandhiji advised and launch a struggle against the government on March 22, 1918.
- Gandhiji with his lieutenants like Vallabh Bhai Patel, the young lawyer of Kheda (who had become Gandhiji follower during this Satyagraha), Indualal Yagnik and many other youth, toured villages to encourage the peasants.
- The "Kheda Satyagraha", wrote Gandhiji, "Marks the beginning of an awakening among the peasants of Gujarat, the beginning of their true political education".
- Through the Kheda Campaign, Satyagraha took firm roots in the soil of Gujarat.
- At the end Gandhiji himself put an end to this Satyagraha due to two reasons:
- Firstly, the peasants badly affected with plague, price rise and famine, were not in a position to carry on the struggle any longer and secondly it came into the notice of Gandhiji that the government had issued secret instructions that revenue should be recovered only from those peasants who could afforded to pay it. Thus, it lessened the woes of the farmers and helped in the achievement of the object for which the Satyagraha had been started.

Significance of Gandhi

- Champaran, Kheda, and Ahmedabad were the testing grounds of Gandhian style of politics in India.
- These were non-violent mass based campaigns. In the process of these campaigns, Gandhi was able to recruit a number of committed political workers who played vital role in the national movement in the years to come. Prominent among them were Rajendra Prasad, JB Kriplani, Vallabhbhai Patel, Mahadev Deasi and Indulal Yagnik.
- By the end of 1918, through three limited campaigns, he had demonstrated that Satyagraha was viable in India. By this time, he also attained considerable public position and achieved some authority in specific areas.

- What distinguished him was his weapon of political agitation which seemed to meet the need of the day. Satyagraha could involve people, bring them directly into the fold of nationalist agitation and then a sense of participation.
- The Satyagraha of Champaran, Kheda and Ahmedabad made Gandhiji very popular among the masses. He started emerging as a leader of the masses and won the admiration and respect of political workers particularly the youth.
- Finally, these struggle brought Gandhiji in close contact with the masses whose interests he espoused all his life.
- In fact, he was the first Indian nationalist leader who identified his life and his manner of living with the life of the common people. Very soon he became the symbol of poor India, nationalist India, and rebellious India and of course the Independent India.

Chapter at a Glance

- The All India Muslim League was established on 3 December, 1906.
- Vasudeo Balwant Phadke created a terror for British authorities in 1878 in Maharashtra.
- The great revolutionary Sri Shyamji Krishna Verma was a great Sanskrit scholar and also been the Dewan of Udaipur and Junagarth States.
- Shyamji Verma, the first man to initiate and fight for India's struggle of independence from outside India started to publish a journal 'Sociologists' from January 1905.
- V.D. Savarkar wrote a book 'Joseph Mazzini-Biography and Politics' in 1906.
- Madam Bhikaji Cama was arrested in 1914 and deported to an island for four years.
- The original name of the Gadar Party was 'Hindi Association of the Pacific Coast'.
- The baranches of Gadar Party was established at Manila, Bangkok, Hong-kong, Shanghai and Panama.
- In 1915 an Indian Independence Committee was formed with the help of German Government to organise invasion of Burma from Siam and China.
- Tilak set up Indian Home Rule league on 28 April, 1916 with Headquarter at Poona.

Previous Year Question Paper (1998-2017)

1. Consider the following statements:
   1. The "Bombay Manifesto" signed in 1936 openly opposed the preaching of socialist ideals.
   2. It evoked support from a large section of business community from all across India.

   Which of the statements given above is/are correct?
   (a) 1 only (b) 2 only
   (c) Both 1 and 2 (d) Neither 1 nor 2
   (2010)
2. Consider the following statements:
   1. Dr. Rajendra Prasad persuaded Mahatma Gandhi to come to Champaran to investigate the problem of peasants.
   2. Acharya J.B. Kriplani was one of Mahatma Gandhi's colleagues in his Champaran investigation.

   Which of the statements given above is/are correct? **(2010)**

(a) 1 only (b) 2 only
(c) Both 1 and 2 (d) Neither 1 nor 2

3. For the Karachi session of Indian National Congress in 1931 presided over by Sardar Patel, who drafted the Resolution on Fundamental Rights and Economic Programme?
   (a) Mahatma Gandhi
   (b) Pandit Jawaharlal Nehru
   (c) Dr. Rajendra Prasad
   (d) Dr. B.R. Ambedkar **(2010)**
4. Who among the following were official Congress negotiators with Cripps Mission?
   (a) Mahatma Gandhi and Sardar Patel
   (b) Acharya J.B. Kriplani and C. Rajagopalachari
   (c) Pandit Nehru and Maulana Azad
   (d) Dr. Rajendra Prasd and Rafi Ahmed Kidwai **(2010)**
5. In the 'Individual Satyagraha', Vinoba Bhave was chosen as the first Satyagarhi. Who was the second?
   (a) Dr. Rajendra Prasad
   (b) Pandit Jawahar Lal Nehru
   (c) C. Rajagopalachari
   (d) Sardar Vallabhbhai Patel **(2009)**
6. Consider the following statements:
   The Cripps Proposals include the provision for:
   1. Full independence for India.
   2. Creation of Constitution-making body.

   Which of the statements given above is/are correct?
   (a) 1 only
   (b) 2 only
   (c) Both 1 and 2
   (d) Neither 1 nor 2 **(2009)**
7. During the freedom struggle, Aruna Asaf Ali was a major woman organizer of underground activity in
   (a) Civil Disobedience Movement
   (b) Non-Cooperation Movement
   (c) Quit India Movement
   (d) Swadeshi Movement **(2009)**
8. Consider the following statements:
   1. The discussions in the Third Round Table Conference eventually led to the passing of the Government of India Act of 1935.
   2. The government of India Act of 1935 provided for the establishment of an all India federation to be based on a Union of the provinces of British India and the Princely states.

   Which of the statements given above is/are correct?
   (a) 1 only (b) 2 only
   (c) Both 1 and 2 (d) Neither 1 nor 2 **(2015)**
9. Who of the following Prime Minister sent Cripps Mission to India?
   (a) James Ramsay Mac Donald
   (b) Stanley Baldwin
   (c) Neville Chamberlain
   (d) Winston Churchill **(2015)**
10. During the Indian Freedom Struggle, why did Rowlatt Act arouse popular indignations?
    (a) James Ramsay MacDonald
    (b) Stanley Baldwin
    (c) Nevile Chamberlain
    (d) Winston Churchill **(2009)**
11. Which one of the following began with the Dandi March?
    (a) Home Rule Movement
    (b) Non-Cooperation Movement
    (c) Civil Disobedience Movement
    (d) Quit India Movement **(2009)**
12. With which one of the following movements is the slogan "Do or die" associated?

(a) Swadeshi Movement
(b) Non-Cooperation Movement
(c) Civil Disobedience Movement
(d) Quit India Movement **(2009)**

13. Who of the following founded the Ahmedabad Textile Labour Association?
(a) Mahatma Gandhi
(b) Sardar Vallabhbhai Patel
(c) N.M. Joshi
(d) J.B. Kripalani **(2009)**

14. In the context of the Indian freedom struggle, 16th October 1905 is well known for which one of the following reasons?
(a) The formal proclamation of Swadeshi Movement was made in Calcutta town hall
(b) Partition of Bengal took effect
(c) Dadabhai Naoraji declared that the goal of Indian National Congress was Swaraj
(d) Lokmanya Tilak started Swadeshi Movement in Poona **(2015)**

15. Who among the following rejected the title of Knighthood and refused to accept a position in the Council of the Secretary of State for India?
(a) Motilal Nehru (b) M.G. Ranade
(c) G.K. Gokhale (d) B.G. Tilak

16. During the Indian Freedom Struggle, who of the following raised an army called 'Free Indian Legion'? **(2015)**
(a) Lala Hardayal
(b) Rashbehari Bose
(c) Subhas Chandra Bose
(d) V.D. Savarkar **(2015)**

17. Which one of the following suggested the reconstitution of the Viceroy Executive Council in which all the portfolios including that of War Members were to be held by the Indian leaders?
(a) Simon Commission
(b) Simla Conference
(c) Cripps Proposal
(d) Cabinet Mission **(2015)**

18. Match List-I with List-II and select the correct answer using the code given below the Lists:

List-I (Author)	List-II (Work)
A. Bankimchandra	1. Shatranj Ke Khilari
B. Dinabandhu Mitra	2. Debi Chaudhurani
C. Premchand	3. Nil-Darpan
	4. Chandrakanta

Code:

	A	B	C
(a)	2	4	1
(b)	3	4	2
(c)	2	3	1
(d)	3	1	4

(2015)

19. Who among the following Gandhian followers was a teacher by profession?
(a) A.N. Sinha
(b) Braj Kishore Prasad
(c) J.B. Kriplani
(d) Rajendra Prasad **(2015)**

20. Which one of the following was a journal brought out by Abul Kalam Azad?
(a) Al-Hilal
(b) Comrade
(c) The Indian Sociologist
(d) Zamindar **(2015)**

21. Where was the First Session of the Indian National Congress held in December?
(a) Ahmedabad (b) Bombay
(c) Calcutta (d) Delhi **(2015)**

22. Who among the following wrote the poem, Subhe-e-Azadi?
    (a) Sahir Ludhiyanvi
    (b) Maulana Abul Kalam Azad **(2015)**
23. **Assertion (A):** The Congress Ministries in all the provinces resigned in the year 1939.
    Reason (R): The Congress did not accept the decision of the Viceroy to declare war against Germany in the context of the Second World War.
    (a) Both A and R are true and R is the correct explanation of A
    (b) Both A and R are true but R is not a correct explanation of A
    (c) A is true but R is false
    (d) A is false but R is true **(2015)**
24. Which one of the following places was associated with Acharya Vinoba Bhave's Bhoodan Movement at the beginning of the movement?
    (a) Udaygiri (b) Rapur
    (c) Pochampalli (d) Venkatagiri
    (2007)
25. **Assertion (A):** According to the Wavell Plan, the number of Hindu and Muslim members in the Executive Council were to be equal.
    Reason (R): Wavell thought that this arrangement would have avoided the partition of India.
    (a) Both A and R are true and R is the correct explanation of A
    (b) Both A and R are true but R is not a correct explanation of A
    (c) A is true but R is false
    (d) A is false but R is true

Answers

1. (a)	2. (b)	3. (b)
4. (c)	5. (b)	6. (b)
7. (c)	8. (c)	9. (d)
10. (c)	11. (c)	12. (d)
13. (a)	14. (b)	15. (c)
16. (c)	17. (c)	18. (c)
19. (c)	20. (a)	21. (b)
22. (b)	23. (a)	24. (c)
25. (c)		

Practice Paper

1. Who was the Governor General of India during the launch of Civil Disobedience Movement?
   (a) Lord Chelmsford
   (b) Lord Reading
   (c) Lord Irwin
   (d) Lord Wavell **(NDA 2007)**
2. Which one of the following movement started from Dandi March?
   (a) Swadeshi Movement
   (b) Quit India Movement
   (c) Civil Disobedience Movement
   (d) Non-Cooperation Movement
   (NDA 2008, WB. PCS (P) 2008)
3. Who prescribed the separate electrorates for India on the basis of the Communal Award in August 1932?
   (a) Lord Irwin
   (b) Ramsay Mac Donald
   (c) Lord Linlithgow
   (d) Winston Churchill
   (NDA 2008, WB PCS (P) 2008)
4. Which one of the following slogans is attributed to Subhash Chandra Bose?
   (a) Jai Jawan Jai Kisan
   (b) Bande Mataram
   (c) Jai Hind
   (d) Inqilab Zindabad **(NDA 2009)**

5. Who among the following has authored the book 'Hind Swaraj'?
   (a) Bal Gangadhar Tilak
   (b) Mahatma Gandhi
   (c) Gopal Krishna Gokhle
   (d) M.G. Ranade **(NDA 2009)**
6. Which one of the following with regard to the Poona Pact, 1932 is NOT correct?
   (a) Adequate representation of depressed sections in Government jobs.
   (b) Reservation of seats for the depressed classes in the provincial legislature
   (c) Acceptance of joint electrorate system
   (d) Reservation of seats for the depressed classes in the central legislature **(NDA 20100)**
7. Who one of the following statements with regard to Direct Action Day is correct?
   (a) Hasan Suhrawardy prescribed over the Direct Action Day.
   (b) Direct Action Day took place in Delhi
   (c) Direct Action Day led to the Bihar riot.
   (d) Direct Action Day was endoresed by the Congress Party. **(NDA 2010)**
8. The Haripura Congress (1938) remains a milestone in Indian freedom struggle, because
   (a) It declared war on the British Empire
   (b) It anointed Jawahar Lal Nehru as the future Prime Minister of India.
   (c) Of the introduction of the idea of a planning commission
   (d) Of the acceptance of the Government of India Act, 1935 by the Congress. **(NDA 2010)**
9. In 'Hind Swaraj', Mahatma Gandhi was critical of railways, because they are
   1. Carriers of plague germs
   2. Instruments for requency of famines
   3. Responsible for creating class division in the society
   4. Accident-prone

   Select correct answer using the codes given below

   Codes:
   (a) 1, 2 and 3
   (b) 1 and 2 only
   (c) 2 and 3 only
   (d) 1 and 4 only **(NDA 2010)**
10. **Assertion (A):** Indian National Congress Boycotted the Simon Commission.

    Reason (R): It was proposed to the composition of the commission.
    (a) Both A and R are true and R is the correct explanation of A
    (b) Both A and R are true but R is not a correct explanation of A
    (c) A is true but R is false
    (d) A is false but R is true **(CDS 2010)**
11. **Assertion (A):** Khalifat Movement started in India after the Second World War.

    Reason (R): Gandhiji had been one of the Presi dents of the All India Khilafat Con ference.
    (a) Both A and R are true and R is the correct explanation of A
    (b) Both A and R are true but R is not a correct explanation of A
    (c) A is true but R is false
    (d) A is false but R is true **(CDS 2002)**
12. Consider the following incidents with reference to the Civil Disobedience Movement during Indian freedom struggle
    1. Chittgong armoury raid
    2. Refusal of a platoon of Garhwal Regiment to open fire on a batch of Khudai Khidmatgars.

3. Strike of textile workers in Sholapur involving attacks to government buildings.
4. Increase the number of Muslim participants in it all provinces

Which of these incidents caused alarm among the British rulers?

(a) 1, 2 and 3 (b) 2, 3 and 4
(c) 1 and 4 (d) 1, 2, 3 and 4

(CDS 2002)

13. During the Indian freedom struggle, which one among the following formed earliest?
   (a) Congress Socialist Party
   (b) Communist Party of India
   (c) Hindustan Republican Socialist Association
   (d) All India State people's Conference **(CDS 2003)**
14. Two independent states of India and Pakistan were created by
   (a) The Simla Conference
   (b) The Cripps Proposal
   (c) The Cabinet Mission plan
   (d) The Indian Independence Act **(CDS 2003)**
15. The lady Congress leader who went underground during the Quit India Movement was
   (a) Sucheta Kripalani
   (b) Vijay Laxmi Pandit
   (c) Aruna Asaf Ali
   (d) Sarojini Naidu **(CDS 2003)**
16. After the elections in 1937, the Congress ministers tendered their resignations because
   (a) The British Government declared India a party to World War II without consulting them
   (b) Of undue interference in their working by the Government
   (c) Of paucity of financial resources which hampered all developmental works
   (d) Of their inexperience to run the administration **(CDS 2004, 2014)**
17. Who was the first woman President of Indian National Congress?
   (a) Annie Besant
   (b) Aruna Asaf Ali
   (c) Sarojini Naidu
   (d) Vijayalaxmi Pandit **(CDS 2004, UP PCS (P) 2007, UPPCS (M) 2007)**
18. Ramsay Mc Donald's Communal Award gave
   (a) Privy purse to native princes
   (b) Communal representation to Muslims
   (c) Reservations to Sikhs in elections
   (d) Separate electorates for depressed classes **(CDS 2005)**
19. Who of the following was known as Deshbandhu?
   (a) Aurobindo Ghosh
   (b) Chitt Ranjan (C.R.) Das
   (c) Dadabhai Naoroji
   (d) Jyotiba Phule **(CDS 2005)**
20. Which one of the following is the correct chronological order?
   (a) First Round Table Conference-Poona Pact-Simon Commission-Gandhi-Irwin Pact
   (b) Simon Commission-First Round Table Conference-Gandhi-Irwin Pact-Poon Pact
   (c) Gandhi-Irwin Pact-Simon Commission-First Round Table Conference-Poona Pact
   (d) Poona Pact- Simon Commission-First Round Table Conference-Gandhi-Irwin Pact **(CDS 2005)**

21. **Assertion (A):** During India's freedom struggle, C.R Das formed Congress-Khilafat Swaraj Party within the Congress which was later known as the Swarajest Party.
   Reason (R): At special Calcutta Session of 1920, C.R. Das opposed Gandhiji.
   (a) Both A and R are true and R is the correct explanation of A
   (b) Both A and R are true but R is not a correct explanation of A
   (c) A is true but R is false
   (d) A is false but R is true **(CDS 2005)**
22. Consider the following statements:
   1. Both Congress andMuslim League refused the offer of the Cripps Mission.
   2. The interim government formed in 1946 had nominees of the Congress only and not those of the Muslim League.

   Which of the statement is/are correct?
   (a) 1 only (b) 2 only
   (c) Both 1 and 2 (b) Neither 1 nor 2
   (CDS 2006)
23. In the year 1946, who among the following joined the Viceroy's Executive Council with finance portfolio?
   (a) Mohammad Ali Jinnah
   (b) Liaqat Ali Khan
   (c) Nawab Salimullah
   (d) Shaukat Ali **(CDS 2006)**
24. During whose tenure as the Viceroy of India were the great martyrs Bhagat Singh, Rajguru and Sukhdev hanged?
   (a) Lord Curzon
   (b) Lord Irwin
   (c) Lord Minto
   (d) Lord Chelmsford **(CDS 2006)**
25. During Indina freedom struggle, which one of the following happened earliest?
   (a) Simon Commission
   (b) Gaya Session of Congress
   (c) Tripuri Session of Congress
   (d) Gandhi-Irwin Pact **(CDS 2008)**
26. The Rani Jhansi Regiment, the women's regiment of Azad Hind Fauj, was under whose command?
   (a) Usha Mehta
   (b) Anne Marcarence
   (c) Annie Besant
   (d) Lakshmi Sehgal **(CDS 2008)**
27. Who among the following was elected as the President of All-India Khilafat Conference met at Delhi in November,1919?
   (a) Moti Lal Nehru
   (b) Mahatma Gandhi
   (c) M.A. Jinnah
   (d) Shaukat Ali **(CDS 2009)**
28. Who among the following was NOT a member of the Cabinet Mission?
   (a) Sir Stafford Cripps
   (b) A.V. Axesander
   (c) Red Cliff
   (d) Pethwick Lawrence **(CDS 2009)**
29. Who among the following Urdu poets was invited to the Second and Third Round Table Conference?
   (a) Faiz Ahmed Faiz
   (b) Josh Malihabadi
   (c) Muhammad Iqbal
   (d) Firaq Gorakhpuri **(CDS 2009)**
30. What is the correct sequence of the following events?
   1. Bardoli Satyagraha
   2. Rajkot Satyagraha
   3. Champaran Satyagraha
   4. Nagpur Satyagraha

   Select the correct answer used the codes given below?
   (a) 1 – 2 – 4 – 3 (b) 4 – 3 – 1 – 2
   (c) 3 – 1 – 4 – 2 (d) 3 – 4 – 1 – 2
   (CDS 2009)

Answers

1. (c)	2. (c)	3. (b)	16. (a)	17. (a)	18. (d)
4. (c)	5. (b)	6. (a)	19. (b)	20. (b)	21. (b)
7. (c)	8. (c)	9. (a)	22. (a)	23. (b)	24. (b)
10. (a)	11. (d)	12. (a)	25. (b)	26. (d)	27. (b)
13. (b)	14. (d)	15. (c)	28. (c)	29. (c)	30. (d)

CHAPTER

14

Struggle for Independence: Third Phase (1927 to 1939)

Introduction

According to a provision of the Government of India Act, 1919, a Royal Commission was to be appointed ten years after the passage of the Act (i.e., in 1929) to enquire into the working of the Act and to purpose further reforms, if needed. The conservative government in London appointed the Commission two years earlier for the fear that a Labour Government, which was seen to be likely o come to power in the forthcoming General Election, might appoint a statutory commission composed of members with liberal and pro-India Views.

Simon Commission

- Lord Birkenhead, secretary of state for India announced the appointment of a statutory commission under the chairmanship of Sir John Simon on November 8, 1927. Simon Commission was officially known as **India Statutory Commission.** All the seven members of the commission were Englishmen, who were members of British Parliament. Party wise there were four conservative, two laborites and one liberal.

- This all White Commission with no Indian representative was greeted with strong protest. The Congress, at its session held in Madras in December 1927, resolved to boycott the commission, everywhere and in every form.
- However, the league led by **Muhammad Safi** as also Justice Party in Madras, Unionist Party in Punjab, Central Sikh Sangh and All India Achut Federation did not oppose the Commission a

section of league led by Jinnah boycotted the Commission.

- The commission paid visits to India (February–March 1928 and October 1928–April 1929), each time it faced boycott. It made extensive tours and prepared a report, which was published in May, 1930.
- The Report was later discussed at the Round Table Conference held at London.
- The report of Simon omitted any mention of **Dominion Status** even as a distant goal and rejected all ideas of transfer of power at the çentre.
- The proposals of Simon Commission were completely rejected by the major political parties in the country, including the Muslim League.
- Even Lord Irwin found its finding as lacking in imagination and sought to divert attention by stressing the independent role of the forthcoming Round Table Conference.
- Beside, the Commission's finding were outpaced by events like the **Nehru Report** as well as the Viceroy's declaration of October 31, 1929 promising Dominion Status for India in the future.
- This is also known as **Deepavali Declaration.**

Nehru Report

- In response to the appointment of Simon Commission and Challenge given by Lord Birkenhead secretary of state for India, an **All Parties Conference was called at Delhi** on February 12, 1928, which was attended by representatives of 29 organizations.
- It was presided by **MA Ansari.**
- On may 19, 1928 at its meeting at Bombay, the all Parties Conference appointed a committee with **Motilal Nehru** as its Chairman.
- The purpose was to consider and determine the principles of the **Constitution for India.**
- The committee consisted of Sir Tej Bahadur Sapru, Sir Ali Imam, M.S. Aney, Mangal Singh, Shuab Oureshi, G.R. Pradhan, N.M. Joshi, M.R. Jayakar and Subhas Chandra Bose.
- The committee presented its report in the fourth session of the All Parties Conference at Lucknow in August 10, 1928. Some important recommendations of the report were as follows:
    - The future Constitution of India should be based on "Full Responsible Government on the model of the Constitution of the self-governing Dominions", and the conceding of the Dominion Status should be "the next immediate step" and not a remote stage of our evolution.
    - The North-west Frontier Province (with its Muslim majority of over 90 percent) should acquire the same status as other Provinces and Sind (With its muslim Majority of over 7 per cent) should be detached from Bombay and became a separate Province.
    - The Committee made no concession to the Muslim standpoint on the question of separate electorates. All election made by joint or mixed electorates.
    - Reservation of seats for Muslims or Hindus wherever they were in

minority. No reservation of seats for Muslim in Punjab and Bengal.

- The Constitution of India should be federal in character and the Indian States should be welcome to joint it.
- There should be inserted in the Constitution a "Declaration of Rights" assuring inter alia, the fullest liberty of conscience profession and practice of one's religion. Provision for adult universal suffrage.
- The new Indian Legislature should be empowered to legislate and budget for the India army, and that its control should be transferred to a responsible Indian Minister of Defence.
- The legislative power of the Commonwealth should be vested in a bicameral legislature and the executive power in the King "exercisable by the Governor-General as the King's representative, acting on the advice of the Executive Council."

On December 2, 1928, the All-Parties Conference met at Calcutta to consider the Nehru Report. There was violent clash between Jinnah (representing the Muslim League) and MR Jaykar (who put forward the view point of the Hindu Mahasabha).

- The Simon Commission reached Bombay on February 3, 1928 and was greeted with the slogan of 'Go back, Simon'. Wherever the commission visited, complete hartal was observed and processions were taken out.
- At many places the police used brute force to crush the agitation. A procession led by Lala Lajpat Rai in Lahore was lathi charged and Lalaji succumbed to his injuires. JL Nehru and GB Pant were lathi charged in Lucknow.
- A revolutionary group led by Bhagat Singh, took the revenge of Lalaji's death by killing the Assistant Police Superintendent Saunders.
- The Annual session of the INC held in Calcutta in December 1928, approved the Nehru Report and also served an ultimatum on the British government to accept the Nehru Report on or before December 31, 1929, failing which the party would launch another mass movement, with a new goal of Poorna Swarajya.
- The open session of the Muslim League meeting at Delhi on March 28, 1929, rejected the Nehru Report and accepted Mr. Jinnah's Fourteen Points.
- **Jinnah** moved a number of amendments and demanded one-third representation of the Muslims in the Central Legislature.
- Whereas **MR Jayakar** questioned Jinnah's locus standi as a representative of the Muslims and warned against going back on the report.
- Finally Jinnah left the All Parties Conference and joined the breakaway group of League led by Agha Khan and Muhammad Shafi after his demands were rejected.
- The British government neither accepted nor rejected the Nehru report. As a result the Congress declared on 31 December that the Nehru Report had ceased to be valid and passed the **Poorna Swarajya Resolution** at its Lahore Session (1929).

Nationalist Muslim Party

- The rise of the nationalist Muslims as an organized group may be traced to the formation of the Congress Muslim Party at Bombay on July 29, 1929. At the same time Maulana Abul Kalam Azad who presided over the first All-India Nationalist Muslim Conference at Allahabad pledged to develop among Muslims a spirit of nationalism.

- Even earlier, at the Muslim League Session at Delhi in March 1929, leaders of the Khilafat Conference had supported the Nehru Report.
- But, some outsider stormed the hall and supporters of the report were thrown out, some of whom decided to form the Nationalist Muslim Party.
- Initiative also came from the Congress, which was naturally anxious that nationalist Muslims should have an independent organization to support its programme and the Nehru Report.
- Finally **Khaliquzzaman,** some representatives from the Punjab and Bengal, as well as Dr. Sheikh Muhammad Alam formed the new Muslim Nationalist Party. Dr. MA Ansari became its president and Khaliquazzaman its secretary.
- Though Maulana Abul Kalam Azad and Rafi Ahamd Kidwai did not oppose the formation of the new party, they kept aloof from it.
- Almost simultaneously there was the emergence in the North-West Frontier Province of the **Khudai Khidmatagars** (Red Shirts) under Khan Abdul Ghaffar Khan and Dr. Khan Sahib, giving a great boost to the nationalist Muslim cause.

Jinnah's "Fourteen Points"

- The "Fourteen Points" were announced by Jinnah in Delhi on **March 28, 1929,** at a meeting of the Muslim League. It did not accept the Nehru Report on the ground that it discarded separate electorates and other demands of minorities.
- Jinnah in view of more safeguards for Muslims, drew up a list of demands (The so called 'fourteen Points'), which represented the Minimum demands of the Muslims. These were as follows:
  - The form of the future Constitution of India should be federal with residuary powers vested in the provinces.
  - A Uniform measure of autonomy-my should be granted to all Provinces.
  - All Legislatures and other elected bodies should be constituted on the definite principle of adequate and effective representation of minorities in every province without reducing the majority in any province to a minority or even equality.
  - In the Central Legislature, Muslim representation should not be less than one-third.
  - Representation of communal groups should continue to be by separate electorates as at present, provided that it should be open to any community at any time to abandon its separate electorate in favour of joint electorate.
  - Any territorial redistribution should not, in any way, affect the Muslim majority in Punjab, Bengal and the NWFP.
  - Full liberty of belief, worship and observance, propaganda, association and education should be guaranteed to all communities.

- No bill or resolution or any party should be passed in any Legislature or any other elected body if three-fourths of the members of any community in that body opposed it as being injurious to the interests of that community.
- Sind should be separated from the Bombay Presidency.
- Reforms should be introduced in the NWFP and Baluchistan on the same footing as in other provinces.
- Adequate share for Muslims should be provided in the Constitution in all services of the state subject to the requirements of efficiency.
- Adequate safeguards for the protection and promotion of Muslim, culture, education, language, religion, personal laws and charitable institutions and for their due share in the grants-in-aid given by the State should be provided in the Constitution.
- No change should be made in the Constitution by the Central Legislature except with the concurrence of the State constituting the Indian Federation.

Lahore Session of Congress (December 1929)

- ❑ The Calcutta Session of the Congress, 1928, had served an ultimatum to the British Government to accept the Nehru Report by the year-end or to face a mass movement.
- ❑ The next annual session of the Congress was held at Lahore, 1929. **Jawaharlal Nehru** was elected President of this historic Session of the Congress. The Lahore session of the Congress passed a series of landmark resolutions:
  - The Nehru Committee Report had lapsed (i.e. Dominion status was now not acceptable) since the one-year time limit set at the Calcutta session passed without a positive reply from the Government.
  - As per the Poorna Swarajya resolution passed at the Lahore Congress the word Swaraj in the Congress Constitution would thenceforth mean complete independence, which was set forth as the goal of the national movement.
  - In pursuance of the above, the Central and Provincial Legislatures and the Committees constituted by the Government were to be completely boycotted. All future elections were to be boycotted.
  - Round Table Conference, decided to be held in London, should be boycotted.
  - A programme of Civil Disobedience was to be launched. The CWC allowed Gandhi to determine the time, place and issue on which CDM was to be launched. Gandhi decided to inaugurate the movement by violating the salt laws on the sea-coast at Dandi.
- ❑ On December 31, 1929, Jawaharlal Nehru, the president of the Congress unfurled the flag of India's independence on the banks of the Ravi in Lahore.
- ❑ The Congress Working Committee, which met on January 2, 1930, decided that January 26, 1930, should be observed as the Poorna Swarajya Day (Independence Day).

- On that day Mahatma Gandhi drafted a Poorna Swarajya Pledge and gave a call to the people that "it was crime against the God and Man to submit to the Satanic British rule".

Civil Disobedience Movement

- Gandhi placed as an ultimatum on January 31, 1930 **"Eleven Points"** of administrative reforms and stated that if Lord Irwin accepted them there would be no need for agitation. The Important demands were:
  - The Rupee-Sterling ratio should be reduced.
  - 50% reduction in land revenue.
  - Abolition of the salt tax and government salt monopoly.
  - 50% cut in military expenditure.
  - Salaries of highest grade services should be reduced by half.
  - Change Arms Act allowing citizens to bear arms for self-protection.
  - Protection for Indian textile industry.
  - Reservation of Coastal shipping for Indians.
  - Release of all political prisoners.
  - Total Prohibition of intoxicants.
- The Congress Working Committee had authorized Mahatma Gandhi to determine the time, place and issue on which the Civil Disobedience Movement was to be launched.
- Gandhi waited for 41 days for the Government to respond to his 11-point ultimatum and then decided to inaugurate the movement by violating the Salt Law.
- Salt was made an issue, because the Government controlled the sale of this indispensable commodity, and imposed a tax on it which was felt most keenly by the poor.
- On **March 12, 1930** Gandhi started the historic march from his Sabarmati Ashram with 78 followers.
- After a 24 day long March he symbolically broke the salt at **Dandi** on April 5, 1930. The breaking of the Salt Law formally inaugurated the Civil Disobedience. Some of the programme outlined for the Civil Disobedience were the following:
  - The violation of the Salt law and other laws.
  - Non-Payment of land revenue, rent or other taxes.
  - Boycott of Law Courts, Legislatures, Elections, Government Functions, Government Schools and Colleges.
  - Boycott of foreign goods and cloths and burning foreign cloth.
  - Peaceful picketing of shops selling liquor and other intoxicants.
  - Organizing mass strikes and demonstrations.
  - Resigning Government jobs and not going the Civil, military or police services.
- Soon the defiance of salt laws started all over the country. In Tamil Nadu **C. Rajagopalchari** led a salt March from Trichinopoly to Vedaranniyam on the Tanjore coast. He was arrested 30th April.
- In Malabar **K. Kelappan,** the hero of the Vaikom Satyagraha walked from Calicut to Payment to break the Salt law.

- NC Kelkar, Satyamurti and MA Ansari were among those who refused to resign from Legislature after the call of the Congress to do so.
- They came to be known as **New Swarajists.** Satyamurti voiced the Council entry programme in October 1933 followed by Bhulabhai Deasi, BC Roy and MA Ansari in April 1934.

Course of the Movement

- In United Province and Gujarat, a no tax campaign was launched. On 18th April the Bengal revolutionaries led a seize to the **Chittagong Armoury** and fought a pitched battle on Jalaba hill on 22 April.
- On may 21st, with Sarojini Naidu, Imam Sahib (Gandhi's comrade of south African struggle) and Gandhi's son, Manilal in front ranks, a band of 2000 marched towards the police cordon that had sealed off the **Dharasana Salt Works.** Here the British repression was most severe upon the Satyagrahis.
- The working Committee in May 1930 sanctioned; Non-Payment of land revenue in Ryotwari areas, Non Payment of Chaukidari (Village police) tax in Zamindari region and Forest Satyagraha i.e. Peaceful violation of forest laws that restricted the age old tribal and poor peasant rights to free fodder, timber and other forest produce.
- Amid all this the viceroy took the initiative of releasing the Congress leaders and invited Mahatma Gandhi for talks which led to the Gandhi for talks which led to the Gandhi-Irwin Pact and the suspension of the Civil Disobedience Movement.

Gaffar Khan and Rani Gaidinliu

- Khan Abdul Gaffar Khan (Popularly known as 'Frontier Gandhi') was active for several years in NWFP.
- His mass work lay behind the formation of the band of non-violent revolutionaries, the khudai khidmatgar (Servants of Gods) popularly known as the Red shirts (After the colour of their uniform) that played an extremely active role in the Civil Disobedience Movement.
- In the Northeast, the Manipuris joined the movement and the young Rani Gaidinliu with her Naga followers actively supported the Movement. In Assam there was a strong student agitation against Cunningham Circular.

Gandhi-Irwin Pact (March 5, 1931)

- During the course of CDM the Simon Commission report was published and to consider its recommendation the **First RTC was called in London in November 1930.**

- The Congress boycotted the conference, however other political parties participated. The British Authorities wanted Congress to join.

- Some of the liberal leaders like Tej Bahadur Sapru, VS Shastri and MR Jayakar on their return for the first RTC tried to persuade Gandhi on the same lines.
- To create an appropriate atmosphere viceroy released Congress leaders and invited Gandhi for Talks; the Congress also authorized Gandhi to Negotiate a settlement with the viceroy.
- Gandhi ji initiated a talk with Irwin in February 14, 1931, which culminated in the Delhi Pact of March 5, 1931. The pact is popularly called Gandhi-Irwin Pact.
- This pact was also largely due to the efforts of Tej Bahadur Sapru, VS Shastri and MR Jayakar.
- According to the pact the Congress agreed to join the second Round Table Conference for drafting the constitutional Reforms on the basis of (a) Federation (b) Responsibility and (c) Safeguards or reservation in the interest of India for such matters as defense, external affairs, minorities and the financial credit of Indian.
- Gandhiji agreed not to press for investigation into police excesses.
- On behalf of the Congress, Gandhiji agreed to discontinue the Civil Disobedience Movement.
- The viceroy agreed to withdraw ordinances promulgated in connection with the Civil Disobedience Movement.
- The government agreed to release all political prisoners, except those guilty of violence and restore the confiscated property of the Satyagrahi's.
- The government agreed to permit the people living within a certain distance of the seashore to collect or manufacture sea salt free of duty.
- The government agreed to permit peaceful picketing of liquor and opium shops.
- Gandhiji's request for remitting the death sentence on **Bhagat Singh, Sukhdev** and **Rajguru** was turned down by the Viceroy.
- The annual session of the Congress, held in **Karachi** from March 26 to 29, 1931 endorsed the pact, and also authorized Gandhi to represent it at the second Round Table Conference.
- Two separate resolutions one of Fundamental Rights and other on National Economic Policy was passed.

Second Phase of Civil Disobedience Movement

- The 2nd RTC (September 1931) failed to satisfy Congress or provide anything substantial to the Country.
- The Gandhi returned to India disheartened and disillusioned. Meanwhile Lord Wellingdon had succeeded Irwin as the Viceroy and had flouted many provisions of the Gandhi-Irwin Pact.
- On January 4th, 1932, a fresh batch of Congress leaders including Gandhiji and Sardar Patel were arrested [Gandhi was kept in **Yervada Prison** (Pune) during CDM and at **Aga Khan Palace** (Pune) during QIM].
- The same day (4th January) Congress and its allied organizations were declared illegal and their offices and funds seized nearly all the Gandhi Ashrams were occupied by the police.
- Wellingdon described Bombay city and Bengal as the 'two black spot' on April 1932. The Government also promulgated ordinances which gave

the authorities unlimited power-thus initiating has been described as 'Civil Martial Law', declaring military rule.

- With the announcement of **Communal Award** (August 16, 1932) by Ramsay Mac Donald (British P.M.) the strength and the pace of CDM began to decline.
- The Delhi Congress Session (April 1932) and the Calcutta Congress Session (March 1933) were held while the official ban was still in force.
- On may 8, 1933 Mahatma Gandhi announced a **self-Purification fast** for 21 days for purification of himself and his associates "For greater vigilance and watchfulness in connection with the Harijan cause".
- In the background of the communal Award and Gandhi's fast unto death, the CDM lost its momentum. After the Poona Pact Gandhi lost interest in the movement and got fully involved in the anti-untouchability struggle, which led to the foundation of **Harjina Sevak Sangh.**
- Gandhiji recommended to the Congress to suspend the movement for a month or six weeks. Accordingly the movement was suspended for about twelve weeks.
- In its place Mahatma Gandhi launched **Individual Civil Disobedience on August 1, 1933.**
- However, the Civil Disobedience Movement continued to liner till early April 1934 when Gandhiji decided to formally (finally) withdraw in April 1934. Gandhiji now decided to make Harjijan work as the main theme of his new rural constructive programme.
- In October 1934 Gandhiji decided to withdraw himself from active politics to devote all his time to the cause of Harijans. He announced his resignation from the Congress to serve it better in thoughts, words and deeds.
- Gandhiji landed in Bombay on 28th December and witnessed government repression in full swing. Most of the important Congress leaders were also arrested.
- The Congress Working Committee met the next day to decided on the question of resuming Civil disobedience if the Government did not make some positive gestures. On the 31st, Gandhiji asked the Viceroy for a meeting, offering to suspend the decision on Civil Disobedience However, the Viceroy reused to see Gandhiji.
- The Congress Working Committee which met on January 1, 1932 decided to resume the Civil Disobedience Movement.

Impact of CDM

- The Congress swept polls in most provinces in 1937.
- The left parties emerged as an-alternative in Politics.
- Some Congress activists formed socialist group.
- Nehru and Subhash Bose emerged as leaders.

The Round Table Conferences

First Round Table Conference

- Sir john Simon (Chairman of Simon Commission) recommended British Government to call a conference consisting of the representatives of both the British India as well as the Indian States so as to take a final decision on the issue of Constitutional Reforms for India.

- Subsequently **Lord Irwin,** the Governor-General of India, made his famous declaration known as the **Deepavali Declaration** (October 31, 1929).
- According to the declaration the objective of British policy was to grant commission Status to India and a round table conference would be held in London after the Simon Commission had submitted its report.
- The conference ended with the Indian princes agreeing for a federation with a weak responsible central government. The absence of congress representation in the First Round Table Conference made it pointless. So it was decided to have a second one.
- The first session of the Round Table Conference began on November 12, 1930. In all 89 persons were invited to attend the conference. Of these 16 represented Princely states. The British India delegation comprised 58 members, Rest were British Officials. Some prominent members who participated were:

Hindu Mahasabha	MR Jayakar, MS Moonje
Sikh	Sardar Sampurna Singh
Christians	KT Paul
Liberal	TB Sapru, CY Chintamani, Srinivas Shastri
Muslim League	Aga khan, Md. Shafi, Jinnah, Muhammad Ali, Fazlul Haq
Depressed Classes	BR Ambedkar
Princes	Akbar Hydari (Diwan of Hyderabad), Mirza Ismali (Diwan of Mysore), Maharaja of Bikaner

Second Round Table Conference

- **Wellingdon** succeded Lord Irwin in Delhi in April 1931. Sir Simuel Hoare, a leading conservative became secretary of state for India. On August 26, 1931, Mac Donald's Labour Cabinet resigned and a new coalition government dominated by the conservatives was formed under him.
- The Congress had suspended Civil Disobedience movement but reiterated Poorna Swaraj as its ultimate political goal.
- Gandhiji sailed for London on August 29, 1931. Against this background the second of the Round Table Conference opened on September 7, 1931. There were altogether 112 Delegates. Some prominent members were:

Congress	Mahatma Gandhi
Muslim	Muhammad Iqbal
Depressed	BR Ambedkar
Liberals	TB Sapru
Capitalist	GD Birla
Others	Sarojini Naidu, MM Malviya, Ali Imam

- The Second session made recommendations such as:
  - The composition of the Indian federation,
  - Structure of the federal Judiciary,

- The mode of accession of states to the federation, and
- Distribution of financial resources.

- Gandhiji returned to India towards the end of 1931, utterly disillusioned. Gandhiji landed in Bombay on 28 December. Gandhiji was soon arrested on January 4, 1932 and the government unleashed a region of terror.
- It was agreed at the Conference that **Responsible Government** would be established immediately, both at the Centre and in the Provinces, including complete control over Finance, Army, Defence and External relations. However the discussion over communal issues disturbed the conference.
- Ultimately the conference broke down since no agreed solution could be formed for solving the communal problems, and Gandhi returned empty handed. Dr. BR Ambedkar demanded a **Separate Electorate for** the depressed classes but Mahatma Gandhi opposed this.
- The Second session ended on December 1, 1931. The communal issues bogged down the proceedings of the conference. The 2nd Round Table Conference having failed to resolve the question of communal issue authorized the British PM to resolve it.
- The conference ended with Ramsay Mac Donald announcing the formation of two New Muslim Majority Province (NWFP and Sind) and the setting up of an Indian consultative committee and three expert committees and holding out the prospect of a unilateral British communal award if the Indians failed to agree on the minority's issue.

Third Round Table Conference

- The Third Round Conference was called on November 17, 1932. The Congress boycotted it. Only 46 delegates attended the session. The prominent members were TB Sapru and Ambedkar (the only persons to attend all there, RTC). The conference lasted till December 24, 1932.
- The British government, on the basis of the discussion at the three sessions, drafted its proposals for the reform of the Indian constitution which were embodied in the white paper published in March 1933.
- The White paper was examined and approved by a joint committee of the British Parliament (October 1934) and a bill, based on the report of this committee, was introduced and passed in the British parliament as the Government of India Act, 1935.

Communal Award and Poona Pact

- On August 16, 1932 Prime Minister Ramsay Mac Donald announced in the British Parliament the proposal on minority representation known as the 'Communal Award'. The award allotted to each minority a number of seats in the Provincial legislature (Lower House Only).
- According to this Award the Muslim, Christian, Anglo Indians, European and Sikh Voters would elect their candidates by voting in separate communal electorates.
- The Award declared the depressed classes (Officially described as Scheduled castes) also to be a minority community entitled to separate electorates and thus separated them from

the rest of the Hindus. They also had the right to vote in the reaming general constituencies also.

- The award recommended:
  - To double the existing seats in Provincial legislatures.
  - To retain the system of separate electorate for the minorities.
  - To grant weightage to Muslims in provinces where they were minority.
  - To recognize depressed classes as minority community and make them entailed to the right of separate electorate.
  - To reserve 3% seats for women in all provincial legislatures except in the NWFP.
  - To allocate seats to labour, landlords and traders and industrialists.
  - Seven seats were reserved for Merchants in certain selected constituency of the Bombay Presidency.
- Mc Donald, however, promised to accept any alternative scheme mutually agreed upon by the Hindus and the depressed classes.
- Gandhiji reacted strongly to the proposal and wrote to the British Prime Minister on August 18, 1932 that he would commence the fast on September 20 in the Yervada Jail, where he was lodged, and it would cease only if the scheme was reviewed and the common electorate restored.
- He went on fast unto death on September 20, 1932 to enforce his demand. The 20th of September was observed as a day of fasting and prayer. Temples, wells, etc were thrown open to the depressed classes all over the country.
- Pandit **Madan Mohan Malviya** summoned a conference of various castes and political parties, including Dr. BR Ambedkar (The Leader of Depressed Class League).
- On September 25, 1932, the sixth day of Gandhiji fast, they arrived at an agreement in Poona, popularly known as Poona Pact. **Poona Pact between Gandhi and Ambedkar** was concluded with the following terms:
  - The Principle of joint/common electorate was accepted, for all Hindus.
  - 148 seats in different Provincial legislature were reserved for the depressed classes in place of 71 (as provided in the Communal Award).
  - 18% of the seats in the central Legislature were reserved for the depressed classes.
  - Adequate representation would be given to the depressed classes in the civil services.
- After the Poona Pact Mahatma Gandhi lost interest in the civil Disobedience Movement and was fully engrossed in the anti-untouchability movement, which led to the foundation of the Harijan Sevak Sangh.

Election of 1937 and Congress Ministries

After the decline of Civil Disobedience Movement there began a search for a new course which the National Movement should take in the immediate future i.e., during the phase of non-mass struggle.

At this stage three perspective were put forward:

First Constructive work on Gandhian lines should be continued.

Second Constitutional struggle and Participation in the forthcoming elections, to keep up the political interest and morale of the people. This advocated by Dr. MA Anasri, Asaf Ali, Bhulabhai Desai, S Satyarmurti, BC Roy and KM Munshi among others.

Third Resumption and continuation of non-constitutional mass struggle, as the situation was still revolutionary owing to continued. Economic crisis and readiness of the masses to fight.

- The **Lucknow session of April 1936,** presided by Jawaharlal Nehru, Congress resolved to contest election. Jawaharlal Nehru admitted, "There was no choice but to contest elections." In his view, this would "educate the masses on the political policies and economic programme of the Congress", which demand for the constituent Assembly in the forefront.
- JL Nehru in his presidential speech (Lucknow session) advocated Socialism and took three Socialists into the Congress Working Committee i.e. Jaiprakash Narain, Acharya Narendra Deo and Achyut Patwardhan.
- The session passed some important resolutions such as:
  - The people of the Princely state should have the same right of self-determination as those of the rest of the India but "The Struggle for liberty" was to be carried out by the people of states themselves.
  - The Provincial units were asked to conduct agrarian enquires.
- The prominent features of the Election Manifesto adopted by the AICC in August 1936 were the following:
  - The purpose of sending congressmen to the legislature was to combat the Act of 1935.
  - To highlight the poverty of Indian masses particularly peasants, workers and artisans.
  - To take all step to end the various regulations, ordinances and Acts which oppress the Indian people.
  - For the industrial workers the policy of the Congress would be to secure for them a decent standard of living, regular hours of work and better condition of labour.
- There were other promises such as:
  - Removal of untouchability
  - Equal status for women
  - Encouragement of Khadi and village industries, and
  - Satisfactory solution on communal problem.

All India Kisan Sabha

- The Lucknow Session was important from another point of view as well. It was during this session that the first meeting of the All India Kisan Sabha was held under the presidentship of Swami Sahajanand Saraswati.
- The Faizpur session held at December 1936, under the Presidentship of Jawaharlal Nehru, attacked Fascism and Congress and Congress passed resolutions condemning Italian aggression of Abyssinia and Japanese aggression of China. In this session Congress demanded the Formation of a Constituent Assembly.

Elections

- The elections to the Provincial Legislatures were held in January-February 1937. Congress won 715 out of 836 seats. In Five Provinces it had a clear majority (Madras, United Province, Central Province, Bihar and Orissa).
- In NWFP, Assam and Bombay Congress emerged as the single largest party. In Bengal, Punjab and Sind the Congress did not have majority. The Congress could not do well in the election to upper houses as the franchise there was limited to the upper strata only. As far as reserved seats were concerned:
- Out of the 38 seats reserved for Labour, the Congress had contested 20 and won 18.
- 482 seats were reserved as Muslim seats. The Congress Contested 58 and could win only 26 seats.
- For commerce and Industry 56 seats were reserved. The Congress contested 8 and could win only 3.
- For Landholders 37 seats were reserved. The Congress contested 8 and won 4.

Conditional Acceptance

- Gandhiji advised Congressmen to hold offices lightly and not tightly.
- The offices were to be seen as "Crown of Thorns" which had been accepted to quicken the pace towards the Nationalist goal.
- In the AICC meet in March 1937, Ranjendra Prasad moved a resolution for 'Conditional acceptance' of office, which was accepted.
- The condition was that the Governors would not use their special powers to intervene with functioning of ministries. The Governor refused to give assurance on the condition put forward by the Congress and therefore the Congress turned down the offer to form ministers.
- The Government therefore formed **Interim Ministries** (e.g., Nawab Chattari of National Agriculture Party formed his ministry in UP and Sir Dhunjishah formed his ministry in Bombay). In some cases the Governor (Like Lord Erskine, the Governor of Madras) suggested dissolution of legislature, to the Viceroy.
- In July 1937 the Congress formed Ministries in the United Provinces, Central Provinces, Orissa, Bihar, Madras and Bombay. Later Assam and the NWFP also came under the Congress rule.
- In Punjab the Unionist Party and the Muslim League formed a coalition Government.
- However, later on the Muslim League established its influence.
- In Sind a Succession of non-Congress Ministries under different leaders held office between 1937–1947.
- The Premiers—Ghulam Hussain Hidayatullah and Allah Bakhsh had strong association with the Congress.
- On June 20, the viceroy clarified the stance of the Government in relation to special powers of the Governors vis-à-vis ministries.
- The CWC met at Wardha in the first week of July and permitted office acceptance. The resignation of the interim ministries was followed by the formation of Congress Ministries.

Congress Ministries in Office (1937-39)

- In all the Congress remained in power in Eight Provinces for 28 months. During this period it made efforts to work for the benefit of Indians.
- In all the Congress ruled Provinces the efforts were to protect the peasant's from the moneylenders and to improve irrigation facilities.

- In the united provinces and Bihar, tenancy Bills were passed.
- The Congress Government in Bombay appointed a **Textile Enquiry Committee** in 1937, which recommended a wage increase, and health and insurance cover to worker.
- The Bombay Ministry also introduced an **Industrial disputes** Act in November 1938, based on the principles of arbitration, to prevent strikes and lockouts. In the field of Civil Liberties; all political prisoners were released and constructive programme undertaken.
- The other major achievements of the Congress Ministries were:
    - Reduction in salaries of Ministries.
    - The declaration of fundamental Rights.
    - Welfare schemes for Tribals.
    - Carrying on Jail Reforms.
    - Carrying out Commercial and economic surveys and uplift of village industries.
    - Promotion of education, especially primary education through the introduction of 'Basic Education'.
- The Congress Government also joined the efforts to develop planning through the **National Planning Committee** appointed in 1938 by the Congress President Subhas Chandra Bose.
- In November 1939, when Britain unilaterally declared India to be belligerent in the Second World War, the congress Ministries resigned. The Muslim league observed the 'Day of Deliverance' on 22nd December.

Chapter at a Glance

- Bhagat Singh and Batukeshwar Dutta threw bombs in the Legislative Assembly at Delhi on 8 April, 1929.
- Jatin Das started a hunger strike to protest the ill treatment of prisoners in Jail. He died on 18 September, 1920 after a fast of 64 days.
- Chandrashekhar died in a skirmish with the police in 1931 at Alfred Park, Allahabad.
- The Hindustan Republic Association was reorganised in September, 1928 as the Hindustan Socialist Republican Association or Army (H.S.R.A.) with provincial units at Bengal, Punjab, U.P. Bihar, Delhi and Madras.

- Suryasen masterminded the Chittagong Armoury Raid and declared himself the president of the provincial Independent Government of India.
- Madan Lal Dhingra shot dead Col. William Curzon Wyllie, political A.D.C. to the Indian office in 1909.
- In 1905, Shyamji Krishan Verma set up the Indian Home Rule Society popularly known as the Indian House.
- The dead bodies of Bhagat Singh, Raj Guru and Sukhadev were cremated at Hussainwala in Ferozpur on 23 March, 1931.
- The slogan of "Inquilab Zindabad" under which the Gandhiji fought the struggle was first popularised by the revolutionaries.
- Barinder Kumar Ghosh was the younger brother of Arbindo Ghosh.
- In 1905 Barinder Ghosh and Pulin Das published a book entitled 'Bhavani Mandir' in 1905. In 1907 they wrote another book called 'Vartaman Rajniti'.
- A periodical 'Yugantar' was started by the leaders of Anusilan Samiti which openly preached armed rebellion against the British.
- Unfortunately two European ladies were killed (30 April, 1908) in place of the unpopular British Judge Kingsford.
- Narendra Gasain was the black sheep who disclosed the secret of the society. He was shot dead by Kanhai Lal Dutta and Satyen Bose.
- Barindar Ghosh, Hemchandra Das, Ullas Duttal Upendra Bannerjee etc. were convicted in the Alipur conspiracy case.
- A member of the Abhinava Bharat, P.N. Bapat, went to Paris to learn the art of Bomb making. Sir Denzi Ibbetson, the Lt. Governor of Punjab described in a minute that terrorists were openly and sedulously preaching an active anti English propaganda in certain towns.

Previous Year Question Paper (1998-2017)

1. Which one of the following aroused a wave of popular indignation that led to the massacre by the British at Jallianwala Bagh?
   (a) The Arms Act
   (b) The Public Safety Act
   (c) The Rowlatt Act
   (d) The Vernacular Press Act **(2007)**
2. At which one of the following places did Mahatma Gandhi first start his Satyagraha in India?
   (a) Ahmedabad (b) Bardoli
   (c) Champaran (d) Kheda **(2015)**
3. The song 'Amar Sonar Bangla' written during the Swadeshi Movement of India inspired the liberation struggle of Bangladesh and was adopted as the National Anthem of Bangladesh. Who wrote this song?
   (a) Rajni Kanta Sen
   (b) Dwijendralal Ray
   (c) Mukunda Das
   (d) Ravindranath Tagore **(2015)**
4. Consider the following statements about Madam Bhikaji Cama:
   1. Madam Cama unfurled the National Flag at the International Socialist Conference in Paris in the year 1907.

2. Madam Cama served as private secretary to Dadabhai Naoroji.
3. Madam Cama was born to Parsi parents.

Which of the statements given above is/are correct?

(a) 1, 2, and 3 (b) 2 and 3 only
(c) 1 and 2 only (d) 3 only **(2006)**

5. Under whose presidency was the Lahore Session of the Indian National Congress held in the year 1929 wherein a resolution was adopted to gain complete independence from the British?
(a) Bal Gangadhar Tilak
(b) Gopal Krishna Gokhale
(c) Jawaharlal Nehru
(d) Motilal Nehru **(2006)**

6. Who among the following was the Chairman of the Union Constitution Committee of the Constituent Assembly?
(a) B.R. Ambedkar
(b) J.B. Kripalani
(c) Jawaharlal Nehru
(d) Alladi Krishnaswami Ayyar **(2005)**

7. Which of the following pairs are correctly matched?

Movement/ Satyagraha	**Person Actively Associated with**
1. Champaran	Rajendra Prasad
2. Ahmedabad Mill Workers	Morarji Desai
3. Kheda	Vallabhbhai Patel

(2005)

Select the correct answer using the code given below:

Codes:

(a) 1 and 2
(b) 2 and 3
(c) 1 and 3
(d) 1, 2 and 3

8. Consider the following statements:
1. Lord Mountbatten was the Viceroy when Simla Conference took place.
2. Indian Navy Revolt, 1946 took place when the Indian sailors in the Royal Indian Navy at Bombay and Karachi rose against the Government.

Which of the statements given above is/are correct?

(a) 1 only (b) 2 only
(c) Both 1 and 2 (d) Neither 1 nor 2
(2015)

9. Who among the following was not associated with the formation of UP Kisan Sabha in February 1918?
(a) Indra Narain Dwivedi
(b) Gauri Shankar Misra
(c) Jawaharl Lal Nehru
(d) Madan Mohan Malviya **(2015)**

10. Who among the following drafted the resolution on fundamental rights in the Karachi Session of Congress 1931?
(a) Dr. B.R. Ambedkar
(b) Pandit Jawahar Lal Nehru
(c) Dr. Rajendra Prasad
(d) Sardar Vallabhbhai Patel **(2005)**

11. In October 1929, who of the following headed a group of Indians gathered at Tashkent to set up a Communist Party of India?
(a) H.K. Sarkar
(b) P.C. Joshi
(c) M.C. Chagla
(d) M.N. Roy **(2005)**

12. At which Congress Session was the Working Committee authorised to launch a programme of Civil Disobedience?

(a) Bombay
(b) Lahore
(c) Lucknow
(d) Tripuri **(2005)**

13. In which one of the following provinces was a Congress ministry not formed under the Act of 1935?
(a) Bihar (b) Madras
(c) Orissa (d) Punjab
(2005)

14. Consider the following statements:
On the eve of launch of Quit India Movement, Mahatma Gandhi
1. Asked the government servants to resign.
2. Asked the soldiers to leave their posts.
3. Asked the Princes of the Princely States to accept the sovereignty of their own people.
Which of the statements given above is/are correct?
(a) 1 and 2 (b) 2 and 3
(c) 3 only (d) 1, 2, and 3
(2015)

15. Consider the following statements:
1. In the First Round Table Conference, Dr. Ambedkar demanded separate electrorates for the depressed classes.
2. In the Poona Act, special provisions for representation of the depressed people in the local bodies and civil services were made.
2. The Indian National Congress did not take part in the Third Round Table Conference.
Which of the statements given above are correct?
(a) 1 and 2 (b) 2 and 3
(c) 1 and 3 (d) 1, 2 and 3
(2015)

16. Which party was founded by Subhash Chandra Bose in the year 1939 after he broke away from the Congress?
(a) Indian Freedom Party
(b) Azad Hind Fauj
(c) Revolutionary Front
(d) Forward Block **(2005)**

17. Consider the following statements:
1. The First Session of the Indian National Congress was held in Calcutta
2. The Second Session of the Indian National Congress was held under the presidentship of Dadabhai Naoroji.
3. Both Indian National Congress and Muslim League held their sessions at Lucknow in 1916 and concluded the Lucknow Pact
Which of the statements given above is/are correct?
(a) 1 and 2
(b) 2 only
(c) 2 and 3
(d) 3 only **(2004)**

18. During the Indian Freedom Struggle, who among the following proposed that Swaraj should be defined as complete independence free from all foreign control?
(a) Mazharul Haque
(b) Maulana Hasrat Mohanti
(c) Hakim Ajmal Khan
(d) Abul Kalam Azad **(2015)**

19. The name of the famous person of India who returned the Knighthood conferred on him by the British Government as a token of protest against the atrocities in Punjab in 1919 was
(a) Tej Bahadur Sapru
(b) Ashutosh Mukherjee
(c) Rabindra Nath Tagore
(d) Syed Ahmad Khan **(2015)**

20. Consider the following events during India's freedom struggle:
    1. Chauri-Chaura Outrage
    2. Minto-Morley Reforms
    3. Dandi March
    4. Montagu-Chelmsford Reforms

    Which one of the following is the correct chronological order of the events given above?
    (a) 1–3–2–4 (b) 2–4–1–3
    (c) 1–4–2–3 (d) 2–3–1–4 **(2004)**
21. **A:** In 1916, Maulana Mohammad Ali and Abul kalam Azad resigned from the Legislative Council.
    R: The Rowlatt Act was passed by the Government in spite of being opposed by all Indian members of the Legislative Council.
    (a) Both A and R are true and R is the correct explanation of A
    (b) Both A and R are true but R is not a correct explanation of A
    (c) A is true but R is false
    (d) A is false but R is true **(2003)**
22. Who headed the Interim Cabinet, formed in the year 1946?
    (a) Rajendra Prasad
    (b) Jawaharlal Nehru
    (c) Sardar Vallabhbhai Patel
    (d) Rajagopalachari **(2003)**
23. With reference to Indian freedom struggle, which one of the following statements is **NOT** correct?
    (a) The Rowlatt Act aroused a wave of popular indignation and led to the Jallianwala Bagh massacre
    (b) Subhash Chandra Bose formed the Forward Bloc
    (c) Bhagat Singh was one of the founders of Hindustan Republicon Socialist Association
    (d) In 1931, the Congress Session at Karachi opposed Gandhi-Irwin Pact **(2008)**
24. An important aspect of the Cripps Mission of 1942 was
    (a) The all Indian States should join the Indian Union as a condition to consider any degree of autonomy for India.
    (b) The creatin of an Indian Union with dominion status very soon after the Second World War.
    (c) The active participation and cooperation of the Indian people, communities and political parties in the British war effort as a condition for granting indepenence with full sovereign status to India after war.
    (d) The framing of a constitution for the entire Indian Union, with no separate constitution for any province, and a Union constitution to be accepted by all provinces. **(2015)**
25. When Congress leaders condemned the Montague-Chelmsford Report, many moderates left the party to form the:
    (a) Swaraj Party
    (b) Indian Freedom Party
    (c) Independence Federation of India
    (d) Indian Liberal Federation **(2015)**

Answers

1. (c)	2. (c)	3. (d)
4. (b)	5. (c)	6. (c)
7. (c)	8. (b)	9. (c)
10. (b)	11. (d)	12. (b)
13. (d)	14. **(?)**	15. (c)
16. (d)	17. (c)	18. (b)
19. (c)	20. (b)	21. (d)
22. (b)	23. (b)	24. (b)
25. (d)		

Practice Paper

1. When Lord Mountbatten became the first Governor General of free India, who among the following became the Governor General for Pakistan?
   (a) Lord Mountbatten
   (b) M.A. Jinnah
   (c) Liaquat Ali Khan
   (d) Shaukat Ali **(CDS 2010)**
2. Which of the following Commissions/ Committees was appointed by the British Government to investigate into the massacre in Jallianwala Bagh?
   (a) Welby Commission
   (b) Hunter Commission
   (c) Simon Commission
   (d) Bulter Committee **(CDS 2010)**
3. October 26, 1947 is an important date in the Indian History because of:
   (a) Maharaja Hari Singh's signing of Instrument of Accession
   (b) Ceasefire with Pakistan
   (c) Merger of Sind
   (d) Declaration of War over India by Pakistan **(CDS 2010)**
4. Cabinet Mission was presided over by:
   (a) Lord Atlee
   (b) Stafford Cripps
   (c) Clement Atlee
   (d) Pathic Lawrence **(45th BPSC 2002)**
5. Jai Prakash Narayan Belonged to which Party?
   (a) Congress (b) Kisan Sabha
   (c) Socialist (d) Raivadi
   (45th BPSC 2002, 48th-52nd BPSC 2008)
6. Who of the following shot dead Dyer responsible for Jallianwala Bagh massacre?
   (a) Khudiram
   (b) Bhagat Singh
   (c) Madan Lal Dhingra
   (d) Udham Singh
   (45th BPSC 2002, UP PCS (P) 2003)
7. Quit India Movement was led by:
   (a) B.R. Ambedkar
   (b) Jawahar Lal Nehru
   (c) Mahatma Gandhi
   (d) None of them **(45 BPSC 2002)**
8. The mantra 'Do or Die' was given by:
   (a) P.C. Roy
   (b) J.C. Bose
   (c) C.V. Raman
   (d) Mahatma Gandhi
   (45th BPSC 2002, WB PCS (P) 2008)
9. Bhagat Singh, Rajguru and Sukhdev were hanged on:
   (a) March 23, 1931
   (b) March 23, 1932
   (c) March 23, 1933
   (d) March 23, 1934 **(45 BPSC 2002)**
10. Where was Azad Hind Fauj set up?
    (a) Japan (b) Burma
    (c) Singapore (d) England
    (45 BPSC 2002)
11. Who is known as 'Lok Nayak'?
    (a) Mahatma Gandhi
    (b) Subhash Chandra Bose
    (c) Jai Prakash Narayan
    (d) Bal Gangadhar Tilak
    (45 BPSC 2004, SSC Mat.2008)
12. At the time of Transfer of Power (1947), one of the following States possessed a well developed Congress Party Organisation, which was:
    (a) Hyderabad (b) Awadh
    (c) Mysore (d) Junagarh
    (46 BPSC 2004)
13. The Congress in Travencore launched a Civil Disobedience Movement against

the autocratic Government of the Dewan of Travancore State, who was:
(a) C.P. Ramaswami Aiyer
(b) J. Krishna Swamy
(c) P.K. Warrier
(d) Bhaskaran Nair **(46th BPSC 2004)**

14. Which incident led Gandhiji to withdraw Non-Co-operation Movement'?
(a) Kakori episode
(b) Chauri-Chaura episode
(c) Jallianwala Bagh episode
(d) Muzaffarpur episode
(46th BPSC 2004, Utt. PSC(P) 2005, MP PSC(P) 2008, CPF Assit Commt.2008)

15. The Poona Pact aimed:
(a) At Hindu- Muslim Unity
(b) To represent to lower cast
(c) At privileges to princes
(d) To review the Dyarchy
(46th BPSC.2004)

16. The object of Butler Committee of 1927 was to:
(a) Modernise the Indian army
(b) Demodernise the Indian army
(c) Impose censorship on National Press
(d) Improve the relationship between Government of India and Indian Princely States **(46th BPSC 2004)**

17. The massacre of the crowd at Jallianwala Bagh at Amritsar took place on-
(a) 1st June, 1918
(b) 13th April, 1919
(c) 14th April, 1920
(d) 6th July, 1921
(46th BPSC 2004, WB PCS (P).2008)

18. The Second Round Table Conference at London was held in the backdrop of the:
(a) Emerson-Gandhi Pact
(b) Hailey-Gandhi Pact
(c) Gandhi-Irwin Pact
(d) Gandhi-Simon Pact
(46th BPSC 2004)

19. Mahatma Gandhi's close English compatriot during the freedom movement was:
(a) Thomas Moore
(b) A.O. Hume
(c) Charlie Freer (C.F.) Andrews
(d) William Wavell **(46th BPSC 2004)**

20. The first and last Indian to hold office as Governor General of Independent India was:
(a) Jamanalal Bajaj
(b) C. Rajgopalachari
(c) Rajendra Prasad
(d) M.A. Ansari
(46th BPSC 2004, SSC CPO SI 2008)

21. The Chairman of Joint Parliamentary Committee of the 1935 Bill that led to the framing of the Government of India Act of 1935 was:
(a) Lord Linlithgow
(b) James Mac Donald
(c) Winston Churchill
(d) Clement Attlee **(46th BPSC 2004)**

22. The Prime Minister of England at the time of Quit India Movement was:
(a) Chamberlain
(b) Churchill
(c) Clement Attlee
(d) Mac Donald **(47th BPSC 2005)**

23. Which Congress President negotiated with both Cripps Mission and Lord Wavell?
(a) Abul Kalam Azad
(b) Jawahar Lal Nehru
(c) J.B. Kripalani
(d) C. Rajagopalachari
(47th BPSC 2005)

24. How many seats were given to depressed classes under Communal Award and Poona Pact?

(a) 74th and 79 respectively
(b) 71 and 147 respectively
(c) 78 and 80 respectively
(d) 78 and 69 respectively

(47th BPSC 2005)

25. Which among the followin g capitalists served as AICC Treasurer for a long time and went to jail in 1930?
(a) G.D. Birla
(b) Jamanalal Bajaj
(c) J.R.D. Tata
(d) Balchand Hirachand

(47th BPSC 2005)

26. At which place in Bihar was the session of Indian National Congress of 1922 held?
(a) Haripura (b) Patna
(c) Gaya (d) Ramgarh

(47th BPSC 2005)

27. Who played an important role in signing of Gandhi-Irwin Pact?
(a) Motilal Nehru
(b) Madan Mohan Malviya
(c) Tej Bahadur Sapru
(d) Chintamani **(47th BPSC 2004)**

28. Why did Mahatma Gandhi support the Khilafat Movement?
(a) Gandhiji wanted to win the support of the Indian Muslims against the British.
(b) The Khalifa had given shelter to Indian revolu tionaries.
(c) The Khalifa support Indian struggle for freedom.
(d) The Khalifa was a personal friend of Gandhiji **(48th-52nd BPSC 2008)**

29. Why did people gather to demonstrate at Jallianwala Bagh?
(a) To protest against the arrest of Gandhiji and Lajpat Rai
(b) To protest against the arrest of Kitchlu and Satyapal
(c) To offer prayers on the Baisakhi Day
(d) To protest against the arbitrarily of inhuman acts of the Punjab Government

(48th 52nd BPSC 2008)

30. At which place of Bihar, Gandhiji started Satyagraha movement for the first time in India?
(a) Patna (b) Gaya
(c) Madhubani (d) Champaran

(48th 52nd BPSC 2008)

Answers

1. (b)	2. (b)	3. (a)	16. (d)	17. (b)	18. (c)
4. (d)	5. (c)	6. (d)	19. (c)	20. (b)	21. (a)
7. (c)	8. (d)	9. (a)	22. (b)	23. (a)	24. (b)
10. (c)	11. (c)	12. (c)	25. (b)	26. (c)	27. (c)
13. (a)	14. (b)	15. (b)	28. (a)	29. (b)	30. (d)

CHAPTER

15

Struggle for Independence: Fourth Phase (1940 to 1947)

Towards Quit India Movement

Following the withdrawal of the CDM, Gandhi wanted to focus upon his village reconstruction programme and Harijan Campaign while many other party members wanted to fight the elections.

In October 1934, Gandhi resigned from the Indian National Congress.

Quit India Movement

In the Elections to the Central Legislative Assembly in November 1934, the Congress won 45 seats out of the 75. The government announced the holding of elections to the provincial legislatures in February 1937 under the Government of India Act 1935 which promised provincial autonomy. At the Lucknow session (April 1936), the Congress decided to contest them. The Congress framed a detailed political and economic programme at the Faizpur session (December 1936) under the Presidentship of Jawaharlal Nehru.

Provincial Elections Under the GoI Act 1935

The Congress won a massive mandate. It formed ministries in 8 provinces–Madras, Bombay, Central Provinces, Orissa, Bihar, UP, NWFP and Assam.

- Haripura Session (Feb 1938) declared Puma Swaraj ideal to cover Princely States.
- Tripuri Congress (March 1939) favoured active participation in the Princely States because of the federal structure of the 1935 Act and due to assumption of office by the Congress after the 1937 elections.
- The Tripuri Session witnessed Bose vs. Sitaramyya (Gandhi's nominee) conflict. Bose resigned to form the Forward Bloc.

August Offer, 1940

The Viceroy (Linlithgow) put forward a proposal that included:

- Dominion Status in the unspecified future
- A post-war body to enact the constitution
- Expansion of Governor-General's Council with representation of the Indians
- Establishing a War Advisory Council.

In this offer he promised the Muslim League and other minorities that the British Government would never agree to a constitution or government in India, to which did not enjoy their support (the Muslim League had demanded Pakistan in its Lahore session of 1940).

The Congress rejected this offer because:

- There was no suggestion for a national government and because the demand for Dominion Status was already discarded in favour of Purna Swaraj.
- It encouraged anti-Congress forces like the Muslim League.

Individual Satyagraha

With the failure of the British government to measure up to the demands, there were two opinions in Congress about the launching of civil disobedience. Gandhi felt that the atmosphere was not in favour of civil disobedience as there were differences and indiscipline within the Congress. However, the Congress Socialists and the All India Kisan Sabha were in favour of immediate struggle.

Convinced that the British would not modify their policy in India, (the Congress having rejected the August Offer), Gandhi decided to start the Individual Satyagraha.

The very reason for confining the movement to individual participation was that neither Gandhi nor the Congress wished to hamper the War effort and this was not possible in a mass movement. Even the aim of the Satyagraha was a limited one i.e. to disprove the British claim of India supporting the War effort whole-heartedly.

On 17 October 1940 Vinoba Bhave became the first satyagrahi followed by Nehru.

The Cripps Mission: March-April 1942

Under the pressure of Allies and the need for gestures to win over Indian public opinion, the Britishers were forced to offer reconciliatory measures. After the fall of Rangoon to the Japanese the British decided to send the Cripps Mission to India for constitutional proposals, which included:

- Dominion status to be granted after the war with the right to secede (Any province could, if it so desired, remain outside the Indian Union and negotiate directly with Britain).
- Constitution making body to be elected from Provincial Assemblies and Princes' nominees after the War.
- Individual princes could sign a separate agreement with the British which in effect accommodated the Pakistan demand.
- British would however, control the defence for war period.

The Congress did not want to rely upon future promises. It wanted a responsible government with full powers and also a control over the country's defence. Gandhi termed the proposals as a post dated cheque in a crashing bank. Cripps Mission failed to satisfy Indian nationalists and turned out to be merely a propaganda device for US and Chinese consumption.

But above all the Cripps Proposals brought in "Pakistan" through the backdoor via the "local option" clause. Though the Cripps Mission failed, Cripps' proposals provided legitimacy to the Pakistan demand by accommodating it in their provision for provincial autonomy.

Quit India Movement

Beginning

- In the backdrop of the failure of Cripps Mission, imminent Japanese threat, the British attitude towards Indians who were left behind in Burma and the prevailing anger and hostility to an alien and meaningless war, Quit India resolution was passed on 8 August 1942 at Gowalia Tank, Bombay.
- Gandhi told the British to quit and "leave India in God's hand". His message was 'Do or die'.
- In the initial stages, the Movement was based on non-violent lines.
- Repressive policy of the government and indiscriminate arrests of the leaders provoked people to violence. (Nehru was lodged in Almora jail, Maulana Azad in Bankura and Gandhi in Agha Khan's Palace, Poona).
- Further, it was the only all-India movement, which was leaderless. In many areas, the government lost all control and the people established Swaraj.

Public Participation

- Parallel governments were established in Satara—(Prati Sarkar under Nana Patil), Talcher (Orissa), parts of eastern U.P and Bihar.
- In Bengal, Tamluk Jatiya Sarkar functioned in Midnapore district. This national government had various departments like Law and Order, Health, Education, Agriculture, etc. along with a postal system of its own and arbitration courts.
- The trend of underground revolutionary activity also started during this phase. Jaya Prakash Narain and Ramnandan Misra escaped from Hazaribagh Jail and organised an underground movement.
- In Bombay, the Socialist leaders continued their underground activities under leaders like Aruna Asaf Ali. The most daring act of the underground movement was the establishment of Congress Radio with Usha Mehta as its announcer.
- The participation was on many levels. School and College students remained in the forefront, women actively participated and workers went on strikes. Though, peasants concentrated their offence on symbols of authority, there was complete absence of anti zamindar violence. There were no communal clashes during the movement. Repression was severe.
- The Movement did not evoke much response from the merchant community. In fact, most of the Capitalists and merchants had profited heavily during the War.
- The Muslim League kept aloof and the Hindu Mahasabha condemned the Movement. The Communist Party of India due to its "People's War" line did not support the movement.

- The Indian Princes and the landlords were supporting the War effort and therefore did not sympathize with the movement.
- Some Congress leaders like Rajagopalachari also did not participate.

Towards Freedom

Rajagopalachari Formula (1944)

- In 1944, C. Rajagopalachari proposed that after the termination of the war, a Commission could be appointed for demarcating contiguous districts in the north-west and east where Muslims were in absolute majority. In the areas thus demarcated, a plebiscite would be held on the basis of adult suffrage that would ultimately decide the issue of separation from Hindustan. If the majority decided in favour of forming a separate Sovereign State, such decision could be accepted.
- In case of acceptance of partition, agreement to be made jointly for safeguarding defence, commerce, communications etc. The above terms would to be operative only if England transferred full powers to India.
- Muslim League was expected to endorse the Congress demand for independence and co-operate with it in the formation of provisional government for the intrerim period.
- Jinnah objected, as he wanted congress to accept two-nation theory and wanted only Muslims of the northwest and east of India to vote in the plebiscite. Hindu leaders led by Y.D. Savarkar condemned the plan.

Shimla Conference

- Proposed by Wavell.
- Talks suggested setting up of a new Executive council with only Indian members. The Viceroy and the Commander in-chief would be the only non-Indian members of the council.
- 'Caste Hindus' and Muslims would have equal representation the executive would work within the existing constitution (i.e. not responsible to the central Assembly) but the door was kept open for discussions on a new constitution.
- The Congress, headed by Maulana Azad, resented being characterized as a caste Hindu organization.
- Talks broke down due to Jinnah's demand for the Muslim League to have absolute choice in choosing all Muslim members and a demand for communal veto, though it had ministries only in Assam and Sind.
- The dissolution of the conference gave Jinnah the Communal Veto in effect. Thereafter, the satisfaction of the League became a pre-requisite to any major settlement.

RIN Mutiny (1946)

- 18 Feb. 1946, Bombay Ratingso HMS Talwar struck work due to flagrant racial discrimination, unpalatable food and abuse after the arrest of BC Dutt who lad scrawled Quit India on the ship. On 19th Feb. HMS Hindustan, in Karachi also mutinied.
- Seventy-four ships, four flotillas and twenty shore establishments in Bombay,

Karachi, Cochin, Vizag, Calcutta and Delhi had come under the command or influence of a Naval Central Strike Committee (headed by M. S. Khan). In Bombay the mutineers hoisted the tricolour on their shipmasts together with a portrait of Subhash Bose and shouted Jai Hind in the barracks. Their demands included release of all political prisoners including those belonging to the Indian National Army.

- Vallabhbhai Patel and Jinnah jointly persuaded the ratings to surrender on 23rd February 1946.

Cabinet Mission (March-June 1946)

- Members—Pethwick Lawrence (secretary of State), Stafford Cripps and Alexander.
- The Mission rejected the demand for a full-fledged Pakistan (Comprising the whole of all the Muslim majority areas). The Mission reasoned that the right of communal self-determination, if conceded to Muslims, also had to be granted to non-Muslims who formed majorities in West Bengal and Eastern Punjab, as well as in Assam proper. The 'truncated' or smaller Pakistan was unacceptable to the League.

1946 Cabinet Mission to India

The Plan Proposed

- Rejection of the demand for a full fledged Pakistan.
- For a very loose union of all the Indian territories under a centre that would control merely the defence, the Foreign Affairs and the Communications, leaving all other subjects to the existing provincial legislatures.
- Provincial legislatures would elect a Constituent Assembly. The members would divide up into three sections—A, B & C while electing the constitutent Assembly. All these sections would have the authority to draw up provincial constitutions and even group constitutions.
- **Section A:** Non Muslim Majority provinces (Bombay, United Provinces, Bihar, Central Provinces, Orissa, Madras)
- **Section B:** Muslim majority provinces in the north-west (Sind, NWFP & Punjab)
- **Section C:** Muslim majority provinces in North east (Bengal, Assam)
- Communal questions in Central legislature were to be decided by a simple majority in both communities
- Provinces were to have full autonomy & residual powers

- Princely states were no longer to be under paramountcy of British. Government.
- After the first general elections, a province could come out of a group and after 10 years a province could call for reconsideration of the group or union constitution
- Each group had powers to set up intermediate level legislature and executive on their own.
- The plan failed on the issue of the nature of grouping- Jinnah was for compulsory while Nehru was for grouping only till the formation of a constituent assembly. On 29th July 1946 Jinnah withdrew his earlier acceptance of the plan and fixed 16 August 1946 as Direct Action Day. Calcutta, Noakhali, Garmukteshwar were the storm centres. Communal massacre weakened the Congress position in the NWFP.

Interim Government (September 1946)

- Came into existence on 2nd September 1946, in accordance with Cabinet Mission's proposal and was headed by J L Nehru. Muslim League refused to join it initially.
- Wavell persuaded the League leaders to join on 26 October 1946.
- 8th December 1946 – Constituent Assembly begins its session with Liaqat Ali Khan of Muslim League as the Finance Minister.
- The Interim government, obstructed by its League members and bureaucracy was reduced to a figurehead and was unable to control the communal carnage.

Attlee's Announcement (February 1947)

- British Prime Minister Atlee on 20 February 1947 announced that the British would withdraw from India by 30 June, 1948 and that Lord Mountbatten would replace Wavell. British powers & obligations vis-a-vis the princely states would lapse with transfer of power but these would not be transferred to any successor Government in British India. Partition of the country was implicit in the provision that if the constituent assembly was not fully representative then power would be transferred to more than one central govt.

Mountbatten Plan (3rd June Plan)

- His earlier Plan Balkan was abandoned for the 3rd June Plan.

- The Plan declared that power would be handed over by 15 August 1947 on the basis of dominion status to India and Pakistan.
- Mountbatten supported the Congress stand that the princely states must not be given the option of independence. They would either join India or Pakistan.
- Boundary commission was to be headed by Redcliffe and the award was to be

announced after Republic day (which was a major cause of massacres).

- Punjab and Bengal Legislative Assemblies would meet in two groups, Hindu's and Muslims, to vote for partition. If a simple majority of either group voted for partition, then these provinces would be partitioned. In case of partition, two dominions and two constituent assemblies would be created.

Indian Independence Act, 1947

- Implemented on 15th August 1947 and Sovereignty of British Parliament was abolished. Dominions of India and Pakistan were created. Each dominion to have a Governor-General. Pakistan was to comprise Sind, British Baluchistan, NWFP, West Punjab and East Bengal.

Chapter at a Glance

- Sister Nevedita, the Irish disciple of Swami Vivekanand supported the Anusilan Samiti.
- Bipin Behari Ganguly founded a secret society Atmonnaati Samiti.
- A Marathi Scholar Sakharam Ganesh Desukar who was proficient in Bengali, provided a link between the revolutionaries of Bengal and Maharashtra.
- Shyamji Krishna Verma founded the Indian Home Rule Society with the object of securing Home rule for India.
- Tarak Nath Das formed the Indian Independence League in 1907 in California.
- Raja Mahendra Pratap and Barkatullah set up a provisional Government of India in Kabul with the support of Russia and Germany.
- Kakori is a wayside Railway Station on the Lucknow-Saharanpur line.
- Ram Prasad Bismil also participated in Mainpuri conspiracy case.
- Michael O' Dyer was shot dead by Udham Singh where he was scheduled to attend a lecture in Caxton Hall, London on 13th March, 1940.
- British philosopher C.E.C. Joad called Gandhi a 'moral genius'.
- The first poetry of Rabindra Nath Tagore was published in Tattva Bodhini Patrika in 1874.
- During the 1905 antipartition of Bengal the song of Rabindra Nath Tagore 'Amar Sonar Bangla' Became very popular.
- In 1911 Rabindra Nath Tagore composed the National Anthem 'Jana Gana Mana'.
- Rabindra Nath Tagore is called the 'Goethe of India' and the 'Leonardo da Vinci' of the Indian Renaissance.
- Gandhi established 'Phoenix Farm' near Durban in South Africa.
- Gandhi was influenced by the writings of John Ruskin.

Previous Year Question Paper (1998-2017)

1. The leader of the Bardoli Satyagraha (1928) was:
   (a) Sardar Vallabhabhai Patel
   (b) Mahatma Gandhi
   (c) Vithalbhai J. Patel
   (d) Mahadev Desai **(2003)**
2. With reference to the Indian freedom struggle, which one of the following statements is not correct?
   (a) Hakim Ajmal Khan was one of the leaders to start a nationalist and militant Ahrar movement
   (b) When the Indian National Congress was formed, Sayyid Ahmad Khan opposed it.
   (c) The All-India Muslim League which was formed in 1906 vehemently opposed the partition of Bengal and separate electrorates.
   (d) Maulana Barakataullah and Maulana Obeidullah Sindhi were among those who formed a Provisional Government of India in Kabul. **(2002)**
3. Which one of the following submitted in 1875 a petition to the House of Commons demanding India's direct representation in the British Parliament?
   (a) The Decan Association
   (b) The Indian Association
   (c) The All-India Muslim League which was formed in 1906 vehemently opposed the partition of Bengal and separate electorates
   (d) Maulana Barakataullah and Maulana Obeidullah Sindhi were among those who formed a Provisional Government of India in Kabul. **(2015)**
4. The President of Indian National Congress at the time of partition of India was:
   (a) C. Rajagopalachari
   (b) J.B. Kriplani
   (c) Jawaharlal Nehru
   (d) Maulana Abul Kalam Azad **(2015)**
5. During the Indian freedom struggle, the Khudai Khidmatgars, also known as Red Shirts, called for
   (a) The Union of Pashtun tribal areas in north-west Afghanistan
   (b) The adoption of terrorist tactics and methods for terrorising and finally ousting the colonial rulers
   (c) The adoption of communist revolutionary ideology for political and social reforms
   (d) The Pathan regional nationalist unity and a struggle against colonialism **(2002)**
6. The last opportunity to avoid the partition of India was lost with the rejection of:
   (a) Cripps Mission
   (b) Rajagopalachari Formula
   (c) Cabinet Mission
   (d) Wavell Plan **(2002)**
7. With reference to the period of extremist nationalist movement in India with its spirit of Swadeshi, which one of the following statements is not correct?
   (a) Liakat Hussain led the Muslim Peasants of Barisal in their agitations
   (b) In 1898, the scheme of national education was formulated by Satish Chandra Mukherjee
   (c) The Bengal National College was founded in 1906 with Aurobindo as the principal
   (d) Tagore preached the cult of Atmashakti, the main plan of

which was social and economic regeneration of the villages **(2015)**

8. **A:** The effect of labour participation in the Indian nationalist upsurge of the early 1930's was weak:
   R: The labour leaders considered the ideology of Indian National Congress as bourgeois and reactionary.
   (a) Both A and R are true and R is the correct explanation of A
   (b) Both A and R are true but R is not a correct explanation of A
   (c) A is true but R is false
   (d) A is false but R is true **(2015)**
9. Who among the following was the President of the All India States People's Conference in 1939?
   (a) Jaya Prakash Narayan
   (b) Jawaharlal Nehru
   (c) Sheikh Abdullah
   (d) Sardar Vallabhbhai Patel **(2001)**
10. Who among the following organised the famous Chittagong armoury raid?
   (a) Laxm Sehgal
   (b) Surya Sen
   (c) Batukeshwar Datta
   (d) J.M. Sengupta **(2001)**
11. Who among the following leaders proposed to adopt Complete Independence as the goal of the Congress in the Ahmedabad session of 1920?
   (a) Abul Kalam Azad
   (b) Jawaharlal Nehru
   (c) Hasrat Mohani
   (d) Mohandas Karamchand Gandhi **(2001)**
12. A London branch of the All India Muslim League was established in 1908 under the presidency of:
   (a) Aga Khan
   (b) Ameer Ali
   (c) Liaquat Ali Khan
   (d) M A Jinnah **(2001)**
13. The Hunter Commission was appointed after the:
   (a) Black-hole incident
   (b) Jalianwalla Bagh massacre
   (c) Uprising of 1857
   (d) Partition of Bengal **(2001)**
14. Consider the following statements about the Indian National Congress:
   1. Sarojini Naidu was the first woman to be the President of the Congress
   2. C.R. Das was in prison when he functioned as the President of the Congress
   3. The first Britisher to become the President of the Congress was Alan Octavian Hume
   4. Alfred Webb was the President of the Congress in 1894 **(2000)**

   Which of these statements are correct?
   (a) 1 and 3 (b) 2 and 4
   (c) 2, 3 and 4 (d) 1, 2 3 and 4
15. **A:** The basic weakness of the early nationalist movement lay in its narrow social base.
   R: It fought for the narrow interests of the social groups which joined it.
   (a) Both A and R are true and R is the correct explanation of A
   (b) Both A and R are true but R is not a correct explanation of A
   (c) A is true but R is false
   (d) A is false but R is true **(2015)**
16. Which one of the following is **NOT** a feature of the Government of India Act of 1935?
   (a) Dyarchy at the Centre as well as in the provinces
   (b) A bicameral legislature
   (c) Provincial autonomy
   (d) An All-India federation **(2015)**

17. The Indian National Army (INA) came into existence in 1943 in
(a) Japan (b) Burma
(c) Singapore (d) Malaya **(2000)**

18. As an alternative to the partition of India, Gandhiji suggested to Mountbatten that he:
(a) Postpone granting of independence
(b) Invite Jinnah to form the government
(c) Invite Nehru and Jinnah to form the government together
(d) Invite the army to take over for some time **(2015)**

19. After returning from South Africa, Gandhiji launched his first successful Satyagaraha in:
(a) Chauri Chaura
(b) Dandi
(c) Champaran
(d) Bardoli **(2000)**

20. **A:** Lord Linlithgo described the August Movement of 1942 as the most serious revolt after the Sepoy mutiny.
R: Peasants joined the movement in large number in some places.
(a) Both A and R are true and R is the correct explanation of A
(b) Both A and R are true but R is not a correct explanation of A
(c) A is true but R is false
(d) A is false but R is true **(2015)**

21. While delivering the presidential address, the Congress President who advocated the introduction of Roman script for Hindi language was:
(a) Mahatma Gandhi
(b) Jawaharlal Nehru
(c) Abul Kalam Azad
(d) Subhash Chandra Bose **(2015)**

22. At the time of partition of India, which one of the following provinces of British India came forward with a plan for a united and independent existence?
(a) Punjab (b) Assam
(c) Bengal (d) Bihar **(2015)**

23. The Balkan Plan for fragmentation of India was the brainchild of
(a) W. Churchill
(b) M.A. Jinnah
(c) Lord Mountbatten
(d) V.P. Menon **(2015)**

24. Which Indian natinalist leader looked upon the war between Germany and Britain as a godsent opportunity which would enable Indians to exploit the situation to their advantage?
(a) C. Rajagopalachari
(b) M.A. Jinnah
(c) Subhash Chandra Bose
(d) Jawaharlal Nehru **(2015)**

25. The first venture of Gandhi in all-India politics was the:
(a) Non-Cooperation Movement
(b) Rowlatt Satyagraha
(c) Champaran Movement
(d) Dandi March **(1999)**

Answers

1. (a)	2. (c)	3. (d)
4. (b)	5. (d)	6. (c)
7. (a)	8. (c)	9. (b)
10. (b)	11. (c)	12. (b)
13. (b)	14. (b)	15. (c)
16. (a)	17. (d)	18. (b)
19. (c)	20. (a)	21. (d)
22. (a)	23. (c)	24. (c)
25. (b)		

Practice Paper

1. When was Rowlatt Act passed?
   (a) 1919 (b) 1920
   (c) 1921 (d) 1922
   (48th 52nd BPSC 2008)
2. Gandhiji launched the Non-Co-operation Movement in-
   (a) 1920 (b) 1919
   (c) 1921 (d) 1922
   (48th 52nd BPSC 2008)
3. Quit India Movement began on:
   (a) 9th August,1942
   (b) 10th August,1942
   (c) 15th August,1942
   (d) 16th August,1942
   (48th 52nd BPSC 2008, WB PCS(P)2008)
4. The correct chronological order of following events is:
   1. C.R. Formula
   2. Cabinet Mission
   3. Gandhi-Jinnah Dialogue
   4. Wavel Plan
   (a) 4 – 3 – 2 – 1 (b) 1 – 2 – 3 – 4
   (c) 1 – 3 – 2 – 4 (d) 1 – 3 – 4 – 2
   (JPSC 2003)
5. Who of the following took the burning of the foreign clothes during the Non-Cooperation Movement as 'insensate waste':
   (a) Rabindra Nath Tagore
   (b) Mohammad Ali
   (c) Lord Reading
   (d) Moti Lal Nehru **(UP PCS (P) 2002)**
6. Find out the correct sequence of the following from the code given below:
   (1) C. Rajagopalachari Plan
   (2) Wavell Plan
   (3) Mountbatten Plan
   (4) Cabinet Mission Plan
   Code:
   (a) 1 – 2 – 3 – 4 (b) 2 – 3 – 4 – 1
   (c) 1 – 2 – 4 – 3 (d) 2 – 1 – 3 – 4
   (UP PCS(P) 2002)
7. The name of the periodical among the following published by Mahatma Gandhi during his stay in South Africa:
   (1) Navjivan (2) India Gazette
   (3) Africaner (4) Indian Opinion
   Code:
   (a) 1 – 2 – 3 – 4 (b) 2 – 3 – 4 – 1
   (c) 1 – 2 – 4 – 3 (d) 2 – 1 – 3 – 4
   (UP PCS (P) 2002)
8. In which of the following did Sardar Vallabhbhai Patel play a leading role?
   (a) Bijolia Movement
   (b) Dandi March
   (c) Bardoli Satyagraha
   (d) Textile Mill Workers strike at Ahmedabad **(UP PCS (P) 2002)**
9. A larg crowd gathered in the Jallianwala Bagh at Amritsar on April 13, 1919 to protest against the arrest of:
   (a) Swami Shradhanand and Mazharul Haq
   (b) Madan Mohan Malviya and Mohammad Ali Jinnah
   (c) Mahatma Gandhi and Abul Kalam Azad
   (d) Dr. Saifuddin Kitchhu and Dr. Satyapal **(UP PCS(P) 2002)**
10. The date April 6, 1930 is known in Indian History for:
    (a) Dandi March by Mahatma Gandhi
    (b) First Round Table Conference
    (c) Gandhi-Irwin Pact
    (d) Jallianwala Bagh massacre
    (UP PCS (P)2002)

11. Which of the following struggles of Mahatma Gandhi was related to industrial workers?
    (a) Champaran Satyagraha
    (b) Ahmedabad Struggle
    (c) Kheda Struggle
    (d) None of these **(UP PCS (P) 2002)**
12. Consider the following statements and select the correct answer from the code given here under:
    Assertion (A): In the wake of Quit India Movement, the British and the Muslims in their common hatred for the Congress closer to each other.
    Reason (R): Jinnah acted as a staunchally of the British Government and told Muslims to keep away from the Congress movement of 1942.
    Codes:
    (a) Both A and R are true and R is the correct explanation of A
    (b) Both A and R are true but R is not a correct explanation of A
    (c) A is true but R is false
    (d) A is false but R is true
    (UP PCS (P) 2003)
13. Match List-I with List-II and select the correct answer using the code given below:

List-I	List-II
A. August Declaration	1. Lord Linlithgow
B. August Offer	2. Montague
C. August Resolution	3. M.A. Jinnah
D. Direct Action	4. Gandhi

Codes

	A	B	C	D
(a)	2	1	4	3
(b)	1	2	4	3
(c)	1	2	3	4
(d)	4	1	2	3

(UP PCS (P) 2003)

14. With which of the following movements was Gandhiji NOT associated?
    (a) Khilafat Movement
    (b) Individual Satyagraha Movement
    (c) Quit India Movement
    (d) Swadeshi Movement
    (UP PCS (P) 2003)
15. The main reason for the boycott of Simon Commission in India was
    (a) Appointment before time
    (b) All the members were Englishmen
    (c) Chairman was a member of the British Liberal Party
    (d) Gandhiji's Non-Co-operation Movement **(UP PCS (P) 2004)**
16. Dyarchy was first introduced in India under
    (a) Government of India Act, 1935
    (b) Morley-Minto Reforms
    (c) Mont-Ford Reforms
    (d) Simon Commission Plan
    (UP PCS (P) 2004, CDS 2010)
17. Poona Pact was signed between
    (a) Gandhiji and Lord Irwin
    (b) Gandhiji and Jinnah
    (c) Gandhiji and S.C. Bose
    (d) Gandhiji and Ambedkar
    (UP PCS (P) 2004)
18. Find the correct chronological order of the following events from the code given below

(1) Civil Disobedience Movement
(2) Individual Satyagraha
(3) Quit India Movement
(4) Cripps Mission

Code:

(a) 1 – 2 – 4 – 3 (b) 1 – 2 – 3 – 4
(c) 2 – 1 – 3 – 4 (d) 2 – 3 – 1 – 4

(UP PCS (P) 2004)

19. The freedom fighter who died in jail due to hunger strike was
(a) Bhagat Singh
(b) Bipin Chandra Pal
(c) Jatin Das
(d) Subhash Chandra Bose

(UP PCS Special (P) 2004)

20. Who of the following said, 'Mahatma Gandhi, like fleeting phantom raises dust but not the level'?
(a) B.R. Ambedkar
(b) M.A. Jinnah
(c) V.D. Savarkar
(d) None of these **(UP PCS (M) 2005)**

21. The province where the Indian National Congress could not get absolute majority during the general election of 1937 was
(a) Bombay (b) Assam
(c) Orissa (d) Bihar

(UP PCS (M) 2004)

22. In which chronological order the following events took place?
(1) Chauri-Chaura Episode
(2) Jallianwala Bagh Massacre
(3) Rowlatt Satyagraha
(4) Champaran Satyagraha

Codes:

(a) 1 – 2 – 3 – 4 (b) 2 – 3 – 4 – 1
(c) 4 – 3 – 2 – 1 (d) 3 – 2 – 4 – 1

(UP PCS (M) 2004)

23. The historic Dandi March is associated with
(a) Boycott of elections
(b) Violation of Salt law
(c) Hindu Muslim Unity
(d) Abolition of Untouchability

(UP PCS (M) 2004, SSC MP JEE 2014)

24. Who among the following decided to launch the Independent Party on 16th December, 1922?
Select the correct answer from the codes given below:
(1) Lala Hardayal
(2) Madan Mohan Malviya
(3) Mohammad Ali Jinnah
(4) Moti Lal Nehru

Codes:

(a) 1 and 2 (b) 2 and 3
(c) 3 and 4 (d) 2 and 4

(UP PCS (M) 2005)

25. Which of the following statements are ture about the Simon Commission?
Select the correct answer from the codes given below the statements:
1. It was appointed to enquire into the working of the 1919 Act
2. It was headed by Sir John Simon
3. It recommended a Federal form of Government
4. It was opposed by the Indian Leaders.

Codes:

(a) 1 and 2 only (b) 1, 2 and 3 only
(c) 2, 3 and 4 only (d) All the above

(UP PCS (M) 2005)

26. Select the correct chronological order of the following events from the codes given below:
(1) Poona Pact
(2) Quit India Movement
(3) Cabinet Mission
(4) Simla Conference

Codes:

(a) 1 – 2 – 4 – 3 (b) 4 – 3 – 2 – 1
(c) 3 – 4 – 1 – 2 (d) 2 – 3 – 4 – 1

(UP PCS (M) 2005)

27. Which of the following institutions were founded during the Non-Co-operation Movement (1920-22)?
    (1) Kashi Vidyapeeth
    (2) Gujarat Vidyapeeth
    (3) Jamia Milia
    Select the correct answer from the codes given below:
    (a) 1 and 2 only (b) 2 and 3 only
    (c) 1, 2 and 3 only (d) All the above
    (UP PCS (M) 2005)
28. Which one of the following was favoured by Nehru but not favoured by Gandhiji?
    (a) Truth
    (b) Non-Violence
    (c) Untouchability
    (d) Heavy industrialisation
    (UP PCS (M) 2006)
29. Consider:
    Assertion (A): Nehru had no regard for Upanishads.
    Reason (R): His attitude was scientific.
    Codes:
    (a) Both A and R are true and R is the correct explanation of A
    (b) Both A and R are true but R is not a correct explanation of A
    (c) A is true but R is false
    (d) A is false but R is true
    (UP PCS (P) 2003)
30. Who among the following Pakistani National was awarded 'Bharat Ratna' by the Indian Government?
    (a) Liaquat Ali Khan
    (b) M.A. Jinnah
    (c) Khan Abdul Ghaffar Khan
    (d) Muhammad Iqbal
    (UP PCS (M) 2006)

Answers

1. (a)	2. (a)	3. (a)	16. (c)	17. (d)	18. (a)
4. (d)	5. (a)	6. (c)	19. (c)	20. (a)	21. (b)
7. (d)	8. (c)	9. (d)	22. (c)	23. (b)	24. (d)
10. (a)	11. (b)	12. (a)	25. (d)	26. (a)	27. (c)
13. (a)	14. (d)	15. (b)	28. (d)	29. (d)	30. (c)

SECTION B

PRACTICE PAPERS

PRACTICE PAPER

1

1. Which of the following laid the foundation of central administration in India?
   (a) Pitt's India Act of 1784
   (b) Regulating act of 1773
   (c) Government of India Act of 1858
   (d) Charter Act of 1833
2. Arrange the following events in chronological order:
   1. Hindu widow remarriage act
   2. Abolition of Sati
   3. Woods Despatch
   4. Macaulay Minute

   Correct code is:
   (a) 1, 2, 3, 4 (b) 2, 4, 3, 1
   (c) 1, 3, 4, 2 (d) 4, 1, 2, 3
3. Which of the following is not a recommendation of Charles Wood's Despatch?
   (a) An education department to be established in every province.
   (b) At least one Government school is opened in every district.
   (c) The Indian native should be given training in the English language.
   (d) Affiliated private schools should be given grant in aid.
4. According to Doctrine of Lapse, when the ruler of a protected state died without a natural heir, his state was not to pass to an adopted heir as sanctioned by the age old tradition of the country. Following states were annexed by applying this doctrine
   1. Nagpur
   2. Satara
   3. Balaghat
   4. Jhansi

   Arrange the above states of annexation in chronological order.
   (a) 2–3–4–5–1 (b) 2–3–1–5–4
   (c) 3–1–2–4–5 (d) 3–1–4–5–2
5. Consider the following statements regarding Alfonso de Albuquerque:
   1. He was the first governor of the Portuguese possessions in the East.
   2. He had made Pondichery the headquarters of the Portuguese Empire in India.
   3. Albuquerque encouraged the marriages of the Portuguese with Indian women.

   Which of the statements given above is/are correct?
   (a) 1 and 3 only (b) 1 and 2 only
   (c) 1 only (d) 3 only
6. Consider the following statements about British East India Company :
   1. In the latter half of the 16th century, it gained control over trade of Indonesia, India, Srilanka and Malaya.

2. The Island of Bombay was acquired by the company from the British government in 1668.

Which of the statement(s) given above is/are correct?

(a) 1 only (b) 2 only
(c) Both 1 and 2 (d) Neither 1 nor 2

7. Raja Rammohan Roy was a pioneer of Indian journalism. He wanted to spread awareness among the people. He brought out journals in which of the following languages:

1. Bengali 2. Persian
3. English 4. French

Code :

(a) 1, 2 and 3 only (b) 1, 2 and 4 only
(c) 1, 3 and 4 only (d) 2, 3 and 4 only

8. In which of the following Viceroy's reign, durand line was demarcated to define border between India and Afghanistan (now between Pakistan and Afghanistan)?

(a) Lord Dufferin
(b) Lord Elgin II
(c) Lord Lansdowne
(d) Lord Ripon

9. **Assertion (A):** The Saraswati was a mighty river in the Vedic and Pre-Vedic time, but disappeared thereafter, probably by the advancing desert.

Reason (R): The Ghaggar is believed to be the present day successor of the river Saraswati.

Select the correct answers from the code given below.

(a) Both (A) and (R) are true and (R) is the correct explanation of (A).
(b) Both (A) and (R) are true but (R) is NOT the correct explanation of (A).
(c) (A) is true but (R) is false.
(d) (A) is false but (R) is true.

10. Arrange the following papers/journals in order of their start of publication year:

1. Sambad Kaumudi
2. Digdarshana
3. Rast Goftar
4. Madras Mail

(a) 4-3-1-2 (b) 2-1-3-4
(c) 4-3-2-1 (d) 2-4-3-1

11. Which of the following statements is not correct?

(a) The permanent settlement guaranteed stability of income for the East India Company.
(b) The permanent settlement was expected to increase agricultural production.
(c) Under permanent settlement, the Company's income increased as income from agriculture also went up.
(d) In parts of Central India and Awadh, the British introduced a temporary zamindari system under which the zamindars were made owner of the land but land revenue rate was revised periodically.

12. Consider the following statements about the two famous battles of the eighteenth century :

The "............." did not decide who was to rule India but rather decided that who was not and ".............." was the most decisive battles of Indian history for it demonstrated the superiority of English arms over the combined army of two of the major Indian powers.

Considering the two famous battles respectively, which of the given options below would correctly fill in the blanks of the statement?

(a) Battle of Plassey, Battle of Buxar
(b) Battle of Buxar, Battle of Plassey
(c) Battle of Buxar, third Battle of Panipat
(d) Third battle of Panipat, Battle of Buxar

13. The Moti Masjid in Agra was built by Shah Jahan whose architectural features are quite similar to that of the Saint Basil's Cathedral in Moscow. Who built Moti Masjid at the Red Fort in Delhi?
(a) Shah Jahan (b) Aurangzeb
(c) Akbar (d) Humayun

14. Which one of the later mughals was captured, imprisoned, blinded, poisoned and ultimately put to death by the Saiyid brothers.
(a) Farrukh Siyar
(b) Zulfikar Khan
(c) Muhammad Shah
(d) Jahandar Shah

15. Consider the following statements:
1. In the second Anglo-Mysore war, the Marathas and the Nizam joined hands with Hiadar Ali against the British.
2. In the first Anglo-Mysore war, the Marathas and the Nizam were with the British against Haidar Ali.

Which of the statements given above is/are correct?
(a) 1 only (b) 2 only
(c) Both 1 and 2 (d) Neither 1 nor 2

16. Consider the following statements with regard to 'Permanent Settlement system' of land revenue:
1. The work related to this system though started by Warren Hastings, was completed by Lord Cornwallis.
2. Lord Cornwallis was assisted by Sir John Shore in adopting this settlement policy.
3. Under this settlement, Zamindars were recognized as the owner of the land.
4. Lord Cornwallis had adopted this settlement to teach a lesson to the peasants of India.

Which of the above given statements is/are incorrect?
(a) 1 only (b) 2 and 3 only
(c) 4 only (d) 2 and 4 only

17. Dada Bhai Naoroji organized 'East India Association' to serve which one of the following purposes?
(a) To promote nationalism among the peasants of India.
(b) To discuss the Indian questions and influence British public to promote India welfare.
(c) To unite all nationalist leader under one organization.
(d) To start an independent organization apart from congress.

18. Which one of the following observations about trade of India, during 18th century is incorrect?
(a) In this period India's industrial and agricultural products had a steady market outside the country.
(b) While sea trade was expanded, overland trade through Afghanistan and Persia was disrupted.
(c) Constant warfare and disruption of law and order in many areas harmed the country's internal trade.
(d) From 1757 began the special phase of company's trade-cum-plunder of Bengal which was called by R.P. Dutt as period of industrial capital.

19. Though they indulged in inhuman cruelties and lawlessness, the possession of the Portuguese in India

survived for one century. Which one of the following factors was not a cause for their territorial control?

(a) Their good trade relations with South-East Asia.
(b) They enjoyed the control over high seas.
(c) Their soldiers and aministration maintained strict discipline.
(d) They did not have to face the might of the Mughal Empire as South India was outside Mughal influence.

20. Consider the following statements in regard to the social and cultural policy of the British Rule in India:
    1. From the beginning the majority of British officials in India were generally of progressive persuasion.
    2. Initially the British followed a policy of non-interference in the religious, social and cultural life of the country but later they took active steps to transform Indian society.
    3. Many English officials, business-men and statesmen, encouraged the modernization of India because it was expected to make Indians better customers for British goods and reconcile them to the alien rule.

    Which of the statements given above are correct?

    (a) 1 and 2 only (b) 2 and 3 only
    (c) 1 and 3 only (d) 1, 2 and 3

21. Consider the following statements in regard to Mughal Emperor Bahadur Shah I:
    1. He accepted the demand of Raja Jai Singh and Ajit Singh for high mansabs and the offices of subahdars of important provinces of Malwa and Gujarat.
    2. He made peace with Bundela chief Chhatarsal.

    Which of the statements given above is/are correct?

    (a) 1 only (b) 2 only
    (c) Both 1 and 2 (d) Neither 1 nor 2

22. Which one of the following statements about the battle of Wandiwash, fought between the English and the French is incorrect?
    (a) In the very beginning of war the English managed to gain control over Bengal.
    (b) The English General Eyre Coot defeated the French commander Lally.
    (c) The war ended with the signing of the Treaty of Ex La Chapelle.
    (d) After the war of Wandiwash, the French lived in India under British protection.

23. **Assertion (A):** In the begining the Indian rulers tolerated and even encouraged the establishment of the East India Company's factories in India.

    Reason (R): The nature of the business of the company initially increased the export of Indian manufacturers and thus encouraged their production.

    Select the correct answer from the codes given below.

    (a) Both (A) and (R) are true and (R) is the correct explanation of (A).
    (b) Both (A) and (R) are true but (R) is NOT the correct explanation of (A).
    (c) (A) is true but (R) is false.
    (d) (A) is false but (R) is true.

24. Which one of the following was the primary cause of majority of civil rebellion against the British Rule before 1857?

(a) Exploitation of the village artisans and farmers by moneylenders along with Britishers.
(b) The rapid changes that the British introduced in the economy, administration and land revenue system.
(c) The colonial policy of intensifying demands for land revenue and extracting as large an amount as possible.
(d) Not even a part of the enhanced revenue was spent on the development of agriculture or the welfare of the cultivator.

25. The most important consequence of the decline of the Mughal Empire in India was that :
(a) The regional powers arose to fulfil their own interests.
(b) The British were able to conquer India.
(c) The Indians had to face the western powers for the supremacy.
(d) None among the Indian powers became competent to replace the Mughals.

26. Consider the following statements in regard to early administrative policies of the East India Company in India :
1. The dominant classes of the British society were keen to preserve the monopoly of lucrative appointments in the Indian Civil Service and other services for their children.
2. Lord Cornwallis had proposed to give the British and Indian officials high salaries to help them resist temptations and to become honest and obedient.
(a) 1 only (b) 2 only
(c) Both 1 and 2 (d) Neither 1 nor 2

27. Consider the following statements in regard to Ryotwari Settlement of land revenue system in India under the British rule.
1. Under the Ryotwari Settlement, the cultivator was recognised as the owner of his plot of land for the payment of land revenue.
2. The Ryotwari Settlement brought into existence a system of peasant ownership over the land.
Which of the statements given above is/are correct?
(a) 1 only (b) 2 only
(c) Both 1 and 2 (d) Neither 1 nor 2

28. Which one of the factors given below did not help the money-lenders to exploit the cultivators under the British rule in India?
(a) The new legal system and new land revenue policy introduced by the British.
(b) The introduction of transferability of land.
(c) The growing commercialisation of agriculture.
(d) Support of money-lending traditions, prevalent for a very long time.

29. Which one of the following statements about Tipu Sultan, the ruler of Mysore is not correct?
(a) He tried to build a modern navy and established two dockyards.
(b) In treaty of Mangalore, Tipu Sultan dictated terms to British.
(c) Tipu Sultan had a rocket brigade called Kushoons in his army.
(d) The economy of Mysore under his rule was free from the contemporary economic backwardness.

30. Lord Dalhousie, the British Governor General of India, to extend direct British rule over maximum possible area in the country, declared that the extinction of all native states of India was just a question of time. The inherent movtie of this extension policy of the British rule over India was :
    (a) To expand the export of the British goods to India.
    (b) To add the Indian economy to the concurrent global market, through the British economy.
    (c) To impose similar rule over maximum part of India for the maintenance of law and order.
    (d) To convert India as a unified economic unit.
31. **Assertion (A):** From the second decade of the 19th century, many British officials, political leaders and traders pleaded to the British Government in India to reduce the land revenue.
    Reason (R): They all wanted to improve the status of the Indian peasants.
    Select the correct answer from the codes given below.
    (a) Both (A) and (R) are true and (R) is the correct explanation of (A).
    (b) Both (A) and (R) are true but (R) is NOT the correct explanation of (A).
    (c) (A) is true but (R) is false.
    (d) (A) is false but (R) is true.
32. Consider the following statements in regard to the modern education system during the British period in India :
    1. The British education system neglected the mass education.
    2. The English medium of education generated a linguistic and cultural distance between the educated persons and masses.
    3. Bethune School founded by D. K. Karve at Pune, was one of the pioneer institutes in India, to provide modern education to the girls.

    Which of the statements given above are correct?
    (a) 1 and 2 only (b) 2 and 3 only
    (c) 1 and 3 only (d) 1, 2 and 3
33. With reference to the Parmanent Settlement system of land revenue in Bengal, which of the following statements is not correct?
    (a) The security of tenure of landlords was guaranteed.
    (b) It was introduced by the British government to increase the yield of the soil.
    (c) It gave rise to the commericialization of land.
    (d) Under this system, small land-holders could be expelled by the new landholders.
34. With regard to Lord Macaulay's Minute, consider the following statements:
    1. It gave preference to western sciences and literature over traditional Indian learning.
    2. It proposed English as a medium of isntruction in schools and colleges.
    3. It forwarded the 'downward filtration theory'.
    4. It led to the opening of a large number of elementary schools.

    Which of the statements given above are correct?
    (a) 1 and 2 only
    (b) 1, 2 and 3 only
    (c) 2 and 3 only
    (d) 1, 2, 3 and 4
35. Which of the following events was associated with Lord Lytton?

(a) Telegraphic communication was opened with Europe.
(b) High Courts were established at Calcutta, Bombay and Madras.
(c) The Doctrine of Lapse was withdrawn.
(d) Grand Durbar was arranged in Delhi, when country was under servere famine.

36. **Assertion (A):** In 1813 the British Government abolished the East India Company's monopoly of Indian trade.
Reason (R): The British traders, who were not partners in the East India Company, powerfully campaigned against the Company's monopoly to get a share in the high profitable trade with India.
Select the correct answer from the codes given below.
(a) Both (A) and (R) are true and (R) is the correct explanation of (A).
(b) Both (A) and (R) are true but (R) is NOT the correct explanation of (A).
(c) (A) is true but (R) is false.
(d) (A) is false but (R) is true.

37. Consider the following statements:
1. Lord Cornwallis laid the foundation of a new judicial system in British India through a hierarchy of civil and criminal courts.
2. Lord Cornwallis separated the posts of the Civil Judge and the Revenue Collector in a district in British India.

Which of the statements given above is/are correct?
(a) 1 only (b) 2 only
(c) Both 1 and 2 (d) Neither 1 nor 2

38. **Assertion (A):** The life of the common Indian people during the first half of eighteenth century was better as compared to the people in the late nineteenth century.
Reason (R): During the first half of the eighteenth century, in India, there was not much inequality in the economic life of the people.
Select the correct answer from the codes given below.
(a) Both (A) and (R) are true and (R) is the correct explanation of (A).
(b) Both (A) and (R) are true but (R) is NOT the correct explanation of (A).
(c) (A) is true but (R) is false.
(d) (A) is false but (R) is true.

39. **Assertion (A):** The caste system was a major element of social disintegration in India, in 18th century.
Reason (R): It was possible for a person to acquire a higher social status by the acquisition of a high office or power.
Select the correct answer from the codes given below.
(a) Both (A) and (R) are true and (R) is the correct explanation of (A).
(b) Both (A) and (R) are true but (R) is NOT the correct explanation of (A).
(c) (A) is true but (R) is false.
(d) (A) is false but (R) is true.

40. **Assertion (A):** A major lacuna in the early education policy of the British rule in India (during 1813 to 1857) was the almost total neglect of the education of girls.
Reason (R): Social discrimination based on sex was prevalent in Britain also up to the 19th century and even the British women were treated as secondary subjects of the British Crown.
Select the correct answer from the codes given below.
(a) Both (A) and (R) are true and (R) is the correct explanation of (A).

(b) Both (A) and (R) are true but (R) is NOT the correct explanation of (A).
(c) (A) is true but (R) is false.
(d) (A) is false but (R) is true.

41. Which of the following Indian rulers supported the British during the revolt of 1857?
1. The Scindias of Gwalior
2. Raja Khan Bahadur Khan of Bareilly
3. Raja Kunwar Singh of Jagdishpur
4. Nana Saheb of Kanpur
5. Nawab of Hyderabad
(a) 1 and 2 only (b) 2 and 3 only
(c) 1 and 5 only (d) 2 and 4 only

42. Which of the following were anti brahmanical movements?
1. The Nair Movement
2. Self Respect Movement
3. The Nadar Movement
4. The Shuddhi Movement
Correct code is:
(a) 1, 2 and 4 only (b) 2, 3 and 4 only
(c) 1, 2 and 3 only (d) 1, 3 and 4 only

43. Which of the following statements is not correct?
(a) The first session of Indian national congress was presided over by W.C. Bonnerjee in December 1885 and attended by 72 delegates.
(b) Surendranath Bonerjee was one of the founder member of Indian National Congress.
(c) Dada Bhai Naoroji organised the East India Association in London to discuss the Indian matters and to influence British people to promote Indian Welfare.
(d) Pherojshah Mehta, K.T. Telang, Badruddin Tyabji and others formed the Bombay Presidency Association in 1885.

44. Portfolio system was introduced in India by:
(a) Lord Curzon (b) Lord Mayo
(c) Lord Canning (d) Lord Ripon

45. The traditional system of justice in India was based on customary laws which arose from long tradition and practice. The British laid the foundation of a new system of dispensing justice through a hierarchy of civil and criminal courts. Who among the following Governor Generals initiated new system of justice in India?
(a) Lord Cornwallis
(b) Lord Ripon
(c) Warren Hastings
(d) William Bentick

46. Surendranath Banerjee, one of the founding fathers of Indian national movement, was the first Indian to go to jail in performance of his duty as a journalist. Which one of the following newspaper is associated with the incident?
(a) Amrit Bazaar Patrika
(b) Banga Nivasi
(c) Bengalee
(d) Indian Mirror

47. Which of the following statements is not correct?
(a) Romesh Chandra Dutta published 'The Economic History of India', in which he examined in minute detail, the entire economic record of colonial rule since 1757.
(b) G.V. Joshi, G. Subramaniya Iyer and G. K. Gokhale also analysed colonial economic policies.
(c) The early nationalist believed that all encompassing poverty was inherent in India and unavoidable.

(d) The early nationalist leaders organized powerful intellectual agitations against important official economic policies.

48. Which of the following correspondents toured India during the revolt of 1857 who mentioned popular support for revolt and said that although people did not rise up in revolt but showed strong sympathy for the rebels?
(a) Bobb Miller (b) W.H. Russel
(c) Samuel (d) P.H. Thomas

49. In 1877 certain heads of expenditure like land revenue, Excise, General administration, Law and Justice were transferred to the provinces in furtherance of separation of Central finances from Provincial finances. Who among the following Governor General was responsible for this act?
(a) Lord Mayo
(b) Lord Lytton
(c) Lord Ripon
(d) Lord Northbrook

50. In which of the following Indian National Congress session, demand for permanent fixation of land revenue was made?
(a) Nagpur session, 1891
(b) Madras session, 1894
(c) Amravati session, 1897
(d) Lucknow session, 1899

51. Match the following :

A. Sewa samiti	1. Behramji M. Malabari
B. Seva sadan	2. Hridyanath Kunzru
C. Mahars movement	3. K. Rama
D. Nair movement	4. B.R. Ambedkar

Code :

	A	B	C	D		A	B	C	D
(a)	4	3	1	2	(b)	2	1	4	3
(c)	4	3	2	1	(d)	1	2	4	3

52. This organization opposed the vices in society, believed in truth, freedom and reason and established the 'Society for the acquistion of General Knowledge'. Identify the organization out of the following options:
(a) Students literary and scientific society
(b) Indian reform association
(c) Deccan education society
(d) Young Bengal movement

53. What was the main contribution of moderates for Indian National Movement?
(a) Appointment of Public Service commission in 1886
(b) Enactment of the Indian Council Act 1892
(c) Appointment of Welby commission on Indian expenditure
(d) Assessment of economic impact of British rule in India.

54. Which of the following books were written on Revolt of 1857?
1. The Indian War of Independence
2. Free Hindustan
3. The Sepoy Mutiny and the Revolt of 1857
4. Civil Rebellions in the Indian Mutinies

Code:
(a) 1, 2 and 3 only (b) 1, 2 and 4 only
(c) 1, 3 and 4 only (d) 2, 3 and 4 only

55. Consider the following statements :
1. Muhammad Qasim Nanotavi and Rashid Ahmad Ganghoi founded the Deoband School.

2. The objectives of Deoband School were to train religious leaders for Muslim community and oppose English education.

Which of the statement(s) given above is/are correct?

(a) 1 only (b) 2 only
(c) Both 1 and 2 (d) Neither 1 nor 2

56. The East Indian Association was founded in London in 1866 with the objective to work for public interest and the welfare of the Indians. In which of the following cities, the East India Association proposed to set up its branches at the time of its establishment?

1. Bombay
2. Madras
3. Calcutta

Correct code:

(a) 1 and 2 only (b) 2 and 3 only
(c) 1 and 3 only (d) 1, 2 and 3

57. Match the following.

(Movement)	**(Founder/Main Leader)**
A. Indian women's association	1. Dhondo Keshav Karve
B. Social service league	2. Saralabala Devi Choudharani
C. Bharat stri mandal	3. Narayan Malhar Joshi
D. Nishkam Karma Math	4. Annie Besant

Code:

	A	B	C	D		A	B	C	D
(a)	4	3	1	2	(b)	2	4	3	1
(c)	4	3	2	1	(d)	2	4	1	3

58. Consider the following statements about Eka Movement :

1. The grass root leadership of Eka Movement came from Madar Pasi and other low-caste leaders.
2. A resolution was passed for refusing to do forced labour and not abiding by panchayat decisions.

Which of the statement(s) given above is/are correct?

(a) 1 only (b) 2 only
(c) Both 1 and 2 (d) Neither 1 nor 2

59. In encouraging the foundation of the Congress the Hume's main purpose was to provide a 'saftey valve' or as safe outlet to the growing discontent among the educated Indians. Considering the above information identify, which of the following given statement is wrong?

(a) A O Hume wanted to prevent the union of a discontented nationalists intelligentsia with a discontented pesantry.
(b) The safety valve theory was completely clear and lucid.
(c) If Hume wanted to use the Congress as a 'safety volve', the early Congress leaders hoped to use him as lightening conductor.
(d) The Indians National Congress was one of the channels through which the stream of nationalism flowed.

60. Which among the following were the causes of failure of Indian handicraft during British rule?

1. Hostile British policies
2. Disappearance of Princely support
3. Emergence of Joint Hindu Family Business
4. Competition from machine made goods

Code:

(a) 1 and 2 only (b) 1, 3 and 4 only
(c) 1, 2 and 4 only (d) All of the above

61. Which of the following were aims and objectives of the Indian National Congress at the time of its establishment in 1885?
    1. Founding a democratic and nationalist movement
    2. Political education of the people
    3. Framing Constitution for the Indian National Congress
    4. Promoting and nurturing Indian Nationhood

    Correct Code:
    (a) 1, 2 and 3 only
    (b) 1, 2 and 4 only
    (c) 1, 3 and 4 only
    (d) 2, 3 and 4 only
62. Which of the following Governor General withdrew the Doctrine of Lapse?
    (a) Lord Mayo
    (b) Lord John Lawrence
    (c) Lord Northbrook
    (d) Lord Canning
63. **Assertion (A):** The Vernacular Press Act 1878 was brought with a view to prevent the criticism of the government policies and the Act excluded English language publications.

    Reason (R): Lord Ripon repealed the Vernacular Press Act, 1878.

    Select the correct answer from the codes given below.
    (a) Both (A) and (R) are true and (R) is the correct explanation of (A).
    (b) Both (A) and (R) are true but (R) is NOT the correct explanation of (A).
    (c) (A) is true but (R) is false.
    (d) (A) is false but (R) is true.
64. Consider the following statements :
    1. The objective behind the Partition of Bengal, 1905 was to weaken the rising sentiments of nationalism.
    2. Partition of Bengal began a transformation of the Indian National Congress from a middle-class pressure group into a nationwide mass movement.
    3. Partition of Bengal suppressed the rising sentiments of the nationalism.

    Which of the statement(s) given above is/are correct?
    (a) 1 only (b) 2 only
    (c) 1 and 2 only (d) 1, 2 and 3
65. **Assertion (A):** Earlier congress leader did not adopt aggressive approach towards the British Government and followed a moderate approach.

    Reason (R): Earlier congress leaders knew the limit of their activity.

    Select the correct answer from the codes given below.
    (a) Both (A) and (R) are true and (R) is the correct explanation of (A).
    (b) Both (A) and (R) are true but (R) is NOT the correct explanation of (A).
    (c) (A) is true but (R) is false.
    (d) (A) is false but (R) is true.
66. Consider the following statements regarding Muslim socio-religious movements:
    1. Fairazi movement was started by Haji Shariatullah and Dudhi Miyan, which gave emphasis on strict monotheism and anti-British ethos.
    2. Taiyuni movement, which was started at Dacca by Maulana Shibli Numani, was opposed to Fairazi movement and supported the British rule.

    Which of the statements given above is/are correct?
    (a) 1 only (b) 2 only
    (c) Both 1 and 2 (d) Neither 1 nor 2

67. **Assertion (A):** After the Revolt of 1857 in India, the British recruited the soldiers in the British Indian Army from Punjabi, Gurkha and Pathan Communities on a large scale and declared them as martial communities.

Reason (R): The soldiers from these communities staunchly secured the British interests outside India on a large scale.

Select the correct answer from the codes given below.

(a) Both (A) and (R) are true and (R) is the correct explanation of (A).
(b) Both (A) and (R) are true but (R) is NOT the correct explanation of (A).
(c) (A) is true but (R) is false.
(d) (A) is false but (R) is true.

68. Consider the following statements in respect of the Theosophical Soceity movement in India :

1. The Theosophical Society movement was led by westerns (Europeans and Americans) who glorified Indian religious and philosophical traditions.
2. This movement tended to give the Indians a sense of false pride in their past greatness.
3. This movement got remarkable success within India as well as outside India.

Which of the statements given above are correct?

(a) 1 and 2 only (b) 2 and 3 only
(c) 1 and 3 only (d) 1, 2 and 3

69. **Assertion (A):** The Indian Councils Act, 1861 provided to incorporate Indians in the Governor General's Executive Council to represent the Indian views.

Reason (R): A statutory commission constituted by the British government under the chairmanship of Charles Wood, in 1859, recommended for the appointment of Indians in the Governor General's Executive Council.

Select the correct answer from the codes given below.

(a) Both (A) and (R) are true and (R) is the correct explanation of (A).
(b) Both (A) and (R) are true but (R) is NOT the correct explanation of (A).
(c) (A) is true but (R) is false.
(d) (A) is false but (R) is true.

70. Which one of the following observations is incorrect about the early moderate nationalists during the Indian Freedom Movement?

(a) They were declared seditious Brahmins by the British officials.
(b) They lost their control over the movement raised in Bengal against its partition.
(c) They could not develop proper communication with the common Indian people.
(d) They could not keep the concurrent young generation with them.

71. **Assertion (A):** Before 1905 the nationalist leaders during the Indian National Movement showed lukewarm attitude towards the interests of the labourer class in India.

Reason (R): The early nationalist leaders belonged to either the middle class or upper class of the soceity and they were not very keen for the welfare of the labour class.

Select the correct answer from the codes given below.

(a) Both (A) and (R) are true and (R) is the correct explanation of (A).
(b) Both (A) and (R) are true but (R) is NOT the correct explanation of (A).

(c) (A) is true but (R) is false.
(d) (A) is false but (R) is true.

72. Which one of the following observations is not true in regard to the Indigo revolt of 1859-60 in India?
(a) It was the most militant and widespread peasants agitation just after the Revolt of 1857.
(b) One of the major reasons for the success of the revolt was the complete unity among Hindu and Muslim peasants.
(c) The Christian Missionaries opposed the indigo peasants in their struggle.
(d) The government's response to the revolt was not as harsh as the case of civil rebellions.

73. Consider the following statements in regard to the famine relief measures taken during British rule in India :
1. Lord Ripon appointed a famine commission, under the chairmanship of Richard Strachey.
2. The Strachey Famine Commission recommended for the appointment of a Famine Commissioner to operate the relief programmes in the area affected by the famine.

Which of the statements given above is/are correct?
(a) 1 only (b) 2 only
(c) Both 1 and 2 (d) Neither 1 nor 2

74. Which of the following pairs are correctly matched?

Provision		Act
1. Creation of Board of Control	:	Government of India Act, 1858
2. All Civil and Military powers vested in Governor General of India	:	Charter Act, 1833
3. Creation of new office of Secretary of state for India	:	Government of India Act, 1861
4. Separate electroate for Sikhs	:	Government of India Act, 1919

Correct code is
(a) 1, 2 and 3 only (b) 2 and 4 only
(c) 1 and 3 only (d) 2, 3 and 4 only

75. Dr. Mukhtar Ahmed Ansari was an Indian nationalist and political leader and former president of the Indian National Congress and the Muslim league during the Indian Independence movement. He was founder member of which of the following universities?
(a) Jamia Millia Islamia University
(b) Aligarh Muslim University
(c) Berkatullah University
(d) Jawahar Lal Nehru University

76. Who had coined the famous slogan "One religion, one caste and one God for mankind"-
(a) Mahatma Gandhi
(b) B. R. Ambedkar
(c) Shri Narayan Guru
(d) Raja Rammohan Roy

77. Which among the following newspapers carried the caption on the masthead: "Angrezi Raj Ka Dushman"?
(a) Ghadar (b) Kesari
(c) Somprakash (d) Udant Martand

78. Which of the following woman had never been a President of Indian National Congress?

(a) Annie Besant
(b) Sarojini Naidu
(c) Nelli Sen Gupta
(d) Vijaya Laxmi Pandit

79. Annie Besant was a prominent theosophist, women's rights activist and supporter of Irish and Indian self rule. She was born in
(a) Germany (b) Scotland
(c) England (d) Ireland

80. Consider the following statements :
1. At Lucknow session of congress, Indian National Congress and Muslim League sank their old differences and put up common political demands before the British Government.
2. The British Government suppressed the publication of the 'Al-Hilal' of Abul Kalam Azad and 'The Comrade' of Maulana Mohamed Ali in 1916.
3. Lucknow pact signed by congress-muslim league was facilitated by Lokmanya Tilak and Mohammed Ali Jinnah.
4. At the Lucknow session of the Indian National Congress moderate and extremist wings of congress were united.

Which of the given statements above are correct?
(a) 1 and 2 only (b) 2, 3 and 4 only
(c) 1, 2 and 3 only (d) 1, 3 and 4 only

81. Match List-I with List-II and select the correct answer using the codes given below the lists:

List I	List II
A. Mujaffar Ahmad	1. Navyug
B. Shripad Amrit Dange	2. The Socialist
C. Gulam Hussein	3. Inqlab
D. M. Singarvellu	4. Lebar Kisan Gazette

Codes:

	A	B	C	D
(a)	1	2	4	3
(b)	4	3	2	1
(c)	1	2	3	4
(d)	4	3	1	2

82. With reference to the Home Rule Movement in India, which one of the following statements is correct?
(a) Annie Besant launched a campaign through two papers, Commonweal and Young India for granting India, self-government status.
(b) Annie Besant succeeded in persuading the Congress and the Muslim League for setting up home rule leagues.
(c) Lokmanya Tilak set up Home Rule League at the Bombay provincial Conference held at Bombay in April 1916.
(d) Tilak's league worked in Maharashtra (excluding Bombay city), Karnataka, the central provinces and Berar.

83. Consider the following statements about Swadeshi Movement :
1. Book 'Thakurmar Jhuli' was written by Dakshinaranjan Mitra Majumdar.
2. Rabindranath Tagore broke the domination of Victorian naturalism over Indian art and incorporated Mughal, Rajput and Ajanta paintings into his works.

Which of the statements given above is/are correct?
(a) 1 only (b) 2 only
(c) Both 1 and 2 (d) Neither 1 nor 2

84. The Ghadar Party was a revolutionary outfit established outside India to carry out revolutionary activities. Which of the following incidents/organizations were reasons for its establishment?
 1. First World War
 2. Establishment of United India House at Seattle
 3. Komagata Maru incident
 4. Establishment of Swadesh Sevak Home at Vancouver.

 Correct code:
 (a) 1, 2 and 3 only
 (b) 1, 2 and 4 only
 (c) 1, 3 and 4 only
 (d) 1, 2, 3 and 4 only

85. Nehru Committee was the first major attempt by the Indians to draft a constitution. The recommendations of Nehru Committee were unanimous in all matters except:
 (a) Rejection of separate electorates
 (b) Responsible government at the centre and in provinces.
 (c) Complete independence.
 (d) Fundamental rights

86. Consider the following pairs :
 1. Mother of Indian Revolution: Sarojini Naidu
 2. Hindu Luther of Northern India during 19th century: Ishwar Chandra Vidyasagar
 3. Father of renaissance of Western India : M.G. Ranade
 4. Founder leader of Muslim Faqirs : Dadu Mian

 Which of the given pairs above are correctly matched?
 (a) 1, 2 and 3 only
 (b) 2 and 3 only
 (c) 3 and 4 only
 (d) 1, 2, 3 and 4

87. Consider the following:
 1. Western liberal thoughts
 2. Belief that the British crown was unworthy of claiming Indian loyalty
 3. Immense faith in the capacity of masses
 4. Demanded constitutional reforms and share in the services

 Which of the ideas the attributes given above were followed by the extremists?
 (a) 1, 2 and 4 only
 (b) 2 and 4 only
 (c) 2 and 3 only
 (d) 1, 2, 3 and 4 only

88. Consider the following statements :
 1. Revolutionary terrorism was a by-product of the process of the growth of militant nationalism in India.
 2. Revolutionary terrorism acquired a more activist form as a fall out of swadeshi and boycott movement.

 Which of the statements given above is/are correct?
 (a) 1 only (b) 2 only
 (c) Both 1 and 2 (d) Neither 1 nor 2

89. The evolution of relations between the British authority and states can be traced under the following broad stages:
 1. Policy of Ring Fence
 2. Policy of subordinate isolation
 3. Policy of subordinate union
 4. Policy of equal federation

 What is the correct chronological order of these stages?
 (a) 1, 2, 4, 3 (b) 2, 4, 1, 3
 (c) 1, 2, 3, 4 (d) 4, 3, 1, 2

90. Consider the following statements :
 1. Following Dandi salt march, Mahatma Gandhi chose Dharasana salt Satyagarha in Mysore as the next non-violent protest against British rule.

2. In Eastern India during Civil Disobedience Movement, people refused to pay chowkidari tax.

Which of the statements given above is/are correct?

(a) 1 only (b) 2 only
(c) Both 1 and 2 (d) Neither 1 nor 2

91. Which of the following events was/were the possible reason/s behind the launch of the Non Co-operation Movement?

1. First World War
2. Rowlatt Act
3. Hunter Commission Report

Correct code :

(a) 1 only (b) 2 only
(c) 1 and 2 only (d) 1, 2 and 3

92. Match List-I with List-II and select the correct answer using the code given below the lists :

List-I
(Acts)

A. Indian Councils Act, 1892
B. Indian Councils Act, 1909
C. Indian Councils Act, 1919
D. Indian Councils Act, 1935

List-II
(Provisions)

1. Election of the members of the council at the centre was introduced
2. Councils were empowered to discuss the budget
3. Division of subjects of administration between centre and provinces.
4. Distribution of legislative powers between the centre and provinces

Code:

	A	B	C	D		A	B	C	D
(a)	1	2	3	4	(b)	1	2	4	3
(c)	2	1	3	4	(d)	2	1	4	3

93. Match the following :

(North-East tribal movements)	(Leader)
A. Naga Movement	1. Zemi
B. Heraka Movement	2. Nunklow
C. Zeliansgong Movement	3. Jadonang
D. Khasis Revolt	4. Gaidinliu

Code:

	A	B	C	D		A	B	C	D
(a)	4	3	1	2	(b)	3	4	2	1
(c)	4	3	2	1	(d)	3	4	1	2

94. In 1940 Mahatma Gandhi initiated limited Satyagraha on individual basis because

(a) He wanted to unite both the left and right wing of the All India National Congress during the national movement.
(b) He wanted to express symbolic oppose against the British Rule as it was appeasing the Fascist Powers in Europe.
(c) He wanted to give the British rule a chance to peacefully accept the Indian demands of freedom and to constitute immediately an interim Indian government.
(d) He wanted to provide his active support to the British Rule to oppose the fascist powers in Europe.

95. With respect to All India States People's Conference (AISPC), consider the following statements :

1. It was formed to co-ordinate political activities in the Princely States.
2. It urged the Princely States to introduce democratic respresentative government.

3. It represented the people of princely states in the First Round Table Conference.
4. It played a major role in the merger of Princely States with the Indian dominion after independence.

Which of the statements given above are correct?
(a) 1 and 3 only
(b) 1, 3 and 4 only
(c) 1, 2 and 4 only
(d) 1, 2, 3 and 4

96. Consider the following statements :
1. Indian National Army (INA) was initially composed of "Indian Prisoners of War" captured by Germany.
2. Ram Singh Thakur who composed the song for INA's regimental march "Kadam Kadam badaye ja.......", had also composed the tune for the post independent Indian National Anthem.
3. Subhash Chandra Bose was posthumously awarded 'Bharat Ratna' in 1992 but this was later withdrawn due to the controversy over the circumstances of his death.

Which of the statements given above are correct?
(a) 1 only (b) 3 only
(c) 1 and 2 only (d) 1, 2 and 3

97. Arrange the following historical events in correct chronology :
1. Attlee's announcement
2. Mountbatten Plan
3. Formation of Constitutent Assembly
4. Interim Government

Code :
(a) 4-3-2-1 (b) 4-3-1-2
(c) 1-2-3-4 (d) 1-2-4-3

98. Two arch-moderates, who were in favour of recognizing the rights of Muslim majority provinces to secede through plebiscites after independence, resigned from the All India Congress Working Committee in July 1942 were :
1. Abbas Tayabji
2. C Rajagopalachari
3. Yusuf Meher Ali
4. Bhulabhai Desai

Correct code :
(a) 1 and 3 only (b) 1 and 2 only
(c) 2 and 4 only (d) 2 and 3 only

99. Which pairs are correct?

Jain Shrines	Location
1. Dilwara temples	Rajasthan
2. Palitana temples	Gujarat
3. Shri Digambarjain	Delhi
4. Sittanavasal	Karnataka

Correct code is:
(a) 2, 3 and 4
(b) 2, 3 and 4 only
(c) 1, 3 and 4 only
(d) 1 and 2 only

100. Match the following:

(Monument)	(Dynasty)
A. Alai Darwaja	1. Slave Dynasty
B. Hauj Khas	2. Mughal Dynasty
C. Shalimar Bagh	3. Khilji Dynasty
D. Arhai din ka jhopra	4. Tughlaq Dynasty

Code:

	A	B	C	D		A	B	C	D
(a)	1	3	2	4	(b)	1	2	3	4
(c)	3	4	2	1	(d)	4	3	1	2

Answer Sheet

1. (b)	2. (b)	3. (c)	52. (d)	53. (d)	54. (c)
4. (a)	5. (d)	6. (b)	55. (c)	56. (c)	57. (c)
7. (a)	8. (c)	9. (b)	58. (a)	59. (b)	60. (c)
10. (b)	11. (c)	12. (d)	61. (b)	62. (d)	63. (b)
13. (b)	14. (a)	15. (a)	64. (c)	65. (a)	66. (a)
16. (c)	17. (b)	18. (d)	67. (b)	68. (a)	69. (c)
19. (a)	20. (b)	21. (b)	70. (b)	71. (b)	72. (c)
22. (c)	23. (a)	24. (b)	73. (d)	74. (b)	75. (a)
25. (b)	26. (a)	27. (a)	76. (c)	77. (a)	78. (d)
28. (d)	29. (d)	30. (a)	79. (c)	80. (d)	81. (c)
31. (c)	32. (a)	33. (d)	82. (d)	83. (a)	84. (d)
34. (b)	35. (d)	36. (c)	85. (c)	86. (b)	87. (c)
37. (b)	38. (c)	39. (b)	88. (c)	89. (c)	90. (b)
40. (b)	41. (c)	42. (c)	91. (d)	92. (c)	93. (d)
43. (b)	44. (c)	45. (c)	94. (c)	95. (c)	96. (c)
46. (c)	47. (c)	48. (b)	97. (b)	98. (c)	99. (d)
49. (b)	50. (d)	51. (b)	100.(c)		

PRACTICE PAPER

2

1. Regarding the Indus Valley Civilization, consider the following statements:
   1. It was predominantly a secular civilization and the religious element, though present, did not dominate the scene.
   2. During this period, cotton was used for manufacturing textiles in India.

   Which of the statements given above is/are correct?
   (a) 1 only (b) 2 only
   (c) Both 1 and 2 (d) Neither 1 nor 2
2. Match List-1 with List-2 and select the correct answer:

List-I (Ancient site)	**List-II (Archaeological finding)**
A. Lothal	1. Ploughed field
B. Kalibungan	2. Dockyard
C. Dholavira	3. Terracotta replica of a plough
D. Banawali	4. An inscription comprising ten large sized signs of the Harappan Script

Codes:

	A	B	C	D
(a)	1	2	3	4
(b)	2	1	4	3
(c)	3	2	1	4
(d)	2	1	3	4

3. Which one of the following animals was not represented on the seal and terracotta art of the Harappan culture?
   (a) Cow (b) Elephant
   (c) Rhinoceros (d) Tiger
4. The religion of early Vedic Aryans was primarily of:
   (a) Bhakti
   (b) image worship and Yajnas
   (c) worship of nature and Yojnas
   (d) worship of nature and Bhakti
5. The "dharma" and "rita" depicit a central idea of ancient Vedic civilization of India. In this context, consider the following statements:
   1. Dharma was a conception of obligations and of the discharge of one's duties to oneself and to others.
   2. Rita was the fundamental moral law governing the functioning of the universe and all it contained.

   Which of the statements given above is/are correct?

(a) 1 only (b) 2 only
(c) Both 1 and 2 (d) Neither 1 nor 2

6. What does Budhayan theorem (Baudhayan Sulva Sutras) relate to?
   (a) Lengths of sides of a right angled triangle
   (b) Calculation of the value of pi
   (c) Logarithmic calculations
   (d) Normal distribution curve
7. Which one of the following four Vedas contains charms and spells?
   (a) *Rig-veda* (b) *Yajur-veda*
   (c) *Atharva-veda* (d) *Sama-veda*
8. The term 'Aryan' denotes
   (a) An ethnic group
   (b) A nomadic people
   (c) A speech group
   (d) A supporter race
9. Between which of the following was the ancient town of Takshasila located?
   (a) Indus and Jhelum
   (b) Jhelum and Chenab
   (c) Chenab and Ravi
   (d) Ravi and Beas
10. Who among the following was not a contemporary of the other three?
    (a) Bimbsara
    (b) Gautama Buddha
    (c) Milinda
    (d) Prasenjit
11. The practice of military governorship was first introduced in India by the.
    (a) Greeks (b) Sakas
    (c) Parthians (d) Mughals
12. Which one of the following dynasties was ruling over North India at the time of Alexander's invasion?
    (a) Nanda (b) Maurya
    (c) Sunga (d) Kanva
13. One consistent feature found in the history of southern India was the growth of small regional kingdoms rather than large empires because of
    (a) The absence of minerals like iron
    (b) Too many divisions in the social structure
    (c) The absence of vast areas of fertile land
    (d) The scarcity of manpower
14. Which one of the following was initially the most powerful city state of India in the 6th century BC?
    (a) Gandhar (b) Kamboj
    (c) Kashi (d) Magadh
15. Which of the following pairs are correctly matched?
    1. Lothal: Ancient dockyard
    2. Sarnath: First Sermon of Buddha
    3. Rajgir: Lion capital of Ashoka
    4. Nalanda: Great seat of Buddhist learning

    Select the correct answer using the codes given below:

Codes:
    (a) 1, 2, 3, and 4 (b) 3 and 4
    (c) 1, 2 and 4 (d) 1 and 2
16. **A:** The Ahm and Puram poems of the Padinen Kilukanakku group formed a continuation of the Sangam composition.

    R: They were included under the Post-Sangam works as against the Sangam works proper.
    (a) Both A and R are true and R is the correct explanation of A
    (b) Both A and R are true but R is not a correct explanation of A
    (c) A is true but R is false
    (d) A is false but R is true
17. Which of the following Kingdoms were associated with the life of the Buddha?
    1. Avanti 2. Gandhara
    3. Kosala 4. Magadha

    Select the correct answer using the code given below:

(a) 1, 2 and 3 (b) 2 and 4
(c) 3 and 4 only (d) 1, 3 and 4

18. Which of the following statements is/ are applicable to Jain doctrine?
    1. The surest way of annihilating Karma is to practice penance
    2. Every object, even the smallest particle has a soul
    3. Karma is the bane of the soul and must be ended

    Select the correct answer using the codes given below:
    (a) 1 only (b) 2 and 3 only
    (c) 1 and 3 only (d) 1, 2, and 3

19. With reference to the history of ancient India, which of the following was/ were common to both Buddhism and Jainism?
    1. Avoidance of extremities of penance and enjoyment
    2. Indifference to the authority of the Vedas
    3. Denial of efficacy of rituals

    Select the correct answer using the codes given below:
    (a) 1 only (b) 2 and 3 only
    (c) 1 and 3 only (d) 1, 2 and 3

20. Lord Buddha's image is sometimes shown with the hand gesture called 'Bhumisparsha Mudra'. It symbolizes:
    (a) Buddha's calling of the Earth to watch over Maya and to prevent Maya from disturbing his meditation
    (b) Buddha's calling of the Earth to witness his purity and chastity despite the temptations of Maya
    (c) Buddha's reminder to his followers that they all arise from the Earth and finally dissolve into the Earth, and thus this life is transitory
    (d) Both the statements (a) and (b) are correct in this context

21. The Jain philosophy holds that the world is created and maintained by
    (a) Universal Law
    (b) Universal Truth
    (c) Universal Faith
    (d) Universal Soul

22. Anekantavada is a core theory and philosophy of which one of the following?
    (a) Buddhism (b) Jainism
    (c) Sikhism (d) Vaishnavism

23. With reference to ancient Jainism, which one of the following statements is correct?
    (a) Jainism was spread in South India under the leadership of Sthulabahu
    (b) The Jainas who remained under the leadership of Bhadrabahu were called Shvetambaras after the Council held at Pataliputra
    (c) Jainism enjoyed the patronage of the Kalinga king Kharavela in the first century BC
    (d) In the initial stage of Jainism, the Jainas worshipped images unlike Buddhists

24. Consider the following statements:
    1. Vardhaman Mahavira's mother was the daughter of Lichchhavi chief Chetaka
    2. Gautama Buddha's mother was a princess from the Kosalan dynasty
    3. Parshvanatha, the twenty-third Tirthankara, belonged to Benaras

    Which of these statements is/are correct?
    (a) Only 1 (b) Only 2
    (c) 2 and 3 (d) 1, 2 and 3

25. In ancient India Buddhist monasteries, a ceremony called Pavarana, used to be held. It was the:
    (a) occasion to elect the Sanghaparinayaka and two speakers, one on Dhamma and the other on Vinaya

(b) Confession by monks of their offence committed during their stay in the monasteries during the rainy season
(c) Ceremony of initiation of new person into the Buddhist Sangha in which the head is shaved and yellow robes are offered
(d) Gathering of Buddhist monks on the next day to the fullmoon day of Ashadha when they take up a fixed abode for the next four months of rainy season

26. **A:** The emphasis of Jainism on non-violence (ahimsa) prevented agriculturalists from embracing Jainism.
R: Cultivation involved killing of insects and pests.
(a) Both A and R are true and R is the correct explanation of A
(b) Both A and R is true but R are not a correct explanation of A
(c) A is true but R is false
(d) A is false but R is true

27. Many of the Greeks Kushanas and Shakas embraced Buddhism rather than Hinduism because.
(a) Buddhism was in the ascendant at that time
(b) They had renounced the policy of war and violence
(c) Caste-ridden Hinduism did not attract them
(d) Buddhism provided easier access to Indian society.

28. The concept of Eight-Fold Path forms the theme of
(a) Dipavamsa
(b) Divyavadana
(c) Mahaparinirvan Sutta
(d) Dharma Chakra Pravartana Sutta

29. The ancient Indian play *Mudrarakshasa* of Visakhadatta has its subject on
(a) A conflict between Gods and Demons of ancient Hindu lore
(b) A romantic story of an Aryan prince and a tribal woman
(c) The story of power struggle between two Aryan tribes
(d) The court intrigues at the time of Chandragupta Maurya

30. **A:** Ashoka annexed Kalinga to the Mauryan Empire.
R: Kalinga controlled the land and sea routes to south India.
(a) Both A and R are true and R is the correct explanation of A
(b) Both A and R are true but R is not a correct explanation of A
(c) A is true but R is false
(d) A is false but R is true

31. The following persons came to India at one time or another:
1. Fa-Hien 2. I-Tsing
3. Megasthenese 4. Hieun-Tsang
The correct chronological sequence of their visits is:
(a) 3, 1, 2, 4 (b) 3, 1, 4, 2
(c) 1, 3, 2, 4 (d) 1, 3, 4, 2

32. Which one of the following ancient Indian records is the earliest royal order to preserve food grains to be utilised during the crises in the country?
(a) Sohogaura Copper-plate
(b) Rummindei pillar-edict of Ashoka
(c) Prayag-Prasasti
(d) Mehrauli pillar inscription of Chandra

33. The given map relates to
(a) Kanishka at the time of his death
(b) Samudragupta after the close of his South Indian campaign

(c) Ashoka towards close of his reign
(d) Empire of Thaneswar on the eve of Harsha's accession

34. **A:** According to Ashoka's edicts, social harmony among the people was more important than religious devotion.
R: He spread the ideas of equity instead of promotion of religion.
(a) Both A and R are true and R is the correct explanation of A
(b) Both A and R are true but R is not a correct explanation of A
(c) A is true but R is false
(d) A is false but R is true

35. The Ashokan major rock edicts which tell us about the Sangam kingdom include rock edicts.
(a) I and X (b) I and XI
(c) II and XIIII (d) II and XIV

36. The Chinese traveler Yuan Chwang (Hiuen Tsang) who visited India recorded the general conditions and culture of India at that time. In this context, which of the following statements is/are correct?
1. The roads and river-routes were completely immune from robbery.
2. As regards punishment for offences, ordeals by fire, water and poison were the instruments for determining the innocence or guilt of a person.
3. The tradesman had to pay duties at ferries and barrier stations.

Select the correct answer using the codes given below:
(a) 1 only (b) 2 and 3 only
(c) 1 and 3 only (d) 1, 2 and 3

37. With reference to the guilds (Shreni) of ancient India that played a very important role in the country's economy, which of the following statements is/ are correct?
1. Every guild was registered with the central authority of the State and the king was the chief administrative authority on them.
2. The wages, rules of work, standards and prices were fixed by the guild.
3. The gild has judicial powers over its own members.

Select the correct answer using the codes given below:
(a) 1 and 2 only (b) 3 only
(c) 2 and 3 only (d) 1, 2 and 3

38. With reference to the invaders in ancient India, which one of the following is the correct chronological order?
(a) Greeks - Sakas - Kushans
(b) Greeks - Kushans - Sakas
(c) Sakas - Greeks - Kushans
(d) Sakas - Kushans - Greeks

39. Consider the following statements:
1. The last Mauryan ruler, Brihadratha was assassinated by his commander-in-chief, Pushyamitra Sunga.
2. The last Sunga King, Devabhuti was assassinated by his Brahmana minister Vasudeva Kanva who usurped the throne.
3. The last ruler of the Kanva dynasty was deposed by Andhras.

Which of these statement (s) is/are correct?
(a) 1 and 2 (b) Only 2
(c) Only 3 (d) 1, 2 and 3

40. Which one of the following pairs is correctly matched?
(a) Harappan Civilization-Painted Grey Ware
(b) The Kushans - Gandhara School of Art.
(c) The Mughals - Ajanta Paintings
(d) The Marathas - Pahari School of Painting

41. Who among the following presided over the Buddhist Council held during the reign of Kanishka at Kashmir? **(2015)**
   (a) Parsva (b) Nagarjuna
   (c) Sudraka (d) Vasumitra
42. From the third century AD when the Hun invasion ended the Roman Empire, the Indian merchants relied more and more on the **(1999)**
   (a) African Trade
   (b) West-European Trade
   (c) South-East Asian Trade
   (d) Middle-Eastern Trade
   (e) West-European Trade
43. The Indo-Greek Kingdom set up in north Afghanistan in the beginning of the second century BC was **(1999)**
   (a) Bacteria (b) Scythia
   (c) Zedraisia (d) Aria
44. **A:** The Gandhara School of Art bears the mark of Hellenistic influence.
   R: Hinayana form was influenced by that art. **(1998)**
   (a) Both A and R are true and R is the correct explanation of A
   (b) Both A and R are true but R is not a correct explanation of A
   (c) A is true but R is false
   (d) A is false but R is true
45. What is the correct chronological order in which the following appeared in India? **(2015)**
   1. Gold coins
   2. Punch-marked silver coins
   3. Iron plough
   4. Urban culture

   Select the correct answer using the codes given below
   (a) 3, 4, 1, 2 (b) 3, 4, 2, 1
   (c) 4, 3, 1, 2 (d) 4, 3, 2, 1
46. With reference to the scientific progress of ancient India, which of the statements given below are correct? **(2015)**
   1. Different kinds of specialized surgical instruments were in common use by 1st Century AD.
   2. Transplant of internal organs in the human body had begun by the beginning of 3rd century AD.
   3. The concept of sine of an angle was known in 5th century AD.
   4. The concept of cyclic quadrilaterals was known in 7th century AD.

   Select the correct answer using the codes given below:
   (a) 1 and 2 only
   (b) 3 and 4 only
   (c) 1, 3, and 4 only
   (d) 1, 2, 3 and 4
47. There are only two known examples of cave paintings of the Gupta period in ancient India. One of these is paintings of Ajanta caves. Where is the other surviving example of Gupta paintings? **(2010)**
   (a) Bagh caves
   (b) Ellora caves
   (c) Lomas Rishi cave
   (d) Nasik caves
48. The Allahabad Pillar inscription is associated with which one of the following? **(2006)**
   (a) Mahapadma Nanda
   (b) Chandragupta Maurya
   (c) Ashoka
   (d) Samudragupta
49. '*Mrichhakatikam*' an ancient Indian book written by Shudraka deals with **(2015)**
   (a) The love affair of rich merchant with the daughter of a courtesan
   (b) The victory of Chandragupta II over the Shaka Kshtrapas of western India

(c) The military expeditions and exploits of Samudragupta
(d) The love affair between a Gupta King and a princess of Kamarupta

50. **A:** The origin of feudal system in ancient India can be traced to military campaigns.
R: There was considerable expansion of the feudal system during the Gupta period.
(a) Both A and R are true and R is the correct explanation of A
(b) Both A and R are true but R is not a correct explanation of A
(c) A is true but R is false
(d) A is false but R is true

51. **Assertion (A):** Muhammad bin Tughluq issued a new gold coin which was called Dinar by the Batutah.
Reason (R): Muhammad bin Tughluq wanted to issue token currency in gold coins to promote trade with West Asian and North African countries. **(2006)**
(a) Both A and R are true and R is the correct explanation of A
(b) Both A and R are true but R is not a correct explanation of A
(c) A is true but R is false
(d) A is false but R is true

52. Which one of the following is the correct chronological order of the Afghan rulers to the throne of Delhi? **(2015)**
(a) Sikandar Shah-Ibrahim Lodi - Bahlol Khan Lodi
(b) Sikandar Shah - Bahlol Khan Lodi - Ibrahmi Lodi
(c) Bahlol Khan Lodi - Sikandar Shah - Ibrahim Lodi
(d) Bahlol Khan Lodi - Ibrahim Lodi - Sikandar Shah

53. Who was the last ruler of the Tughluq dynasty of the Delhi Sultanate? **(2015)**
(a) Firuz Shah Tughluq
(b) Ghiyas-ud-din Tughluq Shah II
(c) Nasir-ud-din Mahmud
(d) Nasrat Shah

54. How did Sultan Qutb-ud-din Aibak die? **(2003)**
(a) He was treacherously stabbed to death by one of his ambitious nobles.
(b) He was killed in a battle with Taj-u-din Yildiz, the ruler of Ghazni who entered a context with him over the capture of Punjab.
(c) He sustained injuries while besieging the fortress of Kalinjar in Bundelkhand and succumbed to it later.
(d) He died after a fall from his horse while playing Chaugan.

55. The Historian Barani refused to consider the state in India under Delhi sultans as truly Islamic because **(2015)**
(a) The majority of the population did not follow Islam
(b) The Muslim theologists were often disregarded
(c) The Sultan supplemented the Muslim law by framing his own regulations
(d) Religious freedom was accorded to non-Muslims

56. With reference to medieval Indian rulers, which one of the following statements is correct? **(2015)**
(a) Allauddin Khilji first set up a separate Ariz's department.
(b) Balban introduced the branding system of horses of his military.
(c) Muhammad bin Tughlaq was succeded by his uncle to the Delhi throne.
(d) Feroze Tughlaq set up a separate department of slaves.

57. **A:** Muhammad bin Tughlaq left Delhi, and for two years lived in a camp called Sarga-dwari.
R: At that time, Delhi, was ravaged by a form of plague and many people died. **(2015)**
(a) Both A and R are true and R is the correct explanation of A
(b) Both A and R are true but R is not a correct explanation of A
(c) A is true but R is false
(d) A is false but R is true

58. The Mongols under Chengez Khan invaded India during the reign of
(a) Balban
(b) Feroz Tughlaq
(c) Iltutmish
(d) Muhammad bin Tughluq

59. The shaded area in the given map shows the empire of **(2001)**
(a) Alauddin Khilji
(b) Mohammad Tughlaq
(c) Shahjahan
(d) Aurangzeb

60. Which of the following pairs is correctly matched? **(2001)**
(a) Dewn-i-Bandaganj: Tughluq
(b) Dewan-i-Mustakhraj: Banlab
(c) Dewan-i-Kohi: Alauddin Khalji
(d) Dewan-i-Arz: Muhammad Tughluq

61. The given map refers to the kingdom of India prior to 1947.
(a) Akbar at the time of capture of Khandesh in 1601
(b) Akbar at the time of his death in 1605
(c) Aurangzeb at the time of capture of Hyderabad
(d) Aurangzeb at the time of his death in 1707

62. Consider the following events: **(2015)**
1. Reign of Krishna Deva Raya of Vijayanagar
2. Construction of Qutub Minar
3. Arrival of Portugese in India
4. Death of Feroz Tughlaq

The correct chronological sequence of these events is:
(a) 2, 4, 3, 1 (b) 2, 4, 1, 3
(b) 4, 2, 1, 3 (d) 4, 2, 3, 1

63. The king was freed from his people and they form their king'. On whose death did Badauni comment thus? **(1999)**
(a) Balban
(b) Allauddin Khilji
(c) Muhammad-bin-Tughlaq
(d) Feroz Shah Tughlaq

64. The first venture of Gandhi in all-India politics was the: **(1999)**
(a) Non-Cooperation Movement
(b) Rowlatt Satyagraha
(c) Champaran Movement
(d) Dandi March

65. Fawazil in the Sultanate period meant **(2015)**
(a) Extra payment made to the nobles
(b) Revenue assinged in lieu of salary
(c) Excess amount paid to the exchequer by the iqtadars
(d) Illegal exactions extracted from the peasants

66. The Sultan of Delhi who is reputed to have built the biggest network of canals in India was **(1998)**
(a) Iltutmish
(b) Ghiyasuddin Tughlaq
(c) Feroz Shah Tughlaq
(d) Sikandar Lodi

67. **A:** At first the Turkish administration in India was essentially military.
R: The country was parcelled out as Iqtas among leading military leaders. **(1998)**
(a) Both A and R are true and R is the correct explanation of A

(b) Both A and R are true but R is not a correct explanation of A
(c) A is true but R is false
(d) A is false but R is true

68. With reference to the religious history of medieval India, the Sufi mystics were known to pursue which of the following practices? **(2015)**
1. Meditation and control of breath
2. Severe ascetic exercises in a lonely place
3. Recitation of holy songs to arouse a state of ecstasy in their audience

Select the correct answer using the codes given below:
(a) 1 and 2 only (b) 2 and 3 only
(c) 3 only (d) 1, 2 and 3

69. Among the following, who was not a proponent of bhakti cult? **(2010)**
(a) Nagarjuna (b) Tukaram
(c) Tyagaraja (d) Vallabhacharya

70. Bhakta Tukaram was a contemporary of which Mughal Emperor? **(2015)**
(a) Babar (b) Akbar
(c) Jahangir (d) Aurangzeb

71. Which one of the following sequences indicates the correct chronological order? **(2015)**
(a) Shankaracharya-Ramanuja-Chaitanya
(b) Ramanuja-Shankaracharya-Chaitanya
(c) Ramanuja-Shankaracharya-Chaitanya
(d) Ramanuja-Chaitanya-Shankaracharya
(e) Shankaracharya-Chaitanya-Ramanuja

72. Who among the following was the first Bhakti saint to use Hindi for the propagation of his message? **(2015)**
(a) Dadu (b) Kabir
(c) Ramananda (d) Ṭulsidas

73. Match List-I with List-II and select the correct answer using the codes given below the lists: **(2001)**

List-I (Bhakti Saint)	**List-II (Profession)**
A. Namdev	1. Barber
B. Kabir	2. Weaver
C. Ravidas	3. Tailor
D. Sena	4. Cobbler

Codes:

	A	B	C	D
(a)	2	3	1	4
(b)	3	2	4	1
(c)	3	2	1	4
(d)	2	3	4	1

74. Which among the following ports was called Babul Makka (Gate of Makka) during the Mughal Period? **(2015)**
(a) Calicut (b) Broach
(c) Cambay (d) Surat

75. Match List-I with List-II and select the correct answer from the codes given below the lists: **(2000)**

List-I	**List-II**
A. Iqta	1. Marathas
B. Jagir	2. Delhi Sultans
C. Amaram	3. Mughals
D. Mokasa	4. Vijayanagara

Codes:

	A	B	C	D
(a)	3	2	1	4
(b)	2	3	4	1
(c)	2	3	1	4
(d)	3	2	4	1

76. The first writer to use Urdu as the medium of poetic expression was **(1999)**
(a) Amir Khusro
(b) Mirza Ghalib
(c) Bahadur Shah Zafar
(d) Fiz

77. Consider the following statements: **(1999)**
The striking feature of the Jama Masjid in Kashmir, completed by Zain-ul-Abidin, include (s)
1. Turret
2. Similarity with Buddhist pagodas
3. Persian style
Which of the above statement (s) is/are corect?
(a) 1 alone (b) 1, 2 and 3
(c) 2 and 3 (d) 1 and 3

78. Consider the following: **(2015)**
1. Tughlaqabad Fort
2. Lodi Garden
3. Qutub Minar
4. Fatehpur Sikri
The correct chronological order in which they were built is:
(a) 3, 1, 4, 2 (b) 3, 1, 2, 4
(c) 1, 3, 2, 4 (d) 1, 3, 4, 2

79. What was the immediate reason for Ahmad Shah Abdali to invade India and fight the Third Battle of Panipat? **(2010)**
(a) He wanted to avenge the expulsion by Marathas of his viceroy Timur Shah from Lahore.
(b) The frustrated governor of Jullundhar Adina Beg Khan invited him to invade Punjab.
(c) He wanted to punish Mughal administration for non-payment of the revenues of the Chahar Mahal (Gujarat, Aurangabad, Sialkot and Pasrur).
(d) He wanted to annex all the fertile plains of Punjab up to the borders of Delhi to his kingdom.

80. Consider the following statements. **(2004)**
1. In the Third Battle of Panipat, Ahmed Shah Abdali defeated Ibrahim Lodi.
2. Tipu Sultan was killed in the Third Anglo-Mysore War.
3. Mir Jafar entered in a conspiracy with the English for the defeat of Nawab Siraj-ud-daulah in the Battle of Plassey.
Which of the statements given above is/are correct?
(a) 1, 2, and 3 (b) 3 only
(c) 2 and 3 (d) None

81. Which one of the following statements is NOT correct? **(2003)**
(a) Ali Mardan Khan introduced the system of revenue farming in Bengal.
(b) Maharaja Ranjit Singh set up modern foundries to manufacture cannons at Lahore.
(c) Sawai Jai Singh of Amber had Euclid's 'Elements of Geometry' translated into Sanskrit.
(d) Sultan Tipu of Mysore gave money for the construction of the idol of Goddess Sarda in the Shringeri temple.

82. **A:** Shah Alam II spent the initial years as an Emperor outside Delhi.
R: There was always a lurking danger of foreign invasion from the north-west frontier. **(2003)**
(a) Both A and R are true and R is the correct explanation of A
(b) Both A and R are true but R is not a correct explanation of A

(c) A is true but R is false
(d) A is false but R is true

83. How did the Mughal emperor Jahandar Shah's reign come to an early end? **(2003)**
(a) He was deposed by his Wazir.
(b) He died due to slip while climbing down steps.
(c) He was defeated by his nephew in a battle
(d) He died of sickness due to too much consumption of wine.

84. Who among the following Indian rulers established embassies in foreign countries on modern lines? **(2015)**
(a) Haider Ali
(b) Mir Qasim
(c) Shah Alam II
(d) Tipu Sultan

85. With reference to Pondicherry (now Puducherry), consider the following statements: **(2010)**
1. The first European power to occupy Pondicherry were the Portuguese.
2. The second European power to occupy Pondicherry were the French.
3. The English never occupied Pondicherry

Which of the statements given above is/are correct?
(a) 1 only (b) 2 and 3 only
(c) 3 only (d) 1, 2 and 3

86. Who among the following Europeans were the last to come to pre-Independence India as traders? **(2015)**
(a) Dutch (b) English
(c) French (d) Portuguese

87. Which one of the following was the first fort constructed by the British in India? **(2007)**
(a) Fort William (b) Fort St. George
(c) Fort St. David (d) Fort St. Angelo

88. In the year 1613, where was the English East India Company given permission to set up a factory (trading post)?
(a) Bangalore (b) Madras
(c) Masulipattam (d) Surat

89. Which one of the following is the correct statement? **(2015)**
(a) The modern Kochi was a Dutch colony till India's Independence.
(b) The Dutch defeated the Portuguese and built Fort Williams in the modern Kochi.
(c) The modern Kochi was first a Dutch colony before the Portuguese took over from them.
(d) The modern Kochi never became a part of the British colony.

90. With reference to the entry of European powers into India, which one of the following statements is NOT correct? **(2003)**
(a) The Portuguese captured Goa in 1499.
(b) The English opened their first factory in South India at Masulipattam.
(c) In Eastern India, the English Company opened its first factory in Orissa in 1633.
(d) Under the leadership of Dupleix, the French occupied Madras in 1746.

91. In India, among the following locations, the Dutch established their earliest factor at **(2015)**
(a) Surat (b) Pulicat
(c) Cochin (d) Qassimbazar

92. Who amongst the following Englishmen first translated Bhagavad-Gita into English? **(2015)**
(a) William Jones
(b) Charles Wilkins

(c) Alexander Cunningham
(d) John Marshall

93. Which one of the following pairs is not correctly matched? **(1999)**
(a) Jahangir William Hawkins
(b) Akbar Sir Thomas Roe
(c) Shahjahan Travernier
(d) Aurangzeb Manucci

94. What was/were the object/objects of Queen Victoria's Proclamation (1858)? **(2015)**
1. To disclaim any intention to annex Indian States
2. To place the Indian administration under the British Crown
3. To regulate East India Company's trade with India.

Select the correct anwer using the code given below:
(a) 1 and 2 only (b) 2 only
(c) 1 and 3 only (d) 1, 2 and 3

95. Which amongst the following provided a common factor for tribal insurrection in India in the 19th Century? **(2011)**
(a) Introduction of a new system of land revenue and taxation of tribal products.
(b) Influence of foreign religious missionaries in tribal areas.
(c) Rise of a large number of money lenders, traders and revenue farmers as middlemen in tribal areas.
(d) The complete disruption of the old agrarian order of the tribal-communities.

96. With reference to the period of colonial rule in India. "Home Charges" formed an important part of drain of wealth from India. Which of the following funds constituted "Home Charges"? **(2011)**
1. Funds used to support the India Office in London.
2. Funds used to pay salaries and pensions of British personnel engaged in India.
3. Funds used for waging wars outside India by the British.

Select the correct answer using the codes given below:
(a) 1 only (b) 1 and 2 only
(c) 2 and 3 only (d) 1, 2 and 3

97. Karl Marx explained the process of class struggle with the help of which one of the following theories? **(2011)**
(a) Empirical liberalism
(b) Existentialism
(c) Darwin's theory of evolution
(d) Dialectical materialism

98. With whose permission did the English set up their first factory in Surat? **(2009)**
(a) Akbar (b) Jahangir
(c) Shahjahan (d) Aurangzeb

99. The ruler of which one of the following States was removed from power by the British on the pretext of misgovernance? **(2007)**
(a) Awadh
(b) Jhansi
(c) Nagpur
(d) Satara

100. Which one of the following is the correct chronological order of the battles fought in India in the 18th Century? **(2005)**
(a) Battle of Wandiwash–Battle of Buxar–Battle of Ambur-Battle of Plassey
(b) Battle of Ambur–Battle of Plassey–Battle of Wandiwash–Battle of Buxar
(c) Battle of Wandiwash–Battle of Plassey–Battle of Ambur–Battle of Buxar
(d) Battle of Ambur–Battle of Buxar–Battle of Wandiwash–Battle of Plassey

Answer Sheet

1. (c)	2. (b)	3. (a)	52. (d)	53. (c)	54. (d)
4. (c)	5. (c)	6. (a)	55. (c)	56. (d)	57. (a)
7. (c)	8. (c)	9. (a)	58. (c)	59. (c)	60. (a)
10. (c)	11. (b)	12. (a)	61. (d)	62. (a)	63. (c)
13. (c)	14. (c)	15. (c)	64. (b)	65. (c)	66. (c)
16. (c)	17. (c)	18. (c)	67. (a)	68. (d)	69. (c)
19. (b)	20. (b)	21. (a)	70. (c)	71. (a)	72. (c)
22. (b)	23. (c)	24. (c)	73. (b)	74. (c)	75. (b)
25. (b)	26. (a)	27. (d)	76. (a)	77. (b)	78. (b)
28. (d)	29. (d)	30. (a)	79. (a)	80. (b)	81. (a)
31. (b)	32. (b)	33. (c)	82. (c)	83. (c)	84. (d)
34. (a)	35. (c)	36. (b)	85. (a)	86. (c)	87. (b)
37. (d)	38. (a)	39. (d)	88. (d)	89. (b)	90. (a)
40. (b)	41. (d)	42. (c)	91. (b)	92. (b)	93. (b)
43. (a)	44. (c)	45. (d)	94. (a)	95. (c)	96. (a)
46. (c)	47. (a)	48. (d)	97. (d)	98. (b)	99. (a)
49. (a)	50. (d)	51. (c)	100. (b)		

APPENDIX

1. Indian History at a Glance
2. Important Dynasties, Founders and their Capitals
3. Important Battles of Indian History
4. Important Indian Rulers, Dynasties and their Titles
5. Summary: Freedom Movement
6. Reforms/Acts during British Period
7. Social and Cultural Awakening—Socio-religious Movements
8. Important Dances/Dramas
9. Mughal Literature
10. Trivia
11. Classical Writers in Indian Languages
12. Important Sessions of INC
13. Newspapers and Journals
14. Important Literary Works of Ancient India
15. Political and National Organisations of Modern India
16. Important Acts and Laws during British Regime
17. Revolutionary Organisations Abroad
18. Important Revolutionary Activities

1. Indian History at a Glance

Ancient Indian History

3000 - 2600 BC	-	Harappa Civilisation
1200 - 500 BC	-	Vedic Era
550 BC	-	Birth of Mahavira
563 - 483 BC	-	Siddhartha Gautama, the Buddha
327 BC	-	The Conquests of Alexander the Great
325 BC	-	Alexander the Great, still goes on
322 BC	-	Rise of the Mauryas, Chandragupta
298 BC	-	Bindusara Coronated
272 BC	-	Ashoka's Reign
180 BC	-	Fall of the Mauryas & Rise of the Sungas
30 BC	-	Rise of the Satvahana Dynasty
50 AD	-	The Kushans and Kanishka
320 AD	-	Chandragupta I establishes the Gupta dynasty

360 AD	-	Samudragupta conquers the North
380 AD	-	Chandragupta II comes to power
415 AD	-	Accession of Kumara Gupta I
467 AD	-	Skanda Gupta assumes power
892 AD	-	Rise of the Eastern Chalukyas
985 AD	-	The Chola Dynasty

Medieval Indian History

1026	-	Ghazni sacks Somnath Temple
1191	-	First Battle of Tarain
1192	-	Second Battle of Tarain
1206	-	Qutbuddin establishes the Slave Dynasty
1221	-	Mongol invasion under Genghis Khan
1232	-	Foundation of the Qutub Minar
1288	-	Marco Polo visits India
1290	-	Jalaluddin Firuz Khalji establishes the Khalji dynasty
1320	-	Ghiyasuddin Tughluk founds the Tughluk dynasty
1325	-	Accession of Muhammad-bin-Tughluk
1336	-	Foundation of Vijayanagar (Deccan)
1398	-	Timur invades India
1424	-	Rise of the Bahmani dynasty (Deccan)
1451	-	The Lodi dynasty established in Delhi
1469	-	Birth of Guru Nanak - The Founder of Sikhism
1489	-	Adil Shah dynasty at Bijapur
1498	-	First voyage of Vasco da Gama
1510	-	Portuguese capture Goa
1526	-	Establishment of the Mughul Dynasty; First Battle of Panipat
1526-1530	-	Reign of Babur
1530	-	Humayun succeeds Babur
1539	-	Shershah Suri defeats Humayun
1555	-	Humayun recovers the throne of Delhi

1556	-	Accession of Akbar/ Second Battle of Panipat
1565	-	Battle of Talikota
1568	-	Fall of Chittor Garh
1576	-	Battle of Haldighati
1577	-	Akbar troops invade Khandesh
1597	-	Akbar completes his conquests
1600	-	Charter to the English East India Company (East India Co. founded)
1605	-	Jahangir becomes emperor
1609	-	The Dutch opens a factory at Pulicat
1615	-	Submission of Mewar to the Mughals
1620	-	Capture of Kangra Fort
1623	-	Shah Jahan revolts against Jahangir
1628	-	Shah Jahan proclaimed Emperor
1636	-	Aurangzeb appointed Viceroy of Deccan
1646	-	Shivaji captures Torna
1658	-	Coronation of Aurangzeb
1666	-	Death of Shah Jahan
1689	-	Execution of Sambhaji
1700	-	Death of Rajaram
1707	-	Death of Aurangzeb
1720	-	Accession of Baji Rao Peshwa at Poona
1742	-	Marathas invade Bengal
1748	-	First Anglo-French war
1750	-	War of the Deccan; Death of Nasir Jang
1756	-	Siraj-ud-daulah captures Calcutta

Modern Indian History

1757	-	Battle of Plassey: The British defeat Siraj-ud-daulah
1760	-	Battle of Wandiwash: The British defeat the French
1761	-	Third battle of Panipat
1764	-	Battle of Buxar: The British defeat Mir Kasim

1765 - The British get Diwani Rights in Bengal, Bihar and Orissa/Treaty of Allahabad

1767-1769 - First Mysore War

1772 - Warren Hastings appointed as Governor of Bengal

1773 - The Regulating Act passed by the British Parliament

1775 -1782 - The First Anglo-Maratha War

1780-1784 - Second Mysore War: The British defeat Hyder Ali

1784 - Pitt's India Act

1790-1792 - Third Mysore War between the British and Tipu

1793 - Permanent Settlement of Bengal by Lord Cornwallis

1799 - Fourth Mysore War: The British defeat Tipu

1802 - Treaty of Bassein

1803-1805 - The Second Anglo-Maratha war

1814-1816 - The Anglo-Gorkha War

1817-1818 - The Pindari War

1824-1826 - The First Burmese War

1829 - Prohibition of Sati by Lord William Bentick

1831 - Mysore administration taken over by East India Company

1833 - Renewal of Company's Charter

1833 - Abolition of Slavery throughout the British Empire

1838 - Tripartite treaty between Shah Shuja, Ranjit Singh and the British

1839-1842 - First Afghan War

1843 - Gwalior War

1845-1846 - First Anglo-Sikh War

1848 - Lord Dalhousie becomes the Governor-General

1848-1849 - Second Anglo-Sikh War

1852 - Second Anglo-Burmese War

1853 - Railway & Telegraph line introduced

1857	-	First War of Indian Independence: The Sepoy Mutiny
1857	-	Jhansi Rani Laxmibai – Freedom struggle in 1857
1858	-	British Crown takes over the Indian Government
1877	-	The Queen of England proclaimed Empress of India
1878	-	Vernacular Press Act
1881	-	Factory Act
1885	-	First meeting of the Indian National Congress
1897	-	Plague in Bombay; Famine Commission
1899	-	Lord Curzon becomes Governor-General and Viceroy
1905	-	The First Partition of Bengal
1906	-	Formation of Muslim League
1911	-	Partition of Bengal modified to create the Presidency of Bengal
1912	-	The Imperial capital shifted from Calcutta to Delhi
1913	-	Educational Resolution of the Government of India
1915	-	Defence of India Act
1916	-	Home Rule League, Foundation of Women's University at Poona
1919	-	Rowlatt Act evokes protests; Jallianwala Bagh massacre;
1920	-	The Khilafat Movement started, Non-cooperation Movement
1921	-	Moplah (Muslim) rebellion in Malabar; First Census of India
1922	-	Civil Disobedience Movement, Chauri-Chaura violence
1925	-	Reforms Enquiry Committee Report
1927	-	Indian Navy Act; Simon Commission Appointed
1928	-	Simon Commission comes to India: Boycott by all parties

1929	-	Lord Irwin promises Dominion Status for India; Trade Union split. Congress demanded complete independence at Lahore session
1930	-	Salt Satyagraha, First Round Table Conference
1931	-	Second Round Table Conference; Irwin-Gandhi Pact
1932	-	Third Round Table Conference, Poona Pact
1934	-	Civil Disobedience Movement called off; Bihar Earthquake
1937	-	Inauguration of Provincial Autonomy
1939	-	Political deadlock in India as Congress ministries resign; second world war started
1942	-	Cripps Mission, Quit India Movement, Indian National Army
1944	-	Gandhi-Jinnah Talks break down on Pakistan issue
1946	-	Interim Government formed, Constituent Assembly's first meeting
1904 - 1947	-	History of Indian Flag
3 June 1947	-	Lord Mountbatten's plan for partition of India
15 Aug 1947	-	Partition of India and Independence

2. Important Dynasties, Founders and their Capitals

Dynasty	Founder	Capital
Haryank Dynasty	Bimbisara	Rajgriha
Shishunaga Dynasty	Shisunaga	Vaishali
Nanda Dynasty	Mahapadmananda	Patliputra
Maurya Dynasty	Chandragupta Maurya	Patliputra
Shunga Dynasty	Pushyramitra Sunga	Patliputra
Kanva Dynasty	Vasudeva	Patliputra

Satvahanas	Simuka	Paithan
Kushanas	Kujula Kadphises	Purushpura
Guptas	Sri Gupta	Patliputra
Hunas	Toraman	Sialkot
Vardhans	Pushyabhuti	Thaneswar/Kannauj
Sena Dynasty	Samanta Sena	Lakhnauti
Parmaras	Upendra	Dhara
Chandellas	Nannuk	Khajuraho/Mahoba
Gahadvalas	Chandradeva	Kanauj
Gurjar Pratiharas	Nagabhatta-I	Kanauj
Pallava Dynasty	Simbhavishnu	Kanchipuram
Chalukyas of Badami	Pulakesin-I	Badami
Chalukyas of Vengi	Vishnuvardhana	Vengi
Chalukyas of Kalyani	Vijayaditya	Manyakhet
Rashtrakutas	Dantidurg	Manyakhet
Slave Dynasty	Qutubuddin Aibak	Delhi
Khalji Dynasty	Jalalludin Khalji	Delhi
Tughlaq Dynasty	Ghiyasuddin Tughlaq	Delhi
Saiyyads	Khizr Khan	Delhi
Lodi Dynasty	Bahlol Lodi	Delhi
Pandayas	Nediyan	Madurai
Cholas	Vijaylaya	Tanjaur
Yadavas	Bhillan	Devagiri
Hoysalas	Vishnuvardhan	Dwarasamudra
Sangam Dynasty	Harihar and Bukka	Vijaynagar
Saluvas	Narsingha	Vijaynagar
Tuluvas	Vir Narsingha	Vijaynagar

Aravidu Dynasty	Tirumala	Penukonda
Bahmani Dynasty	Hasan Gangu	Gulbarga
Qutubshahi Dynasty	Quli Qutubshah	Golkonda
Adilshahi Dynasty	Adilshah	Bijapur
Nizamshahi Dynasty	Malik Ahmad	Ahmednagar
Imadshahi Dynasty	Amir-ud-Barid	Bidar
Solanki Dynasty	Mulraj	Anhilwara
Kalchuris	Kokkal	Tripuri
Sharqui Dynasty	Malik Sarvar	Jaunpur
Mughal Dynasty	Babur	Delhi/Agra
Bhonsle Dynasty	Shivaji	Raigarh
Pala Dynasty	Gopala	Munger
Hyderabad State	Nizam-ul-Mulk	Hyderabad
Karkota Dynasty	Durlabhvardhan	Kashmir
Utpal Dynasty	Avantivarman	Kashmir
Lohar Dynasty	Sangramraj	Kashmir
Vakatakas	Vindhyashakti	Nandivardhan
Faruqi Dynasty	Malik Raza	Burhanpur

3. Important Battles of Indian History

327-326 B.C.	Alexander invades India. Defeats Porus in the Battle of Hydaspes (Jhelum) 326 B.C.
305 B.C.	Chandragupta Maurya defeats the Greek king Seleucus.
216 B.C.	The Kalinga War. Conquest of Kalinga by Ashoka.
155 B.C.	Menander's invasion of India.
90 B.C.	The Sakas invade India.
454 A.D.	The first Huna invasion.
495 A.D.	The second Huna invasion.
711-712 A.D.	The Arab invasion of Sind under Mohammad-bin-Qasim.
1000-1027	Mahmud Ghazni invades India 17 times.

1175-1206	Invasions of Muhammad Ghori. First battle of Tarain, 1191, Prithviraj Chauhan defeats Muhammad Ghori; Second battle of Tarain, 1192, Muhammad Ghori defeats Prithviraj Chauhan; Battle of Chandawar, 1194, Muhammad Ghori defeats Jayachandra Gahadvala of Kannauj.
1294	Alauddin Khalji invades the Yadava kingdom of Devagiri. The first Turkish invasion of the Deccan.
1398	Taimur invades India. Defeats the Tughlaq Sultan Mahmud Shah; the Sack of Delhi.
1526	Babur invades India and defeats the last Lodi Sultan Ibrahim Lodi in the First Battle of Panipat.
1539-1540	Battle of Chausa or Ghaghra (1539) and Kanauj or Ganges (1540) in which Sher Shah defeats Humayun.
1545	Battle (siege) of Kalinjar and death of Sher Shah Suri.
1556	Second battle of Panipat. Akbar defeats Hemu.
1565	Battle of Raktakshasi-Tangadi (Talikota) in which the forces of the empire of Vijayanagar under King Sadasiva Raya and his regent Rama Raya routed by the confederate forces of the Deccan states of Bijapur, Golconda, Ahmednagar, and Bidar.
1576	Batle of Haldighati. Akbar defeats Rana Pratap of Mewar.
1632-1633	Conquest of Ahmednagar by Shah Jahan.
1658	Battles of Ahmednagar by ShahJahan. Samugarh (June 8, 1658). Dara Shikoh, eldest son of Shah Jahan, defeated by Aurangzeb.
1665	Shivaji defeated by Raja Jai Singh and Treaty of Purandhar.
1739	Invasion of India by Nadir Shah.
1746	First Carnatic War
1748-1754	Second Carnatic War
1756-1763	Third Carnatic War
1757	Battle of Plassey. Siraj-ud-daulah, the Nawab of Bengal, defeated by Clive.
1760	Battle of Wandiwash, in which the English under Sir Eyre Coote defeated the French under Lally.
1762	Third battle of Panipat. Marathas defeated by Ahmad Shah Abdali.
1764	Battle of Buxar. The English (under Munro) defeat Mir Kasim, the Nawab of Bengal and Nawab Shuja-ud-daulah of Awadh.
1767-1769	First Mysore War.
1780-1782	Maratha War
1774	The Rohilla War between the Rohillas and the Nawab of Awadh supported by the East India Company.

1775-1782	First Maratha War	1846	Battle of Aliwal between the English and the Sikhs. The Sikhs defeated.
1780-1784	Second Mysore War		
1792	Third Mysore War		
1799	Fourth Mysore War Defeat and death of Tipu Sultan.	1848-1849	Second Sikh War and annexation of the Punjab to British India.
1802-1804	Second Maratha War		
1817-1818	Third Maratha War	1857	The Revolt of 1857 (The First War of Indian Independence).
1845-1846	First Sikh War		

4. Important Indian Rulers, Dynasties and their Titles

Ruler	Dynasty	Title
Ajatshatru	Haryank	Kunika
Bimbisara	Haryank	Shrenika
Mahapadmananda	Nanda	Agrasen
Dhanananda	Nanda	Agramese
Chandragupta Maurya	Maurya	Sandrocottus, Androcottus
Bindusara	Maurya	Amitraghat
Ashoka	Maurya	Devanampiya Piyadarsi
Chandragupta-II	Gupta	Vikramaditya
Harshvardhana	Pushyabhuti	Saliditya
Narsimhavarman-I	Pallava	Vatapikonda
Amoghvarsha	Rashtrakuta	Vir Narayan
Pulakesin-II	Chalukyas (Vatapi)	Parmeshvar
Mahendravarman-I	Pallava	Vichitrachita
Govinda-III	Rashtrakuta	Jagtung
Vikramaditya-IV	Chalukyas (Kalyani)	Tribhuvan, Malla
Vikramaditya-II	Chalukyas (Vengi)	Sikandar
Ibrahim Qutubshah	Qutubshahi	Malik Brahim
Qutubuddin Aibek	Slave Dynasty	Lakh Baksh, Malik

Jauna Khan	Tughlaq	Muhammad-bin-Tughlaq, Ulug Khan
Hala	Satvahana	Kavivatsal
Gautami Putra Satkarni	Satvahana	Kshatriya Darp Mardan
Kanishka	Kushana	Devaputra
Rajraj	Chola	Mummadi Chola, Arumoli, Raj Kesari
Rajendra-I	Chola	Gangaikonda Chola
Mahmud Ghazni	Ghazni	Yamin-ud-Daula
Krishnadevaraya	Tuluva	Andhra Bhoj, Yavanraj Sthapanacharya
Ibrahim Lodi	Lodi	Ibrahim Shah
Babar	Mughal	Ghazi
Sher Shah	Sur	Hazrat-i-Ala
Bairam Khan	Mughal	Khan Baba
Akbar	Mughal	Islam-i-Adil
Jahangir	Mughal	Shekh Salim
Mehrunissa	Mughal	Nurjahan
Dara Shikoh	Mughal	Shah-Iqbal
Aurangzeb	Mughal	Alamgir, Ghazi
Shivaji	Marathas	Chhatrapati
Balaji Bajirao	Marathas	Nana Saheb

5. Summary: Freedom Movement

S. No.	Nomenclature	Year	Led by
1.	Sepoy Mutiny	1857	First War of Independence due to dissatisfaction of the Indian soldiers
2.	Indian National Congress	1885	Initiated by A. O. Hume; first president, W. C. Bannerjee
3.	Swadeshi Movement	1905	Boycott of foreign goods

4.	Home Rule Movement	1916	Led by Dr. (Mrs) Annie Besant
5.	Lucknow Pact	1916	Hindu-Muslim unity which weakened the British
6.	Civil Disobedience	1930	Non-violent non-cooperation movement led by Gandhiji
7.	Khilafat Movement	1920	Mohd Ali and Shaukat Ali led the movement for restoration of Khilafats, alienating Muslims from the British
8.	Chauri-Chaura incident	1922	Mob clashed with police, killing 22 policemen. Gandhiji called off the non-cooperation movement.
9.	Non-cooperation Movement	1920	With Gandhiji's support of the Khilafat movement, Hindus and Muslims launched the non-cooperation movement
10.	Swaraj Party	1922	Gandhiji's decision to call off the non-cooperation movement, led to the formation of the Swaraj party Initiated by Motital Nehru.
11.	Dandi March	1930	Gandhiji launched the movement to break the salt law
12.	Quit India Movement	1942	Led by Gandhiji; asking the British to leave India
13.	Direct Action Campaign	1946	Launched by Muslim League, resulted in heavy riots

6. Reforms/Acts during British Period

S. No.	Nomenclature of the Reforms/Acts	Year	During the term of	Significance
1.	Prohibition of Sati and female infanticide	1829	Lord William Bentinck	Supported by Raja Ram Mohan Roy
2.	Doctrine of Lapse	1848	Lord Dalhousie	Adoption of sons by rulers in the absence of their natural heirs was banned
3.	Indian Legislative Councils Act	1861	Lord Canning	Envisaged association of Indians with the administration at higher level.

4.	Ilbert Bill	1883	Lord Ripon	To bring Indian and European magistracy on equal footing
5.	Indian Councils Act	1892	Lord Lansdowne	Membership of the central legislative councils was enlarged
6.	Morley-Minto Reforms	1909	Lord Minto II	Separate electorates to widen the gulf between Hindus and Muslims
7.	Indian Councils Act	1909	Lord Minto II	(See Morley-Minto reforms)
8.	Dyarchy	1919	Lord Chelmsford	Meaning dual system of Government (See Rowlatt Act)
9.	Jallianwala Bagh Massacre	1919	Lord Chelmsford	Massacre at Jallianwala Bagh in Amritsar by General Dyer
10.	Rowlatt Act/ Montague Chelmsford Reforms	1919	Lord Chelmsford	Extraordinary powers were given to government to suppress the freedom struggle with General Dyer as the Commandant
11.	Simon Commission	1928	Lord Irwin	To report working of the reforms; recommended dyarchy in provinces. India to be constituted as a federation and Indianization of armed forces
12.	Gandhi-Irwin Pact	1931	Lord Irwin	Congress called off the agitation and agreed to participate in the Second Round Table Conference
13.	Communal Award	1932	Lord Willingdon	Envisaged communal representation for depressed classes besides Hindus, Muslims and Sikhs
14.	Separate electorates	1932	Lord Willingdon	(See Communal Award)

15.	Government of India Act	1935	Lord Willingdon	Provided for a federal type of constitution
16.	Cripps Mission	1942	Lord Linlithgow	Proposed Dominion status for India after the Second World War
17.	INA Trial	1945	Lord Wavell	INA prisoners of war were tried at Red Fort Delhi and Jawaharlal Nehru defended them
18.	Wavell Plan	1945	Lord Wavell	Envisaged constitution of executive council in such a way as to give representation to all major communities in India
19.	Cabinet Mission Plan	1947	Lord Wavell	Envisaged establishment of Constituent Assembly to frame the Constitution
20.	Indian Independence Act	1947	Lord Mountbatten	India partitioned and attained independence

7. Social and Cultural Awakening—Socio-religious Movements

Year	Place	Name of the Organization	Founder
1815	Calcutta	Atmiya Samaj	Ram Mohan Roy
1828	Calcutta	Brahrno Samaj	Ram Mohan Roy
1829	Calcutta	Dharma Sabha	Radhakanta Dev
1839	Calcutta	Tattvabodhini Sabha	Debendranath Tagore
1840	Punjab	Nirankaris	Dayal Das, Darbara Singh, Rattan Chand etc.
1844	Surat	Manav Dharma Sabha	Durgararn Manchharam
1849	Bombay	Parmahansa Mandli	Dadoba Pandurang
1857	Punjab	Namdharis	Ram Singh

1861	Agra	Radha Sowami Satsang	Tulsi Ram
1866	Calcutta	Brahmo Samaj of India	Keshab Chandra Sen
1866	Deoband	Dar-ul-Ulurn	Maulana Hussain Ahmed
1867	Bombay	Prarthna Samaj	Dr Atmaram Pandurang
1875	Bombay	Arya Samaj	Swami Dayanand Saraswati
1875	New York (USA)	Theosophical Society	Madame HP Blavastky and Col H. S. Olcott
l878	Calcutta	Sudharam Brahmo Samaj	Anand Mohan Bose
1884	Pune (Poona)	Deccan Education Society	G. G. Agarkar
1886	Aligarh	Muhammadan Educational Conference	Sir Syed Ahmad Khan
1887	Bombay	Indian National Conference	M. G. Ranade
1887	Lahore	Deva Samaj	Shivnarayan Agnihotri
1894	Lucknow	Nadwah-ul-Ulema	Maulana Shibli Numani
l897	Belur	Ramakrishna Mission	Swami Vivekananda
1905	Bombay	Servants of Indian Society	Gopalakrishan Gokhale
1909	Pune (Poona)	Poona Seva Sadan	Mrs Ramabai Ranade and G. K. Devadhar
1911	Bombay	Social Service League	N. M. Joshi
1914	Allahabad	Seva Samiti	H. N. Kunzru

8. Important Dances/Dramas

Name of Dance/Drama	State	Name of Dance/ Drama	State
Bhaka Wata	Orissa	Bhavai	Gujarat
Bidesia	Bihar	Chakri	J & K
Chamar Ginad	Rajasthan	Chappeli	Uttar Pradesh

Chau	West Bengal	Chavittu Natakam	Kerala
Chiraw (Bamboo dance)	Mizoram	Dahi Kala	Maharashtra
Dandanate	Orissa	Devarattam	Tamil Nadu
Gangore	Rajasthan	Garba	Gujarat
Gidda	Punjab	Jhulan Leela	Rajasthan
Jhumar (Ghumar)	Rajasthan	Kaikotti Kalai	Kerala
Kajri	Uttar Pradesh	Kanayala	Himachal Pradesh
Karan	Uttar Pradesh	Kathi	West Bengal
Kayanga Bajayanga	Rajasthan	Koodiyattam	Kerala
Kottam	Andhra Pradesh	Krishnavattam	Kerala
Kumaon	Uttar Pradesh	Lai Haroba	Manipur
Lavani	Maharashtra	Lezim	Maharashtra
Lota	Madhya Pradesh	Maha Rasa	Manipur
Mudiyettu	Kerala	Pandvani	Madhya Pradesh
Poikkal Kudirai Attam	Tamil Nadu	Rasila	Gujarat
Tappatri Kai	Kerala	Therukkoothu	Tamil Nadu
Theyyam	Kerala	Trippani	Gujarat
Wangala Laho	Meghalaya	-	-

9. Mughal Literature

Author	Name of the Work	Remarks
Gulbadan Begum	Humayun Namah	About Humayun's reign
Abul Fazl	Ain-i-Akbari	About Akbar's reign
Abul Fazl	Akbar Namah	About Akbar's reign
Badauni	Muntakhab-ul-Tawarikh	About Akbar's reign
Mulla Daud	Tawarikh-i-Alfi	About Akbar's reign
Nizam-ud-din Ahmad	Tabaqat-i-Akbari	About Akbar's reign
Jahangir	Tuzuk-i-Jahangiri	Autobiography
Mutamad Khan	Iqbal Namah	About Jahangir's reign
Abdul Haqq	Nuriyya-i-Sultaniyya	Theory of kingship

Abdul Hamid Lahori	Padshah Namah	About Shah Jahan's reign
Muhammad Waris	Padshah Namah	About Shah Jahan's reign
Inayat Khan	Shah Jahan Nama	About Shah Jahan's reign
Muhammad Salim	Shah Jahan Nama	About Shah Jahan's reign
Dara Shikoh	Safinat-ul-Auliya	Biographies of Sufi saints
Dara Shikoh	Sakinat-ul-Auliya	Upanishads Translation
Dara Shikoh	Hasanat-ul-Arifin	His religious and
Dara Shikoh	Majma-ul-Bahrain	philosophical ideas
Aurangzeb	Raqqat-i-Alamgiri	A collection of his letters
Khafi Khan	Muntakhab-ul-Lubab	About Aurangzeb's reign

10. Trivia

• 1st President of INC	W C Bannerjee
• Gandhiji became the President in	1924 (Belgaum)
• S. C. Bose became the President in	1938 (Haripura) & 1939 (Tripuri)
• President during Quit India Movmt. (1940)	Maulana Abul Kalam Azad (Ramgarh) and no sessions during 1941-45 due to arrests and jailing of all eminent leaders
• Jawahar Lal Nehru became President for the first time in	1929 (Lahore)

11. Classical Writers in Indian Languages

Author	Work(s)
Abdul Hamir Lahori	Padshahnama
Al-beruni	Kitab-i-Rahla
Ali Muhammad Khan	Mirat-i-Muluk
Amar Simha (Chandragupta II)	Amarkosa
Amir Khusrau	Tarikh-i-Alai
Aryabhatta	Surya Sidhanta

Asvaghosha	Bhuddha Charita
Ayapa Senani	Nrutyaratnakaram
Babur	Tuzuk-i-Baburi
Banabhatta (Harshavardhan)	Kadambari, Harshacharita
Barani	Tarikh-i-Firuzshahi
Bharavi (Simhevishnu)	Kiratharjuneeyam
Bhavabhuti	Uttararamacharita
Bilhana	Vikramanakadeva Charita
Chand Bardoi	Prithviraj Raso
Charaka	Charaka Samhita
Dandin (Narasimhavaraman)	Dasa Kumara Charita
Firdausi	Shahnama
Gona Buddha Reddy	Ranganadharamayanam
Gulbadan Begum	Humayun-nama
Hala	Suptasotka
Harshavardhana	Priyadarsika, Ratnavali, Nagananda
Hulekki Bhaskara	Bhaskararamayanam
Ibn Battuta	Tughlaqnama, Safarnama (Muhammed-bin-Tughlaq)
Ilango Adigal	Silappadikaram
Jayadeva	Gita Govinda
Jayasi	Padmavat
Kalhana	Rahantarangini
Kalidasa (Chandragupta II)	Ritusamhara, Raghuvamsa, Kumarasambhava, Meghaduta, Malavikagnimitra, Vikramorvashi, Sakuntalam
Kautilya	Arthashastra
Kumaragiri Reddy	Vasanta Rajeeyam
Malikarjuna Pandita	Sivatatvasara
Manjhan	Madhumalati

Minhaj-us-Siraj	Tabaqat-i-Firuzahahi
Mirza Muhammad Kasim	Alamgir-nama
Muhammad Manzu	Mirat-i-Sikandri
Nagachandra	Jainaramayanam
Nandi Timmana	Parijatapaharanam
Palkurki Somanatha	Basavapuranam
Panini	Ashtadhyayi
Patanjali	Mahabhasya
Pillalamarri Pina Veerabhadra	Jaimini Bharatam
Pingalisurana	Kalapoornodayam
Prataparudra	Neetisara
Rajashekhara (Mehipel)	Vidha Salabhanjika, Bala Bharata, Kavyamimansa, Bala Ramayana
Ravi Kirti (Pulekesin II)	Aihole Prasasti
Saki Mustaid Khan	Maasir-i-Alamgiri
Shirazi	Tazkirat-i-Muluk
Sri Krishnadeva Raya	Madalasa Charitra, Amuktamalyada
Srinatha Haravilasam, Kasi Khandam	Palnativeeracharitra, Sringara Naishadam
Sudraka	Mrichchakatika
Surdas	Sur Sagar, Sur Sarawali, Sahitya Ratna
Tenali Rama Krishna	Panduranga Mahatyam
Tiruvalluvar	Kural
Tulsidas	Ramacharitmanas
Varamihira	Brihat Sidhanta
Vatsyayana	Kamasutra
Vijnaneswara	Mitakshara
Visakhadatta	Mudrarakshasa
Vishnu Sharma	Sambhava Panchatantra
Yahya-bin-Ahmed	Tarikh-i-Mubarakshahi Sarhindi

12. Important Sessions of INC

Year	Presidents	Venue
1885	W.C. Bannerjee	Bombay
1886	Dadabhai Naoroji	Calcutta
1887	Badruddin Tyabji	Madras
1888	George Yule	Allahabad
1889	Sir William Wedderburn	Bombay
1890	Pherozshah Mehta	Calcutta
1891	P. Anandacharlu	Nagpur
1892	W.C. Bannerjee	Allahabad
1893	Dadabhai Naoroji	Lahore
1894	Alfred Webb	Madras
1895	S. N. Banerjee	Poona
1896	Rahimtulla M. Sayani	Calcutta
1897	C. Sankaran Nair	Amravati
1898	Ananda Mohan Bose	Madras
1899	R. C. Dutt	Lucknow
1900	N. G. Chandavarkar	Lahore
1901	D. E. Wacha	Calcutta
1902	Hasan Imam	Bombay
	S.N. Banerjee	Ahmedabad
1903	Lal Mohan Ghose	Madras
1904	Sir Henry Cotton	Bombay
1905	G. K. Gokhale	Benaras
1906	Dadabhai Naoroji	Calcutta
1907	Dr. Rash Behari Ghosh (Suspended)	Surat
1908	Dr. Rash Behari Ghosh	Madras
1909	Pandit Madan Mohan Malaviya	Lahore
1910	Sir William Wedderburn	Allahabad
1911	Pandit B. N. Dhar	Calcutta
1912	R. N. Modholkar	Bankipore
1913	Nawab Syed Mohammad Bahadur	Karachi
1914	Bhupendranath Basu	Madras
1915	Sir Satyendra Prasad Sinha	Bombay
1916	Ambika Charan Majumdar	Lucknow
1917	Mrs. Annie Besant	Calcutta
1918	Hassan Imam (Special session)	

1918	Pandit Madan Mohan Malaviya	Delhi
1919	Motilal Nehru	Amritsar
1920	Lala Lajpat Rai (Suspended)	Calcutta
	C. Vijayraghavacharia (annual)	Nagpur
1921	C. R. Das (in prison)	Ahmedabad
	Hakim Ajmal Khan (Acting)	
1922	C. R. Das	Gaya
1923	Maulana Abul Kalam Azad (suspended)	Delhi
	Maulana Muhammad Ali (Annual)	Golconda
1924	Mahatma Gandhi	Belgaun
1925	Mrs Sarojini Naidu	Cawnpore
1926	S. Srinivasa Iyengar	Guwahati
1927	Dr. M.A. Ansari	Madras
1928	Pandit Motilal Nehru	Calcutta
1929	Jawaharlal Nehru	Lahore
1930	(No session) but Independence Day Pledge was adopted on 26th Jan. 1930.	
1931	Vallabhbhai Patel	Karachi
1932	R. Amritlal (session was banned)	
1933	Mrs. J. M. Sen Gupta (sesson was banned)	Calcutta
1934	Rajendra Prasad (Continued again for 1935)	Bombay
1936	Jawaharlal Nehru	Lucknow
1937	Jawaharlal Nehru	Faizpur
1938	S. C. Bose	Haripura
1939	S. C. Bose (Re-elected for 1939)	Tripuri
1940	Maulana Abul Kalam Azad	Ramgarh
1941-45	(No sessions, caused by arrests and jailing)	
1946	Acharya J. B. Kriplani	Meerut
1948	B. Pattabhi Sitaramayya	Jaipur

13. Newspapers and Journals

Name of the Paper/Journal	Name of Founder/Editor
Bengal Gazette - 1780	James Augustus Hicky (Irishman)
India Gazette - 1787	Henry Louis Vivian Derozio associated with it.

Madras Courier - 1784 (First paper from Madras)	
Bombay Herald - 1789 (First paper from Bombay)	
Indian Herald - 1795	R. Williams (Englishman) and published by Humphreys
Digdarshan - 1818	(First Bengali monthly)
Calcutta Journal - 1818	J .S. Buckingham
Bengal Gazette - 1818 (First Bengali newspaper)	Harishchandra Ray
Sambad Kaumudi - 1821	Raja Rammohan Roy
Marat-ul-Akbar - 1822 (First journal in Persian)	Raja Rammohan Roy
Jam-i-Jahan Numa - 1822 (First paper in Urdu)	An English firm
Banga-Duta - 1822	Rammohan Roy, Dwarkanath Tagore and others (a weekly in 4 languages English, Bengali, Persian, Hindi)
Bombay Samachar - 1822 (First paper in Gujarati)	
East Indian - 19th Century	Henry Vivian Derozio
Bombay Times - 1838 (The Times of India after 1861)	Foundation laid by Robert Knight, stated by Thomas Bennett.
Rast Goftar - 1851	Dadabhai Naoroji
Hindu Patriot - 1853	Girishchandra Ghosh (later, Harishchandra Mukerji became owner-cum-editor)
Somaprakasha - 1858 (First Bengali political paper)	Dwarkanath Vidyabhushan
Indian Mirror - Early 1862 (first Indian daily paper in English)	Devendranath Tagore
Bengalee - 1862	Girishchandra Ghosh (taken over by S.N. Banerjee in 1879)
Madras Mail- 1868 (First evening paper in India)	
Amrit Bazar Patrika - 1868 (In Bengali and later; an English daily)	Sisirkumar Ghosh & Motilal Ghosh
Bangadarshana - 1873	Bankim Chandra Chatterji
Indian Statesman - 1875 (later; The Statesman)	Robert Knight

The Hindu - 1878	G.S. Aiyar, Viraraghavachari and Subba Rao Pandit
Tribune - 1881	Dayal Singh Majeetia
Kesari and Maharatta - 1881	Tilak, Chiplunkar, Agarkar (before Tilak, Agarkar and Prof Kelkar were the editors respectively.)
Swadeshamitram	G.S. Aiyar
Paridasak - 1886	Bipin Chandra Pal (publisher)
Yugantar - 1906	Barindra Kumar Ghosh and Bhupendranath Dutta
Sandhya 1906	Brahamabandhab Upadhyay
Kal - 1906	
Indian Sociologist - London	Shyamji Krishnavarama
Bande Mataram - Paris	Madam Bhikajl Cama
Talvar - Berlin	Verendranath Chattopadhyay
Free Hindustan - Vancouver	Tarakanth Das
Ghadr - San Francisco	Ghadr Party
Bombay Chronicle - 1913	Pherozeshah Mehta, Editor-B.G. Horniman (Englishman)
The Hindustan Times - 1920	K.M. Panikkar as part of the Akali Dal Movement
The Milap - 1923	M.K. Chand
Leader	Madan Mohan Malaviya
Kirti - 1926	Santosh Singh
Bahishkrit Bharat - 1927	B.R. Ambedkar
Kudi Arasu - 1910	E.Y. Ramaswamy Naicker (Periyar)
Kranti - 1927	S.S. Mirajkar, K.N. Joglekar, S.Y. Ghate
Langal and Ganabani - 1927	Gopu Chakravarti and Dharani Goswami
Bandi Jivan	Sachindranath Sanyal
National Herald - 1938	Jawaharal Nehru
Al-hilal	Maulana Abul Kalam Azad
Comrade	Mohammed Ali
Young India, Harijan	Mahatma Gandhi
Nation	Gopalakrishna Gokhle
Bengali	Surendernath Banerjee
Som Prakash	Ishwar Chandra Vidyasagar
Karmyogi	Arvindo Ghosh
Free Hindustan	Taraknath Das
Zamindar, Lahore	Zafar Ali Khan
New India, Commonweal	Annie Besant

Satpatra Series	Gopal Hari Deshmukh
Din Mitra	Mukundrao Patil
Kudi Arasu	Periyar
Ghulamgiri (Slavery)	Jotirao Phule
Maratha, Din Bandhu	Bhaskar Rao Jadhav
Darpan	Bal Shastri Jambekar
Prabhudha Bharat, Udbodhava	Vivekananda

14. Important Literary Works of Ancient India

Literary Work	Author
Ashthadhyayi	Panini
Mahabhashya	Patanjali
Manu Smriti	Manu
Arthshastra	Kautilya
Chhanda-Sutra	Pingala
Buddhacharita	Ashvaghosha
Saripurta Prakarna	Ashvaghosha
Saundaranand	Ashvaghosha
Kumarsambhavam	Kalidasa
Raghuvansa	Kalidasa
Malvikagnimitram	Kalidasa
Sisupalvadha	Magha
Natyashastram	Bharat Muni
Ratnavali	Harshavardhana
Nagananda	Harshavardhana
Maltimadhav	Bhavabhuti
Uttararamcharita	Bhavabhuti
Meghaduta	Kalidasa
Gita Govinda	Jayadeva

Literary Work	Author
Harshacharita	Banabhatta
Ramcharita	Sandhyakar Nandi
Gaudvaho	Vakpati Raj
Daskumarcharita	Dandin
Vashvadatta	Subandhu
Kathasaritsagar	Somdeva
Panchatantra	Vishnu Sharma
Hitopdesha	Narayan Pandit
Kamasutra	Vatsayan
Mattavilasa Prahasana	Mahendravarman -I
Nitisara	Kamandaka
Charak Samhita	Charak
Dayabhaga	Jimutavahana
Nighantu	Yaska
Mitakshara	Vijneshvra
Brihat Kathamanjari	Kshemendra
Mahaviracharita	Bhavabhuti

15. Political and National Organisations of Modern India

Year	Organisation	Founder	Place
1838	Land Holders Society	Swarika Nath Tagore	Calcutta
1839	British India Society	William Adam	London

1843	British India Society	-	Calcutta
1851	British India Association	Devendra Nath Tagore	Calcutta
1852	Madras Native Association	-	Madras
1852	Bombay Association	Jagannath Shankar	Bombay
1862	London India Committee	C. Purshottam Mudaliyar	London
1866	East India Association	Dadabhai Naoroji	London
1867	National India Association	Mary Carpenter	London
1872	Indian Society	Anand Mohan Bose	London
1876	Indian Association	A.M. Bose, S.N. Bannerji	Calcutta
1833	Indian National Society	Shrish Chandra Bose	Calcutta
1883	Indian National Conference	S.N. Bannerjee	Calcutta
1884	Madras Mahajan Sabha	V. Raghavachari, S. Aiyyar	Madras
1885	Bombay Presidency Association	Ferozshah Mehta, Telang	Bombay
1885	Indian National Congress	A.O. Hume	Bombay
1888	United Indian Patriotic Association	Sir Syed Ahmed Khan	Aligarh
1905	Servants of India Society	Gopal Krishna Gokhale	Bombay
1915	Home Rule League	Annie Besant, Tilak	Pune
1918	U.P. Kisan Sabha	Malviya, Indra Narayan, Gaurishankar	Lucknow
1918	Ahmedabad Textile Labour Association	Mahatma Gandhi	Ahmedabad
1918	National Liberal Federation	S.N. Bannerjee	Calcutta
1920	Servants of People Society	Lala Lajpat Rai	Lahore
1920	Awadh Kisan Sabha	Nehru, Ramchandra Gorishankar	Pratapgarh
1920	Indian Trade Union Congress	N.M. Joshi (Founder), Lala Lajpat Rai (President)	Lucknow
1921	Communist Group of India	Nalini Gupta	Calcutta
1923	Swaraj Party	M.L. Nehru, C.R. Das	Delhi
1924	All India Communist Party	Satyabhakt	Kanpur
1925	Rashtriya Swayamsevak Sangh (RSS)	K.D. Hedgewar	-
1927	All India Women Conference	Lady Sadashiv Ayyar	Madras
1928	Labour Swaraj Party	Kazi Nasrul Islam	-
1929	Khudai Khitmadgar	Khan Abdul Gaffar Khan	Peshawar

1934	Congress Socialist Party	Acharya Narendra Dev, Jai Prakash Narayan	-
1936	Progressive Writers Association	Munshi Premchand	Lucknow
1936	All India Kishan Sabha	N.G. Ranga, Sahjanand	Lucknow
1936	Akhil Bhartiya Vidhyarthi Parishad	Meenu Masani, Ashok Mehra, Dr. Ashraf	-
1939	Forward Bloc	Subhash Chandra Bose	Calcutta
1939	Indian Bolshevik Party	N.D. Majumdar	Calcutta
1940	Radical Democratic Party	M.N. Roy	Calcutta
1941	Indian Bolshevik Lenin Party	Ajit Roy, Indrasena	Calcutta
1942	Krantikari Samajvadi Dal	Saumendra Nath Tagore	Calcutta

16. Important Acts and Laws During British Regime

Year	Act/Law	Founder	Main Provisions
1773	Regulating Act	Warren Hastings	Limited control of British Parliament
1784	Pitt's India Act	Warren Hastings	Establishment of Board of Control
1813	Charter Act	Lord Minto I	Monopoly of trade abolished
1829	Abolition of Sati	William Bentinck	Stopped Sati System
1933	Charter Act	William Bentinck	Bengal Governor came to be known as Governor General of Bengal
1853	Charter Act	Lord Dalhousie	Limited control of East India Company
1856	Hindu Widow Remarriage Act	Lord Dalhousie	Permitted widow remarriage
1858	Act for Good Administration	Lord Canning	Power transferred to the crown
1861	Indian Council Act	Lord Canning	Indian's entry into councils
1891	Consent of Age Law	Lansdowne	Child marriage (below 12 years) was prohibited
1892	Indian Council Act	Lansdowne	Beginning of elective principles
1909	Morley Minto Reforms	Lord Minto II	Communal electorate

1919	Montague-Chelmsford Reforms	Lord Chelmsford	Dyarchy in provinces
1927	Simon Commission	Lord Irwin	Constitution framing plan
1930	Sharda Act	Lord Irwin	Age of Marriage 18 and 14 years for boys and girls respectively
1935	Indian Government Act	Lord Willingdon	Provincial autonomy
1940	August Offer	Lord Linlithgow	Provincial self rule
1942	Cripps Mission	Lord Linlithgow	Plan for Constituent Assembly
1945	Wavell Plan	Lord Wavell	To frame council with the participation of all major political parties
1946	Cabinet Mission Plan	Lord Wavell	Formation of Indian Federation
1947	Mountbatten Plan	Lord Mountbatten	Partition of India

17. Revolutionary Organisations Abroad

Year	Organisation	Founder	Main Provisions
1904	Indian House	Shyam Ji Krishan Verma	London (England)
1906	Abhinav Bharat	V.D. Savarkar	London (England)
1907	Indian Independence League	Taraknath Bose	America
1913	Gadar Party	Lala Hardayal, Ramchandra and Barkatullah	San Francisco (America)
1914	India Independence	Lala Hardayal and Virendra Nath Chattopadhyaya	Berlin (Germany)
1915	Indian Independence League and Government	Raja Mahendra Pratap	Kabul (Afghanistan)
1942	Indian Independence League	Ras Behari Bose	Tokyo (Japan)

1942	Azad Hind Fauz	Ras Behari Bose (In 1943 Azad Hind Fauz was reorganised by netaji Subhash Chandra Bose in Singapore)	Tokyo (Japan)

18. Important Revolutionary Activities

Year	Event	Place	Revolutionaries
1897	Murder of Commissioner Rand and Amherst	Pune	Damodar Chapekar and Balkrishna Chapekar
1908	Attempt to kill vindictive judge Kingsford	Muzaffarpur	Khudiram Bose and Prafulla Chaki
1908	Alipur Conspiracy Case	Alipur	Kanhai Lal Dutta and Satyendra Nath Bose
1909	Murder of Jackson	Nasik	Anant Kanhere
1909	Murder of Col. Villy	London	Madan Lal Dhingra
1912	Attempt to murder Viceroy, Hardinge	Delhi	Ras Behari Bose and Basant Kumar
1927	Kakori Case	Kakori	Bismil, Ashfaqullah
1928	Murder of Saunders	Lahore	Sardar Bhagat Singh
1930	Chittagong Armoury Case	Chittagong	Surya Sen
1940	Murder of General Dyer	London	Udham Singh